THE LAND OF THE VEDA BEING PERSONAL REMINISCENCES OF INDIA

THE
LAND OF THE VEDA

BEING

PERSONAL REMINISCENCES

OF

INDIA

ITS PEOPLE, CASTES, THUGS, AND FAKIRS

ITS RELIGIONS, MYTHOLOGY, PRINCIPAL MONUMENTS, PALACES, AND MAUSOLEUMS

TOGETHER WITH THE

INCIDENTS OF THE GREAT SEPOY REBELLION

ILLUSTRATED

NEW EDITION

BY WILLIAM BUTLER, D.D.

GYAN

Published by

Gyan Publishing House
5, Ansari Road
Daryaganj, New Delhi-110002
Phone: 011-47034999, 9811692060
E-mail: books@gyanbooks.com

Distribution Network
gyanbooks.com
India, USA, Canada, UK, Australia, France

ISBN : 978-81-212-3687-4 (PB)
First Published, 1895

2nd Impression 2020

Printed at: Gyan Press, Delhi.

The
Land of the Veda being Personal Reminiscences of India
Author: William Butler

THE LAND OF THE VEDA

BEING

PERSONAL REMINISCENCES

OF

INDIA

ITS PEOPLE, CASTES, THUGS, AND FAKIRS

ITS RELIGIONS, MYTHOLOGY, PRINCIPAL MONUMENTS, PALACES, AND MAUSOLEUMS

TOGETHER WITH THE

INCIDENTS OF THE GREAT SEPOY REBELLION

ILLUSTRATED

NEW EDITION

BY WILLIAM BUTLER, D.D.

NEW YORK: HUNT & EATON
CINCINNATI: CRANSTON & CURTS
1895

Taj Mahal, Agra—South Facade.

PREFACE.

THE writer of this book has aimed to act toward the reader in the relation of a guide, as though he were going over the ground again, and giving the benefit of his experience, in pointing out the objects of interest with which years and study have familiarized his own mind. The thread of the narrative runs through the work, and, so far as the subject permitted, its continuity has been preserved.

In a theme like that of India, and after the reading and note-taking of fifteen years, it is a difficult task for an author to trace every entry to its source, or adequately to discriminate between what is original and what is borrowed. Every reasonable effort, however, has been made to give proper acknowledgment wherever it was found desirable to use the ideas or language of others.

While the denominational relation of the writer is evident enough, he trusts that there will not be found on these pages a single sentence that can give offense to any member of Christ's Church, but, on the contrary, that their perusal may encourage and strengthen the faith of God's elect in that almighty Power which, even in the idolatrous and conservative East, is so manifestly subduing all things unto Himself. Here may be discerned the dawn of that day, so long foretold, when all Oriental races shall be blessed in a Redeemer who was himself Asiatic by birth and blood and the sphere of His personal ministry—whose cross was erected on that continent, and whose first ministers and members were taken from among that people. The hundreds of millions of their descendants now await this redemption, and shall yet joyously unite to crown him "Lord of all."

The writer has not concealed his conviction that human history, and the movements and changes of thrones, and powers, and kingdoms, can be fully understood only in the light of the doctrine of the Second Psalm. Jesus Christ, the divine and eternal Son of God, who created and redeemed this world, is its "Master and Lord." The number, the malignity, the counsel of his foes, are lighter in his estimation than the chaff of the summer threshing-floor, and as easily swept from the path of his almighty movements. He has not abandoned this world, with its thousand millions of accountable and dying men, to be the victims of the whims and caprice of selfish potentates, deceiving errorists, or wicked spirits in high places, to be forever crushed down beneath their tyranny and misdirection. He has undertaken, and will accomplish, man's redemption in every sense, temporal, spiritual, and eternal.

That repose which the world, and particularly its Oriental portion, so much needs and has so long sighed for, is to be found only in Him ; and it will come when He has overthrown the foes of the world's welfare, and rectified its many wrongs. Then, beneath the benign administration of this "Prince of Peace," humanity at length shall rest, each of them under his own vine and fig-tree, and none shall make them afraid.

The government of Christ alone explains the condition and the history of the world. We acknowledge him to be "The blessed and only Potentate, the KING OF KINGS AND LORD OF LORDS," whose scepter sways "all power in heaven and in earth." At his feet, who is "Prince of the kings of the earth," and "Head over all things to the Church," is laid this humble effort to illustrate his high providence, as one more heartfelt tribute to be added to the many which are already ascribing—"Blessing, and honor, and glory, and power unto Him who sitteth upon the throne, and unto the Lamb for ever and ever!" W. B.

CONTENTS.

CHAPTER I.

THE PEOPLE OF INDIA—CASTE AND ITS IMMUNITIES.

CHAPTER II.

STATISTICS, MYTHOLOGY, AND VEDIC LITERATURE.

CHAPTER III.

ARCHITECTURAL MAGNIFICENCE OF INDIA.

CHAPTER IV.

ORIGINATING CAUSES OF THE SEPOY REBELLION.

CHAPTER VII.

THE CAUSES AND FAILURE OF THE SEPOY REBELLION.

CHAPTER VIII.

RESULTS OF THE REBELLION TO CHRISTIANITY AND CIVILIZATION.

CHAPTER IX.

THE CONDITION OF WOMAN UNDER HINDOO LAW.

CHAPTER X.

OUR CHRISTIAN ORPHANAGES IN ROHILCUND.

CHAPTER XI.

RESULTS THUS FAR OF THIS WORK.

ILLUSTRATIONS.

CHIEFLY FROM PHOTOGRAPHS.

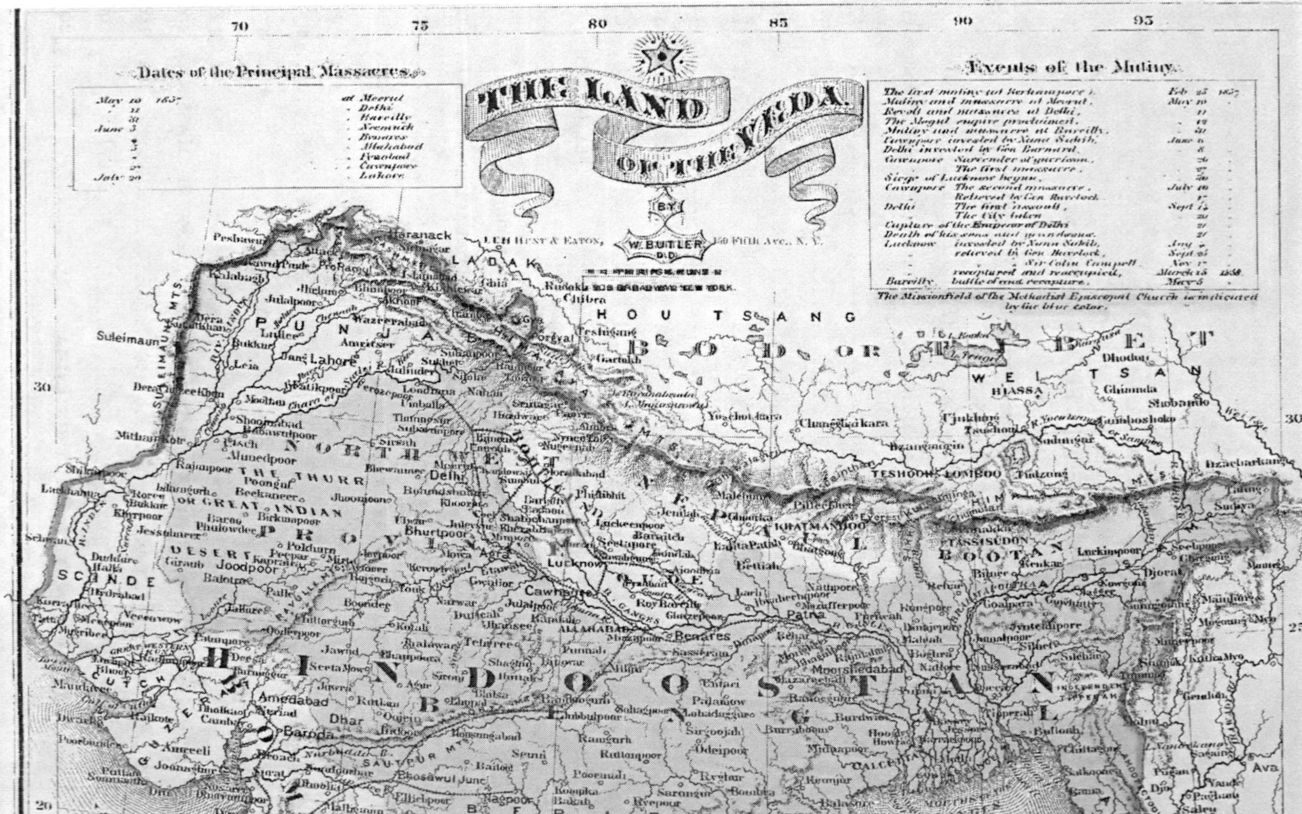
THE LAND OF THE VEDA.
BY
W. BUTLER D.D.
HUNT & EATON, 150 Fifth Ave., N. Y.
Dates of the Principal Massacres.
Events of the Mutiny.
The Missionfield of the Methodist Episcopal Church is indicated by the blue color.
HOU TSANG
BOD OR TIBET
WEI TSAN
LADAK
PUNJAB
NORTH WEST
PROVINCES
THE THURR OR GREAT INDIAN DESERT
SCINDE
CUTCH
HINDOOSTAN
BOOTAN
OUDE
BERAR
Peshawur
Lahore
Umritsur
Delhi
Agra
Lucknow
Cawnpore
Benares
Patna
Moorshedabad
Amedabad
Baroda
Dhar
Joodpoor
Nagpoor
Lassa
Teshoo Lomboo
Ava

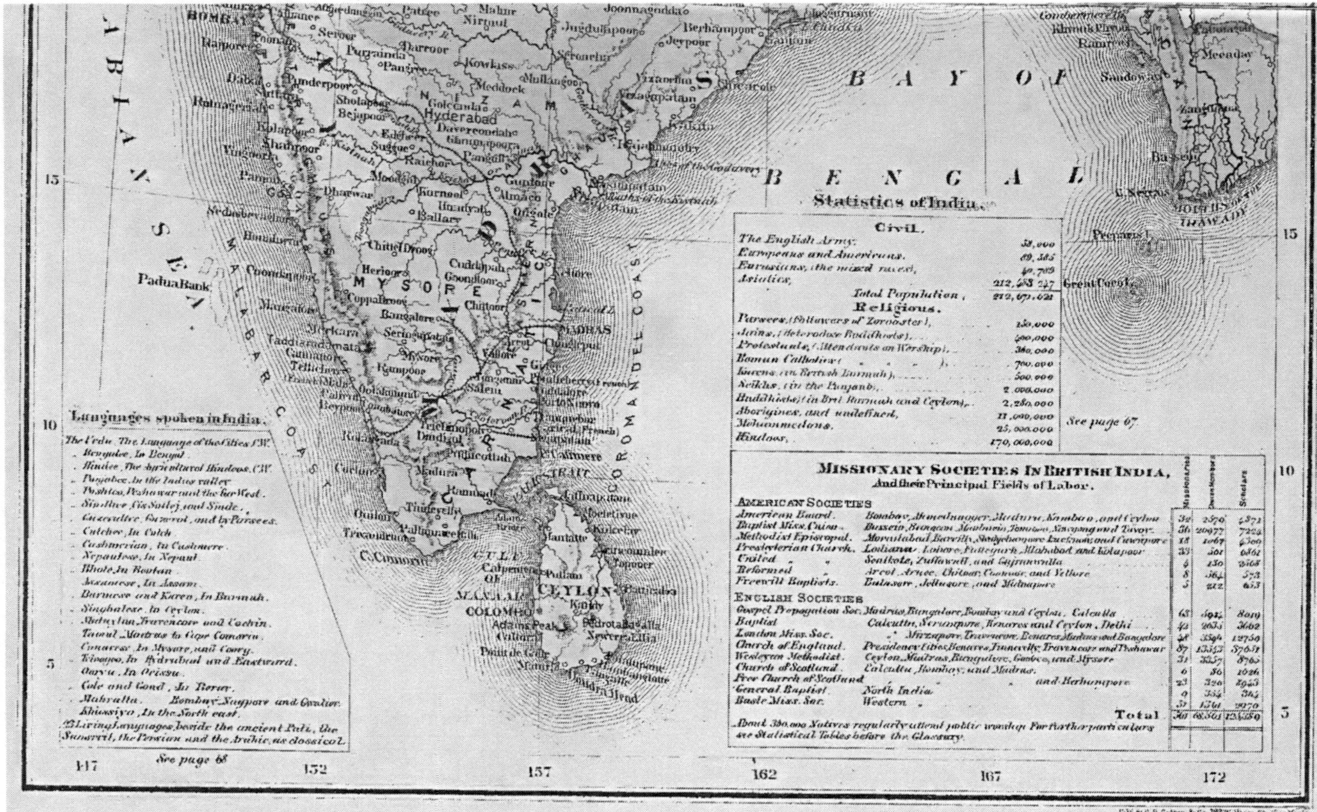
BAY OF BENGAL
ARABIAN SEA
MALABAR COAST
COROMANDEL COAST
MYSORE
CEYLON
COLOMBO
MADRAS
BOMBAY
Hyderabad
Statistics of India.
Civil.
The English Army, 58,000
Europeans and Americans, 69,385
Eurasians, (the mixed races), 40,709
Asiatics, 212,483,247
Total Population, 212,671,021
Religious.
Parsees, (Followers of Zoroaster), 150,000
Jains, (Heterodox Buddhists), 400,000
Protestants, (Attendants on Worship), 360,000
Roman Catholics (...), 700,000
Karens, (in British Burmah), 500,000
Seikhs, (in the Punjaub), 2,000,000
Buddhists, (in Brit. Burmah and Ceylon), 2,280,000
Aborigines, and undefined, 11,000,000
Mohammedans, 25,000,000
Hindoos, 170,000,000
See page 67
Missionary Societies in British India, And their Principal Fields of Labor.
Missionaries / Church Members / Scholars
American Societies
American Board. Bombay, Ahmednuggur, Madura, Kambaro, and Ceylon 32 2570 4871
Baptist Miss. Union. Bassein, Rangoon, Maulmain, Tonngoo, Sandoway and Tavoy. 36 20977 7224
Methodist Episcopal. Moradabad, Bareilly, Shahjehanpore, Lucknow and Cawnpore 18 1067 4300
Presbyterian Church. Lodiana, Lahore, Futtegurh, Allahabad and Kolapoor 33 501 6861
United. Sealkote, Zuffawall, and Gujranwalla 4 130 2568
Reformed. Arcot, Arnee, Chitoor, Coonoor, and Vellore 8 364 573
Freewill Baptists. Balasore, Jellasore, and Midnapore 5 212 653
English Societies
Gospel Propagation Soc. Madras, Bangalore, Bombay and Ceylon, Calcutta 63 4914 8019
Baptist. Calcutta, Serampore, Benares and Ceylon, Delhi 42 2635 3662
London Miss. Soc. Mirzapore, Travancore, Benares, Madras and Bangalore 48 3594 12750
Church of England. Presidency Cities, Benares, Tinnevelly, Travancore and Peshawar 87 13352 37651
Wesleyan Methodist. Ceylon, Madras, Bangalore, Goobee, and Mysore 31 3357 8765
Church of Scotland. Calcutta, Bombay, and Madras. 6 86 1026
Free Church of Scotland. and Berhampore 23 326 8943
General Baptist. North India 9 354 344
Basle Miss. Soc. Western 37 1561 2970
Total 501 68,561 125,350
About 330,000 Natives regularly attend public worship. For further particulars see Statistical Tables before the Glossary.
Languages spoken in India.
The Urdu. The Language of the Cities &c.
Bengalee, In Bengal.
Hindee, The Agricultural Hindoos, &c.
Punjabee, In the Indus valley.
Pushtoo, Peshawar and the far West.
Sindhee, Cis-Sutlej and Sinde.
Guzeratee, Guzerat, and by Parsees.
Cutchee, In Cutch.
Cashmerian, In Cashmere.
Nepaulese, In Nepaul.
Bhote, In Bootan.
Assamese, In Assam.
Burmese and Karen, In Burmah.
Singhalese, In Ceylon.
Malayalam, Travancore and Cochin.
Tamul, Madras to Cape Comorin.
Canarese, In Mysore, and Coorg.
Telugoo, In Hydrabad and Eastward.
Ooriya, In Orissa.
Cole and Gond, In Berar.
Mahratta, Bombay, Nagpore and Gwalior.
Khassiya, In the North east.
23 Living Languages beside the ancient Pali, the Sanscrit, the Persian and the Arabic, as classical.
See page 68
G.W. & C.B. Colton & Co. 182 William St. New York

THE

LAND OF THE VEDA.

CHAPTER I.

THE PEOPLE OF INDIA—CASTE AND ITS IMMUNITIES.

IN my youth I read those amazing descriptions of Oriental magnificence recorded by Sir Thomas Roe—England's first Embassador to India—and others, describing the power and glory of "The Great Mogul" in such glowing terms that they seemed more like the romance of the "Arabian Nights" than the real facts, which they were, of the daily life witnessed in that splendid Court. Europe then heard for the first time of "The Taj," "The Peacock Throne," "The Dewanee Khass," "The Weighing of the Emperor," when on each birthday his person was placed in golden scales, and twelve times his weight of gold and silver, perfumes and other valuables, were distributed to the populace; but the statements seemed so distant from probability that they were regarded by many as extravagances which might well rank with the asserted facts of "Lalla Rookh;" so that the Embassador, who was three years a resident, and the Poet, who had never been there at all, with their authorities, seemed alike to have drawn upon their imagination for their facts, transcending, as their descriptions did, the ability and the taste of European Courts.

How little I then imagined that it would fall to my lot at a future day to be in that very Dewanee Khass, sitting quietly on the side of his Crystal Throne, beholding the last of the Mogul Emperors, a captive, on trial for his life, in that magnificent Audience Hall of his forefathers, where millions have bowed down before them in such abject homage! that I should be there to see him, the last of their line, descending from that throne and $900,000 per annum to a felon's doom and the deck of a convict ship, to breathe out the remnant of his miserable life upon a foreign shore; and then after his departure to behold, as I did, that costly Khass given over to the spoiler's hand, rifled by the English soldiers of its last ornaments, and ruined forever!

Truly has it been said that ofttimes "fact is stranger than fiction;" and the assertion has seldom received more impressive illustrations than are found in the wonderful scenes which I witnessed in the Court of Delhi at the close of 1857.

In reading that stirring account of the great victory won for Christianity near Poictiers on the 3d of October, A. D. 732—when the brave Charles Martel, at the head of his Christian warriors, had to meet Abder Rahman and his Arabian cavalry, 375,000 strong, and there to decide whether Europe should henceforth be Christian or Moslem—one almost trembles as he thinks what would have been the result had Charles failed that day! The hosts of the Arabian Antichrist had already extinguished the seven Churches of Asia, almost swept North Africa of its Christianity, had passed the pillars of Hercules and conquered Spain, crossed the Pyrenees, and were now descending into France and Germany with the intention of completing the circuit of the Mediterranean, and making Europe as Mohammedan as they had made Asia Minor and Palestine. Christendom was terrified, for the Christian Church seemed pressed to the verge of ruin. On the issue of that morning, so far as human eye can penetrate the future, it was then and there to be decided whether Paris and London, and, by consequence, New York and Boston, were to be like Bagdad, Constantinople, and Damascus: whether, instead of the spires of our churches and the sound of our Sabbath bells, our race was to receive, at the sword's point, another faith, whose outward expression would be the Mosque and the Minaret, and the Muezzin's cry calling "the faithful" to the Koran and its prayers!

Well did Christendom bestow the surname of the "Hammer" upon the heroic Charles! From the blows which he dealt out to those foes of Gospel civilization they reeled back, stunned into the keen conviction that for them and their hateful creed there was no home in Europe. They recrossed the Straits of Gibraltar, and, instead of the Gallic and Germanic races, sought an easier prey in the enervated communities of Oriental heathenism. Thus, instead of France and Britain and Germany, the Crescent of the False Prophet subdued, and for nearly a thousand years waved over, Egypt, Persia, Toorkistan, and India. But for the Providence which gave Charles Martel that decisive victory, Arabic had been the classical language, and Islamism the religion of our race and of Europe; and "America and the Cape, the Compass and the Press, the Steam-engine, the Telescope, and the Copernican System, might all have remained undiscovered until the present day."

When reading these thrilling events long years since, how free I was from any anticipation that I should yet have to stand in the center of Asia, amid a similar whirl of confusion and blood, organized by that very creed, as it rose in its might to sweep the Eastern hemisphere of every vestige of the Gospel, and plant its triumphant flag on the ruins of Christianity; that it should be my lot to be lost to sight for months amid the rolling clouds of the conflict, where Henry Havelock, victorious over Nana Sahib, accomplished for Oriental Christianity what Charles Martel did a thousand years before for the same faith, in the West; that at length, emerging unscathed, I should have the high honor to be invited by them to render their thanks to God for their victory, on the last battle-field which his heroes won; and, more wonderful still, that there, amid the utter military downfall of that creed and its chief dynasty, I should be privileged to plant the standard of the Cross in the land of the Sepoy, and live to see Churches founded and native ministers raised up from the very race who sought our life and labored to destroy our faith!

How different would the East and the West have been to-day had either Martel or Havelock *failed!* But God is great for the exigencies of his people, and has often, as in both these instances, shown that he can save by few as well as by many. I am fully of the opinion, and think this work will abundantly show, that Oriental Christianity never passed through such an emergency as that of 1857--8. Even worldly men, ay, the very heathen themselves, declared afterward that it was God alone who saved it from complete annihilation. By every law and rule of power, opportunity, and purpose, it must have perished had it been merely human, and true philosophy as well as Christian faith teaches us that it was only saved by the special interposition of Almighty God, its defender and keeper. During the long and weary months of our siege on the summit of Nynee Tal, the handful of villagers there declared that we were the last of the Christian life left in India—that from where we stood, to the sea on either side, our religion and race had been all swept away. We knew well that if this were so our fate was but a question of time that would soon be consummated.

Cut off and excluded, there we stood, our anxious hearts trying to ponder the terrible question, *Could this be so?* and if so, how fearful must be the *result!* For we felt assured, if it were, that the successful effort of the India Sepoy would have found cruel imitation in Burmah, China, and Japan, and that it was possible that, at that hour—in those terrible days of July and August, 1857—Christianity might have been extinguished in the blood of its last martyrs on the Oriental hemisphere, and the clock of the world been put back for centuries. We could only turn to God, and "against hope believe in hope," while we ourselves "stood in jeopardy every hour." How serious that jeopardy was may be realized by turning to the map, and describing a circle around the geographical center of our mission at Shajehanpore, until its diameter would expand to three hundred miles. That area would encircle nearly the whole of Rohilcund, Oude, and The Doab, and would include the cities of Moradabad, Futtyghur, Bareilly, Lucknow, Cawnpore, Rampore, etc. It would represent the very heart of the great Rebellion. Every city, town, and village within these limits "fell," so that, with the exception of the handful with us at Nynee Tal, one little group that was closely hidden in a Hindoo home in Rohilcund, those in the "Residency" of Lucknow, and those in the intrenchments at Cawnpore—not a white face in all that great valley was left alive. Within that fearful circle on the 31st of May, 1857, were five American missionaries. I am the only one of the number that came out of the terrible vortex; all the rest, with their wives and children, were ruthlessly murdered. We knew them well—Brothers Freeman, Campbell, Johnson, and M'Mullen, and their devoted ladies and little ones, honored and beloved missionaries of the American Presbyterian Church. We alone of the number are left alive to tell the story of the circumstances under which they suffered, and of our own wonderful escape from a similar death! How well we can appreciate the victory of Christian civilization over heathen cruelty and purposes, as well as the amazing strides made by the Gospel and by education since that fearful day!

The reader will well remember how the world stood horrified in the fall of that year as mail after mail brought the tidings of cruelty and massacre, in which neither age nor sex was spared, and also with what anxiety they watched the progress of the feeble bands of heroes who, under such leaders as the gallant and saintly Havelock, fought their dreadful way to our rescue, too late to save even one at Cawnpore, but in time to rescue us and those at Lucknow.

The intervention of the civil war in this country necessarily for the time turned away attention from the horrors which were fourteen thousand miles distant; but the public interest in this subject has not ceased, nor will the story of the "Sepoy Rebellion" ever be forgotten while men admire and honor heroic sufferings, Anglo-Saxon pluck, and sublime Christian courage, exhibited against the most fearful odds and in the face of certain death, in the center of a whole continent of raging foes, while the Prince of the powers of the air marshaled the hosts of hell to annihilate the religion of the Son of God. Doubtless "the rulers of the darkness of this world" had more interest and part in that fearful struggle than was taken by the poor, ignorant Sepoy or his crafty priest. It was earth and hell combined. No other theory can account for its character. Of this the reader will judge for himself from the facts presented.

Fourteen years have passed since closed that great "wrestling with flesh and blood, with principalities and powers, and wicked spirits in high places." Eight of those years were spent by the writer amid the scenes of 1857–8, giving him occasion to verify and examine the facts where they transpired, and correct his judgment by as good an opportunity as could be desired. I feel the responsibility to see that such facts shall not drop into oblivion. They should not be allowed to die, especially associated as they are with the history of the Methodist Church in India, whose foundations were laid in such "troublous times."

It will assist the reader's attention, and promote a more adequate understanding of our subject, to introduce to him at this point the people of whom we are speaking, and also unfold somewhat their character and peculiar civilization. The wood-cuts are mostly from photographs brought from India, and of course are faithful representations of the various classes as they appear there. The first group are Hindoos, as they sit round a Brahmin to listen to the reading of the Vedas.

The Hindoos constitute the great majority of the Empire, and are of the same Caucasian race as ourselves. Their ancestors moved southward from their original home more than three thousand years ago, and occupied the Valley of Scinde, probably on the west bank of the Indus, while only Afghanistan and Persia lay between them and the cradle of the race. There, in that valley, their most ancient *Vedas* were written—manifestly so from the local allusions—and from thence at a later period they migrated into the richer Valley of the Ganges, driving before them the aborigines of India, who sought shelter in the jungles and mountains, where their descendants are found to-day. The Hindoos have long ceased to be a warlike people. The rich land which they conquered, its fertility, the abundance and cheapness of the means of life, and their inclination to indolence, which a warm climate

Hindoos and their Teacher.

fosters, have all been promotive of the effeminacy into which they have so generally sunk.

Their separation into castes and classes have tended to individualism, and to an utter indifference to politics or the public good; so that you seek in vain for what we call patriotism or love of country. The Hindoo, as a general fact, cares not who rules the land if only he is allowed to cultivate his fields and eat his rice in peace. If left to himself, the last thing he would have thought of would have been rebellion; indeed, the Hindoos, as a people, did not rebel. They looked on in astonishment, and left the whole affair to be carried on and fought out by the Sepoys and the *Budmashes* (the thieves and vagabonds) of the cities.

In every respect they are a contrast to the Mohammedans among them. No tendency to amalgamation with them has ever been developed. They regard them as aliens and oppressors, and are even thankful that they are no longer under their control.

About eight hundred years ago there came pouring down into India from the countries of the North-west a hardy, large-boned, intolerant race of men, made up of various nations, who had heard of the "barbaric pearl and gold" of Hindustan, and who panted to extend over its wide realms their religion and rule. Before this Mohammedan invasion the Hindoo race succumbed, though the strangers were not one seventh of their number. But they were a unit; and, taking the Hindoo nations in detail, they conquered. Then, filling the positions of trust and the offices of Government with their own creatures, and as far as they could making a monopoly of education, they continued to compensate for deficiency of numbers by a politic use of their opportunities, and left the Hindoo to till the soil and pay the yearly tribute which they had laid upon him. The usual alternative of the Mohammedan conquerors—conformity to their creed or grinding taxation, or even death—had to be foregone in this instance, as its attempted enforcement over a people so much more numerous would have been too much for even Hindoo patience, and have ended probably in the extermination of their iconoclastic conquerors. The distinctive characteristics of each are religiously kept up. One of them is in the fastening of the outer garment. On meeting either party, though the dress is much the same, you at once distinguish the Mohammedan from the Hindoo by the universal fact that the latter has his tunic made to button on the right side, while the Mohammedan hooks his on the left. There is about the Mohammedan a fierce, haughty aspect, which he takes no trouble to conceal. He cannot forget that he had ruled in India for seven hundred years, until the hated English came and broke the rod of his strength, and he is all the more disposed to show his bitterness of spirit because the Hindoo race, with the exception of a few Brahmins, hailed the change with sincere gladness, and can now set him at defiance. It was on this fact that Englishmen relied for the perpetuity of their rule; and on it they might have depended for long centuries to come, had it not been for a combination of peculiar circumstances which existed in 1857, and which will be detailed in their place.

Taking individual portraits, for the sake of more distinctness, I here present a *Brahmin*, as the acknowledged head of Hindoo society, and an associate of the most exclusive and singular of all earthly orders.

The man here introduced holds himself to be a member of the most ancient aristocracy upon the earth. His dignity is one entirely independent of landed possessions, wealth, or manorial halls. Indeed, these have nothing whatever to do with it. The man may have literally no home, and not be worth five dollars of worldly property; he may have to solicit his next meal of food from those who respect his order; but he is a *Brahmin*, and is prouder of that simple string over his shoulder and across his naked breast than any English Earl is of his coronet. These men laugh at such a mushroom aristocracy as that of Britain or France, created merely by the breath of a human Sovereign, whose word raises the plebeian to the noble order; for the Brahmin holds that his nobility is not an accident, but is in the highest sense "by the grace of God." It is in his nature, in his blood, by the original intention and act of his Creator. He was made and designed by

A Brahmin.

God to be different from and higher than all other men, and that from the first to last of time.

How they hate that republican Christianity which declares that "God hath made of one blood all nations of men," and that Gospel equality which announces that saints "are one in Christ Jesus," and that, having "all one Father," "all we are brethren" in a blessed communion, where no lofty pretensions or imprescriptable rights are allowed to any, but he that would be greatest must be the servant of all.

I have seen a person of this class, on approaching a low-caste man, wave his right hand superciliously thirty yards before they could meet, and so send him off to the other side of the road. The poor despised man meekly bowed and obeyed the haughty intimation. No sacerdotal tyranny has ever been so relentlessly and scornfully enforced as that of the Brahminical rule, and none has been such an unmitigated curse to the nation where it was exercised.

Caste is an institution peculiarly Brahminical. The Sanscrit word is *varna*, which denotes color—probably the ancient distinction between the Hindoo invaders and the aborigines. Caste, from the Portuguese *casta*, a breed, exactly expresses the Brahminical idea. Their account of its origin, abridged from the *Institutes of Menu*, the oldest system of law extant save the Pentateuch, is as follows:

"In order to preserve the universe, Brahma caused the *Brahmin* to proceed from his mouth, the *Kshatriya* to proceed from his arm, the *Vaisya* to proceed from his thigh, and the *Sudra* to proceed from his foot. And Brahma directed that the duties of the Brahmins should be reading and teaching the Veda; sacrificing, and assisting others to sacrifice; giving alms if they be rich, and receiving alms if they be poor. And Brahma directed that the duties of the Kshatriyas should be to defend the people, to give alms, to sacrifice, to read the Veda, and to keep their passions under control. And he directed that the duties of the Vaisyas should be to keep herds of cattle, to give alms, to read the Shasters, to carry on trade, to lend money at interest, and to cultivate land. And he directed that the Sudra should serve all the three mentioned castes, namely, the Brahmins, the Kshatriyas, and the Vaisyas, and that he should not depreciate nor make light of them. Since the Brahmin sprang from the mouth, which is the most excellent part of Brahma, and since he is the first-born and possesses the Veda, he is by right the chief of the whole creation. Him Brahma produced from his own mouth, that he might perform holy rites; that he might present ghee to the gods, and cakes of rice to the Pitris, or progenitors of mankind."—*Code of Hindoo Law*, I, pp. 88, 94.

The *Bhagvat Geeta*, their most sublime treatise, repeats the same arrangement, and makes their observance a condition of salvation and moral perfection. Each class had thus a separate creation, constituting it, in fact, a *distinct species*, involving a denial of the doctrine that "God hath made of one blood all men." The Hindoos thus reject our common humanity, and hold it to be heresy to believe that all men are fellow-creatures, scouting the idea that we should "honor all men," or "love our neighbors as ourselves."

Brahmin is a derivative from *Brahm*, the Deity, and signifies a Theologist or Divine. The caste is analogous to the tribe of Levi under the Mosaic economy, but without the family of Aaron. All the benefits of the Hindoo religion belong to this class, and the code secured to them rights, honors, and immunities that no other order could claim, so that their persons were to be considered sacred and inviolate, and they could not be held amenable to the penalties of law even for the worst of crimes. The intention of the legislator was, that from this learned class alone the nation was to take its astronomers, lawyers, prime ministers, judges, philosophers, as well as priests. They were to hold the highest offices, and to be supreme. The Brahmin is invested with that sacred string of three cotton strands, and the ceremony is called regeneration, and gives the Brahmin his claim to the title of the "twice born." For him, and for him alone, has the law-giver laid down in detail the duties of life, even to his devotions. Each morning he may be

Brahmins at Prayer.

seen, as here represented, on the banks of the Ganges or other "holy" stream.

Any thing more singular and whimsical than the forms prescribed for him were never enjoined upon humanity as religious ritual. In illustration of this, from a paper in the "Asiatic Researches," by Mr. Colebrook, as quoted by Dr. Duff, we ask the reader's attention to the following extract. Speaking of the duties of morning worship, one of which is the religious ablution, as here represented, "the Sacred Books" strictly enjoin as follows:

"He *may* bathe with water drawn from a well, from a fountain, or from the basin of a cataract; but he should prefer water which lies above ground—choosing a stream rather than stagnant water, a river in preference to a small brook, a holy stream before a vulgar river, and above all the water of the Ganges. If the Ganges be beyond his reach he should invoke that holy river, saying, 'O, Gunga, hear my prayers! for my sake be included in this small quantity of water with the other sacred streams.' Then, standing in the water, he must hallow his intended performance by the *inaudible* recitation of certain sacred texts. Next, sipping water and sprinkling some before him, the worshiper throws water eight times on the crown of his head, on the earth, toward the sky; again toward the sky, on the earth, on the crown of his head; and lastly on the ground, to destroy the demons who wage war with the gods. During the performance of this act of ablution he must be reciting these prayers: 'O waters! since ye afford delight, grant us present happiness and the rapturous sight of the Supreme Being. Like tender mothers, make us here partakers of your most auspicious essence. We become contented with your essence, with which ye satisfy the universe. Waters, grant it to us.' Immediately after this first ablution he should sip water without swallowing it, silently praying. These ceremonies and prayers being concluded, he plunges *thrice* into the water, each time repeating the prescribed expiatory texts.

"He then meditates in the deepest silence. During this moment of intense devotion he is striving to realize that 'Brahma, with four faces and a red complexion, resides in nis bosom; Vishnu, with four arms and a black complexion, in his heart; and Shiva, with five faces and a white complexion, in his forehead!' To this sublime meditation succeeds a suppression of the breath, which is thus performed: Closing the left nostril with the two longest fingers of his right hand, he draws his breath through the right nostril; and then, closing that nostril likewise with his thumb, he holds his breath, while he internally repeats to himself the *Gayatri*, the mysterious names of the three worlds, the triliteral monosyllable, and the sacred text of Brahma; last of all, he raises both fingers off the left nostril, and emits the breath he had suppressed through the right. This process being repeated three several times, he must next make three ablutions, with the following prayer: 'As the tired man leaves drops of sweat at the foot of a tree; as he who bathes is cleansed from all foulness; as an oblation is sanctified by holy grass, so may this water purify me from sin.' He must next fill the palm of his hand with water, and, presenting it to his nose, inhale the fluid by one nostril, and, retaining it for a while, exhale it through the other, and throw away the water to the north-east quarter. This is considered as an internal ablution which washes away sin. He then concludes by sipping water with the following prayer: 'Water! thou dost penetrate all beings; thou dost reach the deep recesses of the mountains; thou art the mouth of the universe; thou art sacrifice; thou art the mystic word *vasha;* thou art light, taste, and the immortal fluid.'"

After a variety of genuflections and prayers, of which these are but a mere sample, he concludes his devotions by worshiping the rising sun. The veneration in which the Brahmin is to be held by all classes, the privileges which he is to enjoy, his occupations and modes of life, are laid down with wonderful minuteness in this Code of Hindoo Law. A mere sample of his assumptions, under the head of Veneration, will suffice: "The Brahmin is entitled to the whole of the universe by the right of primogeniture. He possesses the Veda, and is alone permitted to teach the laws. By his sacrifices and imprecations he could destroy a Rajah in a moment, together with all his troops, elephants, horses, and chariots In his wrath he could frame new worlds, with new gods and new mortals. A man who barely assaulted a Brahmin, with the intention of hurting him, would be whirled about for a century in the hell termed *Tamasa.* He who smote a Brahmin with only a blade of grass, would be born an inferior quadruped during twenty-one transmigrations. But he who should shed the blood of a Brahmin, save in battle, would be mangled by animals in his next birth for as many years as there were particles of dust rolled up by the blood shed. If a Sudra (a low-caste man) sat upon the same seat with a Brahmin, he was to be gashed in the part offending."—*Institutes of Menu*, I, 94, etc.

Thus a body of men, supposed to number not more than a few hundred thousand, have held the two hundred millions of their fellow-countrymen for thirty centuries in the terrors of this sacerdotal legislation, enforcing its claims to the last limit of endurance, though at the fearful price of the utter ignorance, degradation, and slavery of their nation. The reader can well appreciate the indignant feelings with which this greedy, proud, and supercilious order of men contemplated the incoming of a Christian Government, which would make all men "equal before the law," and the advent of a Religion whose great glory it is to vindicate the oppressed and "preach the Gospel to the poor."

The Kshatriya caste (derived from *Kshetra,* land) and the Vaisyas (traders) had the privilege of the investiture with the sacred string; but to the Sudras there was to be no investiture, no sacrifice, and no Scriptures. They were condemned by this law to perpetual servitude. Yet this class, with the Outcasts, were necessarily the great majority of the nation, and those who might have been their instructors and guides, heartlessly took away the key of knowledge, made it a legal crime to "teach them how sin might be expiated," and deliberately degraded them for time and eternity. The Vedas expressly state that the benefits of the Hindoo religion are open only to three of the four castes! The fourth-caste man could have no share in religion and hold no property. He was a bondsman, and that forever. No system of human slavery ever equaled this; for it was intense, unalterable, and unending, by the act of God himself.

The distinctions of society, by the ordinances of the Hindoo Lawgiver, were thus indicated: Brahmins, or Priests; Kshatriyas, or Soldiers and Rajahs; Vaisyas, or Merchants and Farmers; Sudras, the servile class.

The arrangements indicate a pastoral condition of society, far removed from the stirring scenes of the life of the nineteenth century. The ordinances made no preparation for the wider wants of men or intercommunication of other nations, or the development of our race. They had no provision for manufacturing, mining, or commercial life, but expected the world to move on forever in their limited conservative methods. These four castes were subdivided, according to the theory, into sixty-four, and in the grooves thus opened the divisions of labor were expected to run, so that even trade should become hereditary; and thus, whatever the genius or ability developed in any man, he was expected to be content to remain in the profession of his father. He might have the germ and the buddings of a mind like Newton's, but, according to "their cast-iron rules of social life, if his father made shoes he too must stick to the last."

No man of one caste can eat, smoke, marry with, or touch the cooking-vessels of a person of another caste. The prohibition is fearfully strict, and guarded with terrible sanctions. And it is as destitute of humanity as it is singular; so that, were a stranger of their own nation, coming into one of their towns, to be taken suddenly ill, and unable to speak and explain of what caste he was, he would certainly be liable to perish, for the high-caste people would be afraid to touch him, lest they should break their caste, and those of the low-caste would be unwilling, lest their contact (on the supposition of his superior order) might irrecoverably contaminate him. In their hands the man would perish unaided.

This unique masterpiece of Brahminism was intended by its framers to be a wall of brass around their system, to secure its unalterable permanency. But, its own heartless selfishness and cruel tendencies had so far overdone the work that it was found practically impossible to sustain the integrity of the arrangements. Innovations crept in and conflicts ensued, and, despite the desperate efforts of the Brahmins, confusion has marred Menu's strange designs, while the introduction of Western civilization, the teachings of Christianity, and the light of true knowledge, have delivered such severe and repeated shocks that the venerable and hideous monstrosity is tottering to its final fall.

Four Stages of Life are marked out by Menu for the Brahmin: 1. The *Brahmachari*, or Studentship of the Veda; 2. The *Grihastha*, or Married State; 3. The *Vanaprastha*, or Hermit Life; 4. The *Sannyasi*, or Devotee Condition.

The Brahmachari stage begins with the investiture of the sacred thread, which act signifies "a second birth." The investiture takes place in his eighth year in case of a Brahmin, the eleventh year for a Kshatriya, and the twelfth for a Vaisya. The investiture introduces the "twice-born" Brahmin boy to a religious life, and is supposed to sanctify him for the study of the Veda.

The thread of the Brahmin is made of cotton and formed of three strings; that of the Kshatriya is made of hemp, and that of the Vaisya is of wool. It is termed the "sacrificial cord," because it entitles the wearer to the privilege of sacrifice and religious services. Certain ceremonies are observed for girls as well as for boys, but neither girls nor women are invested with the sacred thread nor the utterance of the sacred *mantras*. They have consequently no right to sacrifice. Indeed, the nuptial ceremony is considered to be for woman equivalent to the investiture of the thread, and is the commencement of the religious life of the female, (*Menu*, II, 66, 67.) So that, a lady remaining unmarried, has nothing equivalent to their "second birth" here, and can look forward to no certainty of a happy life hereafter. The poor Sudra is entirely excluded. Thus, the Servile Man and the unmarried woman of any, even the highest, caste are equally left outside the pale of Brahminical salvation—exactly that condition to which

High-Church Puseyism consigns all "Dissenters" when they hand them over to "the uncovenanted mercies of God."

In addition to the exclusion of woman and the lower caste, this terrible Code proceeds to sink still deeper vast multitudes of their fellow-creatures. The "Outcasts" are numbered by the million. Some of these are called "Chandalas," and concerning them this heartless and cruel Lawgiver ordains: "Chandalas must dwell without the town. Their sole wealth must be dogs and asses; their clothes must consist of the mantles of deceased persons; their dishes must be broken pots, and their ornaments must consist of rusty iron. No one who regards his duties must hold any intercourse with them, and they must marry only among themselves. By day they may roam about for the purposes of work, and be distinguished by the badges of the Rajah; and they must carry out the corpse of any one who dies without kindred. They should always be employed to slay those who are sentenced by the laws to be put to death; and they may take the clothes of the slain, their beds, and their ornaments."—*Code*, X, 51–58.

Can the Western reader wonder that, tame and subdued though the Asiatics may be, these aristocratic ordinances should have proved too much for human nature, or that the introduction of English rule and fair play, elevating these long-crushed millions to legal equality with these proud Brahmins, was an immense mercy to nearly one sixth of the human family?

As a sample of how this sacerdotal law, framed for his special glorification, discriminated in favor of the Brahmin, it may suffice to quote a sentence or two. On the question of his privileges when called to testify in a Court of Justice, he must be assumed to be the "very soul of honor," and his oath, without exposure to penalty, was to be held sufficient. The Code decreed that "A Brahmin was to swear by his veracity; a Kshatriya by his weapons, horse, or elephant; and a Vaisya by his kine, grain, or gold; but a Sudra was to imprecate upon his own head the guilt of every possible crime if he did not speak the truth."—VIII, 113. "To a Brahmin the Judge should say, 'Declare;' to a Kshatriya he should say, 'Declare the truth;' to the Vaisya he should compare perjury to the crime of stealing kine, grain, or gold; to the Sudra he should compare perjury to every crime in the following language: 'Whatever places of torture have been prepared for the murderer of a Brahmin, for the murderer of a woman, or child, have also been ordained for that witness who gives false evidence. If you deviate from the truth you shall go naked, shorn, and blind, and be tormented with hunger and thirst, and beg food with a potsherd at the door of your enemy; or shall tumble headlong into hell in utter darkness. Even if you give imperfect testimony, and assert a fact which you have not seen, you shall suffer pain like a man who eats fish and swallows the sharp bones."—*Menu*, VIII, 79–95.

The scale of punishments in the case of a Brahmin (in the few instances where he was at all amenable to the law it could only touch his property, never, under any consideration, his person) was equally drawn in his favor, and was all the lighter in proportion to the inferiority of caste of the man whom he had injured; while, on the other hand, it was equally to be increased in severity (for the same crime in both cases) in proportion to the same distinction Says the law, "A Kshatriya who slandered a Brahmin was to be fined a hundred panas; for the same crime a Vaisya was to be fined a hundred and fifty or two hundred panas; but a Sudra was to be whipped." On the other hand, if a Brahmin slandered a Kshatriya "he was to be fined fifty panas; if he slandered a Vaisya he was to be fined twenty-five panas; but if he slandered a Sudra he was only to be fined twelve panas. If, however, a Sudra insulted any man of the twice-born castes with gross invectives, he was to have his tongue slit; if he mentioned the name and caste of the individual with contumely, an iron style, ten fingers long, was to be made red-hot and thrust into his mouth; and if, through pride, he dared to instruct a Brahmin respecting his duty, the Rajah was to order that hot oil should be poured into his mouth and ear."—*Menu*, VIII, 266–276.

The "pana" was then nearly equal to our cent, so his privilege of slandering a Sudra could at any time be exercised with impunity for a dime, while, if it was so done unto him, the law took good care that the plebeian wretch should never repeat the offense, for his tongue was to be slit. How truly could the Almighty, whose name they blasphemously invoke for their outrageous legislation. say of them, "Are not your ways unequal?"

Even in salutations the Code ordained the forms, and gave them a religious significance. "A Brahmin was to be asked whether his devotion had prospered, a Kshatriya whether he had suffered from his wounds, a Vaisya whether his wealth was secure, and a Sudra whether he was in good health."—*Menu*, II, 127.

The food, the privileges, the duties, of this pampered monopolist are all minutely laid down in the Code, but they are too diffuse and too childish to place before the reader, and would not be worth the space occupied. In proof of this I quote one sentence from the fourth chapter, merely remarking that the whimsical injunctions are left without any rhyme or reason. They are as unaccountable as they are singular. "He (the Brahmin) must not gaze on the sun while rising or setting, or eclipsed or reflected in water; he must not run while it rains; he must not look on his own image in water; when he sees the bow of Indra in the sky he must not show it to any man; he must not step over a string to which a calf is tied; and he must not wash his feet in a pan of mixed metal."

In these stages of its development and claims, Brahminism is nothing less than a system of supreme selfishness, and was worthy of the express teaching with which the Brahmin was directed, in an emergency, to sacrifice every thing to his own precious self, in the following rule: "Against misfortune let him preserve his wealth; at the expense of his wealth let him preserve his wife; but let him at all events preserve himself, even at the hazard of his wife and riches."

How little can such a religion or such a law know of disinterested affection, or of that devotion which would risk every thing for the safety and happiness of its beloved object?

His student life ended, the Brahmin commences his married existence with forms and rules which will be referred to when we come to speak of the condition of woman under Hindoo law. In this second stage of his life he is required to have "his hair and beard properly trimmed, his passions subdued, and his mantle white; he is to carry a staff of Venu, a ewer with water in it, handful of Kusa grass, or a copy of the Vedas, with a pair of bright golden rings in his ears, ready to give instruction in the sacred books, or political counsel, and to administer justice."

Then in order would come the third and fourth stages of his life, the rules of which are so unique. Such an amazing contrast to the unbounded privileges of the previous stages, and withal so little like what ordinary humanity would impose upon itself, that we must quote them for the information of the reader. These two stages express the very essence of Brahminism. In the Hermit stage, the theory is a course of life that will mortify the passions and extinguish desire; this being accomplished, the last order, or Devotee stage, is religious contemplation with the view to final beatitude.

Menu says, "When the twice-born man has remained in the order of Grihastha, or householder, until his muscles become flaccid and his hair gray, and he sees a child of his child, let him abandon his household and repair to the forest, and dwell there in the order of Vanaprastha, or Hermit. He should be accompanied by his wife if she choose to attend him, but otherwise he should commit her to the care of his sons. He should take with him the consecrated fire, and all the domestic implements for making oblations to fire, and there dwell in the forest, with perfect control over all his organs. Day by day he should perform the five sacraments. He should wear a black antelope's hide, or a vesture of bark, and bathe morning and evening; he should suffer his nails and the hair of his head and beard to grow continually. He should be constantly engaged in reading the Veda; he should be patient in all extremities; he should be universally benevolent, and entertain a tender affection for all living creatures; his mind should be ever intent upon the Supreme Being; he should slide backward and forward, or stand a whole day on tiptoe, or continue in motion by rising and sitting alternately; but every day, at sunrise, at noon, and at sunset, he should go to the waters and bathe. In the hot season he should sit exposed to five fires, namely: four blazing around him, while the sun is burning above him. In the rainy season he should stand uncovered, without even a mantle, while the clouds pour down their heaviest showers. In the cold season he should wear damp vesture. He should increase the austerity of his devotion by degrees, until by enduring harsher and harsher mortifications he has dried up his bodily frame."—*Code*, VI, 22; *Vishnu Purana*, III, 9, etc.

As regards the life to be pursued by a Sannyasi, Menu lays down the following directions:

"When a Brahmin has thus lived in the forest during the third portion of his life as a Vanaprastha, he should for the fourth portion of it become a Sannyasi, and abandon all sensual affections, and repose wholly in the Supreme Spirit. The glory of that Brahmin who passes from the order of Grihastha to that of Sannyasi illuminates the higher worlds. He should take an earthen water-pot, dwell at the roots of large trees, wear coarse vesture, abide in total solitude, and exhibit a perfect equanimity toward all creatures. He should wish neither for death nor for life, but expect his appointed time, as a hired servant expects his wages. He should look down as he advances his foot, lest he should touch any thing impure. He should drink water that has been purified by straining through a cloth, lest he hurt an insect. He should bear a reproachful speech with patience, and speak reproachfully to no man; and he should never utter a word relating to vain, illusory things. He should delight in meditating upon the Supreme Spirit, and sit fixed in such meditation, without needing any thing earthly, without one sensual desire, and without any companion but his own soul.

"He should only ask for food once a day, and that should be in the evening, when the smoke of the kitchen fires has ceased, when the pestle lies motionless, and the burning charcoal is extinguished; when people have eaten, and when dishes are removed. If he fail to obtain food he should not be sorrowful; if he succeed in obtaining it he should not be glad. He should only care to obtain a sufficiency to support life, and he should not be anxious about his utensils."

As to the character of his thoughts: "A Sannyasi should reflect on the transmigrations of men, which are caused by their sinful deeds; on their downfall into a region of darkness, and their torments in the mansions of Yama, (the God of the dead;) on their separation from those whom they love, and their union with those whom they hate; on their strength being overpowered by old age, and their bodies racked with disease; on their agonizing departure from this corporeal frame, and their formation again in the womb; on the misery attached to embodied spirits from a violation of their duties, and the imperishable bliss which attaches to embodied spirits who have abundantly performed every duty.

"The body is a mansion, with bones for its rafters and beams, with nerves and tendons for cords, with muscles and blood for mortar, with skin for its outward covering, and filled with no sweet perfumes, but loaded with refuse. It is a mansion infested by age and by sorrow, the seat of diseases, harassed by pains, haunted with the quality of darkness, and incapable of standing long. Such a mansion of the vital soul should always be quitted with cheerfulness by its occupier."—*Institutes of Hindoo Law*, VI, 76, 77.

When you look around and inquire for these self-denying recluses, with their sublime superiority to the things of earth and the wants and wishes of the human heart, you will not find them; certainly not among the Brahmins. Few of these have ever adopted in reality a life so like that of the Yogee, or Self-torturer. All testimony goes to show that Menu's ordinances for the third and fourth stages of the Brahmin's life have lain in his law-book with not one Brahmin in ten thousand even commencing to make them a reality of human experience. It was too much for humanity, and could only be embraced by some fanatic of a Fakir, who would voluntarily assume such a condition for self-righteous and self-glorifying ends. Such men can and will do, for such reasons, what other men have not nerve enough to adventure merely in obedience to the theoretic rules of their order.

The Brahmins would fain be regarded as the *learned class* of India. Of course there was a time when, in the earlier ages of the world, they were so, as compared to men in other nations. No scholar can doubt this for a moment. But the world and education are no longer what they once were; both have advanced amazingly, while the Brahmin has not only stood still, but he has retrograded. The ruins of India's colleges, observatories, and scientific instruments, especially in Benares, (once "the eye of Hindustan,") convince the traveler too painfully of this fact. Even there, in that renowned city, there is not a single public building devoted to, or containing, the treasures of India's arts, sciences, or literature; no paintings, sculptures, or libraries; no colleges of learning, no museums of her curiosities; no monuments of her great men; only beastly idolatry, filthy fakirs, shrines of vileness without number, and festivals of saturnalian license, all sustained and illustrated by a selfish and ignorant Brahminhood.

Their learning is in the past, and little remains save their great Epics and the magnificent dead Language in which they were written. Their chronology is a wild and exaggerated falsehood, their geography and astronomy are subjects of ridicule to every schoolboy, their astrology (to which they are specially devoted) a humbug for deluding their countrymen; they had no true history till foreigners wrote it for them, and could not even read the Pali on their own public monuments till such Englishmen as Princeps and Tytler deciphered it. Native education to-day owes more to Macaulay, Dr. Duff, and Trevelyan, than to all the Brahmins of India for the past five hundred years. Every improvement introduced, and every mitigation of the miseries in the lot of woman, and of the lower and suffering classes, has been introduced against their will and without their aid as a class. They feel, they know, that their system is more or less effete; that they are being left

A Lady of India in Full Dress.

behind in the march of improvement on which their country has entered. But there they stand, scowling and twirling their Brahminical string; while the Sudras and the very "Chandalas," whom they tried so hard to doom to eternal degradation, are obtaining in Government and Missionary schools a sanctified scholarship, which is soon to consign the claims and pretensions of this venerable, haughty, and heartless aristocracy to the everlasting contempt which they deserve! One by one, in their ridiculous helplessness, they behold their strong places taken and wrested from their grasp. The very *Veda* in which they gloried, and behind which they falsely defended the vileness and cruelty of their system, has been magnificently collated and published in eight volumes by the scholarship of Max Müller, and then rendered, with equal ability, (the last volume having been published within the past five years,) into English by Wilson & Cowell. So that all the world may now know what the Veda is, and what it teaches, and thus hold these unworthy guardians of it to the fearful responsibility which they have incurred, in pretending to quote its authority for the abominations which characterize their modern Hindooism, with all its grievous wrongs against woman in particular, and against the interests of their own nation, as well as its violation of the common sense and judgment of mankind, for whose opinions, however, the Brahmins of India never showed the least respect.

We now turn from them to introduce the reader to one of the ladies of the land.

The opposite picture is from a photograph for which this lady, Zahore Begum, of Seereenugger, consented to sit. As her face had to be *seen* by the artist, the concession was a very singular one for any lady of her race. It was done to gratify the Queen of England, who, on the assumption of the direct sovereignty of India —on the abolition of the East India Company in 1859—requested that photographs of the people, and their various races, trades, and professions, might be taken and sent to her. Her Majesty graciously consented to have her valuable collection copied, and by the courtesy of Captain Meadows Taylor, the Oriental author, the writer obtained copies of this and several others of much value, which will appear in these pages.

My readers have, therefore, before them a faithful picture of a Hindoo lady of the highest rank, as she appears in her Zenana home, under the best circumstances, having made herself as attractive as silk, and muslin, and cashmere cloth, and a profusion of jewelry, can render her. In the jewel on the thumb of the left hand there is inserted a small looking-glass, of which the fair lady makes good use. The usual gold ring, strung with pearls, is in her nose, lying against her left cheek; and her forehead, ears, arms, fingers, ankles, and toes are crowded with jewelry and tinkling ornaments, the sounds of which proclaim her presence and approach always.

The wood-cut does no justice to her *warm olive color*, many of them being even almost fair. Most of them have a figure of great beauty, and a natural elegance of movement which their drapery and rich clothing well become. But the mind is totally neglected. In fact, until lately, when a gleam of light has begun to shine for women in the Land of the Veda, it might be said, without qualification, that no part of an American definition of education would apply to the culture under which a daughter of India is fitted for future life. It does not, for her, include reading, or writing, or history, or science, or aught else which we include in its meaning. Education, in its proper sense, is denied to the females of India; denied on principle, and for reasons which are unblushingly avowed, and all of which are reflections upon her womanly nature—one of them being the position that education in the hands of a woman would most likely become an instrument of evil power. She is deliberately doomed by modern Hindooism to a life of ignorance because she is a woman.

We have mentioned the present dawn of a better day. It is but the dawn. Dr. Mullen's statistics tell us that already there are now thirty-nine thousand six hundred and forty-seven women and girls receiving an education in the Zenana schools in India. The number is by this time larger and still increasing. Yet it is but

The Nautch Girl of India.

the commencement; for the above number, dividing the one hundred millions of women in India, gives but one in two thousand five hundred and twenty-two who are receiving instruction, a number equal only to what this country would have to-day were but one American lady in five hundred and four blessed with education. What need is there, then, to urge on the glorious toil of rescuing India's daughters from the intellectual abominations which desolate their soul and mind in this fearful manner!

The sad story of the wrongs of woman in India will be told after we have traced the rise and fall of the great Rebellion; for the mitigations of her condition, which Christian law had in mercy enforced, were then put forward by her Brahminical oppressors as one of the reasons why they had renounced their allegiance to British rule.

But there is one class of women, and it is a very large class, in India, who are under no such restrictions and jealous seclusion as the lady on the former page. These court publicity, and you can see them every-where. This order of females are released from the doom of an illiterate mind. They can read, write, and quote the poets, and jest with the conundrums and "wise saws" of the land. The writer has known of attempts made by this class of girls to enter our schools in order to add the English tongue to their acquisitions, to be used by them for the worst of purposes. These are the "Nauch Girls," a portrait of one of whom, from a photograph, is here given as she appears in public.

Their title means dancing-girls. No man in India would allow his wife or daughter to dance, and as to dancing with another man, he would forsake her forever, as a woman lost to virtue and modesty, if she were to attempt it. In their observation of white women, there is nothing that so much perplexes them as the fact that fathers and husbands will permit their wives and daughters to indulge in promiscuous dancing. No argument will convince them that the act is such as a virtuous female should practice, or that its tendency is not licentious. The prevalence of the practice in "Christian" nations makes our holy religion—which they suppose must allow it—to be abhorred by many of them, and often it is cast in the teeth of our missionaries when preaching to them. But what would these heathen say could they enter our operas and theaters, and see the shocking exposure of their persons which our public women there present before mixed assemblies? Yet they would be ten times more astonished that ladies of virtue and reputation should be found there, accompanied by their daughters, to witness the sight, and that, too, in the presence of the other sex! But, then, they are only heathens, and don't appreciate the high accomplishments of Christian civilization! Still, Heaven grant that the future Church of India may ever retain at least this item of the prejudices of their forefathers! Dancing forms, then, no part of a daughter's education in India, and it probably never will, that is, unless they become corrupted by "Christian" example.

All of that sort of thing that they ever desire, on occasions of festivals and ceremonies, they hire from the temples and bazaars. Four or five of these women, tricked out in all their finery and jewelry, and tinkling ornaments on arms, necks, and feet, will, for four or five dollars, dance and jest, and sing India's licentious songs for hours; but even they don't dance except with their own sex. They are prostitutes, and yet they are undoubtedly the only intelligent and cultivated class of Hindoo women. So that the profane and debased have a monopoly of education, while the virtuous and retiring ladies of the land are condemned to a life of ignorance. Such is woman in India as to her mind.

Until within a few years this fearful barrier to woman's education stood sternly across the path of the missionary. A change, in the great mercy of Heaven, is dawning at last even upon India; but as recently as ten years ago, when you spoke to a Hindoo father about educating his daughter, the ideas that are here clearly enough intimated at once presented themselves to his mind, and your proposal seemed to him to be almost profane, as he thought "Would you make my daughter a Nauch girl?" The Temple of Knowledge, with its sacred flame, no longer guarded by the Vestal Virgins, seemed resigned absolutely to the control and occupation

The Maharajah Duleep Singh.

of those polluted beings, whose profession and blandishments are exerted to

> "Make vice pleasing and damnation shine,"

but whose guests are in the depths of hell.

We next present to the reader one of the upper class of Hindoo society just as he would appear at a "Durbar," or State ceremonial, or in receiving guests at his palace, or in connection with some public display.

The dress of a gentleman in India is regulated as to its quality by his wealth and position, and in its variations of form by his creed and locality; but the Maharajah costume here shown may be regarded generally as that of his countrymen.

Their dress is free and flowing, adapted to the climate, and leaving to the limbs a greater freedom of action, with more circulation of air, than the American style of dress can ever know. Although to our imagination it appears somewhat effeminate in its aspect, yet it is eminently graceful and becoming to the wearers, as any one who has seen a company of Hindoo gentlemen together will have observed. There is something so conservative and biblical in the aspect of it, that you feel at once that the fluctuations of the fashions can have no influence upon it. Here is something that is at once suitable and unchanging—a style of comfort and elegance which the past five hundred years has not varied, and which will probably remain unaltered when five hundred more years have passed away.

The dress here represented shows a vest of "Kinkob"—cloth of gold—slightly exposed at the breast; a loose-fitting coat falling below the knees, made of rich yellow satin from the looms of Delhi, bordered with gold embroidery; a Cashmere shawl of great value encircles the loins, and the usual "Kummerbund" binds all to the waist of the wearer. The turban is made of several yards of fine India muslin, twisted round the head, heavily adorned with chains of pearls, and aigrettes of diamonds and precious stones. These, with the pearls encircling his neck, are of large size and extraordinary beauty and value, the heir-looms of many generations.

He holds by his side his State sword, the hilt of which is studded with precious stones. To all this "glory" might have been added the matchless *Koh-i-noor* diamond, for this prince was the heir of "The Mountain Light," his father, the Maharajah Runjeet Singh, having been its last possessor ; but the great diamond was sent as a present to Queen Victoria, and he himself is handsome and happy enough without it.

How significant of the resources of India is the fact that every article on the person of this princely man, from the gold and gems on his head to the embroidered slippers on his feet, is the production of his own country, and all of native manufacture! How quietly in this respect he outshines the Broadway "exquisite" or Parisian belle, whose finery must be sought for in a score of climes and imported from many lands!

The Maharajah is considered one of the handsomest of his countrymen. The excellent wood-cut here representing him does not, however, do justice to his black, lustrous eyes, or his finely formed features and intelligent look.

The education of the gentlemen of India is sadly deficient. Conducted in the Zenana, among ladies ignorant of the most elementary knowledge, their mental training and acquisitions are usually of the most superficial sort, and destitute of healthful stimulus. But the gentleman here represented is one of the exceptions to this rule ; and as he has had the moral courage to separate himself from heathenism and receive the Christian faith, the reader may be pleased with some further notice of him.

He is the first royal person in India who has become a follower of Jesus Christ. His highness is the son and heir of the Maharajah Runjeet Singh, who, from the ferocity and valor with which he conducted his wars and ruled his people, was called "The Lion of the Punjab." The old gentleman's policy left his nation in confusion, and the English power, in the wars that resulted, found his forces to be the sturdiest foe with whom they had ever measured swords in India. Runjeet died in 1839, and his son, this Duleep Singh, then only four years old, was placed upon the throne. His uncles ruled in his name, but the ten years which followed were times of anarchy and bloodshed, the Regents being assassinated in succession, and the country one vast camp. The army superseded the civil power, and in their folly actually crossed the frontier, and in 1845 invaded British India. They were repulsed, but only to renew the effort four years later, when they were overthrown, and the Punjab—the country of the five rivers, as the word means, the rivers named in Alexander's invasion, and which unite to form the Indus at Attock—was annexed to the British Empire. The young Maharajah was pensioned, and placed for education under the care of the Government. God mercifully guided the Governor-general in the selection of guardian and tutor for the little prince. Dr. (now Sir John) Logan, of the medical service, and a member of the Presbyterian Church, was appointed his guardian, and Mr. Guise, of the civil service, was selected as his tutor. To Mr. Guise's other high qualifications for his duties was added a beautiful Christian character. He had need of all his fitness, for the little ex-king had never been used to any restraint, much less to study or to books, and claimed the right to run wild and neglect all mental acquisitions. But the patience and conscientiousness of the faithful tutor overcame every difficulty; good habits and a taste for reading were at length formed. Their home was at Futtyghur, on the Ganges, where the American Presbyterian Church has a Mission, (the missionaries being mentioned by name on a previous page,) in which many young men were receiving a Christian education. The prince expressed a desire to have some one of good birth and talents for a companion, and a young Brahmin, by name Bhajan Lal, who had been educated in the mission-school, and had there, though unconverted, contracted a love for the Christian Scriptures, was chosen for the position. He soon enjoyed the entire confidence of the young Maharajah. Bhajan was in the habit of studying the Bible in his leisure moments, and the prince two or three times having come upon him thus engaged, was led to inquire what book it was that so interested him. He was told, and at his request Bhajan promised to read and explain the Word of God to him, but on condition that it should not be known. The priests of his own religion that had accompanied him from the Punjab, and were training him in the tenets of their faith, were soon seen by him in a new light as he continued to read the Scriptures. When he began to compare them, in all their mummery, immorality, and covetousness, with the purity and spirituality of the Christians around him, whose lives and examples he had carefully noted, a feeling of disgust with heathenism, and a preference and love for the religion of the Bible, sprang up in his heart, to which he soon gave expression. Thus the reading of God's holy Word, taught and explained even by a heathen youth and Brahmin, led the Maharajah to give up idolatry, and to express a desire to break his caste and be baptized.

The priests were amazed and confounded, and offered what resistance they could. But the guardianship of the prince effectually shielded him from all persecution. Yet, as he was so young, and the step contemplated so important, his guardian, though rejoiced at his purpose, and ready to aid it in every proper way, suggested delay till he could more fully study the religion of Jesus and act with fuller deliberation. He accepted the advice, drew nearer to the missionaries, attended the services, and enjoyed the association of the Christians. He was led to embrace Christ as his Saviour, and on the 8th of March, 1853, was baptized and received into the Christian Church. The Rev. W. J. Jay, the chaplain of the station, administered the holy ordinance in the presence of all the missionaries, the native Christians and Europeans at the station, and the servants of the Maharajah. He was clad as here represented, and when he took off his turban, and with much firmness and humility bowed his head to receive the sacred ordinance, every heart in the assembly was moved, and many a prayer went up that he might have grace to fulfill his vows and honor his Christian profession.

He has faithfully done so to the present time. Immediately after his baptism he established relief societies at Futtyghur and Lahore, placing them under the control of the American missions at both places. Besides assisting in the support of the missions, he established, and still sustains, a number of village schools for the education of the people, and has been a liberal contributor to every good object brought to his notice. When the writer was at Futtyghur he had the opportunity of witnessing the results which were being accomplished by the Christian liberality of the Maharajah in and around that station. He was then aiding the cause of Christ and the poor to the extent, probably, of fully one tenth of his whole income annually, and I presume his liberality is no less now.

Some time after his baptism, with a desire to improve his mind by foreign travel, he visited England. He took with him a devoted Christian, who had formerly been a Hindoo Pundit, named Nil Knath, by whose instructions he was more fully established in the doctrines of the Gospel, and with whom he enjoyed daily prayer and other religious privileges. On his arrival in London the Government placed a suitable residence in Wimbledon at his disposal, and the Queen and Prince Albert showed him much attention and kindness.

The Sepoy Rebellion of 1857 distressed him exceedingly, and probably alienated him from his native land. His entire severance from the religion of his countrymen, and, most of all, probably, reasons of State in view of the English rule in his country, which he would not wish by his presence there to disturb in any way, led him to prefer England as a residence. A magnificent home has been provided for him near London, and there, on the allowance of his rank paid yearly by the British Government, he is spending the present portion of his life, honored and respected by all around him. He has probably ere now come to the conclusion that the loss of the throne of the Punjab may have been for him a good providence. During the rebellion his life might have been sacrificed. In the peace and honor that surround him he is not only entirely free from the evil influences of an Oriental court, and the distractions of irresponsible government, but he may reflect, judging the present from the past, that, had he remained and reigned, he might very probably, like his uncles and predecessors, have met a violent death.

Gentlemen in other lands having the means and leisure of the higher classes of Hindoo society would be cultivating their minds, enlarging and enriching the literature of their times by their authorship, by foreign travel, by collections of books and works of art, and institutions for developing the resources of their great country. But there are no authors in India, no libraries in its homes; not one in a thousand of its aristocracy ever saw the outside of his native land. Learned societies, museums, or fruits of genius are not to be found there. Education, when acquired, is restricted mostly to the mere ability of reading and writing and talking in courtly style, while there are multitudes of wealthy men that cannot do that much; nay, there are even kings without the power to write their own names, who can give validity to State documents only by stamping them with "the signet on their right hand." The sovereign of the Punjab—father of the Maharajah here represented—was one such. He was unable to write or read his own name, and to the day of his death could not tell one figure from another.

The little information of general news which they acquired from time to time had been obtained by a singular arrangement. Each great family, or king's court, had its "editor." He was expected to furnish the news daily, or as often as he could. So he collected from any source within his reach, and got his newspaper ready. But he had no press, nor type, nor office, nor newsboy to aid him. He simply enters on his broad sheet, in writing, one after another, all the news or gossip he could collect, until his paragraphs fill his pages, and he sallies forth in the morning to circulate the news, commencing with the members of the household, and thence to the servants, and so on to the neighbors, reading for each circle the news he had previously collected and written out, and receiving his fees from each company as he goes round the neighborhood. Of express trains, telegraphs, associated press, pictorial papers, and all our Christian appliances for collecting and distributing the news of the wide world, he is utterly ignorant. But the poor editor is on a par with the education of his patrons, and he can rest assured they are not likely to outstrip him in the race for knowledge. And so it goes on from generation to generation, until now, when this wonderful innovator, Christianity, has walked right into the midst of this venerable ignorance, and, to the horror of these editorial oracles, has lifted many even of the Pariah youth of their bazaars to a plane of education and knowledge up to which millions look with amazement as they wonder what is going to happen now, when boys "whose fathers they would have disdained to set with the dogs in their flocks" are actually becoming possessed of an education which even their Pundits do not enjoy!

The habits of the India aristocracy are in many respects decidedly peculiar. The residence, for instance, is usually very mean, as compared with the wealth of the parties. While they will spend millions upon a temple or tomb, they are content to dwell in a house which a man in America, with one fiftieth of their income, would scorn to inhabit. A Rajah with a rent-roll of say fifty thousand dollars or more per annum will sometimes pass his life in a residence built of sun-dried brick, with a tiled roof, that cost less than two thousand dollars, surrounded on all sides with mud hovels, and in the midst of a bazaar where the din and smoke and effluvia would be intolerable to any decent American.

No doubt this want of appreciation of surrounding circumstances in their life is caused by their inability while heathens justly or truly to estimate that idea of *home* which Christianity has created for man, especially in the "honorable estate" of the married life which she ordains and blesses, and to which she leads the grateful, loving husband to bring his means and ingenuity to adorn it, to make it a convenient, cheerful, happy dwelling for the blessed wife whom he loves and the dear children whom God has given them. Such a home, with its joy and honor, the heathen or polygamist can never know or appreciate. His residence is but a convenience, not the sanctuary of the affections, and his estimate of home must be, and is, defective and perverted.

They eschew furniture, in our sense of the word—tables, chairs, knives and forks. They eat with the fingers alone, and generally sleep on a charpoy or mat. When you enter a Hindoo home you are at once struck with the naked look of the room—no chair or sofa to sit upon, no pictures on the walls, no piano or musical instrument, no library of books, no maps, no table with the newspaper or periodical or album upon it, and you wonder how they can bear to live such a life; to you it would be a misery and a blank. But you are a Christian, and your holy religion has made you to differ, and taught you the nature and value of a Christian home and its conveniences and joys.

Nothing would more surprise them in visiting our Western world than to see how generally, according to the ability of each, we beautify and adorn our residences, and surround them with flowers and verdure and neatness. They would think this all very artificial, and perhaps unnecessary, and could not enter into the feelings of those whose constant effort seems to be to make their abode on earth, in its purity, companionship, and peace, a type of the home in heaven.

Woman alone in heathenism, even where she has possessed peculiar wealth and power and opportunity for the effort, cannot make this earthly paradise; she requires Christianity to be successful. Cases have occurred where European ladies have been induced —in Delhi, Lucknow, etc.—to enter even royal zenanas as wives. But though knowing the difference, and probably fondly hoping they could by their presence and ability constitute a happy social state, they soon realized that the very atmosphere forbid the development of the home they hoped to cultivate, and the fair experimenters had, in utter despair, to abandon their efforts and their hopes, and not only so, but themselves to sink to the sad level of the heathenish community into which they had ventured!

"Home is the sacred refuge of our life."

True, but India's sons can never learn the sentiment and experience which Dryden's line thus expresses till the daughters of India receive the Christianity which alone can cultivate their minds and hearts, and take under its divine guardianship their sacred mission in India, as in America, to

"Give to social man true relish of himself."

The men of India have never known woman's high power as "a helpmeet" in mind, heart, social life, or usefulness, and until they do they cannot enjoy the blessed home which only honored and elevated women can create.

If there be any one thing, short of salvation, in which America and India contrast each other most vividly, it is woman's high position in her home, and man's consequent happiness resulting therefrom—as wife, living for the husband whom she loves; as mother, making her abode a nursery for the Eden on high; the friend and patron of all that is lovely, virtuous, and of good report; her plastic influence of mind and heart and character molding those within her sphere into sympathy with her own goodness, while she thus sweetly

"Allures to brighter worlds, and leads the way."

In presence of this excellence—and, thank Heaven! Christianity has thousands such—every thing beautiful on earth brightens. The holiest and happiest men in this world bask in this blessed social sunshine, and are led by it to the contemplation and earnest hope of those "better things" which it typifies; their sanctified domestic joy becoming a sign and promise of the felicity that will be endless when they come to realize at last what they so often sing below—

"My heavenly home is bright and fair."

The food and manner of eating is quite Oriental, with the peculiarity on the part of the stricter Brahminical caste that they never touch flesh of any kind; but the rich variety of fruits and vegetables, and other products of the field and garden, with milk, butter, etc., enables them to enjoy a full variety. The favorite dish of India is the "curry," and natives and foreigners alike seem to agree that it is the king of all dishes. If it was not the "savory meat" that Isaac loved, the latter was probably very like it; but the dish itself is never equal, in piquancy and aroma out of India to what you receive there. The eating is done without the aid of knives or forks, the fingers alone being used. This is the mode for all, no matter how high or wealthy. The writer saw the Emperor of Delhi take his food in this way. When they have finished, a servant lays down a brass basin before them and pours water on their hands, and presents a towel to wipe them, reminding one of Elisha "pouring water on the hands of Elijah," acting as his attendant in honor of the man of God.

The amusements of the India aristocracy are very limited. The enervation of the climate may have something to do with this, but it is probably more due to a want of that developed manliness and self-assertion which belongs only to a higher civilization. They hardly ever think of going out hunting, or fishing, or fowling. Of the chase they know nothing, and I presume there is not one base-ball club in the country; gymnastic exercises they never take, their music is barbarous, and they do not play. When a feast or marriage requires entertainment they hire professional musicians, dancers, jugglers, or players to perform before their guests, but take no part whatever personally. Operas and theaters and promiscuous dancing they hold in abhorrence, as too immoral for them or their families to witness. They are fond of formal calls upon their equals, or social and civil superiors, and like display and exhibitions of their standing and wealth. They are regularly scientific in the art of taking their ease, being bathed and shampooed, fanned to sleep and while asleep. They love to be decorated with dress and jewelry, enjoy frequent siestas, and divide the remainder of their leisure time in the society of women whom they choose to entertain in their zenanas; but of public spirit and efforts, disinterested devotion to the welfare of others, intellectual enjoyments, the culture and training of their children's minds or morals, or the exalting influence of communion with a refined and intelligent wife or mother, they know but little or nothing, because they are utter strangers to the inspiration of the holy religion whose fruits these joys and virtues are.

When they undertake to pay a visit of ceremony it is, to our views, very singular what form and punctiliousness they deem to be indispensable. The whole establishment seems turned out for the purpose, for the larger the "following" so much the more you are expected to be impressed with the standing and dignity of the great man who has come to honor you with his call. An outrunner or two reaches your door in advance, and announces the master's approach; then come an armed squad, and his confidential servant, or "vakeel," and behind them the great man himself on his elephant, or in his palanquin; another crowd of retainers bring up the rear, the whole train numbering from thirty to sixty persons, or even more. Often, as I have looked at them, have I been reminded of the figure in the Revelations, where the blessed dead are represented as accompanied on their way into the kingdom of heaven by the escort of the good deeds of their faithful lives, which rise up to accompany them as so many evidences of their devotion to God—"Their works do follow them." The interview is merely a ceremony. The lady of the house is not expected to make her appearance; but where the visit is to a missionary family the lady generally does show herself, and, joining in the conversation, watches the opportunity to say a word for the truth of the Gospel. The native gentleman is evidently amazed, though he conceals it as well as he can, at her intelligence and her self-possession in the presence of another man than her husband, so unlike the prejudices that fill his mind about the female members of his own household. No doubt, amazing are the descriptions he carries home of what he has seen and heard on such an occasion.

But it is in connection with "*durbars*," governmental levees and marriage festivals, that the whole force of the native passion for parade and ostentation develops itself. As a sample: At the durbar some time ago in the Punjab, Diahn Singh, one of the nobles, came mounted on a large Persian horse, which curveted and pranced about as though proud of his rider. The bridle and saddle were covered with gold embroidery, and underneath was a saddle-cloth of silver tissue, with a broad fringe of the same material, which nearly covered the animal. The legs and tail of the horse were dyed red—the former up to the knees, and the latter half-way to the haunches—an emblem, well understood by the crowd, of the number of enemies which this military chief was supposed to have killed in battle, and that their blood had covered his horse thus far. The chief himself was dressed with the utmost magnificence, loaded with jewels, which hung, row upon row, round his neck, in his turban, on the hilt of his sword and dagger, and over his dress generally, while a bright cuirass shone resplendent on his breast. Add to this a face and person handsome and majestic, and you have the man as he delighted to be seen on the occasion.

But even this was outdone a few months ago on the occasion of the visit of one of Queen Victoria's sons, the Duke of Edinburgh, to India. A part of the pageant was the procession of elephants. These animals, one hundred and seventy in number, and the finest in size and appearance in India, were each decorated in the richest housings, and ridden by the Nawabs and Rajahs who owned them, each trying hard to outvie the other. Perhaps the Maharajah of Putteallah carried off the palm. The housings of his immense elephant were of such extraordinary richness that they were covered with gold and jewels. The Maharajah, who rode on him, wore a robe of black satin embroidered with pearls and emeralds. The *howdah*—seat on the elephant's back—in which the Rajah of Kuppoorthullah sat, was roofed with a triple dome made of solid silver.

This passion of ostentation and show breaks over all bounds on the occasion of their marriage ceremonies, and is permitted to know no limit but their means, nor sometimes even that. Sleeman narrates of the Rajah of Bullubghur—whom the writer saw in such different circumstances twenty years after these events, on trial for his life in the Dewanee Khass of Delhi, in 1857, as will be described hereafter—that on the occasion of his marriage in 1838 the young chief mustered a cortege of sixty elephants and ten thousand followers to attend him. He was accompanied by the chiefs of

The Mohammedans of India.

Ludora and Putteallah, with forty more elephants, and five thousand people.

It was considered necessary to the dignity of the occasion that the bridegroom's party should expend at least six hundred thousand rupees—$300,000 gold—during the festival. A large part of this sum was to be distributed freely in the procession ; so it was loaded on elephants, and persons were appointed to fling it among the crowds as the cavalcade passed on its way. They scattered copper money all along the road from their home till within seven miles of Bullubghur. From this point to the gate of the fort they scattered silver, and from the gate of the fort to the door of the palace they scattered gold and jewels. The son of the Putteallah chief, a lad of about ten years, had the post of honor in the distribution. He sat on his elephant, and beside him was a bag of gold mohurs — each mohur is worth eight dollars gold — mixed up with an immense variety of gold ear-rings, pearls, and precious stones. His turn for scattering began as they neared the palace door. Seeing some European gentlemen, who had come to look at the procession, standing on the balcony, the little chief thought they should have their share, so he heaved up vigorously several handfuls of the pearls, mohurs, and jewels, as he passed them. Not one of them, of course, would condescend to stoop to take up any, but the servants in attendance upon them showed no such dignified forbearance.

The costs of the family of the bride are always much greater than that of the bridegroom. They are obliged to entertain, at their own expense, all the bridegroom's guests which go with him for his bride, as well as their own, as long as they remain.

From this running description of the superficial, self-glorifying, and aimless lives which these men follow, the reader may easily imagine what must be the condition of their minds, their morals, and their characters.

The Mohammedans, a picture of whom we present here, are a more energetic people than the Hindoos. Their aspect is haughty and intolerant, and in meeting them you are under no liability to mistake them for the milder race whom they have so long crushed down and ruled. They are descended from original Asiatics of Persia, Arabia, etc., while the Hindoos are of western stock.

"The natives of India attach far more weight to form and ceremony than do Europeans. It is considered highly disrespectful to use the left hand in salutation or in eating, or, in fact, on any other occasion when it can be avoided. To remove the turban is disrespectful; and still more so not to put off the shoes on entering a strange house. Natives, when they make calls, never rise to go till they are dismissed, which among Mohammedans is done by giving betel and sprinkling rose essence, and with Hindoos by hanging wreaths of flowers around the visitor's neck, at least on great occasions. Discourteous Englishmen are apt to cut short a long visit by saying *Ab jao*—'Now go!' than which nothing can be more offensive. The best way is to say, 'Come and see me again soon,' or, 'Always make a practice of visiting my house,' which will be speedily understood. Or to one much inferior you may say, *Rukhsat lena*—'Leave to go,' or, better, *Rukhsat lijiye*—'Please to take leave.' A letter closed by moistening the wafer or the gum with the saliva of the mouth should not be given to a native. The feet must not be put upon a chair occupied by them, nor must the feet be raised so as to present the soles to them. One must avoid touching them as much as possible, especially their beards, which is a gross insult. If it can be avoided, it is better not to give a native three of any thing. Inquiries are never made after the female relations of a man. If they are mentioned at all it must be as 'house.' 'Is your house well?' that is, 'Is your wife well?' There are innumerable observances to avoid the evil eye; and many expressions seemingly contradictory are adopted for this purpose. Thus, instead of our 'Take away,' it is proper to say, 'Set on more;' and for 'I heard you were sick,' 'I heard your enemies were sick.' With Mohammedans of rank it is better not to express admiration of any thing they possess, as they will certainly offer it; in case of acceptance they would expect something of more value in return. To approach a Hindoo of high caste while at his meal is to deprive him of his dinner; to drink out of his cup may deprive him of his caste, or seriously compromise him with his caste-fellows. Leather is an abomination to Hindoos; as is every thing made from the pig, as a riding-saddle, to the Moslem. When natives of a different rank are present you must be careful not to allow those to sit whose rank does not entitle them, and to give each his proper place."—*Murray's Handbook.*

Such are the people of that land toward whom for ages the attention of outside nations has been directed with so much interest. We will now consider briefly their composition and numbers, and some of those singular chronological, historical, and religious views which they have entertained so tenaciously, and so long.

CHAPTER II.

STATISTICS, MYTHOLOGY, AND VEDIC LITERATURE.

EVEN among educated men there is a very inadequate idea of what INDIA really is. It is spoken of as though it were one country, with one language and one race of men, just as persons would speak of England or France; whereas India ought to be regarded as a number of nations, speaking twenty-three different languages, and devoted to various faiths and forms of civilization.

During the long period from the time of William the Conqueror till Clive fought the battle of Plassey in 1756, the Hindoos and Mohammedans maintained their diversity, and were as far from any unity or amalgamation when England entered the country, as they were when Mahmoud of Ghizni conquered Delhi. While the nations of Europe tended to unity, and fused their tribes and clans into homogeneous people, who gloried in a common faith and fatherland, these millions of hostile men have retained the sharp outlines of race, religion, language, and nationality as distinctly as ever.

The diversity of race is shown in the Coles, the Jats, the Santhals, the Tartars, the Shanars, the Mairs, the Karens, the Affghans, the Paharees, the Bheels; in religion, we have the Mohammedans, the Hindoos, the Buddhists, the Jains, the Parsees, the Pagans, and the Christians. While in nationality, there are the Bengalese, the Rohillas, the Burmans, the Mahrattas, the Seikhs, the Telugoos, the Karens, and many others.

India is thus, in fact, a congregation of nations, a crowd of civilizations, customs, languages, and types of humanity, thrown together, with no tendency to homogeneity, until an external civilization and a foreign faith shall make unity and common interest possible by educating and Christianizing them.

In regard to the real numbers of these wonderful people we are now able, from a census taken by the English Government last year, and also from Missionary Reports and other authorities, to furnish reliable civil and religious statistics of the Indian Empire. A few items are approximations, but they come as near to accuracy as is now necessary. India has an area of 1,577,698 square miles. It is nearly 2,000 miles from North to South, and 1,900 miles from East to West. The country is divided into 221 British Districts, and 153 Feudatory States, with a population of 212,671,621 souls.

The average density of this population to the square mile is 135 persons. But in Oude and Rohilcund (the mission field of the Methodist Episcopal Church) the density is 474 and 361 respectively, and is therefore probably the most compact population in the world. England has 367, and the United States only 26, persons to the square mile. As to race, this vast multitude of men are divided as follows:

The English army	58,000
Europeans and Americans (civil, mercantile, and missionary life)	89,585
Eurasians (the mixed races)	40,789
Asiatics	212,483,247

In religion the native population are distributed, as nearly as we can approximate them, into

Parsees (followers of Zoroaster)	150,000
Jains (Heterodox Buddhists)	400,000
Syrian and Armenian Christians	140,000
Protestants (attendants on Worship)	350,000
Roman Catholics (attendants on Worship)	760,000*
Karens (in British Burmah)	500,000
Seikhs (in the Punjab)	2,000,000
Buddhists (in British Burmah and Ceylon)	3,280,000
Aborigines, and undefined	11,000,000
Mohammedans	30,000,000
Hindoos	165,000,000

* The Roman Catholic Bishop of Madras in 1869 estimated the whole number of native Romanists in their communion at 760,623, supervised by the Bishops, and 734 priests, in addition to 124,000 with 128 priests under the jurisdiction of the almost schismatic and Portuguese Archbishop of Goa. But Dr. George Smith, one of the highest authorities on India statistics, regards these figures as unworthy of trust, and sets down the numbers for both as not over 700,000.—*Friend of India, May* 10, 1871, p. 554.

There are a few Jews, Chinese, Portuguese, French, Armenians, Nestorians, and others in the country, but of these we make no account here.

The vastness of this wonderful country may be further illustrated by the amazing number of languages spoken throughout its wide extent; and these are living languages, separate and distinct from each other, so that even the characters of their alphabets have no more similarity than the Greek letter has to the Roman. Nor do I include dialects of tongues, or languages of limited and local use, but those which are well known and extensively employed. Of such there are not less than *twenty-three* spoken in the various provinces of India. They are

1. The *Urdu*, (the Hindustanee proper,) the French of India, the language of the Mohammedans, of trade, etc.; spoken in Oude and Rohilcund, the Doab, and by traders generally; 2. The *Bengalee*, spoken in Bengal and eastward; 3. The *Hindee*, used in Oude, Rohilcund, Rajpootana, Bundlecund, and Malwa by the agricultural Hindoos, etc.; 4. The *Punjabee*, in the great Indus valley; 5. The *Pushtoo*, in Peshawar and the far West; 6. The *Sindhee*, in the Cis-Sutlej States and Sinde; 7. The *Guzerattee*, in Guzerat, and by the Parsees; 8. The *Cutchee*, in Cutch; 9. The *Cashmerian*, in Cashmere; 10. The *Nepaulese*, in Nepaul; 11. The *Bhote*, in Bootan; 12. The *Assamese*, in Assam; 13, 14. The *Burmese* and *Karen*, in Burmah and Pegu; 15. The *Singhalese*, in Ceylon; 16. The *Malayalim*, in Travencore and Cochin; 17. The *Tamul*, from Madras to Cape Comorin; 18. The *Canarese*, in Mysore and Coorg; 19. The *Teloogoo*, in Hydrabad, and thence to the East Shore; 20. The *Oorya*, in Orissa; 21. The *Cole* and *Gond*, in Berar; 22. The *Mahratta*, in Bombay, Nagpore, and Gwalior; and 23. The *Khassiya*, in the North-east. Add the English, and there are *twenty-four living languages* extensively spoken in India to-day! Nor is this all: the great classics of the leading tongues, the ancient and venerable *Pali*, the *Sanscrit*, the *Persian*, and the *Arabic* are studied and used by the scholarship of India, because they hold in their charge the venerable treasures of their volumi-

nous literature, and are as important to their faiths as sacred Greek is to Christianity.

Compare India with Europe, leaving out Russia, and she has more States, languages, and people. The principal tongues of Europe are the English, French, Portuguese, Spanish, Italian, German, Russ, Polish, Turkish, Greek, Dutch, Danish, Swede, Norwegian, and Finn—15. There were (according to the Census of 1861) in Europe 52 States, 15 languages, and 198,014,432 people; but, in India, there are 374 States, 23 languages, and 212,483,247 people. Giving India more States, more languages, and more population than all the great Western nations combined!

To understand what India is, and what was the force and importance of her great Sepoy Rebellion, and what is likely to be her relation to Christianity, and to the magnificent future which awaits her Hemisphere, the reader needs to understand and bear these facts in mind.

Of course, such a people are not destitute of national conceit. Indeed, the Hindoos hold up their heads with a sovereign sense of superiority above all other people on the earth. Admit their claims, and their system of chronology, and the assumptions of their history, and all other nations must hang their heads as modern novelties, and bow down in humility in the presence of a civilization of divine origin and a venerable aristocracy that counts its life and honors by millions of years! No Hindoo doubts but that his country is, or has been, the fount of all the blessings which have spread over the world, and in this rich conceit they hold it as a maxim that

> "Min-as-shark talata ba kudrat ar-rahman,
> Anwar-ud-din wa al-ilm, wa al-umran."

That is,

> "From the East, by the power of the Merciful One,
> Lights of Science, Religion, and Culture have shone."

The name India is apparently derived from the river Indus, and may have originated in the fact that that river divided this then unknown land from Persia and the world of ancient classical literature. The country is called in Sanscrit *Bharatkund*, from a dynasty of ancient kings; *Punya Dhurma*, "The Holy Land," and also *Djam-bhu-dwip*, the "Peninsula of the Tree of Life."

The *trade* of India is immense. The Imports are cotton cloth, jewelry, watches, stationery, hardware, metals, salt, silk, books, woolens, *American ice*, bullion, etc., etc.; and the Exports are coffee, tea, raw cotton, (in 1861 to England alone 3,295,000 cwt., producing there $47,500,000,) indigo, opium, ($50,000,000 annually,) saltpeter, jute, seeds, sugar, wool, (23,432,689 lbs. in 1865,) rice, raw silk, ivory, lac, oils, etc. The balance of trade is in favor of India, and the difference has to be paid in cash; so that the specie of England, Germany, and America is drained off to the East, and wealthy India grows richer all the time on a foreign commerce which has now risen to $577,000,000 (gold) per annum. The tonnage is at present 4,268,666 tons, and the revenue $249,646,040, which is only about $1 18 per head—an easier rate of taxation than is levied upon its people by any other civilized Government, while the proportion of the revenue spent on the Administration itself is equally economical. Deduct the annual charges for roads and bridges, police, jails, and courts of justice, education, canals, reservoirs, and irrigation, army, navy, telegraphs, public works, interest on Government securities, and it seems remarkable that the scanty remainder could meet all the charges of the Administration. The Hindoos well know that they were never so well and so cheaply governed as they are now. Their own testimony to this fact will be presented further on. If it were not for the extent to which the cultivated land is almost exclusively made to bear the burden, with its uncertain tenure, (though this is the practice in most Oriental Governments,) and the growth and sale of that vile opium, there would be little now to rebuke in the government of British India. Yet none are more earnest than some of the English themselves for the abolition of this reproach upon their fair fame.

There are seven railroads now running in different parts of the country, with an entire extent of 4,039 miles, and the total traffic receipts of which for the week ending April 22, 1871, was £140,220 11*s*. 4*d*., or $701,102, gold. Other lines are in process of construction. The telegraphs, 14,000 miles long, run all through India, while roads as feeders to the railways are being made over the land. But all has been done or furthered by the Government, and the whole has been accomplished during the past fifteen years.

The wealth of India has been proverbial since the time of Solomon, who imported therefrom his "ivory, apes, and peacocks." It has also seemed to be inexhaustible. From the earliest antiquity, the merchants of Persia, Arabia, Syria, and Egypt sought to enrich themselves by her commerce; and when Europe awoke from her sleep of ages, and entered upon her career of improvement, her first efforts were directed toward gaining a share of the trade of the East. England, at length, entered the field, and soon outstripped all her rivals, Dutch, Portuguese, and French. Agreeably to the policy of the times, the East India Company was chartered by Queen Elizabeth, and vested with the monopoly of the commerce of the East. And advancing by a steady progress, this giant Company, under the patronage of the Imperial power, at length held and governed, or protected, all that immense region.

A leading American journal very justly remarked on this subject, at the time of the great Sepoy Rebellion, that "the achievements by which these stupendous results have been effected are among the marvelous realities of history, compared with which the tales of romance are tame and spiritless. In future times they will, perhaps, constitute the most deeply-interesting portion of the history of our age. We believe that in the present troubles the cause of Great Britain, notwithstanding the many and grave abuses which have been practiced or tolerated by the East India Company, is nevertheless the cause of humanity and Christian civilization. It is this fact, no doubt, which has awakened no small share of the fierce invectives against the proceedings of the English in India. For a long time that region has been the field of an extensive and successful missionary enterprise, to which the British rulers have extended, at least, a protection from Hindoo and Moslem violence, and so afforded an opportunity for the free exercise of Christian philanthropy. This is, doubtless, the head and front of their offending in the minds of many of those who are loudest in their outcries against British cruelty and reckless ambition. We are very far from approving all that has been done by British agents in India, but we are equally clearly convinced that it is much more for their good deeds than their faults that they are most intensely disliked."

Any man who has resided in India, and known the condition of the people and the actions of that Government in regard to them, and the encouragement extended to efforts for the welfare of the natives, especially of late years, will be prepared to accept these words as a fair, and yet generous, statement of the situation. The position of England in India was a very peculiar one, and, in all candor, should be clearly understood before forming an opinion upon the merits of the case. For instance, in India there is no such thing as patriotism, no capability of self-government. If the English rule were withdrawn to-morrow, the last thing the natives would think of would be to unite and form a general Government. Each Rajah and Nawab would simply set up for himself, hold all he had, and take all he was able to seize. Then would begin a renewal of those religious and national contentions which form such a sad part of India's history, and the bloody exercise of which Britain terminated when she took control of the country, ever since holding the peace between those hostile elements.

The natives, especially the more military races, caring little for love of country, are willing to fight for compensation, and to serve any master ; so they were found very ready to wear the livery of England, to bear her weapons, and receive her pay. These men were called "Sepoys," (the Hindustanee for soldier,) each regiment being officered by English gentlemen. By degrees this force rose up to be an immense power, so that in 1856, there were two hundred thousand of them, constituting the regular Sepoy army, besides as many more called "Contingents," maintained by native courts under treaty, having English officers in command. Then there were the armed police ; making altogether a force of about four hundred thousand trained men, with the best weapons of England in their hands.

The total of British troops in all India in 1856 was not much over forty thousand, and they were scattered on the frontier and in a few of the leading cities, seldom more than one regiment in a place, and sometimes only half a regiment.

By degrees the Sepoy army, especially that of Bengal, became what might be called "a close service," a high caste Brahminical force, to whose notions constant concessions were made by the Government. They were a fine body of men, invincible to any thing in the East so long as they were led by their English officers, these officers and their ladies and children being afterward the first victims of the Rebellion. The Sepoys were utterly uneducated, as superstitious as they were ignorant, and entirely under the control of their Fakirs and Priests. This weak-minded and fanatical body of men had won for England her Oriental empire, and she chiefly relied on them for its defense and preservation. She could well do so, as long as they were faithful to her rule, but not a day longer. By degrees her policy changed, and, instead of maintaining a mixed army of all castes and creeds and nationalities, the "Bengal Army," as it was called, grew more and more Brahminical, united, and fanatical.

It has been asked, Why did not England let India go when she threw off her allegiance, and free herself from the care and risk of governing a people who thus disdained her rule? Two answers may be given to this question. One would be the secular reason of men who valued India for what she was to England in the way of profit and power. Millions of British money were invested in the funds and reproductive works of India; then, there was the vast, increasing, and lucrative market for English goods, one item alone of which will express its importance. The clothing of the Hindoo is not very voluminous, yet, what a business was it for Lancashire to have the right to supply cotton cloth for one sixth of the human family! But, besides the merchant and the manufacturer, the politician, the military and the educated man had a deep interest in the retention of this "brightest jewel of the British crown," for here was furnished the most splendid patronage that ever lay in the gift of a statesman. Hundreds of the cultured classes of England had careers of position and emolument as civil servants of the Government, under "covenants" that secured them munificent compensation, and which enabled them, when their legal term of service expired, to retire on pensions equal to about one half their splendid pay; so that Montgomery Martin estimates that the money remittances to Great Britain from India averaged five million sterling ($25,000,000) per annum for the past sixty years. Landed property in England has been largely enhanced in value by the investments of fortunes, the fruit of civil, military, and commercial success in Hindustan. A nation controlling the resources of such a dependency, with such a noble field in which to elicit and educate the genius of its youth and display the ability of its commanders, with the profitable employment of its mercantile shipping in the boundless imports and exports of such a country as India, could not lightly resign, or throw it away without a mighty struggle for its retention.

But, the man who would present no further reasons than these for British resolution to keep India in its control, would do injustice to the better section of English society, and to many of her noble representatives in the East. There is another and a better reason than what was measured by the pounds, shillings, and pence of mere worldly men, underlying the determination of England in this matter. The Christians of Britain hold firmly that, the Ruler of heaven and earth, in so wonderfully subjecting that great people to their rule, has done so for a higher than secular purpose; that he has given them a moral and evangelical mission to fulfill in that land for him; and that it is their high and solemn duty to maintain that responsibility until, by education and Christianity, they shall attach those millions by the tie of a common creed to the English throne, or fit them for assuming for themselves the responsibilities of self-government. For such men Montgomery Martin (one of their most voluminous Oriental writers) speaks when, in his last edition of his "Indian Empire," (4 vols. octavo,) dedicated by permission to the British Queen, he so distinctly declares to his Government and countrymen their high accountability before God and man in this respect, when he asks, "On what principle is the future government of India to be based? Are we simply to do what is right, or what seems expedient? If the former, we may confidently ask the Divine blessing on our efforts for the moral and material welfare of the people of India, and we may strive, by a steady course of kind and righteous dealing, to win their alienated affections for ourselves as individuals, and their respect and interest for the religion which inculcates justice, mercy, and humility as equally indispensable to national as to individual Christianity."

Those who know India best, know that I speak the truth when I assert, that these words are represented by deeds as honorable in the lives, and devotion to India's welfare, of many of the men who represent Great Britain there. I do not know a community of public men where you can find a greater number of "the excellent of the earth," than among the civil and military officers of England in India; men who have stood up for Jesus and for humanity, loving the poor, degraded race whom they ruled, and pleading, toiling, and giving munificently for their elevation to a better condition. Such names as Bentinck, Lawrence, Herbert Edwards, Havelock, Muir, Tucker, Ramsay, Gowan, Durand, and scores of others, amply justify this statement. The Annual Missionary Reports of the Methodist Episcopal Church (and this is equally true of the other missions as well) bear witness to this fact for many years past. During that time, such was the sympathy for the work which we attempted, in helping them to educate and enlighten the people of our own mission field, that noble-hearted Englishmen in all stations of life, from the Governor-General down to the private soldier, have aided us as freely as though we were of their own nation or Church, so that their contributions since 1857 will be found to aggregate over $150,000 in gold to our mission alone; while this assistance is all the time increasing, and is also equally extended by these good men to the missions of any Church or nation which goes there, and whose labors are aiming to elevate the benighted natives, and prepare them by education and a public conscience for self-government.

The Hindoo *Chronology* and division of time are very singular, and even whimsical. They hold to four great Ages of the world, called *Yugs.* Each of these Yugs is inferior to its immemediate predecessor in power, virtue, and happiness. These divisions are denominated the *Satya,* the *Treta,* the *Dwarper,* and the *Kali* Yugs, whose united length amounts to the prodigious sum of 4,320,000 years; yet this sum of the Ages is but a *Kalpa,* or one "Day of Brahma," at the end of which this sleepy deity wakes up to find the universe destroyed, and which he has then to create anew for another "Day" ere he goes to sleep again.

The *Satya Yug,* they tell us, lasted 1,728,000 years, and was the Age of Truth—the Golden Age—during which the whole race was virtuous, and lived each of them 100,000 years, and men attained the stature of "21 cubits" (37 feet) in height!

The *Treta Yug* lasted 1,296,000 years; this was the Silver Age, (using the same figures as the Greek and Roman poets,) during which one third of the race became corrupt, the human stature was lowered, and its life shortened to 10,000 years.

The *Dwarper Yug* extended to only 864,000 years—their Brazen Age—when fully one half of the race degenerated, and their height was again reduced, and their lives shortened to 1,000 years each.

The *Kali Yug* is the one in which we now live, and is regarded by them as the last—the Iron Age—in which mankind has become totally depraved, and their stature further reduced, and their life limited to 100 years. This Yug, according to them, began 4,950 years ago, and is to last exactly 427,050 years longer, which will close this Kalpa, or "Day of Brahma."

They assert that one patriarch called Satyavrata, or Vaivaswata, had an existence running the whole period of the Satya Yug,

(1,728,000 years!) and that he escaped with his family from a universal deluge, which destroyed the rest of mankind. He is regarded by Indian archæologists as the same person as the Seventh Menu, and by Colonel Tod, in his "Annals of Rajasthan," as designating the patriarch of mankind, Noah.

The "Night of Brahma" is held to be of equal length with his "Day," and that in the life of Brahma there are 36,000 such nights and days. At the end of each "Day" there is a partial destruction of the universe, and a reconstruction of it at the close of each "Night." During that long night, "sun, moon, and stars are shrouded in gloom; ceaseless torrents of rain pour down; the waves of the ocean, agitated with mighty tempests, rise to a prodigious height—the seven lower worlds, as well as this earth, are all submerged. In the midst of this darkness and ruin, and in the center of this tremendous abyss, Brahma reposes in mysterious slumber upon the serpent *Ananta*, or eternity. Meanwhile the wicked inhabitants of all worlds utterly perish. At length the long night ends, Brahma awakes, the darkness is instantly dispelled, and the universe returns to its pristine order and beauty."

This amazing chronology further states, that when these 36,000 "days" and "nights" (each of them 4,320,000 solar years in duration) have run their course, Brahma himself shall then expire, amid the utter annihilation of the universe, or its absorption into the essence of Brahm. This they call a *Maha Pralaya*, or great destruction. After this, Brahm, (the original spirit,) who had reposed during the whole duration of the creation's existence, awakes again, and from him another manifestation of the universe takes place, all things being reproduced as before, and Brahma, the Creator, commences a new existence. Each creation is coextensive with the life of Brahma, and lasts over three hundred billions of years, (311,040,000,000 years,) and the people of India believe that thus it has been during the past eternity, and thus it will continue to be in the eternity to come, an alternating succession of manifestations and annihilations of the universe at regular intervals of this inconceivable length. Truly does Wheeler call this daring reckoning "a bold attempt of the Brahmins to *map out eternity!*"

Trevor has remarked that the present age (the Kali Yug) being 432,000 years, the other three Yugs are found simply by multiplying that number by 2, 3, and 4, respectively. The number itself is the tithe of the sum total of the four *Yugs*. The "divine year," being computed like the prophetic, at a year for a day, (counting 360 days to the year,) is equal to 360 ordinary years; and these, multiplied by the perfect number 12,000, makes 4,320,000 years, the sum of the Ages, and a *Kalpa*, or "Day of Brahma."

Trevor supposes, that as this chronologic scheme is too absurd for reception, it must have been originally designed as a sort of arithmetical allegory, expressing the *character*, rather than the duration, of the periods referred to; while the descending ratios of 100,000, 10,000, 1,000, and 100 may indicate only the gradual shortening of the term of human life since the creation of man, as the corresponding proportions of the virtuous and vicious denote the spread of moral evil, till in the present age "they are altogether become filthy." This theory I leave to the learned reader, having introduced the topic chiefly to illustrate the mental characteristics of the people of India, and to show into what vagaries the human intellect, albeit cultivated and subtile, can be drawn in the day-dreams of a people on whom the light of Revelation never dawned. "Professing themselves to be wise, they became fools."

Their divisions of time are singular: 18 Mimeshas (twinkling of an eye, the standard of measure) are equal to 1 Kashta; 30 Kashtas to 1 Kala; 30 Kalas (48 of our minutes) to 1 Muhurtta; 30 Muhurttas to 1 day and night; 1 Month of Men to 1 day and night of the Pitris, (ancestors;) 1 Year of Men to 1 day and night of the Gods. The Hindoos have four watches of the day, and the same at night; these are called *Pahars*, and are three hours long, the first commencing at six o'clock in the morning. The day and night together are also divided into sixty smaller portions, called *Ghurees*, so that each of the eight Pahars consists of seven and a half Ghurees. They have twelve months in the year, each month having thirty days. Half the month, when the moon shines, is called *Oojeeala-pakh*, and the other half, which is dark, they call *Andhera-pakh*, and these distinctions they recognize in writing and dating their letters. They reckon their era from the reign of Bikurmaditt, one of their greatest and best kings, the present year of their era being 1934. The Mohammedans date their era from the Hejira, or flight of Mohammed from Mecca, which took place in A. D. 622; this is therefore their 1249th year.

I saw a very primitive method of measuring time, or ascertaining the "ghuree," in India. It was a small brass cup, with a hole in the bottom, immersed in a pan of water, and watched by a servant. When the cup sinks from the quantity of water its perforation has admitted the *ghuree* is completed, and the cup is again placed empty on the top of the water to measure the succeeding *ghuree*. Great attention is, of course, required to preserve any moderate degree of correctness by this imperfect mode of marking the progress of the day and night, and establishments are purposely entertained for it when considered as a necessary appendage of rank. In most other cases, the superior convenience and certainty of our clocks and watches are making considerable strides in superseding the Hindustanee *ghuree*.

A brief glimpse at the wonderful Mythology, Geography, and Astronomy of these people will be expected here, as also some notice of their venerable Vedas and their voluminous literature. Their "Sacred Books" gravely teach as follows:

"The worlds above this earth are peopled with gods and goddesses, demi-gods and genii—the sons and grandsons, daughters and granddaughters, of Brahma and other superior deities. All the superior gods have separate heavens for themselves. The inferior deities dwell chiefly in the heaven of Indra, the god of the firmament. There they congregate to the number of *three hundred and thirty millions*. The gods are divided and subdivided into classes or hierarchies, which vary through every conceivable gradation of rank and power. They are of all colors: some black, some white, some red, some blue, and so through all the blending shades of the rainbow. They exhibit all sorts of shape, size, and figure: in forms wholly human or half human, wholly brutal or variously compounded, like many-headed and many-bodied centaurs, with four, or ten, or a hundred or a thousand eyes, heads, and arms. They ride through the regions of space on all sorts of etherealized animals: elephants, buffaloes, lions, deer, sheep, goats, peacocks, vultures, geese, serpents, and rats! They hold forth in their multitudinous arms all manner of offensive and defensive weapons: thunderbolts, scimetars, javelins, spears, clubs, bows, arrows, shields, flags, and shells! They discharge all possible functions. There are gods of the heavens above, and of the earth below, and of the regions under the earth; gods of wisdom and of folly; gods of war and of peace; gods of good and of evil; gods of pleasure, who delight to shed around their votaries the fragrance of harmony and joy; gods of cruelty and wrath, whose thirst must be satiated with torrents of blood, and whose ears must be regaled with the shrieks and agonies of expiring victims. All the virtues and the vices of man, all the allotments of life—beauty, jollity, and sport, the hopes and fears of youth, the felicities and infelicities of manhood, the joys and sorrows of old age—all, all are placed under the presiding influence of superior powers."—*Duff's India.*

The *Geography* and *Astronomy* of the Hindoos are on a par with their Theology. It would be a waste of time and patience to crowd these pages with their wild, ridiculous, and unscientific nonsense upon these topics. Yet it may be a duty to say something in order to convey a general idea of the subject to such persons as have not made their system a study. Dr. Duff has had the patience to epitomize it; and from him we quote a passage or two, which the reader will deem to be all sufficient, and which he may be assured is only a sample of the monstrous extravagances of Hindoo "science," falsely so called.

Speaking of the constitution of the physical universe, as revealed in the Sacred Books of the Brahmins, he says: "It is partitioned into *fourteen worlds*—seven inferior, or below the world which we inhabit, and seven superior, consisting—with the exception of our own, which is the first—of immense tracts of space, bestudded with glorious luminaries and habitations of the Gods, rising, not unlike the rings of Saturn, one above the other, as so many concentric zones or belts of almost immeasurable extent.

"Of the seven inferior worlds which dip beneath our earth in a regular descending series, it is needless to say more than that they are destined to be the abodes of all manner of wicked and loathsome creatures.

"Our own earth, the first of the ascending series of worlds, is declared to be 'circular or flat, like the flower of the water-lily, in which the petals project beyond each other.' Its habitable portion consists of seven circular islands or continents, each surrounded by a different ocean. The central or metropolitan island, destined to be the abode of man, is named Jamba Dwip, around which rolls the sea of salt water; next follows the second circular island, and around it the sea of sugar-cane juice; then the third, and around it the sea of spirituous liquors; then the fourth, and around it the sea of clarified butter; then the fifth, and around it the sea of sour curds; then the sixth, and around it the sea of milk; then the seventh and last, and around it the sea of sweet water. Beyond this last ocean is an uninhabited country of pure gold, so prodigious in extent that it equals all the islands, with their accompanying oceans, in magnitude. It is begirt with a bounding wall of stupendous mountains, which inclose within their bosom realms of everlasting darkness.

"The central island, the destined habitation of the human race, is several hundred thousand miles in diameter, and the sea that surrounds it is of the same breadth. The second island is double the diameter of the first, and so is the sea that surrounds it. And each of the remaining islands and seas, in succession, is double the breadth of its immediate predecessor; so that the diameter of the whole earth amounts to several hundred thousand millions of miles—occupying a portion of space of manifold larger dimensions than that which actually intervenes between the earth and the sun! Yea, far beyond this; for, if we could form a conception of a circular mass of solid matter whose diameter exceeded that of the orbit of Herschel, the most distant planet in our solar system, such a mass would not equal in magnitude the Earth of the Hindoo Mythologists!

"In the midst of this almost immeasurable plain, from the very center of Jamba Dwip, shoots up the loftiest of mountains, Su-Meru, to the height of several hundred thousand miles, in the form of an inverted pyramid, having its summit, which is two hundred times broader than the base, surmounted by three swelling cones—the highest of these cones transpiercing upper vacancy with three golden peaks, on which are situate the favorite residences of the sacred Triad. At its base, like so many giant sentinels, stand four lofty hills, on each of which grows a mango-tree several thousand miles in height, bearing fruit delicious as nectar, and of the enormous size of many hundred cubits. From these mangoes, as they fall, flows a mighty river of perfumed juice, so communicative of its sweetness that those who partake of it exhale the odor from their persons all around to the distance of many leagues. There also grow rose-apple trees, whose fruit is 'large as elephants,' and whose juice is so plentiful as to form another mighty river, that converts the earth over which it passes into purest gold!"—*Duff's India and India Missions*, p. 116.

Such is a brief notice of the *Geographical* outline, furnished by their sacred writings, of the world on which we dwell. In turning to the superior worlds we obtain a glimpse of some of the revelations of Hindoo *Astronomy*.

"The second world in the ascending series, or that which immediately over-vaults the earth, is the region of space between us and the sun, which is declared, on divine authority, to be distant only a few hundred thousand miles. The third in the upward ascent is the region of space intermediate between the sun and the pole star. Within this region are all the planetary and stellar mansions. The distances of the principal heavenly luminaries are given with the utmost precision. The moon is placed *beyond* the sun as far as the sun is from the earth. Next succeed at equal distances from each other, and in the following order, the stars, Mercury, (beyond the stars,) Venus, Mars, Jupiter, Saturn, Ursa Major, and the Pole Star. The *four* remaining worlds (beyond the Pole Star) continue to rise, one above the other, at immense and increasing intervals. The entire circumference of the celestial space is then given with the utmost exactitude of numbers.

"In all of these superior worlds are framed heavenly mansions, differing in glory, destined to form the habitation of various orders of celestial spirits. In the seventh, or highest, is the chief residence of Brahma, said by one of the "divine sages" to be so glorious that he could not describe it in *two hundred* years, as it contains, in a superior degree, every thing which is precious, or beautiful, or magnificent in all the other heavens. What then must it be, when we consider the surpassing grandeur of some of these? Glance, for example, at the heaven which is prepared in the *third* world, and intended for Indra—head and king of the different ranks and degrees of subordinate deities. Its palaces are 'all of purest gold, so replenished with vessels of diamonds, and columns and ornaments of jasper, and sapphire, and emerald, and all manner of precious stones, that it shines with a splendor exceeding the brightness of twelve thousand suns. Its streets are of the clearest crystal, fringed with fine gold. It is surrounded with forests abounding with all kinds of trees and flowering shrubs, whose sweet odors are diffused all around for hundreds of miles. It is bestudded with gardens and pools of water; warm in winter and cool in summer, richly stored with fish, water-fowl, and lilies, blue, red, and white, spreading out a hundred or a thousand petals. Winds there are, but they are ever refreshing, storms and sultry heats being unknown. Clouds there are, but they are light and fleecy, and fantastic canopies of glory. Thrones there are, which blaze like the coruscations of lightning, enough to dazzle any mortal vision. And warblings there are, of sweetest melody, with all the inspiring harmonies of music and of song, among bowers that are ever fragrant and ever green.'"—P. 118.

The reader will remember that these descriptions are not to be taken as figurative and emblematic, as is appropriate to a state of glory of whose nature and details the heart of man cannot conceive, but that they are to be understood, as they are taught, in the strictest literality.

The Vedas are undoubtedly the oldest writings in the world, with the exception of the Pentateuch. Colebrook supposes that they were compiled in the fourteenth century before Christ. Sir William Jones assigns them to the sixteenth century. They are certainly not less than three thousand years old. Veda is from the Sanscrit root *vid*, to know, the Veda being considered the fountain of all knowledge, human and divine. A Veda, in its strict sense, is simply a *Sanhita*, or collection of hymns. There are three Vedas, the *Rig-Veda*, the *Yajur Veda*, and the *Sama-Veda*. The fourth, the *Atharva Veda*, is of more modern date and doubtful authority. The Hindoos hold that the Vedas are coeval with creation. As to their several contents, the *Rig-Veda* consists of prayers and hymns to various deities ; the *Yajur Veda*, of ordinances about sacrifices and other religious rites ; the *Sama-Veda* is made up of various lyrical pieces, and the *Atharva Veda* chiefly of incantations against enemies.

The *Rig-Veda* is the oldest and most authentic of all, and many scholars consider that from it the others were formed. The Hindoo writers attach to each Veda a class of compositions, chiefly liturgical and legendary, called *Brahmanas*, and they have besides a sort of expository literature, metaphysical and mystical, called *Upanishads*. They have also an immense body of Vedic literature, including philology, commentaries, *Sutras* or aphorisms, etc., the study of which would form occupation for a long and laborious life. The remote antiquity of the Vedas is indicated, among other reasons, by the entire absence of most of the modern doctrines of Hindooism, such as the worship of the Triad, the names of the modern deities, the doctrines of transmigration, caste, incarnations, suttee, etc., which are now the cardinal points of Hindooism, and the personified Triad of divine attributes, Brahma, Vishnu, and Shiva, in their capacities of Creator, Preserver, and Destroyer.

with the popular forms of the two latter, *Krishna* and the *Linga*, and all the manifestations of the bride of Mahadeva certainly were utterly unknown to the primitive texts of the religion of the Hindoos.

The *Rig-Veda Sanhita* (a complete copy of which is before us as we write) was translated from the original Sanscrit by Horace H. Wilson, and published in English in four volumes, the first being issued in 1850, and the last in 1866. The learned Introduction which the translator attached to the first volume, and an extensive and discriminating notice in the Calcutta Review for 1859, assist us in our description of these venerable writings.

The *Rig-Veda* is a miscellaneous collection of hymns. Each hymn is called a *Sukta.* The whole work is divided into eight books, or *Ashtakas.* Each *Ashtaka* is subdivided into eight Adhyayas, or chapters, containing an arbitrary number of *Suktas* The whole number of hymns in the Rig-Veda is about a thousand. Each *Sukta* has for its reputed author a *Rishi*, or inspired teacher, by whom, in Brahminical phraseology, it has been originally *seen*, that is, to whom it was revealed; the Vedas being, according to mythological fictions, the uncreated dictation of Brahma. Each hymn is addressed to some deity or deities.

Who are the gods to whom the prayers and praises are addressed? Here we find a striking difference between the mythology of the *Rig-Veda* and that of the heroic poems and *Puranas*, which come so long after them. The divinities worshiped are not unknown to later systems, but they there perform very subordinate parts, while those deities who are the great gods—the *Dii Majores* —of the subsequent and present period, are either wholly unnamed in the Veda, or are noticed in an inferior and different capacity. The names of Shiva, of Mahadeva, of Durga, of Kali, of Rama, of Krishna, never occur, and there is not the slightest allusion to the form in which, for the last ten centuries at least, Shiva seems to have been almost exclusively worshiped in India, that of the *Linga* or *Phallus;* neither is there any hint of another important feature of later Hindooism, the *Trimurti*, or Triune combination of Brahma, Vishnu, and Shiva, as typified by the mystical syllable *Om*, although, according to high Brahminical authority, the *Trimurti* was the first element in the faith of the Hindoos, and the second was the *Linga*.

The deities mentioned in the Vedas are numerous, and of different sexes. The leading ones are Indra, Agni, and Surya; and the female deities are Ushas, Saraswati, Sinivali, etc. "The wives of the gods" are spoken of as a large number, and are often invoked. The operations and powers of nature are deified, as the Murats, the winds; the Aswins, the sons of the sun; and even the cows are invoked in a special Sukta.—Vol. iii, p. 440. In fact, the deities, inferior and superior, of the Vedas may be counted by the dozen, and the work is manifestly *polytheistic* to the core in its teaching and tendencies. The evidence of this is on every page.

For the general reader, the mystery that covered the Vedas is a mystery no longer; all that they contain stands out for public view in the common light of day. Except as to grammatical construction and translation into modern words, *we* are far abler to discover and understand what story these ancient documents tell than is any of the Pundits. For, in ascertaining their sense, we have to deal with questions of race, of language, of history, of chronology, and external influences; questions unknown, and therefore unintelligible, to the Hindoo mind. Forbidden to the Sudras, inaccessible from their rarity and high price to most of the Brahmins, for that very reason they are the objects of a more profound and superstitious veneration; and, if any thing can be supposed, *a priori*, to startle and excite all Hindustan, it is surely the announcement that the Vedas have become public property, and that Sudra and *Mlechcha* (barbarian) may read them at his will.

It was almost entirely from such writings as these that European scholars had to undertake the compilation of a true chronology and history for India. The task was certainly not an easy one. It was like this: Given the Psalms of David, to discover from *these alone* the manners, customs, religions, arts, sciences, history, chronology, and origin of the Jewish nation; to classify the hymns too, and assign to each its time and author, with no other help than the heading to each Psalm, added by a later hand. Knowing, as we do, that they range almost from Moses till after the captivity—at least seven hundred years—the later parts of the task alone would demand all the resources of scholarship. It is true that the Vedic hymns are ten times more numerous than the Psalms, but they are at the same time ten times more monotonous, and full of wearisome repetitions, under which even Professor Wilson's patience gives way. In *our* Sacred Books the Code precedes, and the history precedes, accompanies, and follows the Psalms. With the Hindoo the Code comes after the hymns, and has to do with a different stage of society, and *the history never comes at all!* Nevertheless, the Vedas, with all their difficulties, throw a flood of light upon the origin and early state of the Hindoos.

The people among whom the Vedas were composed, as here introduced to us, had evidently passed the nomadic stage. Their wealth consisted of horses, cattle, sheep, goats, and buffaloes. Coined money, and indeed money in any shape, was unknown. We meet but two allusions to gold, except for the purpose of ornaments. The cow was to the Vedic Hindoo at once *food* and money. It supplied him with milk, butter, ghee, curds, and cheese. Oxen ploughed his fields, and carried his goods and chattels. He preserved the *Soma-juice* in a bag of cow-skin, (*Rig-Veda*, vol. I, p. 72,) and the cow-hide girt his chariot. (Vol. III, p. 475.) No idea of *sacredness* was connected with the *cow;* and it is quite clear, however abhorrent and revolting the truth may appear to their descendants, that in the golden age of their ancestors the Hindoos were a *cowkilling and beef-eating people*, and that cattle are declared in the Vedas to be *the very best of food!* Yet modern Hindooism holds it to be a deadly sin to kill a cow, or eat beef, or to use intoxicating drink, and they dare to assert that this was always their creed. We quote texts which leave no room for a doubt on this, to them, important fact:

"Agni, descendant of Bharata, thou art entirely ours when sacrificed to with pregnant kine, barren cows, or bulls."

"Agni, the friend of Indra, has quickly consumed three hundred buffaloes."

"When thou hast eaten the flesh of the three hundred buffaloes."

"Bestow upon him who glorifies thee, divine Indra, food, the chiefest of which is cattle."—Vol. II, p. 225; III, p. 276.

"Sever his joints, Indra, as butchers cut up a cow."—Vol. III, p. 458; I, p. 165.

What an amount of beef-eating is implied in a sacrifice of *three hundred buffaloes!* the greater part, as usual, being devoured by the assistants. The cooking is very minutely and graphically described in vol. II, pp. 117, etc. Part was roasted on spits, while the attendants eagerly watched the joints, sniffing up the grateful fumes, and saying, "It is fragrant." The queens and wives of the sacrificers assisted in cooking and preparing the banquet, which, on particular occasions, alluded to in the text, consisted of *horse-flesh!* All was washed down with copious libations of a strong spirit, made from the juice of the soma plant. *Rishi Kakshivat* had in every way most unclerical propensities. He thanks the *Aswins* most cordially for giving him a cask holding a hundred jars of wine, (vol. I, p. 308;) and *Rishi Vamadeva*, who was taken out of his mother's side, solicits Indra (vol. III, p. 185) for a hundred jars of soma-juice. *Rishi Agastya* also, in a queer, half-crazy Sukta, (vol. II, p. 200,) writes of "a leather bottle in the house of *a vender of spirits*." These were the men that fought Alexander the Great. After such a feast of the gods, Indra puts forth all his might, and destroys the fiercest of the Asuras, (the evil spirits.)

The social position of woman, this Veda demonstrates, was considerably higher than it is in modern India. She is spoken of kindly and pleasantly as "the light of the dwelling." The *Rishi* and his wife converse on equal terms, go together to the sacrifice, and practice austerities together. Lovely maidens appear in a procession. Grown-up unmarried daughters remain without reproach in their father's house. Now, all this is the reverse of the Hindooism of the present day. On the other hand, we have a case of polygamy of the most shameful kind. *Kakshivat*, one of the most illustrious of the Rishis, married ten sisters at once, (vol. II, p. 17;) and, if the tone of female society is to be judged of from the wife even of a *Rishi*, or from a lady who is herself the author of a Sukta, women in those days were no better than they should be.

A gallant, deep-drinking, high-feeding race were the wild warriors of the Indus, and very unlike their descendants.

The picture of Hindoo life and manners, at the time of the Macedonian invasion, (326 B. C.,) was darkly shaded. The Hindoo even then had degenerated; and the "Life of an Eastern King" on the banks of the Indus differed little in its shameless details from that of his modern successor at Lucknow, on the banks of the Goomtee.

Rufus Curtius Quintus, the historian of Alexander, writes of the Hindoos thus: "The shameful luxuries of their prince surpasses that of all other nations. He reclines in a golden palankeen, with pearl hangings. The dresses which he puts on are embroidered with purple and gold. The pillars of his palace are gilt; and a running pattern of a vine, carved in gold, and figures of birds, in silver, ornament each column. The durbar is held while he combs and dresses his hair; then he receives embassadors, and decides cases. . . . The women prepare the banquet and pour out the wine, to which all the Indians are greatly addicted. Whenever he, or his queen, went on a journey, crowds of dancing girls in gilt palankeens attended; and when he became intoxicated they carried him to his couch."—*Liber* VIII, 32. And, if we are to believe his biographer, into such a vile, sensual thing as this the great Alexander himself was rapidly degenerating at that very time!

The religion of the Vedas, then, was *Nature worship;* light, careless, and irreverent, utterly animal in its inmost spirit, with little or no sense of sin, no longings or hopes of immortality, nothing high, serious, or thoughtful. There was no love in their worship. They cared only for wealth, victory, animal gratification, and freedom from disease. The tiger of the forest might have joined in such prayers, and said, "Grant me health, a comfortable den, plenty of deer and cows, and strength to kill any intruder on my beat!" "The blessings they implore," says Professor Wilson, "are for the most part of a temporal and personal description—wealth, food, life, posterity, cattle, cows, and horses; protection against enemies, victory over them, and sometimes their destruction. There are a few indications of a hope of immortality and of future happiness, but they are neither frequent, nor, in general, distinctly announced. In one or two passages Yama, and his office of ruler of the dead, are obscurely alluded to. There is little demand for moral benefactions."—Vol. I, p. 25.

So merely fanciful, so wearisome and monotonous, so contemptuously irreverent are the great bulk of these Vedic prayers, (to Indra especially,) that Professor Wilson, with all his patience, can scarce believe them to be *earnest.* Take, for instance, the following Hymn. It is addressed to the goddess Anna Devata, personified as Pitu, or material food, and is recited by a Brahmin when about to eat. Pitu is also identified with the Soma juice, mentioned below. The Rishi is Agastya, and the reader can judge if any utterances (and this, too, professing to be sacred and inspired) that he has ever seen, more fully illustrates the words of Holy Writ, "Whose God is their belly, whose glory is their shame, who mind earthly things:"

"1. I glorify Pitu, the great, the upholder, the strong, by whose invigorating power Trita slew the mutilated Vritra.

"2. Savory Pitu; sweet Pitu; we worship thee: become our protector.

"6. The thoughts of the mighty gods are fixed, Pitu, upon thee: by thy kind and intelligent assistance Indra slew Ahi.

"8. And since we enjoy the abundance of the waters and the plants, therefore, Body, do thou grow fat!

"9. And since we enjoy, Soma, thy mixture with boiled milk or boiled barley, therefore, Body, do thou grow fat!

"10. Vegetable cake of fried meal, do thou be substantial, wholesome, and invigorating; and, Body, do thou grow fat!

"11. We extract from thee, Pitu, by our praises, the sacrificial food, as cows yield butter for oblation; from thee, who art exhilarating to the gods; exhilarating also to us."—*Rig-Veda*, Vol. II, p. 194. Sukta viii.

In a similar strain the *Soma-plant* is addressed.

It was bruised between two stones, mixed with milk or barley juice, and, when fermented, formed a strong, inebriating, ardent spirit—probably not very unlike the *whisky* of the present day.

It appears that the *Rishis* of the Vedas introduced this custom, or belief, into religion. Indra and all the other gods are everywhere represented as unable to perform any great exploit *without* the inspiration of the Soma, or, in plain English, until they were more or less *drunk!* Hear the Veda:

"May our *Soma* libation reach you, exhilarating, invigorating, inebriating, most precious. It is companionable, Indra, enjoyable, the overthrower of hosts, immortal.

"Thy inebriety is most intense: nevertheless thy acts are most beneficent."—Vol. II, p. 169.

"Savory indeed is this Soma; sweet it is, sharp, and full of flavor: no one is able to encounter Indra in battle, after he has been quaffing this—by drinking of it Indra has been elevated to the slaying of Vritra," etc.—Vol. III, p. 470.

"The stomach of Indra is as capacious a receptacle of Soma as a lake."—Vol. III, p. 60. "The belly of Indra, which quaffs the Soma juice abundantly, swells like the ocean, and is ever moist, like the ample fluids of the palate."—Vol. III, pp. 17, 231, 232. "Indra, quaff the Soma juice, repeatedly shaking it from your beard."—Vol. II, p. 233. What common revelry is expressed in the following verse: "Saints and sages, sing the holy strain aloud, like screaming swans, and, together with the gods, drink the sweet juice of the Soma."—Vol. III, p. 86.

This license runs riot, and "the goddesses, the wives of the gods," (Vol. III. p. 316,) with earthly ladies, one of them (Viswavara) herself a Rishi and compiler of a Sukta (Vol. III, p. 273) in which she prays for "concord between man and wife," all are joined—gods, goddesses, and "divine Rishis"—in high carousal. But, then, mark what Rishi Avatsara says of this lady, Viswavara, and of his brother Rishis, and the rest of the boisterous crew, all "gloriously drunk" together:

"11. Swift is the excessive and girt-distending inebriation of Viswavara, Yajata, and Mayin: by drinking of these juices they urge one another to drink: they find the copious draught the prompt giver of intoxication!"—Vol. III, p. 311.

And this was the worship of Ancient India! Jolly and easy are the terms on which deity and worshiper meet together for their wassail! Prajapate addresses his god thus: "Indra, the showerer of benefits, drink the Soma offered after the other presentations, for thine exhilaration for battle; take into thy belly the full wave of the inebriating Soma, for thou art lord of libations from the days of old!" (Vol. III, p. 75.) But the Rishi Viswamitra evidently thought that, under the circumstances, there was no use in standing upon even Hindoo ceremony, so he says to his deity: "Sit down, Indra, upon the sacred grass—and when thou hast drunk the Soma, then, Indra, *go home!*" finishing up the address by reminding him that the hungry steeds in his car at the door need consideration, and require their provender!—Vol. III, p. 84.

How melancholy and degrading is all this—god, worshiper, and the traffic between them! But one grade above the beasts that perish; yet *these* are the teachings of the most sacred of the so-called "Holy Vedas?" This drunken worship realizes and surpasses Dionysius and the Bacchanals themselves.

These besotted mortals had evidently reached that stage of debasement when men can suppose that the Almighty "was altogether such a one as themselves," and when they can "call evil good" and "put darkness for light." Well might the reviewer exclaim, from the abundant and fearful evidence before him that, "*No worship ever mocked the skies more miserable and contemptible than the religion of the Veda!*"

But, what are we to think of professedly enlightened Hindoos, like Rajah Rammohun Roy, or this modern Baboo, *Keshub Chunder Sen*, who, if they ever *read* the Vedas, of which they talk so glibly, must surely have dared to presume upon the ignorance of their auditors, when they had the temerity, in a day like this, and before a London audience, to assert that "the worship of Almighty

God in his unity," and "a pure system of theism" are taught in the *Vedas?*—Men, who after all this have the impertinence to assume a patronizing aspect toward Christianity, and superciliously inform us that, however good or pure our faith is in itself, its doctrine and services are not needed in India, because "the Holy Vedas" contain all that is requisite for the regeneration of their country! Yet this is said and repeated, and Miss Carpenter and her Unitarian friends clap their hands, applaud the assertions, and lionize the man who utters them, and commend the *Brahmo Somaj*, of which he is the High Priest! Do not such people deserve to be deceived? and is it really a violation of Christian charity to fear that such persons must be given over to "strong delusion" when they can believe such "a lie" as *this?*

After a careful examination, from beginning to end, of this venerable and lauded work, (the doors of which have so lately opened for the admission of mankind,) with the remembrance in my mind of the long years when men have listened to the reiterations of its holiness, as the very source of all Hindoo faith—the oracle from which Vedantic Philosophy has drawn its inspiration, the temple at whose mere portal so many millions have bowed in such awe and reverence, with its interior too holy for common sight, containing, as it was asserted, all that was worth knowing, the primitive original truth that could regenerate India, and make even Christianity unnecessary—well, with no feelings save those of deep interest and a measure of respect, we have entered and walked from end to end, to find ourselves shocked at every step with the revelations of this mystery of iniquity and sensuality, where saints and gods, male and female, hold high orgies amid the fumes of intoxicating liquor, with their singing and "screaming," and the challenging by which "they urge one another" on to deeper debasement, until at length decency retires and leaves them "glorying in their shame!"

The sad samples which we have presented are taken at random, and can be matched by hundreds of passages equally contemptible; while we have purposely avoided quoting Suktas and verses whose indelicacy is even worse than these ; nor have we found, because it is not there, any thing pure, sublime, or good, with which to offset the vileness here laid before the reader. Coming out again from the gloomy scenes of these "works of darkness" into the light and purity of our blessed Bible, with all its "fruits of the Spirit," never before were we so thankful for our holy religion, nor have we ever felt as deep a compassion for the millions so shamefully and so long deluded by the false and hollow pretensions of the Vedic teaching.

Before dismissing the subject I will, for the sake of such readers as may not have seen an entire Sukta of the Veda, quote one in full, so that he may have a complete view of the "holiest" and most venerable of all India's "Scriptures," selecting one, however, that may be regarded as respectable in its ideas and language. I take the fifth Sukta, on page 38 of volume I of the Rig-Veda. The *Rishi* (or author) is Medhalithi, the son of Kanwa, and the hymn is addressed to *Indra*, their God of the Heavens :

"SUKTA V.

"1. Indra, let thy coursers hither bring thee, bestower of desires, to drink the Soma juice ; may the priests, radiant of the sun, make thee manifest.

"2. Let his coursers convey Indra in an easy-moving chariot hither, where these grains of parched barley, steeped in clarified butter, are strewn upon the altar.

"3. We invoke Indra at the morning rite, we invoke him at the succeeding sacrifice, we invoke Indra to drink the Soma juice.

"4. Come, Indra, to our libation, with thy long-maned steeds ; the libation being poured out, we invoke thee.

"5. Do thou accept this our praise, and come to this our sacrifice, for which the libation is prepared ; drink like a thirsty stag.

"6. These dripping Soma juices are effused upon the sacred grass ; drink them, Indra, to recruit thy vigor.

"7. May this our excellent hymn, touching thy heart, be grateful to thee, and thence drink the effused libation.

"8. Indra, the destroyer of enemies, repairs assuredly to every ceremony where the libation is poured out, to drink the Soma juice for exhilaration.

"9. Do thou, Satakratu, accomplish our desire with cattle and horses: profoundly meditating, we praise thee."

As the Greeks and Romans had their Homer and Virgil, so the Hindoos have had their Valmiki and Vyasa. The great epics of India are the *Ramayana* and the *Mahabarata*. These stand peerless in their voluminous literature, and have held control of the minds of the people since long before the Incarnation.

The Ramayana is probably the most ancient and connected epic poem in the Sanscrit, and exceeded only by the Vedas in antiquity. It contains the mythical history of Rama, one of the incarnations of the god Vishnu, and was written by the great poet Valmiki. For a very brief epitome of this wonderful and venerable development of Hindoo literature we are indebted to Speir's "Ancient India."

The style and language of the Ramayana are those of an early heroic age, and there are signs of its having been popular in India at least three centuries before Christ. The original subject of the poem is sometimes considered as mythological, and sometimes as heroic; but the mythological portions stand apart, and have the air of after-thoughts, intended to give a religious and philosophical tone to what was at first a tale rehearsed at festivals in praise of the ancestors of kings. The mythological introduction states that *Lanka*, or Ceylon, had fallen under the dominion of a prince named *Ravana*, who was a demon of such power that by dint of penance he had extorted from the god Brahm a promise that no immortal should destroy him. Such a promise was as relentless as the Greek Fates, from which Jove himself could not escape; and Ravana, now *invulnerable to the gods*, gave up the asceism he had so long practiced, and tyrannized over the whole of Southern India in a fearful manner. At length, even the gods in heaven were distressed at the destruction of holiness and oppression of virtue consequent upon Ravana's tyrannies, and they called a council in the mansion of Brahma to consider how the earth could be relieved from such a fiend. To this council came the "god Vishnu, riding on the eagle *Vain-a-taya*, like the sun on a cloud, and his discus and his mace in hand." The other gods entreat him to give his aid, and he promises, in consequence, to be *born* on earth, and to accomplish the destruction of the terrific Ravana Vishnu therefore became incarnated (his Seventh Avatar) as *Rama* or *Ramchundra*, and his life and exploits as the celebrated King of Ayodhya, form the subject of this, the earliest epic poem of India. According to this work, Rama was born as the son of Dasharatha, King of Ayodhya, the modern Oude. In early life Rama married Seeta, the lovely daughter of the King of Mithili. But domestic trouble, caused by the intrigues of his mother-in-law in behalf of her own son, caused Rama and Seeta to retire to the forests, and there they lived the lives of hermits for years, till the time for his action should come. While in this seclusion, Ravana, the demon King of Lanka, (Ceylon,) who had heard of the *beauty* of Seeta, resolved to steal her from Rama. Finding it in vain to hope to succeed without the aid of stratagem, he took with him an assistant sorcerer, disguised as a deer; and as Rama took great pleasure in the chase, it was not difficult for the deer to lure him from his cottage in pursuit. He did not leave his beloved Seeta without requesting Lakshman, his brother, to remain in charge; but the wily deer knew how to defeat his precaution, and, when transfixed by Rama's arrow, he cried out in the voice of Rama, "O, Lakshman, save me!" Seeta heard the cry, and unentreated Lakshman to fly to his brother's rescue. He was unwilling to go, but yielded to her earnestness, and she was left alone. This being the state of affairs which Ravana desired, he now left his hiding-place, and came forward, disguised as an Ascetic Brahmin, in a red, threadbare garment, with a single tuft of hair upon his head, and three sticks and a pitcher in his hand. In the rich, glowing poetry all creation is represented as shuddering at his approach; birds, beasts, and flowers were motionless with dread; the summer wind ceased to breathe, and a shiver passed over the bright waves of the river. Ravana stood for awhile looking at his victim, as she sat weeping and musing over the unknown cry; but soon he approached, saying, (we quote the metrical translation here,)

"O thou that shinest like a tree
With summer blossoms overspread,
Wearing that woven *kusa* robe,
And lotus garland on thy head,
Why art thou dwelling here alone,
Here in this dreary forest's shade,
Where range at will all beasts of prey,
And demons prowl in every glade?
Wilt thou not leave thy cottage home,
And roam the world, which stretches wide—
See the fair cities which men build,
And all their gardens and their pride?
Why longer, fair one, dwell'st thou here,
Feeding on roots and sylvan fare,
When thou might'st dwell in palaces,
And earth's most costly jewels wear?
Fearest thou not the forest gloom,
Which darkens round on every side?
Who art thou, say! and whose, and whence,
And wherefore dost thou here abide?"

Even a lady alone is not supposed to be necessarily alarmed at meeting "a holy Brahmin," and the fiend's disguise was so complete that only a temporary flush of excitement followed his sudden address. So the poet continues:

"When first these words of Ravana
Broke upon sorrowing Seeta's ear,
She started up, and lost herself
In wonderment, and doubt, and fear;
But soon her gentle, loving heart
Threw off suspicion and surmise,
And slept again in confidence,
Lull'd by the mendicant's disguise.
'Hail, holy Brahmin!' she exclaimed;
And, in her guileless purity,
She gave a welcome to her guest,
With courteous hospitality.
Water she brought to wash his feet,
And food to satisfy his need,
Full little dreaming in her heart
What *fearful guest* she had received."

She even tells him her own story, how Rama had won her for his bride and taken her to his father's home, and how the jealous Kaikeyi had cast them forth to roam the woods; and after dwelling fondly on her husband's praise, she invited her guest to tell his name and lineage, and what had induced him to leave his native land for the wilds of the Dandaka forest, inviting him to await her husband's return, for "to him are holy wanderers dear." Suddenly Ravana declares himself to be the demon monarch of the earth, "at whose name Heaven's armies flee." He has come, he says, to woo Seeta for his queen, and to carry her to his palace in the island of Ceylon! Astonished and indignant at his character and proposal, the wrath of Rama's wife burst forth in these words:

"*Me* would'st thou woo to be thy queen,
Or dazzle with thy empire's shine?
And didst thou dream that Rama's wife
Could stoop to such a prayer as thine?
I, who can look on Rama's face,
And know that there my husband stands,—
My Rama, whose high chivalry
Is blazoned through a hundred lands!
What! shall the jackal think to tempt
The lioness to mate with him?
Or did the King of Lanka's isle,
Build upon such an idle dream?"

But vain was poor Seeta's indignant remonstrance. Ravana's only answer was to throw off his disguise, and, "with brows as dark as the storm-cloud," he carried off the shrieking Seeta as an eagle bears its prey, mounting up aloft and flying with his burden through the sky. The unhappy Seeta calls loudly upon Rama, and bids the flowery bowers and trees and rivers all tell her Rama that Ravana has stolen his Seeta from his home. In Rama's time the woods were inhabited by demons and monkeys. On returning and ascertaining his great loss, Rama did not feel strong enough to recover Seeta single-handed. He therefore entered into an alliance with the monkeys. First, the monkey-king *Sugriva* dispatched emissaries in all directions to ascertain where Seeta was concealed; and when the monkey-general *Hunooman* (the Mars of India) ascertained that she was in a palace in Ceylon, Rama and all the allied monkey forces marched down to the Coromandel coast, and, making a bridge by casting rocks into the sea, passed quickly into Lanka. After fighting a few battles the Rakshasas (demons) were defeated, Ravana was put to death by Rama, and Seeta rescued from her palace prison. Rama will, however, have nothing to say to his recovered wife until she has gone through "the ordeal of fire;" but as she passed through the blazing pile unhurt, and Brahma and other gods attested her fidelity, her husband once more received her with affection, and, the term of exile over, the whole party returned in happiness to Ayodhya. Such, in brief, is the story of the Ramayana, which is spun out into details and episodes of great length. It is read very extensively to listening crowds in India, who believe every word, no matter how improbable, as we would the most authentic records of our own history or our Holy Bible.

The *Mahabarata* is the second famous epic of India. We have only room to say that it describes a contest between the two branches of the Chundra, or Moon dynasty, for the sovereignty of the Ganges territory. The "Great War" (as the word Mahabarata expresses) is generally regarded as having taken place about two hundred years before the siege of Troy.

Princes are enumerated as taking part in the struggle from the Deccan, and the Indus, and even beyond the Indus, especially the Yarases, thought to be Greeks. Fifty-six royal leaders were assembled on the field of battle, which raged for eighteen days with prodigious slaughter—another proof of the division of India into many separate States, though occasionally combined, as in this poem, under the leadership of some great general on either side. The contest was waged between the sons of Pandu, the deceased Rajah, and their cousins the Kooroos, who denied their legitimacy—a never-failing subject of dispute in Hindoo successions. It ended in the victory of the Pandus; but what they gained by arms they lost through gaming. Yudisthira, the Agamemnon of the poem, departs with his brothers and the beautiful Draupadi into exile on the Himalayas. Their evil deeds prevailing, they drop dead, one after another, by the way-side. Yudisthira is the last, and when Indra comes to admit him to *Swarga* (Paradise) he demands to be accompanied by his faithful dog. The poem follows the hero into the other world. Arrived in Indra's paradise, and finding his enemies there before him, with none of his party, he refuses to stay, and, descending to the shades in quest of Draupadi and his brothers, succeeds in rescuing them from torment. The gods applaud his virtue, and he is permitted to convey himself and all his party to Swarga. The hero of this poem is Krishna, the great ally of the Pandus, and generally regarded as the eighth incarnation of Vishnu.—*Trevor's India*, p. 52.

CHAPTER III.

ARCHITECTURAL MAGNIFICENCE OF INDIA

THE missionary authorities of the Methodist Episcopal Church resolved, in the year 1854, to found a mission in India, and they advertised during that year and the next for a man to go forth and commence the work. The writer, after waiting in the hope that some one else, better suited for the duty and less cum bered with family cares, would answer to the call, offered himself for the service. This involved one of the keenest trials through which himself and wife had ever passed—no less than a separation from their two elder boys. The necessity for this, in the case of children over the age of seven years exposed to the climate and moral influence in India, as well as the educational need, are all understood.

Having no personal friends to whose care they could be intrusted, they had to be placed at a boarding-school in the hands of strangers. God only knows the feelings with which we resigned them, fearing (what proved too true in the case of one of them) that we might see them no more on earth ; but, so far as we could understand, it was either this, or for our Church to fail of her duty to perishing men in India. We understood that such sacrifices were contemplated by the Head of the Church when he instituted a missionary ministry for the salvation of the world. He was well aware what this would involve to the souls of many parents in the future, and therefore, to sustain them under the peculiar cross, he had put on record one of his most glorious promises. There can be no mistake as to the circumstances contemplated. "Peter said, Lo, we have left all and followed thee And He said unto them, Verily, verily, I say unto you, There is no man that hath left house, or parents, or brethren, or wife, *or children*, for the kingdom of God's sake, who shall not receive manifold more in this present time, and in the world to come life everlasting." With hearts bleeding at the sacrifice which we were called to make, we clung to the precious and appropriate promise of our divine Master, committed our little ones to his care, and went forth to fulfill his commission to the best of our ability.

With my wife and two younger children I sailed from Boston on the 9th of April, 1856. I was instructed to proceed by way of England, and there obtain from the secretaries of the different missionary societies all the information available in regard to those unoccupied portions of India where we might labor without interference with existing missions, "to preach the Gospel, not where Christ is named, lest we should build upon another man's foundation," and there labor for the enlargement of the kingdom of God.

Having attended to this duty, and obtained all the light that the secretaries and returned missionaries could impart, I resolved to proceed to Calcutta, and from that to move westward into the heart of the country and examine the Valley of the Ganges. We left Southampton on the 20th of August in the steamship Pera. Just as we were departing, the consort ship of the same line, the Ripon, came in with the mails and passengers from India, and on board of her was the Queen of Oude, coming to place before the British Queen her protest against the annexation of Oude, and to plead for the restoration of the sovereignty to her family.

Apart from the singularity of the fact that she was probably the first lady of her race who had ever come to a western clime, her presence there occasioned me no particular interest; yet, as God looked down upon the objects of each, how much she and I, thus meeting casually for a moment, really depended upon each other's movements! Had she succeeded in her mission, I must necessarily have failed in mine, so far as our present mission field is concerned, for I was unconsciously going to the kingdom which she had ruled, and to the very capital whose gates she had left ajar five weeks before—gates that had been closed by Mohammedan bigotry against Christianity for ages. Her success on this expedition would have closed them again indefinitely, and I should have had to go elsewhere; but He whose holy providence guided my steps took care of the issues. She failed, and I succeeded, yet not without "a great fight of afflictions," as the sequel will show.

We landed at Calcutta on the 23d of September, and were most cordially welcomed by the missionary brethren there, and aided by their opinions and advice in regard to the unoccupied territory of the country. We soon realized, in the brotherly kindness of their intercourse, and the gladness with which they regarded the incoming of another mission, what real evangelical union, and what freedom from sectarianism, exist among Christians in a heathen land. Dr. Duff was especially kind to us. He seemed so thankful that the Lord was sending more help to redeem the India he loved so well, and for which he had labored so long and so faithfully. As we parted from the great and good man, I little imagined that within a year, counting us among the slain, he would write a sort of biography of me, (in his work "The Indian Rebellion,") or that I should live to thank him, at his own table, for the peculiar privilege of knowing what my friends would say of me when I was dead. Yet so it proved.

Proceeding at once up the country, we reached the city of Agra, the seat of government for the North-west, and soon realized that we were now amid the splendid evidences of the power and glory of the "Great Moguls." This imperial city, and the adjoining one of Delhi, were full of those reminiscences, and the interest which they at once awakened was something intense and peculiar.

We were in blissful ignorance of any cause for anxiety—knew not what a volcano of wrath was quietly preparing beneath our feet, or how surely the titled and decorated "Nawabs," whose courteous salaams we returned, were thirsting for our blood, and resolving to have it, too; but we will let that subject rest here, until we share with the reader our interest and delight as we survey some of those magnificent, those matchless, monuments of Patan skill and wealth with which we now found ourselves surrounded. This will also give him a better idea than any thing else could do as to what those imperial people *risked* in their desperate enterprise, when pensions, palaces, titles, ancestral monuments, and mausoleums, with all their gorgeous traditions, were the mighty stakes ventured in the frantic and final struggle of their dynasty with a superior civilization and the strength which accompanies it. We were, though we knew it not, contemplating many of these glories for the last time in which men could gaze in admiration upon them, for most of them, save the *Taj* and the *Kootub*, were destined to destruction by the ruin which war was so soon to bring. When we saw them again, one year afterward, "the glory had departed," save in the cases given. The *Taj*, especially, seemed as though self-protected by its own purity and loveliness; even ravaging war respected it, friend and foe alike agreeing that its beauty should remain unsullied forever.

The first permanent conquest by a Mohammedan sovereign in India was that made by Mahmoud of Ghuznee in the year 1001. Sixty-five rulers of that faith, during the following eight centuries, tried to maintain their authority over the great Hindoo nations. It may be doubted whether any part of the world was ever so cursed by a line of bigoted, ferocious wretches as, with two or three exceptions, were these Mohammedan despots of India during that time. To many of them may be truly applied the terrible lines of Moore:

"One of that saintly, murderous brood,
To carnage and the Koran given,
Who think through unbelievers' blood
Lies their directest path to heaven;
One who will pause and kneel unshod
In the warm blood his hand hath poured,
To mutter o'er some text of God
Engraven on his reeking sword;
Nay, who can coolly note the line,
The letters of those words divine,
To which his blade, with searching art,
Had sunk into its victim's heart!"

And all this transacted by these "bloody men" under the professed sanction and authority of a holy and merciful God, whose

Mohammed Suraj-oo-deen Shah Gezee, Emperor of Delhi, the Last of the Moguls.

special favor and reward they asserted awaited them in Paradise for blasphemous cruelties like these! The reference in the lines is to their habit of engraving texts from the Koran upon their swords. What millions, during the past eight centuries, have been destroyed by Mohammedanism and Romanism in the name of religion, till humanity sighs to be relieved of their baneful presence, and the true Christian looks forward solemnly to the awful hour when He "to whom vengeance belongeth" will call "the beast and the false prophet" to their dread account—partners in punishment as they have been in guilt!

The character and cruelties of Popery recorded in Motley's recent histories are equaled in India's records by those Moslem scourges, Hyder Ali, Tippoo, Tamerlane, Nadir Shah, and Aurungzebe. The creed of the Koran is utterly unfit for civil government. It is a system of moral and political bondage, sustained only by military power and despotic rule, naturally corrupting those who administer it, while it has ever pauperized and demoralized the people who have been subjected to its sway. The Moguls have done in India what the Turks have accomplished in Asia Minor; and yet, while destroying and impoverishing, neither race have taken root in either land. In the former the power of the Moguls crumbled to pieces, and in the latter that of the Turks is now "ready to vanish away."

The last century closed upon Shah Alum—the grandfather of the monarch whose portrait we here present—engaged in a terrible struggle with the Rohillas of the North and the Mahrattas of the South. The long examples of perfidy and blood were then bearing their fruit, and had made these once subject-races the remorseless and inveterate enemies of the Mogul rule. Their power had been rising as that of the Emperor was in its decadence. Destitute of the means, which were once so abundant, to repress these conflicts, the aged Emperor had to witness these fierce and powerful parties contending with each other for the possession of his person and his capital, and the power to rule in his name.

In 1785, Sindia, the Mahratta, became paramount; but a few years after, while engaged in a war with Pertalo Sing, of Jeypoor, advantage was taken of his absence by Gholan Kadir Kahn, the Rohilla, to obtain possession of Delhi and the Emperor. This he accomplished by the treachery of the *Nazir*, or chief eunuch, to whom the management of the imperial establishment was intrusted. The inmates of the palace were treated by the usurper with a degree of malicious barbarity which it is hardly possible to conceive any human being could evince toward his fellow-creatures, unless actually possessed by Satan.

After cruelties of almost every description had been practiced, to extort from the members and retainers of the imperial family every article of value that still remained in their possession, Gholan Kadir continued to withhold from them even the necessaries of life, so that several ladies perished of hunger, and others, maddened by suffering, committed suicide. The royal children were compelled to perform the most humiliating offices; and when at last the wretched Emperor ventured to remonstrate indignantly against the atrocities he was thus compelled to witness, the fierce Rohilla sprang at him with the fury of a wild beast, flung the venerable monarch to the ground, knelt on his breast, and, with his dagger, pierced his eye-balls through and through!

The return of Sindia terminated these terrible scenes. Gholan Kadir fled, but was followed and captured by the Mahratta chief, who cut off his nose, ears, hands, and feet, and sent him in an iron cage to the Emperor—a fearful, though not uncommon, example of Asiatic retributive barbarity. He perished on the road, and his accomplice, the treacherous Nazir, was condemned, and trodden to death by an elephant—a mode of execution long practiced at Delhi.

The condition of the imperial family, though ameliorated, remained barely tolerable during the supremacy of Sindia; for the stated allowance for the support of the Emperor and his thirty children, though liberal in its nominal amount, was so irregularly paid that the imperial household often wanted the necessaries of life.

The real authority of the Moguls had passed away, and it now became a question, *Who* shall seize the fallen scepter—some one of these contending chiefs, or the English power, which had already established itself in the South and East of the country? The latter alone had the ability to give peace to the distracted land, and, at the same time, might be relied upon to grant the most generous terms to the falling dynasty. Accordingly, on the 10th of September, 1803, Shah Alum, the last actual possessor of the once mighty throne of the Moguls, thankfully placed himself and his empire under the protection of the British commander, Lord Lake, and thus delivered himself from the cruelty and tyranny of his enemies.

The General, on his entrance to the palace, found the Emperor "seated under a small tattered canopy, his person emaciated by indigence and infirmity, his countenance disfigured by the loss of his eyes, and bearing marks of extreme old age and settled melancholy." The arrangements made with him, under the directions of the Marquis Wellesley, then English Governor-General, were, no doubt, far beyond in liberality what the poor old man could have expected. Of this more hereafter, in its place.

The gigantic genius of Tamerlane, and the distinguished talents of the great Akbar, with the magnificent taste of Jehan, have thrown a sort of splendor over the crimes and follies of their descendants; and men kept reverence for the ruins of such greatness, and for the ideas which we have all associated in our childhood with the boundless wealth and glory suggested by the title of "The Great Moguls."

Under the new rule India began to return to peace, and such prosperity as was possible, with a still brighter day dawning upon her. Shah Alum enjoyed his honors and emoluments till 1806, when he was succeeded on his titular throne by his son, Shah Akbar, who held it until 1836, when its last possessor—the man whose portrait is here given—commenced his occupancy, and retained it till 1857, when a mad and hopeless infatuation led him to violate his treaty, and defy the power of the actual rulers of his empire, and precipitated him from the height to which his ambition had for a few weeks soared, into the depths of ignominious and unpitied exile.

A few facts in explanation are necessary here. This monarch, Mohammed Suraj-oo-deen, succeeded his father in 1836. The father, at the instigation of one of his wives, the favorite Begum, had done his best to deprive his son of his inheritance, and to have her own son, Mirza Saleem, acknowledged as his successor by the British Government. To this injustice that Government would not consent; so his rights were protected, and he mounted the throne of his ancestors.

The beautiful steel engraving on the opposite page gives a faithful picture of the wife, or, rather, one of the wives, of this old gentleman—the last of "The Great Moguls." Her name is Zeenat Mahal—the Ornament of the Palace—which was conferred on her when she was married to the Emperor in 1833. She was then sixteen years of age, and he was sixty—a disparity by no means uncommon in a land where polygamy prevails, and where such prejudice exists against marrying a widow, no matter how young or fair she may be. Her sexagenarian husband had other wives than Zeenat Mahal, but the beautiful and ambitious girl soon gained a complete control over the mind and heart of her aged lord, and this was made all the more influential when she had added the claims of a mother to the attractions of a wife.

Then commenced those intrigues, which she carried on up to the year 1856, to secure the succession to the throne for her child, Mirza Jumma Bukht, to the exclusion of Mirza Furruk-oo-deen, the elder son, whose prior claims the English Government recognized and sustained, as in duty bound. Her hostility to British influence, therefore, became intense; and her hopes of gaining her object were identified with the efforts of the Sepoy conspiracy to overthrow the English power in India. Poor lady! she utterly failed; and she and the son for whom every thing was risked are to-day wanderers in a foreign land, with the bitter reflection of the utter desolation which has overwhelmed the dynasty of which she thus became the last empress. She is the daughter of the Rajah of Bhatneer, a territory about one hundred and eighty miles north-west of Delhi.

Zeenat Mahal, Empress of Delhi.

The pictures of the Emperor and Empress here presented were painted on ivory by the Court portrait-painter twenty years ago, and are beautiful specimens of native art, and very correct likenesses of them both.

We will now turn from these royal persons to their home, and some of their splendid surroundings; and, first of all, let us look at their historical and beautiful *Dewan Khass.* There was something remarkably significant in the fact that the magnificent and famous Audience Hall of the Moguls should sink to ruin with the dynasty which had so long adorned it. For two hundred and fifty years they had shed luster upon each other; but, when we remember the crimes which had so long cried to Heaven for vengeance from the polished floor of this marble hall, it did seem fitting that the Most High, who ruleth in the kingdoms of men, in the hour when their judgment came should, with the same blow, strike down both the Mogul line and their magnificent memorial. When their cup of iniquity was full, and their hands were red with Christian blood, then came the day of vengeance.

It was my lot to be a witness of the wondrous ruin—to behold this imperial head of Oriental Mohammedanism, this "Light of the Faith," as he was designated, sinking into utter ruin and darkness;

> "Falling, like Lucifer,
> Never to hope again."

When I reached the Mogul capital of Hindustan, in the autumn of 1856, the Dewan Khass was still the center of state and pageantry, and its imperial master living in Oriental style on his salary of eighteen lakhs of rupees—$900,000 gold—per annum. Within one year from that day I was again in the Dewan Khass, where he used to sit in his gorgeous array, to witness his trial, and that of his princes and nobles, before a military commission of British officers, by whom he was condemned to be banished as a felon to a foreign shore for the remnant of his miserable life, there to subsist on a convict's allowance; and within a few weeks after, when I again visited the once magnificent Dewan Khass, I found it despoiled of its glory, its marble halls and columns whitewashed.

and the whole turned into a hospital for sick soldiers! Has the world ever witnessed a ruin more prompt, more complete, more amazing than this?

For seven hundred years the Mohammedan dynasties—of whom this wretched old man was the last representative—had tried to hold the reins of power over India, alien alike in race, language, and religion from the people whom they ruled. Mahmoud of Ghuznee—a contemporary for five years of William the Conqueror—was the founder of this line of monarchs; and yet such was their character, that when these long centuries of selfish and bigoted misrule were ending, and this old man was in circumstances that might well have evoked compassion and sympathy from those around him, he was allowed to sink out of sight, not only without regret or condolence, but amid the expressed sense of relief of the race over whom he and his ancestors had dominated—a people with whom they had ever refused to amalgamate, whom they had never tried to conciliate, and from whom his race never realized either loyalty or affection.

It may be doubted if any royal line on earth has had such a sad record to present to the historian. Of the sixty-five monarchs who thus conquered and ruled India, only twenty-seven of the number died a natural death; all the rest were either exiled, killed in battle, or assassinated, while the average length of each reign was only eleven years. Truly has it been said, "Delhi has been the stage of greatness—men the actors, ambition the prompter, and centuries the audience." It was my opportunity to come in at the close, and behold destruction drawing the curtain over the scene, and writing upon it the realized sentence, and the warning to the nations: "Thou shalt break them with a rod of iron; thou shalt dash them in pieces like a potter's vessel. Be wise now therefore, O ye kings: be instructed, ye judges of the earth. Serve the Lord with fear, and rejoice with trembling. Kiss the Son, lest he be angry, and ye perish from the way, when his wrath is kindled but a little."

This was all the more significant, because the men by whose instrumentality God wrought out his purposes were the very race whose new monarchy opened with their own in the tenth century; but a race who received the faith which those Mohammedans repelled and persecuted, and who have consequently risen to supremacy among the nations; so that, while one portion of them rules the New World, the other inherits the empire of the fallen Moguls, and are there with confidence expecting that the promise of the Almighty shall ere long be made as true as his threatenings now consummated: "Ask of me, and I shall give thee the heathen for thine inheritance, and the uttermost parts of the earth for thy possession." How expressively does the history of these eight hundred years declare, "Blessed are all they that put their trust in Him!"

True religion was the only thing this guilty but magnificent race needed for perpetuity. No dynasty ever had a grander opportunity than they—a rich land, the sixth of the world's population, boundless wealth, almost a millennium of time for the trial, with a civilization all their own, and a splendid cultivated taste, which they had the will and the ability to gratify to the utmost, as its memorials in Agra, and Delhi, and elsewhere, attest, to the surprise and delight of the traveler and tourist from many lands.

The Emperor Shah Jehan—A. D. 1627—alone, for his portion, laid out in Alipoor the celebrated Gardens of Shalimar, at a cost of $5,000,000. They were about two miles and a half in circumference, and were almost like Paradise in beauty. He then built the world-renowned Taj Mahal, expending upon it nearly $60,000,000, the present value of money. He also erected the Dewan Khass, the most gorgeous audience hall in the East. This latter we here illustrate.

This imperial hall was a gorgeous accessory of the Palace of Delhi. The front opened on a large quadrangle, and the whole stood in what was once a garden, extremely rich and beautiful. This unique pavilion rested on an elevated terrace, and was formed entirely of white marble. It was one hundred and fifty feet long, and forty in breadth, having a graceful cupola at each angle. The roof was supported on colonnades of marble pillars. The solid and polished marble has been worked into its forms with as much delicacy as though it had been wax, and its whole surface, pillars, walls, arches, and roof, and even the pavement, was inlaid with the richest, most profuse, and exquisite designs in foliage and arabesque; the fruits and flowers being represented in sections of gems, such as amethysts, carnelian, blood-stone, garnet, topaz, lapis lazuli, green serpentine, and various colored crystals. A bordering ran around the walls and columns similarly decorated, inlaid with inscriptions in Arabic from the Koran. The whole had the appearance of some rich work from the loom, in which a brilliant pattern is woven on a pure white ground, the tracery of rare and cunning artists. Purdahs (curtains) of all colors and designs hung from the crenated arches on the outside to exclude the glare and heat. (These purdahs are omitted in the engraving for the sake of the interior view.)

In the center of the hall stood the *Takt Taous*, or Peacock Throne, of Shah Jehan, on the erection of which Price's History tells us he expended thirty millions sterling, ($150,000,000.) This wondrous work of art was ascended by steps of silver, at the summit of which rose a massive seat of pure gold, with a canopy of the same metal inlaid with jewels. The chief feature of the design was a peacock with his tail spread, the natural colors being represented by pure gems. A vine also was introduced into the design, the leaves and fruit of which were of precious stones, whose rays were reflected from mirrors set in large pearls. Beneath all this "glory" sat the Great Mogul.

No wonder that the fame of this wealth and extravagance should attract the notice and cupidity of a man like Nadir Shah, the Persian, who, in 1739, invaded Hindustan, and carried off this Peacock Throne among his trophies. His estimate of it may be understood from the fact that he had a tent constructed to contain it, the outside of which was covered with scarlet broadcloth and the inside of violet-colored satin, on which birds and beasts, trees and flowers, were depicted in precious stones. On either side of the Peacock Throne a screen was extended, adorned with the fig-

The Dewan Khass: or, Hall of Audience. Palace of Delhi.

ures of two angels, also represented in various colored gems. Even the tent-poles were adorned with jewels, and the pins were of massive gold. The whole formed a load for several elephants. The gorgeous trophy was afterward broken up by Adil Shah, the nephew and successor of the captor. Its place in the Dewan Khass was afterward supplied by another of inferior value, and by the Crystal Throne, which the writer saw in 1857.

Inside of the entrance of the Khass, inscribed in black letters upon a slab of alabaster, is the Persian couplet, in the hyperbolical language of the East, quoted by Moore in his Lalla Rookh.

> "If there be an elysium on earth,
> It is this, it is this."

Moore introduces it in "The Light of the Harem," where the Emperor Jehangeer and his beloved and beautiful Nourmahal, in their visit to the Valley of Cashmere, happen to fall into a sort of lovers' quarrel, and in the evening she vails herself, and takes her place among the beautiful female singers who have come to entertain the reclining Emperor—one of whom seems disposed to avail herself of the opportunity to attract the wounded and wandering love of Jehangeer in a wrong direction, when the vailed Nourmahal, at the pause, strikes her lute and sings sweetly:

> "There's a bliss beyond all that the minstrel has told,
> When two that are linked in one heavenly tie,
> With heart never changing, and brow never cold,
> Love on through all ills, and love on till they die!
> One hour of a passion so sacred is worth
> Whole ages of heartless and wandering bliss;
> And O, if there be an elysium on earth,
> It is this, it is this!"

Jehangeer's heart is touched, and there ensues a happy reconciliation. Unfortunately, however, for the poet, there is an anachronism here, and a violation of historic truth, as well as an inadequate translation, for Shah Jehan, who built the Dewan Khass, and inscribed the words on the slab of alabaster over the entrance, was the son of Jehangeer, and it is not likely that his father's wife could quote the words before they were composed. Moore's picture of Jehangeer and Nourmahal is the very reverse of what truthful history, corroborated by the personal observation of Sir Thomas Roe, tells us of that cruel sot and his talented but unprincipled Empress. And she could cherish but little true love for the man that had her noble husband, Sheer Afghan, so basely assassinated in order to gain possession of her person.

It is a pity that poetry should be so often perverted and its elegancies made to adorn the unworthy and the vile. Nevertheless, we know that "the judgments of God are according to truth," and we see here that no wealth, or power, or magnificence, or human adulation, can shield the guilty when the inevitable hand of the Divine verdict has come.

"Elysium" is too European, too Northern, a term to express Shah Jehan's word. But Moore, for a good part of his life a Romanist, may have thought the term over-biblical for his use, and chose the heathen phrase "elysium" in preference to the plain rendering of the word. The inscription runs exactly as follows, expressed in English letters:

> "Ugur Firdousi ba-roo-i-zameen ust,
> Ameen ust, ameen ust, ameen ust."

And the rendering is:

> "If there be a *paradise* on the face of the earth,
> This is it, this is it, this is it!"

(The original Persian may be found quoted by Dr. Clarke in his Commentary on Nehemiah i, verse 8.)

In or near Persia was the region of Paradise, and the fame of the first garden, planted by God, near the banks of the Euphrates, lingered as a tradition in its own vicinity for four thousand years, and led to those imitations of it in the "paradises of Oriental despots." Most of the invasions of India were from the regions of the ancient Eden, and the invaders carried with them their ideas of paradise to the land of the Ganges, and tried to reproduce them there. This Dewan Khass was the central object of the most costly one ever planted in India, or perhaps anywhere else.

Standing in the midst of it, how easy it seemed to transport one's self in thought to that similar scene mentioned in the book of Esther i, 4, 7, where, nearly five hundred years before Christ, Ahasuerus, the Persian, "who reigned from India even unto Ethiopia," displayed his magnificence during the seven days' feast "in the court of the garden of the king's palace, where were white, green, and blue hangings fastened with cords of fine linen and purple to silver rings and pillars of marble; the beds [or seats] were of gold and silver, upon a pavement of red, and blue, and white, and black marble." Verses 5 and 6.

As Dr. Clarke has remarked, the term paradise "is applied to denote *splendid apartments*, as well as *fine gardens*; in a word, any place of pleasure and delight." And is not this exactly the idea of the paradise described in the twenty-first and twenty-second chapters of Revelation — the golden city, with its jasper walls and gates of pearl, in the midst of the garden of God, with the river of the water of life, clear as crystal, and the tree of life yielding its fruit every month?

In speaking of it Jesus says, "In my Father's house are many mansions." "I go to prepare a place for you." "They shall walk with me in white." "To him that overcometh will I give to eat of the tree of life which is in the midst of the paradise of God." How Oriental are all these thoughts! I have seen the princely Asiatic host, with his guests around him in their white flowing robes, moving through his beautiful garden, as he entertained them with his fellowship, with music, and the freest use of the bounties around them; and the earthly scene has been a vivid image of what the heavenly paradise will be to the redeemed, when they shall find themselves at last in the garden of God, with Jesus as their host, having the right of entrance to his glorious audience hall, and the amazing honor of sitting down with him upon his sapphire throne, in the presence of the host of heaven! See Exod. xxiv, 10; Ezek. i, 26; Rev. iii, 21.

The crown worn on the head of the Great Mogul was worthy of the Khass and the throne on which he sat. It was made by the great Akbar, in the fashion of that worn by the Persian kings, and was of extraordinary beauty and magnificence. It had twelve points, each surmounted by a diamond of the purest water, while the central point terminated in a single pearl of extraordinary size, the whole, including many valuable rubies, being estimated at a cost equivalent to £2,070,000 sterling, or $10,350,000. Add one thing more, the *Koh-i-noor* diamond, on his brow, and you have the Mogul "in all his glory," as he sat on the Peacock Throne in his Dewan Khass, surrounded by Mohammedan princes, by turbaned and jeweled rajahs, amid splendor which only "the gorgeous East" could furnish, and the fame of which seemed to the poor courts of Europe of that day like a tale of the *Arabian Nights.*

Soon the Portuguese were found making their way around "the Cape of Storms" into the Indian Ocean, and thence to the capital of the Moguls. James I. of England, in 1615, sent as his embassador Sir Thomas Roe, whose chaplain has left us a record of the embassy in *A Voyage to the East Indies.* Sir Thomas felt keenly the contrast afforded by the unpretending character of the presents and retinue with which his royal master had provided him, to the magnificent ceremonial which he daily witnessed, and in which he was permitted to take part. He remained two years at Jehangeer's Court. One of the greatest displays occurred on the Emperor's birthday, when, amid the ceremonies, the royal person was weighed in golden scales twelve times against gold, silver, perfumes, and other valuables, the whole of which were then divided among the spectators. His description of the splendors of the scene sounds like the veriest romance.

On one of the pillars of the Audience Hall is shown the mark of the dagger of the Hindoo Prince of Chittore, who, in the very presence of the Emperor, stabbed to the heart one of the Mohammedan ministers, who made use of some disrespectful language toward him. On being asked how he presumed to do this in tne presence of his sovereign, he answered in almost the very words of Roderic Dhu,

"I right my wrongs where they are given,
Though it were in the court of Heaven."

Weighing of the Emperor in the Dewan Khass.

Alas! what scenes of perfidy and blood have been witnessed within the walls of this Dewan Khass! Sleeman and others have narrated some of them, but the half has not been told, and all are only known to Heaven. The last of them, in 1857, exhausted the patience of the Almighty, and the dynasty and their Khass were destroyed by that "stone" which then fell upon them, and ground them to powder.

Here in this hall, which he himself had built, sat the great Shah Jehan, obliged to receive the insolent commands of his own grandson, Mohammed, when flushed with victory, and to offer him the throne, merely to disappoint the expectations of the youth's rebel father. Here sat Aurungzebe—Shah Jehan's fourth son—when he ordered the assassination of his own brothers, Dara and Morad, and the imprisonment and destruction by slow poison of his own son Mohammed, who had so often fought bravely by his side in battle. Here, too, stood in chains the graceful Sooleeman, to receive his sentence of death, with his poor young brother, Sipeher Shekoh, who had shared all his father's toils and dangers, and witnessed his brutal murder. And here sat the handsome, but effeminate, Mohammed Shah, in March, 1739, bandying compliments with his ferocious conqueror, Nadir Shah, the Persian King, who had destroyed his armies, plundered his treasury, appropriated his throne, and ordered the murder of nearly one hundred thousand of the helpless inhabitants of his capital, men, women, and children, in a general massacre. The bodies of these people lay unburied in the streets, tainting the air, while the two sovereigns sat here sipping their coffee in the presence of their courtiers, and swearing to the most deliberate lies in the name of their God, prophet, and Koran!

Sleeman relates that on this occasion the coffee was brought into the Dewan Khass upon a golden salver, and delivered to the two sovereigns by the most polished gentleman of Mohammed Shah's Court. Precedence and public courtesies are, in the East, managed and respected with a tenacity and importance that to us of the Western world seems positively ridiculous.

Nevertheless, they are vital to the Oriental, and life or death have often hung upon their manifestations. All present on this occasion felt its significance. The movements of the officer, as he entered the gorgeous apartment, amid the splendid trains of the two Emperors, were watched with great anxiety; if he presented the coffee first to his own master, the furious conqueror, before whom the sovereign of India and all his courtiers trembled, might order him to instant execution; if he presented it to Nadir first, he would certainly insult his own sovereign out of fear of the stranger. To the astonishment of all, he walked up, with a steady step, direct to his own master. "I cannot," said he, "aspire to the honor of presenting the cup to the king of kings, your majesty's honored guest, nor would your majesty wish that any hand but your own should do so." The Emperor took the cup from the golden salver, and presented it to Nadir Shah, who said with a smile as he took it: "Had all your officers known and done their duty like this man, you had never, my good cousin, seen me and my Kuzul Bashus at Delhi. Take care of him for your own sake, and get around you as many like him as you can."

All these are now dust—the oppressor and the oppressed gone to their account before God; but the spirit of bigotry, and recklessness of human suffering and life, engendered by the Moslem creed, clung to the place until its gems ceased to shine, and its glory was extinguished forever. For here, too, sat its last occupant—this man whose portrait we present, Mohammed Suraj-oo-deen—on the 12th of May, 1857, and issued those orders under which England's embassador and his chaplain, with every Christian whom they could find in Delhi, male and female, native or European, were butchered amid barbarities the enormity of which has never been exceeded by any of the edicts of cruelty which have gone forth, even from the Dewan Khass.

Humanity heaves a sigh of relief to know that this is the last. The house of Tamerlane is no more; their Dewan Khass is in ruins; their pomp, and glory, and power, have gone down to the grave forever.

The Taj Mahal viewed from the River Jumna.

From these, with all their crimes, changes, and sufferings, we turn now to the peaceful and lovely monument which is India's architectural glory, and one of earth's great wonders—the existence of which is probably the only valid apology remaining for the vast revenues squandered by these irresponsible despots during so many hundred years.

About six miles before the traveler reaches the city of Agra the dome and minarets of the world-renowned *Taj Mahal* burst upon his view from behind a grove of fruit-trees near the road. The effect is wonderful! The long-anticipated pleasure of beholding earth's most beautiful shrine is now within his reach, and the gratified and delighted sight rests upon this first view of its harmony of parts, its faultless congregation of architectural beauties, with a kind of ecstasy. Of the thousands who have traveled far to gaze upon it, it may safely be asserted that not one of the number has been disappointed in the examination of its wondrous beauty. The Queen of Sheba would probably have admitted, had she seen it, that the "half had not been told her."

We first look at it from the north side, on the river bank, where the scene is fully presented. The building to the right of the Taj is a Mosque for religious services, and that to the left is a Travelers' Rest House, where visitors can be accommodated. We next go around to the gate of entrance on the other side. The inclosure, including the gardens and outer court, is a parallelogram of one thousand eight hundred and sixty feet by more than one thousand feet, with a system of fountains, eighty-four in number, along the central avenue, and a marble reservoir in the middle about forty feet square, in which are five additional fountains, one in the center, and one at each corner. On either side of this beautiful sheet of water, into which are falling the silvery jets of spray from the fountains, are rows of dark Italian cypress, significant of the great design of the shrine. The river Jumna flows mildly by, and the birds, encouraged by the delicious coolness and shade of the place, forget their usual lassitude, and pour forth their songs, while the odor of roses, and of the orange, and lemon, and tamarind trees, perfume the air.

Amid all this loveliness the Taj rises before your view, upon an elevated terrace of white and yellow marble, about thirty feet in height, and having a graceful minaret at each corner. On either side are the beautiful Mosque and the Rest House, facing inward, and corresponding exactly with each other in size, design, and execution. That on the left side is the one used for service, as it allows the faces of the worshipers to be set toward the tomb of their prophet, to the west, at Mecca. The one to the right is used for the accommodation of visitors who come from various parts of the world to enjoy this great sight, and who here receive free quarters as long as they choose to remain.

From the center of this great platform springs up the Taj itself. A detailed description of its general appearance is rendered unnecessary, as our readers have that before them in the beautiful engraving here given. The mausoleum itself, the terrace upon which it stands, and the minarets, are all formed of the finest white marble, inlaid with precious stones. The marble was brought from the Jeypore territory, a distance of nearly three hundred miles, and the sandstone for the walls, from Dholepore and Futtehpore Secree. A Persian manuscript, preserved in the Taj, professes to give a full account of the stones and materials used in its construction. The white marble was brought from Jeypore, the yellow marble from the Nerbudda, the black from Charkoh, crystal from China, jasper from the Punjab, carnelian from Bagdad, turquoises from Thibet, agate from Yemen, lapis lazuli from Ceylon, diamonds from Punah, rockspar from the Nerbudda, loadstone from Gwalior, amethyst and onyx from Persia, chalcedony from Villiat, and sapphires from Lanka—and this does not exhaust the list.

The dome, "shining like an enchanted castle of burnished silver," is seventy feet in diameter, the Taj itself is two hundred and forty-five feet in altitude, and the *cullice*, or golden spire on the summit, is thirty feet more, making a height of two hundred and seventy-five feet from the terrace to the golden crescent.

It is asserted that the whole of the Koran is inlaid upon the building in the Arabic language, the letters being beautifully formed

The Gate of the Taj.

in black marble on the outside, and in precious stones within. Nearly all the external ornamentation which the reader sees in the engraving are these texts.

The writer's earnest desire is, that his description may in some measure be worthy of the pictures; yet, though conscious of having done his best, and venturing to assert that he has here brought together the most complete account of the Taj that has yet appeared, still he realizes to himself how tame and imperfect is any effort to convey to those who never had the privilege of seeing it an adequate idea of what its beauty really is, or of the effect it produces upon the mind of the beholder as he stands within its sacred inclosure and realizes its loveliness as fully displayed before him. Like piety, or like heaven, it may be said of the beauty of the Taj, that "no man knoweth it save him that receiveth it." Let our readers judge of this enthusiasm by the views before them, and by what follows.

The beautiful wood-cut opposite, presenting the view of the gate of the Taj, and the steel engraving which follows, are both made from photographs of the originals, taken in India, so that our readers may be assured that they have here before them the most perfect and worthy representation of this matchless structure that has ever appeared.

The Taj is a mausoleum, built by the Great Mogul, Shah Jehan, over his beautiful Empress. It is situated in the midst of a garden of vast extent and beauty, three miles from Agra. The entrance to the garden is through the gateway here shown. This superb entrance is of red sandstone, inlaid with ornaments and with texts from the Koran in white marble, and is itself a palace, both as regards its magnitude and its decoration. The lofty walls that surround the garden are of the same material, having arched colonnades running around the interior, and giving an air of magnificence to the whole inclosure. The garden is laid out with rich taste Its paths are paved with slabs of freestone, arranged in fanciful devices. Noble trees, affording a delightful shade and pleasant walks, even in the middle of the day, are planted in sufficient number through the various spaces, while the fruit-trees, with the graceful palm, the banyan, and the feathery bamboo, mingle their foliage, and are ornamented by the sweet-scented tamarind and by flowers of the loveliest hue, which bloom in profusion around.

It is difficult to determine whether the exterior or the interior is the more fascinating; each has its own matchless claim, and each is perfect in its loveliness. Externally, the best times to see the Taj are by sunrise or by moonlight. The midday sun shining upon its polished surface is too brilliant for the eye to bear with satisfaction: for a position from whence to view it, the gallery on the top of the entrance-gate inside is decidedly the best point of observation An hour before the sun rises you may see persons taking their places in that gallery, and there, elevated about sixty feet, they wait for the opening day, and the effect produced is thus well described: "The gray light of morning had not yet appeared when we reached the Taj and made our way up to the top of the gate, to look upon it as it gradually grew into shape and form at the bidding of the rising sun. The moon had just hidden her face beneath the western horizon, and the darkness was at its deepest, presaging the approaching break of day. We looked down upon the immense inclosure crowded with trees mingled together in one undistinguishable mass, gently surging and moaning in the night breeze. Above rose, apparently in the distance, a huge gray-blue mass, without shape or form, which rested like a cloud on the gloomy sea of foliage. Soon a faint glimmer of light appeared in the eastern horizon; as the darkness fled away before its gradually increasing power, the cloud changed first to a light blue, and then developed into shape and proportion; and the minarets, and the cupolas, and dome defined themselves in clearer lines upon the still dark sky beyond. Soon the first rosy tint of the dawn appeared, and as if by magic the whole assumed a roseate hue, which increased as the sun made its appearance, and the Taj stood before us, dazzlingly brilliant in the purest white, absolutely perfect in its fairy proportions. It is impossible to describe it. I had heard of perfection

The Taj Mahal.

of outline and of graceful symmetry of proportion, but never realized the true meaning of the words until the morning when I watched the Taj burst into loveliness at the touch of the sun's magic wand."

Under the softened light of the moon the beautiful structure develops fresh beauties. The dazzling effect has ceased, and you gaze upon every part of it as it appears bathed in a soft amber-light that seems to enter your own soul, and impart its peace and serenity till you wonder that outside these walls there can be a world of sin, and strife, and sorrow. You are conscious of abandoning yourself to the delightful, if brief, enjoyment of that poetic and mental peace which the charming scene was designed to produce upon the beholder.

Let us now enter the wonderful shrine itself, and gaze upon its internal beauty. Before entering the central hall we descend to the vault below, where the real sarcophagi are, in which lie the remains of the Emperor and Empress. Her tomb occupies the very center, and his is by her side. The light is made to fall directly upon her tomb, which is of white marble and beautifully decorated. But the especial splendor is reserved for the tombs in the rotunda above, directly over these, and which, as it were, officially represent them.

We ascend to them, and stand amid a scene of architectural glory which has no equal on earth. Above us rises the lofty dome, far up into the dim distance. The floor on which we tread is of polished marble and jasper, ornamented with a wainscoating of sculptured marble tablets inlaid with flowers formed of precious stones. Around are windows or screens of marble filigree, richly wrought in various patterns, which admit a faint and delicate illumination—what Ritualists would love to call "a dim, religious light"—into the gorgeous apartment. In the center are the two tombs, surrounded by a magnificent octagonal screen about six feet high, with doors on the sides. The open tracery in this white marble screen is wrought into beautiful flowers, such as lilies, irises, and others, and the borders of the screen are inlaid with precious stones, representing flowers, executed with such wonderful perfection that the forms wave as in nature, and the hues and shades of the stems, leaves, and flowers appear as real almost as the beauties which they represent.

These ornamental designs are so carefully and exquisitely executed that several of the flowers have as many as eighty different stones entering into their composition, all polished uniform with the marble, into which they are so delicately inserted that you can hardly trace their joinings. They seem as though they had grown there, instead of being separately prepared and placed in their positions by the hands of the "cunning workman," who designed and executed this imperishable and magnificent memorial of human love.

But the richest work of all is on the cenotaph of the Empress within the screen. Upon her tomb—according to universal Mohammedan usage—is a slate or tablet of marble, while on the Emperor's is a small box representing a pen-holder. These always distinguish a man's or a woman's grave among these people; the idea being that a woman's heart is a tablet on which lordly man can write whatever pleases him best. And this mark of feminine inferiority was not spared even the beloved occupant of the Taj Mahal.

But her tomb—how beautiful! The snow-white marble is inlaid with flowers so delicately formed that they look like embroidery on white satin, so exquisitely is the mosaic executed in carnelian, blood-stone, agates, jasper, turquoise, lapis lazuli, and other precious stones. Thirty-five different specimens of carnelian are employed in forming a single leaf of a carnation; and in one flower, not larger than a silver dollar, as many as twenty-three different stones can be counted. Yet these are but specimens of the beauties that are spread in unparalleled profusion over this entire chamber. Indeed, Long asserts that he found one flower upon her tomb to be composed of no less than three hundred different stones.

Her name and date of death, with her virtuous qualities, are recorded in the same costly manner, in gems of Arabic—the sacred language of the Mohammedans—on the side of her tomb. There are other inscriptions upon it, which we will hereafter refer to when we come to examine who this lady was that was thus honored in death beyond all her sex.

The Emperor's tomb is plainer than the other, has no passages from the Koran, but merely a similar mosaic work of flowers, and his name, with the date of his death, upon it.

Over all this richness and beauty rises the magnificent dome, which is so constructed as to contain an *echo* more pure, and prolonged, and harmonious than any other in the world, so far as known. A competent judge has declared, "Of all the complicated music ever heard on earth, that of a flute played gently in the vault below, where the remains of the Emperor and his consort repose, as the sound rises to the dome amid a hundred arched alcoves around, and descends in heavenly reverberations upon those who sit or recline on the cenotaphs above, is perhaps the finest to an inartificial ear. We feel as if it were from heaven, and breathed by angels. It is to the ear what the building itself is to the eye; but unhappily it cannot, like the building, live in our recollections. All that we can in after life remember is, that it was heavenly and produced heavenly emotions." An enthusiast thus more glowingly describes it: "Now take your seat upon the marble pavement beside the upper tombs, and send your companion to the vault underneath to run slowly over the notes of his flute or guitar. Was ever melody like this? It haunts the air above and around. It distills in showers upon the polished marble. It condenses into the mild shadows, and sublimes into the softened, hallowed light of the dome. It rises, it falls; it swims mockingly, meltingly around. It is the very element with which sweet dreams are builded. It is the melancholy echo of the past—it is the bright, delicate harping of the future. It is the atmosphere breathed by Ariel, and playing around the fountain of Chindara. It is the spirit of the Taj, the voice of inspired love, which called into being this peerless wonder of the world, and elaborated its symmetry and composed its harmony, and, eddying around its young minarets and domes, blended them without a line into the azure of immensity."

Let us imagine, if we can, the *effect* produced here when the funeral dirge was chanted over the tomb of the lovely Empress, and the answering echoes, in the pauses of the strains, would seem to fall like the responses of angel choirs in paradise!

Princely provision was made by the gifted originator of the Taj for its care and services. The light that fell upon that tomb day and night was from perfumed oil in golden lamps; fresh garlands of nature's flowers were laid upon it daily; Mogul musicians furnished appropriate music; five times in each twenty-four hours the Muezzin's cry to prayers resounded from these minarets; and a eunuch of high station, with two thousand Sepoys under his orders, held watch and ward without ceasing over the entire place and all its approaches. None but men of Mohammedan faith were permitted to come within these precincts, or to draw near her tomb; and the entire shrine was by the Emperor's orders expressly held sacred from the approach of any Christian foot.

Arrangements were made for occasionally exhibiting its loveliness by light adequate to bring out its perfect beauty. Rests were provided on the eight corners of the shrine for blue or Bengal lights, and when these were simultaneously fired, as the writer has seen them, the effect was magical. The candles had been previously extinguished and the building left in total darkness, when, at the signal, the brilliant illumination burst forth, and every point and ornament, even to the top of the rich dome itself, was displayed more gloriously than the light of day could ever have exhibited their rich colors. The inlaid ornamentation and filagree of the scenes, now like transparent and delicate lace-work, all seemed, to the astonished vision, like a palace of enchantment, and the mind of the beholder was awed into homage of that rare intellect which could devise and execute this the most beautiful monument on which the human eye can ever gaze on earth!

Perhaps no one has ever rendered such perfect justice to the beauty of this mausoleum as the unnamed author quoted by

Stocqueler. He thus sketches it: "I have been to visit the Taj. I have returned full of emotion. My mind is enriched with visions of ideal beauty. When first I approached the Taj, eleven years ago, I was disappointed. In after days, when my admiration for the loveliness of this building had grown into a passion, I often inquired why this should have been? And the only answer I can find is, that the symmetry is too perfect to strike at first. It meets you as the most natural of objects. It, therefore, does not startle, and you return from it disappointed that you have not been startled. But it grows upon you in all the harmony of its proportions, in all the exquisite delicacy of its adornment, and at each glance some fresh beauty or grace is developed. And, besides, it stands so much alone in the world of beauty. Imagination has never conceived a second Taj, nor had any thing similar ever before occurred to it.

"View the Taj at a distance! It is as the spirit of some happy dream, dwelling dim, but pure, upon the horizon of your hope, and reigning in virgin supremacy over the visible circle of the earth and sky. Approach it nearer, and its grandeur appears unlessened by the acuteness of its fabric, and swelling in all its fresh and fairy harmony until you are at a loss for feelings worthy of its presence. Approach still nearer, and that which, as a whole, has proved so charming, is found to be equally exquisite in the minutest detail. Here are no mere touches for distant effect. Here is no need to place the beholder in a particular spot to cast a partial light upon the performance; the work which dazzles with its elegance at the *coup d'œil* will bear the scrutiny of the miscroscope; the sculpture of the panels, the fretwork and mosaic of the screen, the elegance of the marble pavement, the perfect finish of every jot and iota, are as if the meanest architect had been one of those potent genii who were of yore compelled to adorn the palaces of necromancers and kings.

"We feel, as our eye wanders around this hallowed space, that we have hitherto lavished our language and admiration in vain. We dread to think of it with feelings which workmanship less exquisite has awakened, and we dare not use, in its praise, language hackneyed in the service of every-day minds. We seek for it a new train of associations, a fresh range of ideas, a greener and more sacred corner in the repository of the heart. And yet, wherefore should this be, since no terms applying to other works of beauty, excepting the most general, can be appropriated here? For those there be phrases established by usage, which their several classifications of style render intelligible to all acquainted with similar works of art. But in the Taj we fall upon a new and separate creation, which never *can* become a style, since it can never be imitated. It is like some bright and newly discovered winged thing, all beauteous in a beauty peculiar to itself, and referable to no class or order on the roll of zoology, which the whole world flocks to gaze upon with solemn delight, none presuming to designate the lovely stranger, nor to conjecture a kindred for it with the winged things of the earth. Suffice it—Love was its author, Beauty its inspiration."

There never was erected in this world any thing so perfect and lovely, save Solomon's Temple. In gazing down upon the scene, as the writer did in the closing days of the terrible rebellion in 1858, the effect was wonderful, and akin to those emotions that must thrill the soul which looks out for the first time upon the plains of heaven. Every thing that could remind one of ruin and misery seemed so far away, that as we sat, and the delighted eyes drank in the scene before them, terminated by the gorgeous fane as it rose up toward the blue and cloudless sky, we thought, if John Bunyan could have shared the opportunity, he would surely have imagined his dreams realized, and believed himself looking over the battlements of the New Jerusalem, and viewing that "region of eternal day" where holiness and peace are typified by pearls and gold, and all manner of precious stones, with the fountain of life, clear as crystal, proceeding from the throne of God and the Lamb!

Two questions now remain to be answered: Who was the lady to whom the Taj was erected? and, Who was the architect who designed and executed it?

There has been much misunderstanding upon these subjects. The wrong lady has been named by authors who might have understood better, had they consulted the proper authorities, and it has alsc been asserted that the architect was unknown. Bayard Taylor, for instance, in his *India, China, and Japan*, informs his readers that "Shah Jehan—the 'Selim' of Moore's poem—erected it as a mausoleum to his Queen Noor Jehan, the 'Light of the World,'" and he several times repeats this blunder. Mr. Taylor is not profound in Indian history. Every statement in the above quotation is incorrect. The Selim of Moore's poem was not Shah Jehan, but his father; Noor Jehan was not Shah Jehan's wife, but his stepmother; and Noor Jehan was not buried in the Taj, but beyond the Attock, in the North-west, where her tomb is to-day a mere ruin. That Bayard Taylor should write in this superficial style is not very unusual with him: but that such authors as Montgomery Martin and Bishop Heber should say it was for Noor Jehan is indeed surprising: for they had acquaintance with the history of India, and had not to depend upon ignorant guides and guide books for the information they would give their readers

Our description of Etmad-od-Doulah's Tomb will present the facts, showing that the infant born in the desert afterward became the wife, first of Sheer Afghan, and then of Prince Selim, after he mounted the throne, taking the name of Jehangeer, when he conferred upon her the title of Noor Jehan. These were the hero and heroine of Moore's poem. Shah Jehan, who built the Taj, was the son of Jehangeer by a different wife than Noor Jehan. Noor Jehan's brother, Asuf Jan, had a daughter whom Shah Jehan married, and to whom he gave the title of Moomtaj-i-Mahal, and it was to *her* memory that he built the Taj, long after his father was dead, and while he held his stepmother, Noor Jehan—who died in 1646—in a state of honorable captivity. Moomtaj-i-Mahal died in 1631, fifteen years before her aunt, Noor Jehan.

The history of Moomtaj is very interesting, and we may give a few of the facts here. She was very beautiful, and obtained an unbounded influence over the mind of the Emperor, exhibiting such capacity for the management of State affairs, that her husband seems for years to have resigned the reins of government into her hands, while he was consuming his time over the wine bottle in the company of a favorite French physician.

From this dream of pleasure, the history tells us, Shah Jehan was suddenly awakened by the fatal illness of his beautiful Empress. She died in giving birth to a daughter, who is said to have been heard crying in the womb by herself and her other daughters. She sent for the Emperor, and told him that she believed no mother had ever been known to survive the birth of a child so heard, and that she felt her end was near. "She had," she said, "only two requests to make: first, that he would not marry again after her death, and have children to contend with hers for his favors and dominions; and, secondly, that he would build for her the tomb with which he had promised to perpetuate her name." Both her dying requests were granted. Her tomb was commenced immediately. No woman ever pretended to supply her place in the palace, nor had Shah Jehan children by any other.

But Moomtaj might well, in her dying hours, make the request she did, for she could not be ignorant that Shah Jehan had secured the throne to himself, from the other children of his father, by the use of the dagger and the bow-string. And it was not without reason; for before she was many years laid in the Taj her own children, even, contended for the throne; and the magnificent Shah Jehan, realizing that "as he had done so God rewarded him," died in prison in 1666, a captive in the hands of his son, Aurungzebe, who had already followed the example of his father in hunting down and destroying his brothers and nephews in order to secure the throne undisputed to himself.

But we return to the peaceful Taj. The Empress Moomtaj was a Khadija in her day, a Mohammedan devotee, and a bitter foe of Christianity—such Christianity as she knew. She took care that this animosity should go with her to the grave, and even be inserted on her tomb; and there it is to-day, in the Taj, amid the flowers and inscriptions on her cenotaph—a prohibition and a prayer against

Christ's followers, which her race has now forever lost the power to enforce, and which God Almighty has taken providential care shall not only remain unanswered, but be reversed to the very letter.

The circumstances were these: Prior to the days of Shah Jehan and his wife, the Portuguese, attracted by the fame and the wealth of the great Akbar and his sons, had found their way to India, establishing themselves as traders and merchants, on the west coast at Goa and on the east at Hooghly, near the present Calcutta. Some, who were artisans, reached Agra, the imperial city, where they were employed by the Government chiefly in the duties of the artillery, the arsenals and founderies, and a few as artists. The emoluments of office, for arts which they were thus introducing, were very large, and soon attracted great numbers to Agra, so that Monsieur Thevenot, who visited Agra in 1666, tells us that the Christian families there were estimated to have been about twenty-five thousand—an exaggeration doubtless. Still their number must have been large; and among them were some Italians and Frenchmen, as is evident from their tombs, which are still extant in the Roman Catholic cemetery at Agra, where the dates of several are still visible on the head-stones, ranging from the year 1600 to 1650.

Akbar and Shah Jehan allowed these people the free exercise of their religion. Indeed, the former built them a church, and used to take pleasure in presiding at discussions where he matched the Romanist priests against his Pundits and Moulvies, and seemed to enjoy the theological battles between them. Feeble as the light was which thus penetrated the imperial household, it did not shine in vain, for some of Akbar's household were actually baptized and professed the Christian faith.

Roman Catholicism never had a grander opportunity than it enjoyed at Agra during those sixty years. Had it been a pure Christianity it might have won over the house of Tamerlane to the faith, and perhaps have saved all India long since. But it failed utterly, and won only a grave-yard at Agra. These thousands of families soon vanished away and left no succession, for Hindoos and Mohammedans learned to perform duties which they saw bringing to the Christians so much honor and profit, and, as they did so, they necessarily hastened the removal of a religion which they detested. What is needed in India is a Christianity independent of the emoluments of office—one that shall take root in the soil, and be self-sustaining. But Romanism failed, and not from this cause alone, or even chiefly; its weak point was the fearful charge of *idolatry* which the Moulvies triumphantly urged against its priests on all occasions. The skeptical but honest Akbar—the Oriental head of a faith iconoclastic to the core—was confused, as well he might be, when he saw his own Moulvies able to quote the Christian Bible against professed Christian ministers to sustain this terrible charge. Denial of it would not avail; there were their own teachings and acts: worship and prayers to the Virgin Mary, invocation of saints, and prostrations before pictures and images. The subterfuge of a qualified homage was rejected in view of the prohibition of the Second Commandment of Almighty God, forbidding not only the act, but also its semblance, "Thou shalt not *bow down* to them, nor worship them." The priests were worsted; and Akbar and his people, knowing no Christianity but this, concluded that the religion of the Son of God was on a par with Paganism, and that Christians were idolaters. A revulsion set in, which the Empress Moomtaj afterward fully shared. In her case, the hatred of the Christian name was intensified by the remembrance of some insolence shown by the Portuguese at Hooghly, several years before her husband ascended the throne, and when he was a fugitive, after an unsuccessful rebellion against his father. When the power passed into her hands her hatred against "the European idolaters," as she called them, led her to demand their expulsion, at least from Hooghly.

Accordingly, the Governor of Bengal received from Shah Jehan the laconic command, "Expel those idolaters from my dominions." It was done. Hooghly was carried by storm, after a siege of three months and a half, involving a terrible destruction of life on the side of the Portuguese, whose fleet was almost entirely annihilated. The principal ship, in which about two thousand men, women, and children had taken refuge, with all their treasure, was blown up by her captain sooner than surrender to the Moguls. From the prisoners five hundred young persons of both sexes, with some of the priests, were sent to Agra. The girls were divided among the harems of the court and nobles, the boys circumcised, and the priests and Jesuits threatened with torture if they refused to accept the Koran. After some months of imprisonment, however, they were liberated and sent off to Goa, and the pictures and images, which had excited the ire of the Empress, were all destroyed by her orders. Such wrong did Romanism do Christianity in India, and the name of our God and Saviour was blasphemed among the heathen through its idolatry.

The Empress Moomtaj, even in death, could not forget her enmity to every form of Christianity, and secured that it should be expressed upon her very tomb, and there it remains to-day, and will remain while the world stands or the Taj exists. The inscription on the tomb, translated, is as follows: "*Moomtaj-i-Mahal, Ranee Begum, died* 1631:" and on the end of the tomb which faces the entrance, so that all may see it as they approach, are these words: "*And defend us from the tribe of unbelievers*"—Kafirs; the word "Kafirs" being a bitter term of contempt for Christians and all who lack faith in Mohammed and the Koran.

Heaven would not answer the fanatical prayer of this mistaken woman; but, instead, has placed even her shrine in the custody of those she hated; and that very "tribe" now gather from all parts of the civilized world, to enter freely and admire the splendors of the tomb which was raised over her remains, and smile with pity at the impotent bigotry which asked Heaven to forbid their approach! The writer had the privilege, with a band of Christian missionaries, of standing around her tomb, and, in the presence of these words, of joining heartily in singing the Christian Doxology over her moldering remains, while the echo above sweetly repeated the praise to "Father, Son, and Holy Ghost."

An article on the Taj, without some account of its *architect*, would be indeed incomplete. But the record, assuming its correctness, enables us to supply this information also. The wonderful man whose creation the Taj is, was, it is believed, a Frenchman, by the name of Austin de Bordeux, a man of great ability. The Emperor, who had unbounded confidence in his merit and integrity, gave him the title of "Zurrier Dust"—the Jewel-Handed—to distinguish him from all other artists; but by the native writers he is called "Gostan Esau Nadir ol Asur"—the Wonderful of the Age. For his office of "Nuksha Nuwes," or architect, he received a regular salary of one thousand rupees per month—$6,000 gold per annum—with perquisites and presents, which made his income very large. He built the palace at Delhi and the palace at Agra, as well as the Taj.

Tavernier, the traveler, who saw this building commenced and finished, tells us that the Taj, in its erection, occupied 20,000 men for twenty-two years. Its cost, we are told, was "threescore, seventeen lakhs, forty-eight thousand and twenty-six rupees;" that is, £3,174,802 sterling, or, in American money, $15,874,010 gold, of the money of that time, equal to about $60,000,000 of our money! But many of the precious stones in the mosaic were presented by different tributary powers, and are not included in the above estimate. Having finished the Taj, the architect was engaged in designing a silver ceiling for one of the galleries in the palace at Agra when he was sent by the Emperor on business of great importance to Goa. He died at Cochin on his return, and is supposed to have been poisoned by the Portuguese, who were jealous of his influence at Court. Shah Jehan had commenced his own tomb on the other side of the Jumna, and it and the Taj were to have been united by a bridge; but the death of Austin de Bordeux, and the wars between Shah Jehan's sons, which then broke out, prevented the completion of these magnificent works, and so the Emperor was laid beside his consort, when he died in 1666, and the Taj contains the remains of both.

The Empress's title, translated, is, The Ornament of the Palace,

Tomb of Asuf Khan, Agra.

for so Shah Jehan esteemed her. The name of the tomb, Taj Mahal, means, The Crown of Edifices, or Palaces — from Taj, a crown, and Mahal, a palace. It is worthy of its title, and is under the special care of the English Government, and will no doubt be preserved in its present perfect and stainless condition for its own sake, and because it is and must ever remain—notwithstanding the sins and frailties of the couple who beneath its dome await the call to judgment—the most perfect and beautiful testimonial to the virtues of a wife ever raised by an affectionate husband.

Among the thousands of her sex who have visited the Taj, and felt its peculiar fascination over the susceptible heart of sentimental women, Lady Sleeman was not the first, as she certainly will not be the last, to realize the emotion which is recorded of her. Retiring from the Taj, lost in reflection and admiration, she was asked by her husband what she thought of the Taj? Her prompt reply was, "I cannot tell you what I think, for I know not how to criticise such a building; but I can tell you what I feel—*I would die to-morrow to have such another put over me!*"

A short distance from the Taj we reach the beautiful tomb of the Premier of the great Emperor Akbar. This splendid pile of white marble, delicately carved into fret-work, its screens and tessellated enamels being very fine, is situated on the right hand of the road as you enter the city of Agra.

The tomb is not only beautiful in itself, and one of the most interesting specimens of Mogul architecture to be met with, even in a city so replete with artistic triumphs as was once imperial Agra, the creation of the renowned Akbar; but there is a history connected with it so romantic, illustrated by Sleeman and Martin, that it is worthy of its high place among the curiosities of Oriental life.

This structure was raised by the famous Noor Jehan, in loving remembrance of her father, Khwaja Accas, one of the most prominent characters in the history of India during the reign of Akbar. The liberality and fame of the greatest monarch that ever ruled India, and the patronage he extended to men of genius and worth, attracted to his Court from Persia and the adjacent nations those who in his service found wealth and honor. Khwaja Accas was a native of Western Tartary. He had some relations at the Imperial Court of India who encouraged him to join them, under the expectation that they could secure his advancement in life. He was of good ancestry, but of reduced means, and possessed of abilities which needed only a fair opportunity for development to insure his success. He left Tartary for India at the close of the sixteenth century, accompanied by his wife and children; their only means for their journey having been provided by the sale of his little property. The incidents of their long and weary emigration are given with much simplicity. Their stock of money had become exhausted, and, in crossing the Great Desert, they were three days without food, and in danger of perishing. In this fearful emergency, the wife of Khwaja Accas gave birth to a daughter; but, worn out with fatigue and privation, the miserable parents concluded to abandon the poor infant. They covered it over with leaves, and toward evening pursued their journey. One bullock remained to them, and on this the father placed his wife, and tried to support her on their way, in hope to reach the cultivated country and find relief. They had gone about a mile, and had just lost sight of the solitary shrub under which they had left their child, when Nature triumphed, and the mother, in an agony of grief, threw herself from the bullock upon the ground, exclaiming, "My child, my child!" Accas could not resist the appeal. He returned to the spot which they had left, took up his infant, and brought it to its mother's breast.

Shortly after a caravan was seen in the distance coming toward them; their circumstances were made known, and a wealthy merchant took compassion upon them, relieved their necessities, and safely conducted them to their destination; he even lent his influence to advance them in life when they reached Lahore, where the Emperor Akbar was then holding his Court.

That little group of five persons, the father and mother, the babe and her two brothers, were destined to fill a place in the page of history more influential than that of any family that ever emigrated to India; for, leaving out of view for the present the high positions afterward attained by the father and his sons, that babe of the desert became, a few years subsequently, Empress of India, and bore the famous title of "Noor Jehan"—the Light of the World—while her brother, Asuf Jan, became the father of the equally celebrated Moomtaj-i-Mahal—to whose memory her husband, Shah Jehan, built the matchless *Taj Mahal*—the noblest monument ever erected to woman.

Asuf Khan, a distant relative of Khwaja Accas, held a high place at Court, and was much in the confidence of the Emperor. He made his kinsman his private secretary. Pleased with his ability and diligence, Asuf soon brought his merits to the special notice of Akbar, who raised him to the command of a thousand horse, and soon after appointed him Master of the Imperial Household. From this he was subsequently promoted to that of Etmad-od-Doulah, or High Treasurer of the Empire, and first minister. His legislative ability soon produced beneficial results in public affairs, while his modest yet manly bearing conciliated the nobility, who learned to appreciate the value of the control which he exercised over the ill-regulated mind of the Emperor.

His daughter, born in the desert, developed into one of the most lovely women of the East, as celebrated for her accomplishments as she was for her beauty, and ultimately she became the wife of the Prince Selim, known afterward by his title of Jehangeer, by whom she was raised to the throne, and had lavished upon her honors and power never before enjoyed by the consort of an Oriental potentate, even to the conjunction of her name with that of Jehangeer on the coins of the realm.

On the death of her venerable and honored father she erected this tomb over his remains. The building, rising from a broad platform, is of white marble, of quadrangular shape, flanked by octagonal towers, which are surmounted by cupolas on a series of open columns. From the center of the roof of the main building springs a small tomb-like structure, elaborately carved and decorated, the corners terminating in golden spires. Immediately below this, on the floor of the hall, is the tomb inclosing the body of Etmad-od-Doulah. Interiorly and exteriorly this fairy pile is covered, as with beautiful lace, by lattice-work, delicately wrought in marble, covered with foliage and flowers, and intermingled with scrolls bearing passages from the Koran. Every portion of the mausoleum is thus enriched, and all that wealth could furnish, or Oriental art suggest, or genius execute, in the completion of the structure, was devoted to its adornment. The original idea in the mind of the Empress, as Martin and others relate, was to construct her father's shrine of solid silver; and she was only dissuaded from this purpose by the assurance that if marble was not equally costly, it was certain to be more durable, and less likely to attract the cupidity of future ages.

The photograph of this building, when examined by a good glass, brings out its singular loveliness as no mere engraving can present it. Each slab of white marble is wrought in rich tracery in the most delicate manner, pierced through and through so as to be the same when seen from either side; the pattern of each slab differs from the next one, and the rich variety, as well as beauty of the designs, fixes the attention of the beholder in amazement at the taste and patient skill that could originate and execute this vision of beauty, which seems like an imagination rising before the fancy, and then, by some wondrous wand of power, transmuted into a solid form forever, to be touched, and examined, and admired. Standing within the shrine, it seems as though it was covered with a rich *vail,* wrought in curious needle-work, every ray of light that enters coming through the various patterns. You approach and touch it, and find it is of white marble, two inches in thickness! What mind but that of a lady could have suggested a design so unique and feminine?

According to the usages of the Moguls, a lovely garden was planted around the fair shrine, and ample provision made for its care and preservation in the future. Rare and costly trees, fragrant evergreens, shady walks, and tanks and fountains, all added their charms to set off the central pile. A small mosque was added, and such religion as they knew lent its influence to the sacredness of the locality; while the beautiful birds of India, their plumage bearing

"The rich hues of all glorious things,"

made the calm and sweet retreat more gorgeous by their presence.

The Daughter of the Desert, forgetting forever the unnatural desertion of him whom she so lavishly honored, thus made a paradise of the abode of the dead. Let her have the credit of whatever estimable qualities the great act expressed; she needs this, and every other allowance that fairly belongs to her history, as some offset to the sadder parts of a life and character that, two hundred and fifty years ago, surprised all India by its singularity, its magnificence, and its less worthy qualities—a fame that lingered in their legends and history, and which, after such long interval, settled so fascinatingly on the imagination of Tom Moore, and came forth in his romance of Lalla Rookh. But the poet left out more than half the life of his heroine; he gave her loves and fascinations, but omitted her labors, and those brilliant exploits which, quite as much as her beauty, commended her to the admiration of Jehangeer and his subjects.

Looking at such persons, and their brilliant, yet abused, opportunities, one may well say, "I have seen an end of all perfection." How transitory, at best, is the fame that rests on such foundations! While we admire the taste, accomplishments, and achievements of this magnificent woman, we seek in vain for any evidence of benevolence or goodness in what she did. She seems to have left God and humanity entirely out of her calculations. In all the tombs and palaces built by her and for her, personal glory and selfish ends—for self and family—alone appear. On these the revenues of a whole people were squandered, and their hard earnings demanded to enable her to exhibit, on this lavish scale, her magnificent caprices. But no hospitals, or schools, or asylums for suffering humanity, exist to call her blessed, or to hand down her name as a pattern or promoter of purity and goodness. How much more "honorable and glorious" is the character, or the lot, of the humblest saint of God who lives to do good to her fellow-creatures! Her grave may be as lowly and lone as that of Ann Hazeltine Judson, on the rock at Amherst, and without a stone to mark it, as I saw it in 1864; but, when Noor Jehan's marble edifices have returned to the dust, those who have thus employed their time and abilities to save the perishing will be "had in everlasting remembrance," and "shine as the stars for ever and ever."

Few men have visited the East who possessed so highly as did Bishop Heber the capacity to appreciate the taste and skill exhibited in the gorgeous buildings of India. Truly and appropriately does he exclaim, while contemplating their wondrous works, "These Patans built like giants, and finished their work like jewelers." The highest illustration of this eulogium is found in the matchless Taj Mahal.

We present one more evidence of their taste and skill in the wonderful *Kootub Minar*.

It has been well observed that this Minar is, among the towers of the earth, what the Taj is among the tombs, something unique of its kind, that must ever stand alone in the recollection of him who has gazed upon its beautiful proportions, its chaste embellishments, and exquisite finish. About eleven miles south-west of the modern city of Delhi stands the desolate site of ancient Delhi. This city is supposed to have been founded about 57 B. C. The height of prosperity to which it rose may be imagined from its only memorials—the tombs, columns, gateways, mosques, and masonry, which lie strewn around in silent and naked desolation. Where rose temple and tower now resounds only the cry of the jackal and the wolf; for the voice of man is silent there, and the wanderings of the occasional tourist alone give any sign of human life or presence in the once "glorious city." The ruins cover a circle of about twenty miles in extent.

In the midst and above all this wild ruin, like a Pharos to guide the traveler over this sea of desolation, rises the tall, tapering cylinder of the *Kootub Minar*. To archæologists like Cunningham, travelers like Von Orlich, and learned observers like General Slee-

The Kootub. From a Photograph.

man, Mr. Archer, and Bholanauth Chunder, and the pages of the "Asiatic Researches," we are indebted for the best descriptions of this wonderful relic of antiquity. These authors have necessarily borrowed largely from each other in representing this city of the dead and its wonderful and unequaled pillar, the towering majesty of which has looked down for centuries only upon ruin and the wild jungle which now grows where once stood the great center of India's glory—its magnificent metropolis.

The Kootub forms the left of two minars of a mosque, which, in size and splendor, was to be peerless on the earth as a place of worship, and from the character of this single shaft it is evident that, had the design been completed, it would have been all that its imperial founder intended in that respect. But death, war, and human vacillation make sad havoc of men's hopes and intentions, and this great memorial stands in attestation of the fact.

For nearly a century a controversy has existed in India as to the architectural honors of the wonderful Kootub. The Hindoos would fain claim that they built it, and Bholanauth Chunder, on their behalf, makes the best case he can to prove that the honor of its design and creation belongs to his race, and not to the hated Moslem; yet even he has to concede that the evidences of its Mohammedan origin are so decided that the Hindoos must give up the claim to the glory of its origination. The Baboo's description is very vivid, and as he corrected the measurements of General Sleeman and others, and has made his examinations within the past five years, and was also well qualified for the task which he undertook, we quote him with confidence in the following description:

"The Kootub outdoes every thing of its kind—it is rich, unique, venerable, and magnificent. It 'stands as it were alone in India;' rather, it should have been said, *alone in the world;* for it is the highest column that the hand of man has yet reared, being, as it stands now, two hundred and thirty-eight feet and one inch above the level of the ground. Once it is said to have been three hundred feet high, but there is not any very reliable authority for this statement. In 1794, however, it had been actually measured to be two hundred and fifty feet eleven inches high. The Pillar of Pompey at Alexandria, the Minaret of the Mosque of Hassan at Cairo, and the Alexandrine Column at St. Petersburg, all bow their heads to the Kootub.

"The base of this Minar is a polygon of twenty-four sides, altogether measuring one hundred and forty-seven feet. The shaft is of a circular form, and tapers regularly from the base to the summit. It is divided into five stories, round each of which runs a bold, projecting balcony, supported upon large and richly-carved brackets, having balustrades that give to the pillar a most ornamental effect.

"The exterior of the basement story is fluted alternately in twenty-seven angular and semicircular faces. In the second story the flutings are only semicircular; in the third they are all angular. The fourth story is circular and plain; the fifth again has semicircular flutings. The relative height of the stories to the diameter of the base has quite scientific proportions. The first, or lowermost story, is ninety-five feet from the ground, or just two diameters in height; the second is fifty-three feet farther up, the third forty feet farther. The fourth story is twenty-four feet above the third, and the fifth has a height of twenty-two feet. The whole column is just five diameters in height. Up to the third story the Minar is built of fine red sandstone. From the third balcony to the fifth the building is composed chiefly of white Jeypoor marble. The interior is of the gray rose-quartz stone. The ascent is by a spiral staircase of three hundred and seventy-six steps to the balcony of the fifth story, and thence are three more steps to the top of the present stone-work. Inside it is roomy enough, and full of openings for the admission of light and air. The steps are almost 'lady-steps,' and the ascent is quite easy. The ferruginous sandstone has been well selected to lend a rich, majestic appearance to the column. The surface of that material seems to have deepened in reddish tint by exposure for ages to the oxygen of the atmosphere. The white marble of the upper stories sits like a tasteful crown upon the red stone; and the graceful bells sculptured in the balconies are like a 'cummerbund' around the waist of the majestic tower. The lettering on the upper portions has to be made out by using a telescope." The Kootub does not stand now in all the integrity of its original structure. It was struck by lightning and had to be repaired by the Emperor Feroz Shah in 1368.

In 1503 the Minar happened to be again injured, and was repaired by the orders of Secunder Lodi, the reigning sovereign, a man of great taste and a munificent patron of learning and the arts.

Three hundred years after its reparation by Secunder Lodi, in the year 1803, a severe earthquake seriously injured the pillar, and its dangerous state having been brought to the notice of the British Government on their taking possession of the country, they liberally undertook its repair. These repairs were brought to a close in twenty-five years. The old cupola of Feroz Shah, or of Secunder Lodi, that was standing in 1794, having fallen down, had been substituted by a plain, octagonal red-stone pavilion. To men of artistic taste this had appeared a very unfitting head-piece for the noble column, so it was taken down by the orders of Lord Hardinge in 1847, and the present stone-work put up in its stead. The condemned top now lies on a raised plot of ground in front, as shown resting on the platform on the right-hand side in the engraving.

Now, as to the origin of the Kootub, a subject on which much speculation has been wasted.

Theories professing a Hindoo origin are maintained by one party: theories professing its Mohammedan origin are propounded by the other. The Hindoo party believes the Minar to have been built by a Hindoo prince for his daughter, who wished to worship the rising sun and to view the waters of the Jumna from the top of it every morning. The Mohammedan party repudiates this as an outrageous paradox, and would have the Kootub taken for the unmistakable *Mazinah* of the Musjeed-i-Kootub-ul-Islam. "No man who sees the Minar can mistake it for a moment to be any other than a thoroughly Mohammedan building—Mohammedan in design, and

Mohammedan in its intents and purposes. The object is at once apparent to the spectator—that of a Mazinah for the Muezzin to call the faithful to prayers. The adjoining mosque, fully corresponding in design, proportion, and execution to the tower, bears one out in such a view of the lofty column, and there is the recorded testimony of Shams-i-raj and Abulfeda to place the fact beyond a doubt."

In addition to its structure, and the vast mosque near which it stands, and of which it so manifestly forms a part, we have the conclusive fact that the history of the Kootub is written in its own inscriptions. None dares to impeach these records, and the Kootub thus seems to have been commenced in about 1200 A. D., and finished in 1220.

In the "Asiatic Researches" (vol. XIV, p. 481) is given the following translation of the fourth inscription upon the Minar: "The erection of this building was commenced in the glorious time of the great Sultan, the mighty King of kings, the Master of mankind, the Lord of the monarchs of Turkestan, Arabia, and Persia, the Sun of the world and religion, of the faith and of the faithful, the Lord of safety and protection, the heir of the kingdoms of Suliman —Abu Muzeffa Altemsh Nasir Amin ul Momenin."

Such was the style and title affected by these high and haughty sovereigns of Oriental Mohammedanism when, reveling in pride and power, like Nebuchadnezzar, they looked around at the "great Babylons" which they had built. How little they imagined with what utter desolation their works would be overthrown, to leave behind only a name and a ruin, and that so nearly undistinguishable that men in future ages could only ascertain the shadowy record by making it a special study!

For six hundred and forty-six years has the gigantic Kootub weathered the rude assaults of the elements, and thousands of strangers from distant lands have come to gaze upon the mighty monument of a departed glory and a dying faith. How many, as they have stood in its shadow, have realized that there must be an adequate supernatural *cause* to account for all this wondrous decadence and death, which so quietly, but effectively, has prostrated its hopes and heaped confusion upon its intentions (despite its boundless wealth, military power, and fierce religious fanaticism) to defend and diffuse its dominating faith! Yet, after all, thus it sinks and thus it dies in its chosen homes.

The instability and the doom that seems ever impending over the institutions and structures raised by the worshipers of Allah, of Vishnu, of Buddha, or the Virgin Mary, come not causeless. They are Heaven's maledictions upon the fearful crime of false religions, which, while they defy God, degrade and dishonor men—cursing their conditions by poverty, miserable homes, and wretched compensation for their toil; wasting their revenues, sinking them in ignorance, destroying their morals, depriving them of liberty, and ruining their souls; till at length, when they have filled up their measure of iniquity, it turns the very centers and cradles of their faiths into the abodes of material or moral ruin, "the hold of every foul spirit, and a cage of every unclean and hateful bird."

Whether the religion be utterly false or only a perversion of the true, its influence is equally pernicious and manifest. He who runs may read this on its very face in India and in Ireland, in Egypt and Burmah, in Delhi and Rome, in Benares and Mexico; in the Sepoy, the Gazee, and the Jesuit; in Tamerlane, Cesare Borgia, and the Nana Sahib; in Cawnpore, Canton, and St. Bartholomew. All equally evince the direful influence of false religions upon the conditions of men and nations.

On the other hand, the holy, living faith of a divine Jesus regenerates the hearts and the communities which yield themselves to its influence—confers freedom, light, education, equal rights, temporal prosperity, moral purity, domestic joy, and every thing lovely, virtuous, and of good report—rears up the temples of a true Christianity, and, without a stain of decadence upon its bright prospects of final universality, presents no ruins or desolations amid its evangelical conquests or their results.

Those once powerful religions and nations that marched so proudly and resolutely to conquest and ascendency under their

Antichristian banners, and raised their vainglorious monuments on the sites of their cruel victories, and then looked forward to such perpetuity of power and glory—where are they now? "How are the mighty fallen!" How fast they rushed on to their inevitable ruin, while those behind are to-day sinking into the same desolation! And why? Because there were higher laws than their own which they dared to violate—an authority against which they vainly dashed themselves—a power which they had the temerity to oppose, but which, nevertheless, numbered their kingdoms and finished them, by the terrible penalties which they had incurred, and the fearful evidences of which are strewn around in India and so many other localities.

How can these facts and results be understood or explained save on the New Testament assumption that Jehovah Christ has all power in heaven and on earth—that he has a dominion here which he must maintain and vindicate, though earth and hell oppose him, till his enemies are put beneath his feet, and He, the blessed and only Potentate, shall stand at last, amid the overthrow of all opposition, the Conqueror of the world!

"In righteousness he doth judge and make war" upon these enemies of his faith. Before his Holy Word the Veda and the Bana, the Koran and the Missal, must fall. Until that is done he will make good his own awful declaration, that "out of his mouth goeth a sharp sword, that with it he should smite the nations; and he shall rule them with a rod of iron. He treadeth the winepress of the fierceness and wrath of Almighty God, and he hath on his vesture and on his thigh a name written, KING OF KINGS AND LORD OF LORDS."

The Kootub Mosque stands deserted; snakes and lizards now crawl in its ruins, amid which the Mazinah yet stands, solitary, grand, and majestic, as though heaven spurned the attempt to rear up and perpetuate a peerless sanctuary, where Moslem blasphemy against the Christ of God might be continually uttered in a grand center toward which all Oriental Islamites might turn, and in which they might glory. God dashed their hopes to pieces like a potter's vessel, and changed their ambition and glory into a tomb and a ruin.

The unfinished Minar to the right hand has twice the dimensions of the Minar here shown. This column was evidently intended for a second mazinah, without which a Mohammedan mosque is essentially defective.

The second Minar—or Minaret, to use the modern phrase—is considerably larger in the base than the one shown in the engraving. It stands at a proper distance from the first, and was carried up about thirty feet above ground, and then discontinued. Antiquarians have been greatly puzzled to account for the variations from the dimensions of the first and finished one ; but it is not necessary to trouble the reader with their theories or debates, as Sleeman's solution has been accepted as highly probable and satisfactory.

His explanation is, that the unfinished minaret was commenced first, but upon too large a scale, and with too small a diminution of the circumference from the base upward. It is two fifths larger than the finished minaret in circumference, and much more perpendicular. Finding these errors, when the builders had gone up with it thirty feet from the ground, the royal founder began the work anew, and on qualified and corrected dimensions, and this is the finished one before the reader. Had he lived he would no doubt have carried up the second minaret in its proper place on the same scale, and so completed his mosque ; but his death occurring, and being followed by fearful revolutions—so that five sovereigns sat upon the throne of Delhi in the succeeding ten years—works of peace were suspended in the presence of war, while the succeeding monarchs sought renown in military enterprises, and thus the building of the second minaret was never proceeded with.

The great mosque itself, with that exception, seems to have been completed. Nearly all the arches are still standing in a more or less perfect state. They correspond with the magnificent minaret in design, proportion, and execution, it evidently having been the intention of the founder to make them all sustain and illustrate the matchless grandeur of the finished work. It was in this condition when Tamerlane invaded India A. D. 1398. That "firebrand of the universe," as he was called, was so enchanted with the great mosque and its minar that he had a model of it made, which he took back with him, along with all the masons that he could find in Delhi, and it is said that he erected a mosque exactly upon this plan at his capital of Samarcund, before he again left it for the invasion of Syria.

The west face of the quadrangle, in which the minar stands, was formed by eleven large alcoves, the center and greatest of which contained the pulpit.

The court to the eastward is inclosed by a high wall, bordered by arcades formed of pillars carved in the highest style of Hindoo art. Those on the opposite side are dissimilar, and the fair inference is, that the Moslem monarch built his mosque, in part, by materials taken from the great Hindoo temples, which he must have desecrated for the purpose. This was after their fashion, and laid the foundation for those bitter feuds and hatreds of the one people against the other, which have lasted to this day.

Close to the minar are the remains of one of those superb portals, so general in the great works of the Patans. The archway of this gate is sixty feet high, and the ornaments with which it is embellished are cut with the delicacy of a seal engraving, retaining, after the lapse of six hundred years, their sharp, clear outlines.

Few who visit the Kootub, if they have strength for the toilsome ascent, fail to go to the summit, and well does it repay the effort. It is sublime to look up to the unclouded heavens, to which you seem so near, while beneath and beyond, the eye wanders over not merely the city beneath, but across to modern Delhi, with its white and glittering mosques and palaces, the silvery Jumna gently pouring along, the feudal towers of Selimghur, and the mausoleums of Humayun and Sufter Jung, all in the soft light of the India sunset ; but what must that view have been when imperial splendors, and cultivation like earthly paradises, or "the gardens of God," combined all their wealth of beauty beneath its shadow, and then away as far as the eye could reach on every side!

The writer visited the Kootub, on the last occasion, in 1864, in company with Bishop Thomson. The Bishop's description may be found in his "Oriental Missions," Vol. I, p. 65. He justly calls the Minar "the grandest column of the world." It is so. Except the tower of Babel, probably nothing ever erected by human hands has produced the same effect, as one stands awe-struck at its base and gazes up upon its majestic form towering to the skies.

It has not been without its tragic incidents. General Sleeman, writing in 1844, tells us that five years previously, "while the Emperor was on a visit to the tomb of Kootub-ad-deen, an insane man got into his private apartment. The servants were ordered to turn him out. On passing the Minar he ran in, ascended to the top, stood a few moments on the verge, laughing at those who were running after him, and made a spring that enabled him to reach the bottom without touching the sides. An eye-witness told me that he kept his erect position till about half-way down, when he turned over, and continued to turn till he got to the bottom, where his fall made a report like a gun. He was, of course, dashed to pieces."

Close to the Kootub stands the famous *Iron Pillar*—the palladium of Hindoo dominion—and which, there is evidence for believing, has stood there for fifteen hundred years.

The Iron Pillar is a solid shaft of mixed metal resembling bronze, upward of sixteen inches in diameter and about sixty feet in length. The greater part of it is under-ground, and that which is above is less than thirty feet high. The ground about it has marks of excavation, said to have been carried down to twenty-six feet without reaching the foundation on which the pillar rests, and without loosening it in any degree. The pillar contains about eighty cubic feet of metal, and would probably weigh upward of seventeen tons.

The Iron Pillar, standing nearly in the middle of a grand square, "records its own history in a deeply-cut Sanscrit inscription of six lines on its western face." Antiquaries have read the characters, and the pillar has been made out to be "the arm of fame—Kirtibhuja—of Rajah Dhava." He is stated to have been a worshiper of Vishnu, and a monarch who "had obtained with his own arm an undivided sovereignty on the earth for a long period." The letters upon the triumphal pillar are called "the typical cuts inflicted on his enemies by his sword, writing his immortal fame." "It is a pity that posterity can know nothing more of this mighty Rajah Dhava than what is recorded in the meager inscription upon this wonderful relic of antiquity. The characters of the inscription are thought to be the same as those of the Gupta inscriptions, and the success alluded to therein is supposed to have been the assistance which that Rajah had rendered in the downfall of the powerful sovereigns of the Gupta dynasty. The age in which he flourished is, therefore, concluded to have been about the year 319 A. D., the initial point of the Balabhi or Gupta era."

Antiquarians have tried very earnestly to solve the mystery of this metallic monument. The most probable conclusion is, that it marked the center of the great Rajah's city, and stood in a splendid temple. But on the invasion and conquest of Delhi by the Mohammedan power the Emperor chose that center for his own purposes, and threw his great mosque across the very site of that temple, taking its marble columns for his colonnades, permitting the Iron Pillar to remain, but erecting the Minar near it, forever to dwarf its proportions and interest. But all are alike in ruin now—their rage, contention, and emulation in the dust, while the Pillar and the Minar alone remain.

How little did either the proud Rajah or the fierce Emperor anticipate what a wreck the Ruler of heaven and earth would make of their hopes, and that where they built and embellished, and set forth their glory, would yet be as naked as ruin itself, and that the wild beasts of the forest would howl in their desolate palaces!

That desolation is the more marked, when we remember that very probably, after all these high anticipations, carried out so despotically, and with the lavish expenditure of such untold millions, this mosque and minar may never have answered, even in a single instance, the purposes for which they were so proudly intended. According to their customs and rules, the mosque would probably not be used till completed. The second minar, being unfinished, would very likely prevent the dedication; so that ere another hand could consummate the great design, the death of the founder, the long and fierce wars that followed, and finally the imperial fickleness which chose the banks of the Jumna, eleven miles away, as the site of new Delhi, leading to the utter forsaking of the grand old city, with all its monuments, temples, mosques, and palaces, consigned the Kootub forever to desolation, and after all left it, very likely, a mosque where no prayer was ever offered, and a minaret from whose lofty summit no muezzin's voice ever called the sons of the Koran to their vain devotions.

Though fifteen hundred years have gone over it, the Iron Pillar shows no sign of decay; it is smooth and clean. The metal of which it is composed was so fused and amalgamated that it defies all oxidation, while the characters engraven upon it remain to-day clear and distinct as when they were first cut by the hand of the engraver.

The great antiquity, the enormous size, and the interesting inscriptions upon the pillar of Rajah Dhava have led to great reverence toward it by all Hindoos, and legends are not wanting to account tor its origin and position. One tradition is, that it is the veritable club that great Bheema wielded in the battles of the Mahabharata, and which was left standing there by the Pandus after their contest. But the more popular story is, that it is a pillar so long that it pierced the entire depth of the earth, till it rested on the head of the gigantic snake called Vasuki, who supports the world —that its stability was the palladium of Hindoo dominion in India

Such were some of the magnificent and unique surroundings of the Mogul Court in 1856; and all this, with much more that might be mentioned, they were then about to risk the possession of in a fearful struggle with the white-faced race.

CHAPTER IV.

ORIGINATING CAUSES OF THE SEPOY REBELLION.

WHILE moving amid the gorgeous scenes of the previous chapter, we were happily unconscious of the circumstances of danger by which we were surrounded, and which could so easily have victimized us all. We knew not then of that peculiar combination and concurrence of favoring circumstances for the accomplishment of the purposes which are now well understood and can be explained, and a knowledge of which is essential to those who would comprehend the great Sepoy Rebellion. We will now state them, and, in doing this, will show how it was possible for such a rebellion to be then originated and carried out.

1. The first and most important fact was the position of the Emperor of Delhi—he in whose name and for whose interests it was inaugurated. We have already noticed the circumstances under which the alien power of the Mogul entered India, and at last came to rule from Calcutta to Cabul. With the sense of cruelty, injustice, and wrong that rankled in the hearts of the Hindoos against these foreigners, no length of time had ever reconciled them to their presence in their country. Thus, the last thing we could have imagined possible in 1857 was, that these two peoples could find a common ground of agreement on which they could stand together; and that expectation was the confidence of Englishmen in India. They leaned with confidence upon the Hindoos, whom they had elevated from the rule of Mohammedan injustice, believing that so long as they were content and satisfied the English empire was safe, no matter how the Mohammedans might rage. So they thought, and did not even dream that these ancient and inveterate foes were finding a ground of agreement, and were wide

awake, plotting the terrible arrangements that were so soon to burst in fire and bloodshed over the land.

In the East, where there are no constitutions or popular governments, personal influence in a sovereign is every thing; the despotic powers have only their individual adaptation and prestige to depend upon to commend their rule. It is a maxim with them, that "a king who has no eyes in his head is useless." In reference to the poor, old, mutilated Emperor of Delhi, (grandfather of the one whose portrait is herein given,) it had much more than a metaphorical meaning. Its literal truth led to that state of general conviction of Mogul imbecility, and the necessity of having the paramount power of India in hands able to maintain its peace, and which would at the same time respect the rights of the falling dynasty, and all others concerned, which led soon after to the consummation of that Treaty between the Emperor and the English Government, in which his Imperial Majesty consented to surrender to them his authority and power (a poor show it then was) for certain considerations. That is, he agreed that the British were to assume the government of the country, and rule in his name, on condition that they would guarantee to himself and his successors forever the following compensations:

(1.) He was to be recognized as titular Emperor. His title was sounding enough to become a higher condition. How absurd it seems, when we quote its translation in full: "The Sun of the Faith, Lord of the World, Master of the Universe and of the Honorable East India Company, King of India and of the Infidels, the Superior of the Governor-General, and Proprietor of the Soil from Sea to Sea!" This is surely enough for any mortal, especially when it is connected with a safe salary nearly as large as itself!

(2.) He was still to be the fountain of honor, so that all the sunnuds (patents) of nobility, constituting Rajahs, Nawabs, etc., were to be made out in his name, and sealed with his signet.

(3.) An embassador of England was to reside at his Court, to be the official organ of communication between himself and the English Government.

(4.) He was to retain his royal residences, the one in Delhi being regularly fortified, and occupying probably one fourth of the area of the city. And,

(5.) His imperial revenue was to be made sure, and punctually paid from the British Treasury.

He was asked how much that revenue must be? He replied, "Thirteen and a half lakhs of rupees annually"—$675,000 per annum. And as matters go in the East, where kings are supposed to own the soil, and can levy their own jumma (tax) upon every cultivated acre of it, this was not considered an unreasonable or unusual demand.

The terms were accepted, and the British moved their authority west of the Kurrumnasa, assumed the civil, political, and military control of Hindustan proper, and the Mogul Emperor resigned the heavy cares of State and went to house-keeping on his $675,000 per year. He assuredly might think that he had made a good bargain for himself and his family with his commercial patrons, the East India Company, while the whole resources of Great Britain were pledged to every item of the engagement—and he certainly might have done tolerably well under the circumstances. But one thing stood in the way. He and his outraged the laws of Heaven; the result was a ruin which in its completeness has had hardly a parallel in the history of any earthly dynasty.

With idleness and fullness of bread came mischief and vileness for three generations, increasing in their terrible tendencies, as the sins of the fathers were shared by, and visited upon, their children, until hideous ruin engulphed the whole concern, and left not a wreck behind.

To the American reader it must seem amazing to state that the $675,000 per annum proved utterly insufficient to enable the last Emperor to live and keep out of debt; yet so it was. He really could not "make ends meet" from year to year on this splendid allowance, paid to the day, and paid in gold. But the explanation is at hand.

Had the duality of the marriage relation been recognized at the

Court of Delhi, it is very probable that it might have escaped the guilt and misery which hastened its destruction. Men in high or low station cannot violate the laws of God, even when their creed sanctions that violation, without incurring the penalty which is sure to come, sooner or later. Of this truth there never was a more marked example than was exhibited within these high and bastioned walls. The three generations during which this wrath was "treasuring up" its force but made it more overwhelming when its overthrow of desolation came. It was expressly stipulated in the treaty that the munificent provision made for the Emperor was to cover all claims. Out of the $675,000 per annum he was required to support the retinue of relations and dependents collected within the walls of the imperial residence. But fifty years of idleness, and the license of a sensual creed, which permitted unlimited polygamy, made that which would have been easy to virtue impossible to vice.

The Eden of God had but one Eve in it, and she reigned as queen in the pure affections of the happy and noble man for whom God had made her. Within the walls of that Delhi palace Shah Jehan could inscribe the words,

> "If there be a paradise on the face of the earth,
> It is this—it is this—it is this!"

For he loved one only, and was faithful to her, and has enshrined her memory while the world stands in the matchless Taj Mahal. Few, if any, of his race imitated his virtue in this regard; and least of all his last descendants. Fifteen years ago the Delhi "paradise" had become changed into a very *pandemonium.* Here were crowded together twelve hundred *kings* and *queens*—for all the descendants of the Emperors assumed the title of "Sulateens"—with ten times as many persons to wait upon them, so that the population of the palaces were actually estimated at twelve thousand persons. Glorying in their "royal blood," they held themselves superior to all efforts to earn their living by honest labor, and fastened, like so many parasites, upon the old Emperor's yearly allowance. "But what was that among so many," and they so constantly on the increase? So here the "kings" and "queens" of the house of Timour were found lying about in scores, like broods of vermin, without sufficient food to eat, or decent clothing to wear, and literally eating up each other. Yet, notwithstanding, their insolence and pride were exactly equal to their poverty; so that one of these *kings*, who had not more than fifty shillings per month for his share wherewith to subsist himself and his family, in writing to the Representative of the British Government at the Court, would address him as "Fidwee Khass," *our particular slave;* and would expect to be addressed in reply with, "Your Majesty's commands have been received by your slave!"

Living in royalty on twenty-five dollars per month, or less, each of these worthies, on choosing a wife, or adding another to those he had before, would feel it necessary, for *his rank's sake*, to settle upon her a dowry of five lakhs of rupees, (two hundred and fifty thousand dollars,) while actually the royal scamp did not own fifty dollars in the world. His only accomplishment or occupation was playing on the "Sitar," and singing the King's verses, for this king was ambitious of a poet's title, and they flattered the old gentleman's whim. Did the world ever witness such a farce!

Perhaps at the time I first saw the palace of Delhi, with this state of things then in full operation, the eye of God did not look down upon a mass of humanity more dissatisfied, more vile, more proud, and more mean, than the crowd of hungry Shazadahs who pressed against each other for subsistence within the walls of that fortification. All being royal blood, of course they could not soil their hands to gain an honest living; every man and woman of them must be supported out of the imperial allowance.

It was a simple impossibility for the English Government to meet the necessities of this case, or satisfy the demands of this greedy, hungry, and rapidly increasing crew. Twice had the Emperor's appeal been yielded to, and the grant increased from thirteen and a half, to eighteen lakhs, so that in 1857 they were receiving $900,000 per annum; but the limit had been reached at last. The English would neither pay the debts which they contracted nor increase the yearly allowance. The country would not endure it.

The humiliating ceremonies, so tenaciously required by the Emperor on receiving any member of the English Government, had become increasingly irksome and annoying as time rolled on and this condition of things developed, until it began to be felt that the Great Mogul pageant was a bore. Lord Amherst, a former Governor-General, at length refused to visit the Emperor if expected, according to Delhi court etiquette, to do so with bare feet, bowed head, and joined hands. He declared he would only visit him on terms of honorable equality, and not as an inferior. Both he and Lord Bentinck refused any longer to stand in "the Presence," but demanded a State chair on the right hand of the Emperor, and to be received as an equal. This shocked the Emperor's feelings, but he had to give in. Then came the suspension of the "Nuzzer"—the yearly present—a symbol of allegiance or confession of suzerainty. The value was not withheld, but added to the yearly allowance; but the Emperor refused to accept it in this form.

In 1849, on the death of the heir apparent, Lord Dalhousie, then Governor-General, opened negotiations designed to abolish this pageant of the Great Mogul, and offered terms to the next heir to abdicate the throne, vacate the Delhi Palace, and sink their high titles, retiring to the Kootub Palace and a private position, so that the large family might be placed under proper restrictions and required to obtain education, and fit themselves for stations where they could earn their living. But the merciful and wise proposal was misapprehended by them: instead of appreciating it, it thoroughly alarmed them. They chose to consider that their very existence was attacked. They would rather continue to fester and starve together within those walls than to separate and rouse themselves to action and honest employment; so they began to talk louder than ever about their "wrongs," and the "insults" offered them by the English Government, prominent among which was the refusal any longer to give to each of these princes, whenever he chose to show his face in public, the royal salute of his "rank." But the English had deliberately come to the conclusion that this was a foolish and ridiculous waste of the national powder, and ought to cease forever.

Thus the Court — Emperor Begums, Sultans and Sultanas, Shazadas, Eunuchs, and followers, all in a ferment of dissension and hatred of English rule—became a center to which all disaffected elements naturally tended.

These men became the life and soul of the great conspiracy for the overthrow of the English power and the expulsion of Christianity from India, and for the elevation once more of Mohammedan supremacy over the Hindoo nations. Yielding to their influence, and that of the Sepoys, as will be narrated in our next chapter, the old Emperor committed himself fully, without counting the cost, to the fearful struggle.

The reader can well understand what an "elephant" the English Government had here on its hands, and in what perplexity they were as to what they should do with it.

This "high-born" population thus pressed for the means of subsistence within these walls, instead of being required to shift for themselves and quietly sink among the crowd without. When the writer reached India, in 1856, this state of things was ripening to its natural consummation. The different members of the Emperor's great family circle were fast becoming rallying points for the dissatisfied and disaffected. Let loose upon the community, they were every-where disgusting people by their insolence and knavery, so that the English magistrates in Delhi had to stand between them and their victims. The prestige of their names was fast diminishing, and they were falling into utter insignificance and contempt. This was true even of the highest of them. It was these "idle hands" that Satan employed to do much of the "mischief" wrought during the fearful rebellion of 1857—an event which consummated their own ruin, and sent scores of them to the gallows.

In the "good old days" of their rule they had their own way of relieving any financial pressure, as soon as it was felt, by "loans" which were never paid, or by exactions from which there was no appeal or escape. But in 1857 it was no longer possible to practice in this way. The palace people had to let other men's money alone, and were required to live within their means, and those who trusted them had now to do so on their own responsibility. The Government of England refused to pay a dollar of their debts or grant any further increase to their allowance. How they raged over this resolve! Exhortations to do something, or fit themselves for positions which would support them, were all thrown away upon them, or, worse, they held the advice to be an insult. They were royal, and could not think of work; so they raged against the Government that stood between them and those whom they used to victimize, and sighed for the days when they could have relieved their necessities at the expense of other men. It need not be wondered at that such people hated English rule, and resolved that, if ever the opportunity came within their reach, they would be revenged upon the race who compelled them to be honest.

Just in proportion to this impotent rage, of which the Government was well aware, most of the Hindoo princes around were exultant to think that the Great Mogul had found a master at last—that there was a strong hand on the bridle in his jaws, to hold him back from trampling on the rights of other people. The Shroffs (native Bankers) and moneyed men in the bazaars were in high glee, knowing that the rupees in their coffers were all safe under the protection of England's power, and that none could make them afraid.

To all this, if you add the *religious* hate, you have the entire case of the Delhi Court. How these men raged as they remembered that their Crescent had gone down before the hated Cross; that where they had ruled and tyrannized for seven hundred years Christianity was now triumphant. They detest England: they will always do so: not because of her nationality, but for her faith. They would hate Americans all the same if we were there. To

Christianity they are irreconcilably antagonistic. They detest the doctrine of a divine Christ, and his followers have to share his odium at their hands. Alas, it is simple truth to say, that if the Lord Jesus were to come down from heaven to-day, and put himself in their power, they would as assuredly crucify him afresh in the streets of Delhi for saying he was "the Son of God," as did the Jews in Jerusalem eighteen hundred years ago. You have only to read their "Sacred Kulma" to be assured of this spirit, and understand their rage against him; while their fearful deeds in 1857–8 upon his followers were a commentary on the Kulma, written with Christian blood; a record over which they gloat, and in the extent of which they still glory. Sad and abundant evidence of this fact is to follow in these pages; yet all this hatred and determination would have been utterly powerless had it stood alone—had the Hindoos not so strangely and unexpectedly united themselves with it.

2. This leads us to the consideration of the peculiar fact which, for once, brought the Moslem and Hindoo elements of the country into union and a common interest.

Lord Lake, the English General, had defeated the Mahratta chief, Bajee Rao, whose title, the Peishwa, was derived from a Brahmin dynasty founded at Poonah by Belajee Wiswanath. This title formerly meant Prime Minister, but its holders rose from that position to sovereign authority by usurpation and opportunity, and, in view of the high-caste assumptions of the Mahratta nation, their sovereign seems to have laid claim to a sort of headship in Hindooism, and so "Peishwa" became a religious as well as a secular title, and carried a great influence with it in the estimation of the Hindoos.

Duff, the historian of the time, gives a fearful picture of the licentiousness which prevailed at Bajee Rao's capital in 1816, and of his perfidy in attempting the assassination, by treachery, of Mr. Elphinstone, the English Embassador, and in the death of several Europeans whom he caused to be killed in cold blood, as well as the families of the native troops in their service. His ferocious

The "Nana Sahib."

and vindictive orders, issued on the 5th of November, 1817, foreshadowed too truly other orders of a similar nature issued in July, 1857, by him to whom he transferred his home and fortune. The adopted son was worthy of his putative father. That son was *Nana Sahib.* The name of the *author* of the Cawnpore massacre is, of course, well known.

The picture of him here presented was drawn by Major O'Gandini, and sent home from India. He was fat, with that unhealthy corpulence which marks the Eastern voluptuary, of sallow complexion and middle height, with strongly marked features. He did not speak a word of English. His age at the time of the massacre was about thirty-six years. As this man will ever be identified with the sanguinary fame of Cawnpore, it seems appropriate to give the reader a more definite account of who he was, and his antecedents, as furnished by Trevelyan.

His full name was *Seereek Dhoondoo Punth,* but the execration of mankind has found his cluster of titles too long for use, and prefers the more familiar appellation of "*The Nana Sahib.*"

Bajee Rao, the Peishwa of Poonah, was the last monarch of the Mahrattas, who, for many years, kept Central India in war and confusion. The English Government being driven by his faithlessness and treachery to dethrone the old man, assigned him a residence at Bithoor, a few miles from Cawnpore, which he occupied until his death, in 1851. With his traditions, his annuity of eight lakhs of rupees ($400,000) yearly, and his host of retainers, Bajee Rao led a splendid life, so far as this world was concerned. But the old Mahratta had one sore trial: he had no son to inherit his possessions, perpetuate his name, and apply the torch to his funeral pyre. This last office, according to the Hindoo faith, can only be performed properly by a filial hand. In this strait he had recourse to adoption, a ceremony which, by Hindoo law, entitles the favored individual to all the rights and privileges of an heir born of the body. His choice fell upon this Seereek Dhoondoo Punth, who, according to some, was the son of a corn merchant of Poonah, while others maintain that he was the offspring of a poor Konkanee Brahmin, and first saw the light at Venn, a miserable little village near Bombay. The Nana was educated for his position ; and, on the death of his benefactor, he entered into possession of his princely home and his immense private fortune. But this did not satisfy the Nana. He demanded from the British Government, in addition, the title and the yearly pension which they had granted to his adoptive father. His claim was disallowed, as the pension was purely in the form of an annuity to the late King. But the Nana was not to be foiled. Failing with the Calcutta authorities, he transferred his appeal to London, and dispatched an agent to prosecute it there. This opens another amazing chapter in the history of this man. The person selected, and who had so much to do afterward with the massacre of the ladies and children, was his confidential man of business, *Azeemoolah Khan*, a clever adventurer, who began life as a kitmutgar—a waiter at table. He thus acquired a knowledge of the English tongue, to which he afterward added French, and came at length to speak and write both with much fluency. Leaving service to pursue his studies, he afterward became a school-teacher, and in this latter position attracted the notice of the Nana, who made him his Vakeel, or Prime Agent, and sent him to London to prosecute his claims. Azeemoolah arrived in town during the height of "the season" of 1854, and was welcomed into "society" with no inquiry as to antecedents. Passing himself off as an Indian prince, and being abundantly furnished with ways and means, and having, withal, a most presentable contour, he gained admission into the most distinguished circles, making a very decided sensation. He speedily became a lion, and obtained more than a lion's share of the sweetest of all flattery—the ladies voted him "charming." Handsome and witty, endowed with plenty of assurance, and an apparent abundance of diamonds and Cashmere shawls, the ex-kitmutgar seemed as fine a gentleman as the Prime Minister of Nepaul or the Maharajah of the Punjab, both of whom had been lately in London.

In addition to the political business which he had in hand, Azeemoolah was at one time prosecuting a suit of his own of a more delicate nature; but, happily for the fair Englishwoman who was the object of his attentions, her friends interfered and saved her from becoming an item in the harem of this Mohammedan polygamist. He returned to India by Constantinople, and visited the Crimea, where the war was then raging between England and Russia. He bore to his master the tidings of his unsuccessful efforts on his behalf, but consoled him with the assurance that the youthful vigor of the Russian power would soon overthrow the decaying strength of England, and then a decisive blow would be sufficient to destroy their yoke in the East. Subtle and bloodthirsty, Azeemoolah betrayed no animosity until the outburst of the Rebellion, and then he became the presiding genius of the assault and final massacre. Meanwhile he moved amid English society at Cawnpore with such deep dissimulation as to awaken no suspicion; and he was even the whole time carrying on correspondence with more than one noble lady in England, who had allowed herself, in her too confiding disposition, to be betrayed into a hasty admiration of this swarthy adventurer: so that, on the first day of Havelock's entrance, when he and his men came straight from "the Slaughter-House" and fatal Well, to the Palace of Bithoor, they discovered, among the possessions of this scoundrel, the letters of these titled ladies, couched in terms of the most courteous friendship. How little they suspected the true character of their correspondent! and how bitter and painful were the emotions which, under such circumstances, their letters raised in the breasts of Havelock's men! And yet this sleek and wary wretch was educated and courtly, even to fascination, while the heart beneath his gorgeous vest cherished the purposes of the tiger and the fiend. So much for education and refinement without religion or the fear of God.

Dr. Russell, "the Times' Correspondent," mentions having met Azeemoolah in the Crimea, seeing with his own eyes how matters were going on there. He was fresh from England, where, a few weeks before, he might have been seen moving complacently in London drawing-rooms, or cantering on Brighton Downs, the center of an admiring bevy of English damsels; but in the Crimea the secret of his soul was betrayed when, one evening, in a large party, he was incautious enough to remark that the Russians and the Turks should cease to quarrel, and join and take India. The remark caused some feeling, but aroused no suspicion of the lurking vengeance. India could gain nothing by such a change of masters. He knew this well enough; but such a change would humble England, and probably suspend or annihilate Christian missions there: and these results would be to him a full compensation for the change.

The sensual and superstitious Maharajah of Bithoor—as Nana Sahib was called—had thus found an agent after his own heart to work out his will. Bithoor Palace, where the Nana resided, was spacious, and richly furnished in European style. All the reception-rooms were decorated with immense mirrors, and massive chandeliers in variegated glass, and of the most recent manufacture; the floors were covered with the finest productions of the Indian looms, and all the appurtenances of Eastern splendor were strewed about in amazing profusion; but it would be impossible to lift the vail that must rest on the private life of this man. Nowhere was the mystery of iniquity deeper and darker than in this Palace of Bithoor. It was a nest worthy of such a vulture. There were apartments in that palace horribly unfit for any human eye, where both European and native artists had done their utmost to gratify the corrupt master, who was willing to incur any expense for the completion of his loathsome picture-gallery.

In the apartments open to the inspection of English visitors there was, of course, nothing that could shock either modesty or humanity, though a person of fastidious taste might take exception to the arrangement of the heterogeneous collection of furniture and decorations with which the Nana Sahib had filled his house when he aimed to blend the complicated domestic appliances of the European with the few and simple requirements of the Oriental.

The Maharajah had a large and excellent stable of horses, elephants, and camels; a well-appointed kennel; a menagerie of pigeons, falcons, peacocks, and apes, which would have done credit to any Eastern monarch from the days of Solomon downward. His armory was stocked with weapons of every age and country; his reception-rooms sparkled with mirrors and chandeliers that had come direct from Birmingham; his equipages had stood within a twelvemonth in the warehouses of London. He possessed a vast store of gold and silver plate, and his wardrobe overflowed with Cashmere shawls and jewelry, which, when exhibited on gala days, were regarded with longing eyes by the English ladies of Cawnpore: for the Nana seldom missed an occasion for giving a ball or a banquet in European style to the society of the station, although he would never accept an entertainment in return, because the English Government, which refused to regard him as a royal personage, would not allow him the honor of a salute of twenty-one guns. On these occasions the Maharajah presented himself in his panoply of kincob and Cashmere, crowned with a tiara of pearls and diamonds—as here represented—the great ruby in the center, and girt with old Bajee Rao's sword of State, which report valued at three lakhs of rupees, ($150,000.) The Maharajah mixed freely with the company, inquired after the health of the Major's lady, congratulated the Judge on his rumored promotion to the Supreme Court, joked the Assistant Magistrate about his last mishap in the hunting-field, and complimented the belle of the evening on the color she had brought down from the hills of Simla.

All this was going on when the writer was in Cawnpore in the fall of 1856. These costly festivities were then provided for and enjoyed by the very persons—ladies, children, and gentlemen—who were, before ten months had passed, ruthlessly butchered in cold blood by their quondam host. Till his hour arrived nothing could exceed the cordiality which he managed to display in his intercourse with the English. The persons in authority placed implicit confidence in his friendship and good faith, and the young officers emphatically pronounced him "a capital fellow." He had a nod, a kind word, for every Englishman in the station; hunting parties and jewelry for the men, and picnics and Cashmere shawls for the ladies. If a subaltern's wife required change of air the Maharajah's carriage was at the service of the young couple, and the European apartments at Bithoor were put in order to receive them. If a civilian had overworked himself in court, he had but to speak the word, and the Maharajah's elephants were sent to the Oude jungles for him to go tiger hunting; but none the less did he ever, for a moment, forget the grudge he bore the English people. While his face was all smiles, in his heart of hearts he brooded over the judgment of the Government, and the refusal of his despised claim.

The men who, with his presented sapphires and rubies glittering on their fingers, sat there laughing around his table, had each and all been doomed to die by a warrant that admitted of no appeal. He had sworn that the injustice should be expiated by the blood of ladies who had never heard his grievance named, of babies who had been born years after the question of that grievance had passed into oblivion. The great crime of Cawnpore blackened the pages of history with a far deeper stain than Sicilian vespers or St. Bartholomew massacres, for this atrocious deed was prompted neither by diseased nor mistaken patriotism, nor by the madness of superstition. The motives of the deed were as mean as the execution was cowardly and treacherous. Among the subordinate villains there might be some who were possessed by bigotry and class hatred, but Nana Sahib was actuated by no higher impulses than ruffled pride and disappointed avarice.

The Hindoos, and particularly the military class of them, looked up to this man as their Peishwa. His position gave him immense influence. They would go with him to the side which he espoused. It is understood that he was tampered with, and made a tool of, by the Delhi faction under promise that when the English were expelled the country the Emperor would recognize his claims, and give him the throne of his reputed father at Poonah; so he threw in his lot with the conspiracy and bided his time.

3. The Mohammedan monopoly of place and power is another

consideration to be remembered in understanding the character and extent of this vast combination against Christian civilization.

This gave them their opportunity to organize their plans and work up the conspiracy. The Sepoy army, with the "Contingents" at native courts, native police, and, we may also add, the armed followers of the Rajahs and Nawabs who favored the rising, constituted an armed body of men fully five hundred thousand strong —the life and soul of the whole being the native "Bengal Army," very largely Brahminical. Over these ignorant, superstitious, and fanatical forces, whether as military, commissariat, civil, legal, or financial subordinate officers, were these Mohammedan officials, so that a perfect organization, from Delhi throughout the whole land, was being formed, and it only now needed safe means of communication between the several parts, so that the central conspiracy could receive information or send its arrangements through men whom it could entirely trust, and who were its willing and ready agents. But this, too, was supplied, as we shall see.

The Sepoy army mounted guard upon the forts, the magazines, and the treasuries of India; and when their hour had come, and all was prepared, they held in their own hands the key of the coined millions of the public money, its vast stores of munitions of war, and its strong places. The total of European troops then in India was exactly 45,522, of all arms; but of these 21,156 were away in Madras and Bombay, leaving only 24,366 for the East, center, and Punjab, and more than two thirds of these were off on the Western frontiers and in Burmah, so that in the entire Valley of the Ganges there were but two half regiments, one with Sir H. Lawrence in Lucknow, and the other at Cawnpore.

4. India was then not only without railroads, but was even destitute of common roads, while the rivers were unbridged, and there was every natural difficulty in the way of an army of white men moving through the land, with the heavy *impedimenta* which they require in such a climate, and in which respect the native troops, being so much less encumbered, so much more at home in the heat, and so well acquainted with the country, had their enemy at

every disadvantage, and especially as they sprung the struggle upon them in the very midst of the hot season, when sun-stroke would be sure to lay low more than were prostrated by the bullet.

To show the importance of one aspect of this difficulty: In 1856 there was but one made road in North India—"the Grand Trunk," so called, from Calcutta to the Punjab. General Anson, the English Commander-in-chief, on the first alarm on the 10th of May, commenced to collect his forces and march upon Delhi. The distance was under four hundred miles; but so wretched were the roads, and having to drag his artillery through rivers, it was the 8th of June when his army reached Delhi, and nine tenths of all the massacre and mischief were accomplished during those twenty-eight days. On the other side the river the conditions of travel were equally bad. The Soane River is crossed by this Grand Trunk Road. There was, in 1856, no way but to drag through its deep sands and widespread waters with bullocks—I have been four hours going from one side to the other; and the wise Government, that for one hundred years had neglected to build a bridge, had erected a dak Bungalow (Travelers' Rest House) on either bank, to meet the clear necessity that if you had breakfasted on one side you would need your dinner when you reached the other! What it was to take troops, artillery, and commissariat through such a country the reader can imagine.

It is a consolation to add, as a sign of that wonderful progress toward a better state of things on which India has since entered, that I had the satisfaction of crossing that same Soane River in 1864 in a few minutes on a first-class railroad bridge, and to-day General Anson could come from Umballa to Delhi in twenty-four hours.

5. The annexation of Oude—the home of the Sepoy—and where, while it was under native administration, the military classes that took service under the British Government had peculiar privileges that annexation would annul, leaving them equal before the law with the rest of the people: this, with the turbulent character of the Talookdars (or Barons) of Oude, who held themselves above

law, and defied their King to collect revenue from them, or exact their obedience, along with the thousands of persons who made a living by the Court, and their relation to its duties, intrigues, necessities, and vices, and whose occupation would be gone were the country annexed and British rule introduced—all these were aroused to a pitch of frenzy when the plot was actually consummated, and were ready to join in any enterprise, no matter how wild or desperate, that promised an overthrow of the new condition of things. And, finally,

6. To these elements of disturbance and eager watchfulness for a change, has to be added the great fact of the growing fear of the extension of the Christian religion, and the founding of new Missions in the land, with the consequent and widespread fear that their own faiths were in imminent danger of overthrow. Confounding every white man with the Government, and regarding him as most certainly in the service and pay of the English, they looked upon each Missionary as an emissary, backed up by the entire power and resources of the Administration, and to be correspondingly feared. This was the general view, (of course the more enlightened knew better,) and the interested parties took good care to intensify it to the utmost of their ability.

The very pains taken by the English officials to deny it, and present the Government doctrine of "Neutrality," only made matters worse; for Hindoos and Mohammedans could not imagine a ruling power without a religion, or without zeal for diffusion of its own faith. The denial, therefore, was not believed; it only intensified the conviction of the people that these words were used to conceal the truth, and could only be used as a pretext to blind them for the present, till the English were fully prepared for the most determined action against their castes and their faiths. So that every movement was watched, and every act misinterpreted; and those in high places were distracted by prejudices which were too blind and fanatical to allow them to listen to reason.

My own appearance in Lucknow and Bareilly as a Missionary, and the pioneer of a band soon to follow, caused a great deal of talk and excitement, and was pointed to as a part of the plan which the Government was maturing against their religions.

They could also refer to the steady encroachments of Christian law upon their cherished institutions. Suttee had been prohibited, female infanticide made penal, the right of a convert to inherit property vindicated, the remarriage of widows made lawful, self-immolation at Juggernaut interdicted, Thuggeeism suppressed, caste slighted—and they dreaded what might come next, ere they should be entrapped into an utter loss of caste, and forced to embrace the Christian faith.

Such was the peculiar combination of circumstances that in 1856 gave to the disaffected portion of the people of India the opportunity to concentrate their energies, under the most favorable conditions of success, to strike a blow that would at once overthrow Christianity and English rule forever, and restore, as they thought, native supremacy and the abrogated institutions of their respective faiths. They really imagined that if they could but wipe out the few thousand English in the land their work would be done, and that Great Britain either could not, or would not, replace them, especially in view of the resistance to a re-occupation which they could then present.

In addition to the elements of preparation which have been already presented, there was needed, for their safety and success in their terrible enterprise, that the conspirators should have a medium of communication between the various parts of the country and those who were working with them, as, also, an agency to win over the wavering and consolidate the whole power, so that it might be well in hand when the time for action should come.

The post-office was soon distrusted as a medium of communication; nor did it quite answer their purpose. They needed a living agency. This was essential, and one, too, whose constant movements would occasion no surprise; but just such emissaries as they required were ready at hand in the persons of the *Fakirs*, or wandering saints of Hindustan.

No account of India, or of the Sepoy Rebellion, would be complete which did not include a proper description of these *Fakirs*. They are the saints of the Mohammedan and Hindoo systems. These horrible looking men, with their disheveled hair, naked bodies, and painted breasts and foreheads, are constantly roving over the country, visiting shrines, making pilgrimages, and performing religious services for their disciples. The Sepoys greatly honored and liberally patronized these spiritual guides. The post-office failing them, the chiefs of the conspiracy linked these Fakirs into the enterprise as the medium of communication; and they were so stationed that the orders transmitted, or the information desired, could be forwarded with a celerity and safety that was amazing.

It may be desired, for the sake of the information on this singular topic, to digress a little just here, before proceeding with the narrative. Of all the curses under which India and her daughters groan, it may safely be said that this profession of the Fakirs is one of the heaviest and most debasing. The world has not often beheld a truer illustration of putting "darkness for light" than is afforded in the character and influence of these ignorant, beastly-looking men —fellows that in any civilized land would be indicted as "common vagrants," or hooted out of society as an intolerable outrage upon decency. But they swarm in India, infesting its highways, crowding its ghats and temples, creeping into its homes, and leading captive its poor, silly women. They hold the general mind of India in such craven fear that the courtly Rajah, riding in his silver howdah on the back of his elephant, and surrounded by his retinue, will often rise from his seat and salaam to one of these wretches as he goes by.

The Law-giver of India, while so jealously providing for the seclusion of the ladies of the land, expressly relaxes the rules in favor of four classes of men—Fakirs, Bards, Brahmins and their own servants—in the following section of the Code: "Mendicants, encomiasts, men prepared for a sacrifice, cooks, and other artisans are not prohibited from speaking to married women."—Sec. 360. chap. viii. They can exercise their discretion how far they shall unvail themselves before them, though in their intercourse with Brahmins and Fakirs all restriction is usually laid aside. They are as absolutely in their power as the female penitents of the Romish Church are in that of their priesthood, and even more so.

This state of things has lasted for long ages past. Alexander the Great, in his invasion of India, 326 B. C., found these very men as we see them there to-day. The historians of his expedition give us accurate descriptions of them. The Greeks were evidently amused and astonished at the sight of these ascetics, and, having no word in their language to describe them, they invented a new term, and called them *Gymnosophists*, (from *gumnos*, naked, and *sophos*, wise.) The patient endurance of pain and privation, the complete abstraction of some, the free quotations of the Shaster *Slokes* and maxims of their philosophy by the others, led the amazed Alexander and his troops to designate them as "Naked Philosophers," more literally so than the pictures here presented, for, though in my possession, I did not dare to have those engraved whose nudity would have more fully justified the Greek designation ; but they are still there, and of that class of the Fakirs a few words farther on will be in place.

The word "Fakir" (pronounced Fa-keer, with the *a* broad) is an Arabic term signifying "poor," or a "poor man," because they profess to have taken the vow of poverty, and, in theory, hold themselves above the necessity of home, property, or money, realizing their living as a religious right from the people wherever they come.

Some wander from place to place, some go on pilgrimages, and others locate themselves under a great banyan tree, or in the depths of a forest in some ruinous shrine or tomb, or on the bank of a river, and there receive the homage and offerings of their votaries.

I have often stood and looked at them in the wild jungle, miles away from a human habitation, filthy, naked, daubed with ashes and paint, and thought how like they seemed to those wretched creatures whom a merciful Saviour released from the power of evil spirits, and so compassionately restored to decency, to friends, and to their right minds.

The Fakirs of India. From a Photograph.

Some few of these Fakirs are undoubtedly sincere in their profession of giving up the world, and its social and domestic relations, to embrace lives of solitude, mortification, or self-torture, or to devote themselves to a course of religious contemplation and asceticism ; others of them do it from a motive of vain-glory, to be honored and worshiped by their deluded followers ; while both of these classes expect, in addition, to accumulate thereby a stock of merit that will avail them in the next transmigration, and hasten their absorption into Brahm. But no one who has seen and known them can doubt that the great majority of the Fakirs are impostors and hypocrites.

A glance at the picture will enable the reader more fully to understand the descriptions which follow. These wear some clothing, but not much. The hair of the head is permitted to grow—in some cases not cut, and evidently not combed—from the time when they enter upon this profession. It grows at length longer than the body, when it is wound around the head in a rope-like coil, and is fastened with a wooden pin. The figure on the left hand of the picture in front is one of these. Having some doubts whether there was not some "make-believe" in the huge roll, I questioned a Fakir one day about it. Seizing the big pin, he pulled it out, and down fell the long line of hair trailing after him. It was, sure enough, all his own hair.

But even these are not the worst of the class. Quite a number of them give up wandering and locate, and engage in the most amazing manifestations of endurance and self-torture. A few must be mentioned. One will lash a pole to his body and fasten the arm to it, pointing upward, and endure the pain till that limb becomes rigid and cannot be taken down again. The pole is then removed. I saw one of them with *both* arms thus fixed, his hands some eighteen inches higher than his head, and utterly immovable. Some of them have been known to close the hand, and hold it so until the nails penetrated the flesh, and came out on the other side. Tavernier and others give engravings of some who have stood on one leg for years, and others who never lie down, supported only by a stick or rope under their armpits, their legs meanwhile growing into hideous deformity, and breaking out in ulcers. Sticking a spear through the protruded tongue, or through the arm, is practiced, and so is hook-swinging—running sharp hooks through the small of the back deep enough to bear the man's weight—when he is raised twenty or thirty feet into the air and swung around. Some will lie

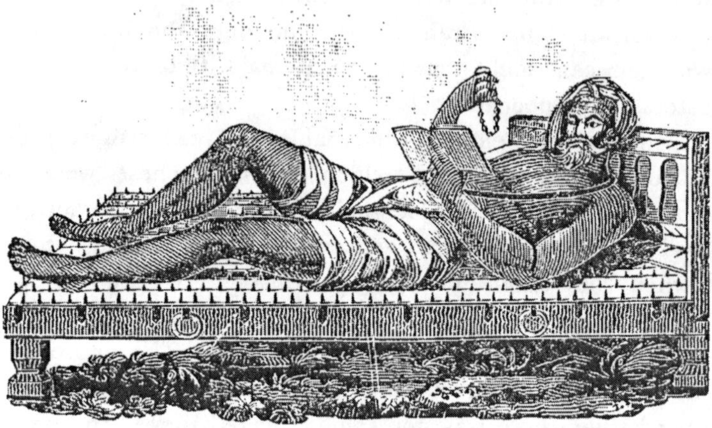

A Self-torturing Fakir.

for years on beds of iron spikes, like the one here represented, reading their Shaster and counting their beads; while their ranks furnish many of the voluntary victims who have immolated themselves beneath the wheels of Juggernaut. But there are tens of thousands of them who take to the profession simply because it gives them a living off the public, and who are mere wandering vagabonds.

Many of them are animated by another class of motives. These hunger for *fame*—they have become Fakirs for the honor of the thing—are willing to suffer that they may be respected and adored by those who witness in wonder the amazing self-tortures which they will endure. An instance which may be worth relating will illustrate this aspect of the subject. It was turned into verse by a humorous Englishman when the case occurred, and we present it here. One of these self-glorifying Fakirs, after graduating to saintship by long years of austerities and extensive pilgrimages, took it into his head that he could still further exalt his fame by riding about in a sort of Sedan chair with the seat stuck full of nails. Four men carried him from town to town, shaking him as little as possible. Great was the admiration of his endurance which awaited him every-where. At length (no doubt when his condition had become such that he was for the time disposed to listen to some friendly advice) a rich native gentleman, somewhat skeptical as to the value and need of this discipline, met him and tried very earnestly to persuade him to quit his uncomfortable seat, and have mercy upon himself. But here let Mr. Cambridge give the reasoning of the kind-hearted native, and point the moral of the story. He says to the Fakir:

> "'Can such wretches as you give to madness a vogue?
> Though the priesthood of *Fo* on the vulgar impose
> By squinting whole years at the end of their nose—
> Though with cruel devices of mortification
> They adore a vain idol of modern creation—
> Does the God of the heavens such a service direct?
> Can his Mercy approve a self-punishing sect?
> Will his Wisdom be worshiped with chains and with nails,
> Or e'er look for his rites in your noses and tails?
> Come along to my house, and these penances leave,
> Give your belly a feast, and your breech a reprieve.'
> This reasoning unhinged each fanatical notion,
> And staggered our saint in his chair of promotion.
> At length, with reluctance, he rose from his seat,
> And, resigning his nails and his fame for retreat,
> Two weeks his new life he admired and enjoyed;
> The third he with plenty and quiet was cloyed;
> To live *undistinguished* to him was the pain,
> An existence unnoticed he could not sustain.
> In retirement he sighed for the fame-giving chair,
> For the crowd to admire him, to reverence and stare:
> No endearments of pleasure and ease could prevail,
> He the saintship resumed, and new-larded his tail."

The reference in the third line—to "squinting whole years at the end of his nose," is a serious subject, and will be explained hereafter.

Sometimes Fakirs will undertake to perform a very painful and lengthened exercise in measuring the distance to the "sacred" city of Benares from some point, such as a shrine or famous temple, even hundreds of miles away, though months or years may be required to complete the journey. I had once the opportunity of seeing one of these men performing this feat. When I met him he was on the Grand Trunk Road, over two hundred and forty miles from Benares. He had already accomplished about two hundred miles. A crowd accompanied him from village to village, as men turn out here to see Weston walk. He was a miserable-looking object, covered from the crown of his head to his feet with dust and mud. He would lay himself down flat on the road, his face in the dust, and with his finger would make a mark in front of his head on the ground; then he would rise and put his toes in that mark, and down he would go again, flat and at full length, make another line, rise, and put his toes in that, and so on, throughout the live-long day. When tired out he would make such a mark on the side of the road as he could safely find next morning, and then go back with the crowd to the last village which he had passed, where he would be *fêted* and honored, and next day would return to his mark and renew his weary way. I could not find out how much progress he usually made. It must have been very slow work—certainly less than one mile per day; and what weary months of hard toil lay between him and Benares is apparent. These wretches thus choose, and voluntarily lay upon themselves, penalties that no civilized government on earth would venture to inflict upon its most hardened criminals.

Some of these Yogees, in view of their supposed sanctity and superiority to all external considerations, hold themselves above obedience to law or the claims of common decency. I have myself seen one of them in the streets of Benares, in the middle of the day, when they were crowded with men and women—a man evidently over forty years of age—as naked as he was born, walking through the throng with the most complete shamelessness and unconcern! And if it were not for the terror of the English magistrate's order and whip, instead of one in a while, hundreds of these "naked philosophers" would scandalize those streets every day in the year, and "glory in their shame."

A Yogee, or Silent Saint of India.--From a photograph.

There is a further aspect of this subject, and one so singular and serious that the reader will be as much surprised at the alleged divine law which requires it, as the sole and only path to moral purity and ultimate perfection, as he will be that men have ever been found who would undertake to conform themselves to the amazing and unique discipline by which it is to be attained. We may talk of self-denial and cross-bearing, but did the history of human endurance ever present any thing equal to the requirements of the following teachings?

In all the wide range of Hindoo Literature it is conceded that there is nothing so sublime, and even pure, as the disquisitions contained in the *Bhagvat Geeta,* (*Bhagvat,* Lord, *Geeta,* song—"the Song of the Lord.") This book is an episode of the celebrated *Mahabarata,* and consists of conversations between the divine Kreeshna, (the incarnate God of the Hindoos, in his last *avatar,* or descent to earth in mortal form,) and his favorite pupil, the valiant Arjoona, commander-in-chief of the Pandoo forces.

Arjoona is religious as well as heroic, and in deep anxiety to know by what spiritual discipline he may reach perfection and permanent union with God. His Incarnate Deity undertakes to enlighten him in the following instructions.

To assist the reader in comprehending the teachings of this whimsical method of reaching "the higher life," as practiced by the most sincere and yearning of India's religious devotees, I present a faithful picture of one of the class described, and who is at the same time one of the most celebrated of the Yogee order, just as I have seen him in Delhi, where the photograph was taken. The Yogee is the central figure. The Fakir standing is his attendant; the man to the right is one of the Yogee's devotees or worshipers, come to pay him the usual homage, expressed by his clasped hands. The Saint is silent, engaged in the meditation and abstraction, the rules of which we are going to present. His body is daubed with ashes till he looks as if covered with leprosy; the marks on his forehead are red, as they are on the face, and breast, and arms of his attendant. He holds no converse with mortal man, nor has he done so for years. The Governor-General of India might pass by, but he would not condescend to look at him, nor deign a word of reply were he to speak to him. He is supposed to be dead to all things here below, and to have every sense and faculty absorbed in the contemplations enjoined in the following words of the Deity:

Kreeshna says to Arjoona: "The man who keepeth the outward accidents from entering his mind, and his eyes fixed in contemplation between his brows—who maketh the breath to pass through both his nostrils alike in expiration and inspiration—who is of subdued faculties, mind, and understanding, and hath set his heart upon salvation, and who is free from lust, fear, and anger—is forever blessed in this life; and being convinced that I am the cherisher of religious zeal, the lord of all worlds, and the friend of all nature, he shall obtain me and be blessed.

"The Yogee constantly exerciseth the spirit in private. He is recluse, of a subdued mind and spirit, free from hope, and free from perception. He planteth his own seat firmly on a spot that is undefiled, neither too high nor too low, and sitteth on the sacred grass which is called Koos, covered with a skin and a cloth. Here he whose business is the restraining of his passions should sit, with his mind fixed on one object alone, in the exercise of his devotion for the purification of his soul, keeping his head, his neck, and body steady without motion, *his eyes fixed on the point of his nose*, looking at no other place around. The peaceful soul released from fear, who would keep in the path of one who followed god, should restrain the mind, and, fixing it on me, depend on me alone. The Yogee of an humble mind, who thus constantly exerciseth his soul, obtaineth happiness incorporeal and supreme in me."—*Bhagvat Geeta*, pp. 46–48.

It was one of these men, sitting thus naked, filthy, and supercilious, upon the steps of the Benares Ghat, receiving the homage and worship of the people, that drew from Bishop Thomson that strong remark which made such an impression upon those who heard him utter it.

The reader will bear in mind that *Yog* means the practice of devotion in this special sense, and a *Yogee* is one devoted to God; and such a man as the one here presented is the highest style of saint that Hindoo theology or its *Patanjala* (School of Philosophy) can know. The demands of these tenets, and the amazing supremacy which their practice confers on such a devotee as this, are so extraordinary and beyond belief, that, instead of my own language, I prefer to state them in the words of Professor H. H. Wilson, the translator of the Veda. Describing the discipline of the Yogees, and the exaltations which they aim at, he says: "These practices consist chiefly of long-continued suppression of respiration; of inhaling and exhaling the breath in a particular manner; of sitting in eighty-four different attitudes; of fixing their eyes on the tips of their noses, and endeavoring by the force of mental abstraction to effect a union between the portion of vital spirit residing in the body and that which pervades all nature, and is identical with Shiva, considered as the supreme being, and source and essence of all creation. When this mystic union is effected, the Yogee is liberated in his living body from the clog of material encumbrance, and acquires an entire command over all worldly substance. He can make himself lighter than the lightest substances, heavier than the heaviest; can become as vast or as minute as he pleases; can traverse all space; can animate any dead body by transferring his spirit into it from his own frame; can render himself invisible; can attain all objects; become equally acquainted with the past, present, and future; and is finally united with Shiva, and consequently exempted from being born again upon earth. The superhuman faculties are acquired in various degrees, according to the greater or less perfection with which the initiatory processes have been performed." All this is implicitly believed of them by their devotees, and they are honored accordingly with a boundless reverence.

The number of persons in the various orders of Yogees and Fakirs all over India must be immense. D'Herbelot, in his *Bibliothèque Orientale*, estimates them at 2,000,000, of which he thinks 800,000 are Mohammedan Fakirs. Ward's estimate seems to sustain this. But the influence of the British Government and its laws, and the extension of education and missionary teaching, are steadily tending to the reduction of the number, by lowering the popular respect for the lazy crew that have so long consumed the industry of the struggling and superstitious people.

The expense of supporting them, at the lowest estimate—say two rupees per month for each Fakir—involves a drain of $12,000,000 per annum upon the industry of the country—a sum equal to what is contributed for the support of all the Christian clergy of the United States. Yet this is only one item of what their religion costs the Hindoos. Besides this come the claims of the regular priesthood, then of the Brahmins, then of the astrologers, encomiasts, etc., which this system creates—and Ward says they, with the Fakirs, make up in Bengal about one eighth of the population—millions of men year after year thus sponging upon their fellows, and engendering the ignorance, the superstition, the vice, the mendicity, the sycophancy, that necessitate a foreign rule in their magnificent land, as the only arrangement under which the majority could know peace, and be safe in possession of the few advantages which they enjoy. Truly heathenism—and above all Hindoo heathenism—is an *expensive* system of social and national life for any people. Error and vice don't pay. They are dearer far than truth and virtue under any circumstances.

Welcoming to their ranks, as they did, every vagabond of ability who had an aversion to labor, before the introduction of the British rule, these Fakirs, under pretenses of pilgrimages, used to wander, like the Gypsies of the West, over the country in bands of several thousands, but holding their character so sacred that the civil power dare not take cognizance of their conduct; so they would often lay entire neighborhoods under contribution, rob people of their wives, and commit any amount of enormities. In Dow's "Ferishta," Vol. III, there is a singular account of a combination of them, twenty thousand strong, raising a rebellion against the Emperor Aurungzebe, selecting as their leader an old woman named Bistemia, who enjoyed a high fame for her spells and great skill in the magic art. The Emperor's general was something of a wit. He gave out that he would resist her incantations by written spells, which he would put into the hands of his officers. His proved the more powerful, for a good reason: a battle, or rather a carnage, ensued, in which the old lady and her Fakir host were simply annihilated. Aurungzebe met his general, and, the historian tells us, had a good laugh with him over the success of his "spells." Even as late as 1778 these militant saints thought themselves strong enough to measure swords with English troops, attacking Colonel Goddard in his march to Herapoor. But the Colonel, though much more merciful than the Mohammedan General, taught them by the sacrifice of a score or more of their number that they had better let carnal weapons alone. Though still saucy enough to the weak, they have ceased to act together in masses, or carry a worse weapon than a club in their peregrinations.

Usually each wandering Fakir has a religious relation to the high priest of some leading temple, and to him he surrenders some portion of the financial results of each tour at its termination. In view of this fact, they claim free quarters in all the temples which they pass. Their wide range of intercourse tends to make them well acquainted with public affairs—they hear all that is going on, and know the state of feeling and opinion, and communicate to their patron priests the information which they gather as they go. This, then, was "the secret service" organized by the conspirators of the Sepoy Rebellion to convey their purposes and instructions—when they concluded that the post-office was no longer safe to them—and a very efficient and devoted "service" it proved to be for their objects.

One of Havelock's soldiers gave me a string of praying beads which he took from one of these Fakirs before they executed him They intercepted him on his way to a Brigade of Sepoys, who had not yet risen, with a document concealed on his person from the Delhi leaders, directing the brigade to rise at once and kill their officers and the ladies and children of their station, and march immediately for Delhi to help the Emperor against the English. With this missive upon him, the Fakir—a stout, able fellow—was passing Havelock's camp, when his movements attracted attention, and he was stopped. The interpreter was sent for, and the man interrogated. He gave a plausible account of himself—was a Holy Fakir, on his way to a certain shrine beyond, to perform his devotion—all the time twirling his beads in mental prayer, and so abstracted he could hardly condescend to reply to their inquiries. Some were for letting him go; others, who did not like his looks, thought it better to search him before doing so, when the terrible missive that was to plunge into a sudden and cruel death some forty English people, more than half of them ladies and children, was found upon him, and he was at once told to prepare for death. They gave him five minutes, and then dropped him by the roadside with the bullet. He held his beads to the last, and the soldier who took them from his hands gave them to me. But there were thousands of such agents at their command, and the loss of a few made little difference to the enterprise.

Out of the Presidency cities (Calcutta, Madras, and Bombay) there were then no hotels, and, save the Dak Bungalows (Travelers' Rest Houses) on the leading roads, a stranger was thrown entirely upon the hospitality of the civil and military officers of the English Government as he moved through the country. Freely and cordially was this hospitality extended to all comers, our kind hosts seeming to regard each visitant as conferring a favor rather than receiving it. On his departure they furnished him with a note of introduction to a friend in the next station, and there the same courtesy and attention were repeated.

Thrown thus so much and so constantly into the society of these gentlemen and their families, we were especially, as American strangers and missionaries, regarded with considerable interest, and our future success discussed from a variety of stand-points, according to the degree and character of the religious views and feelings of our kind entertainers. We had gone to India under the idea that it was a country whose tranquillity was fully assured, and whose peace could not be disturbed by any events likely to arise from any quarter. Our amazement may be imagined when we discovered, as we so soon did, that there were apprehensions in the minds of many of these gentlemen of the existence of something unsafe, and even dangerous, around them; but as others of them treated the matter very lightly, and even ridiculed the idea of any necessity for anxiety, we, on our part, concluded that it was no particular business of ours, so we went on with our duty, leaving the future to be guided and controlled by the great Protector whom we were serving.

On reaching Lucknow, November 29, 1856, we found, rather to our surprise, that our note of introduction was to billet us in the "Residency," (so famous for its siege and relief by General Havelock ten months later.) Lucknow was the splendid capital of the kingdom of Oude, whose sovereign, Wajid Ali Shah, had just been removed to Calcutta, and his dominions annexed by the British Government, on account of the long-continued misrule and oppression that had made Oude a neighborhood of misery and rapine to all the country around it. What the condition of its King and Court were is stated, without exaggeration, in a work issued from the American press about 1854, entitled "The Private Life of an Eastern King," and also in Sleeman's "Recollections," and other publications. Few sovereigns have ever been so utterly forgetful of the duties of a governor of men, or more thoroughly steeped in selfishness and sensuality, than was Wajid Ali Shah. His territories at length, from his misrule and neglect, became an unequaled scene of outrage and bloodshed, and a refuge for the *dacoits* (robbers) of Northern India, who would cross the Ganges at night and plunder in the British Territories all around, making good their retreat into Oude before daylight. Complaints were presented for years, and threats of annexation were served upon him, till they ceased to be heeded by the besotted and reckless man, whose cruelties and neglect of his people (in which, however, he only imitated each of his predecessors) led at last to his being removed from the throne he disgraced. He was transferred to Calcutta in the spring of 1856, and there, on a pension about equal to his royal revenues, he prosecutes his debaucheries without ruining a kingdom any longer. The British Government annexed Oude to their territories, greatly to its relief and advantage. I present a picture of this royal sot, as he loved to display himself in all his jewels and finery.

During the week that we remained at Lucknow we were kindly entertained by a member of the new Government, (at the head of which was the celebrated Sir Henry Lawrence.) Every facility was afforded me in prosecuting my inquiries, and all information that I needed about the country, its condition and statistics, were freely communicated.

Lucknow then well deserved the character, so far as its external aspect was concerned, which Bayard Taylor gives it in his "India, China, and Japan," when, standing on the iron bridge which spans the Goomtee, he exclaims, "All was lovely as the outer court of Paradise!" But, in what moral corruption were its five hundred thousand inhabitants seething! I had never before seen any thing approaching its aspect of depravity and armed violence. Every man carried a weapon—even the trader's sword lay beside his goods, ready to defend them against the lawless. I had not supposed there was a community of men in this world, such ferocious Ishmaelites, as I saw in that city. It was not safe for an unarmed man, black or white, to move among them. And, indeed, when I wanted to see the city thoroughly, it was considered essential to my safety that I should not go alone or unattended, so they kindly mounted me on the back of an elephant in a Government howdah, and gave me a Sepoy escort; and thus elevated, so that I could see every thing on the flat-roofed houses, and in the courts and streets below, I made my first acquaintance with the city of Lucknow, and saw heathenism and Mohammedanism in their unutterable vileness. I returned to the Residency in the evening sick at heart, and, for the moment, discouraged at the fearful task which we were undertaking, to save and Christianize such people.

Outside the city the whole country was a sort of camp. The Sepoy army was drawn chiefly from this military class of men. Indeed, the city of Lucknow was the capital of the Sepoy race.

Wajid Ali Shah, last King of Oude.

The Talookdars (barons) of Oude (each in his own talook, setting up for himself, holding all he had, and taking all he was able to snatch from his neighbors) often defied their King, and refused to pay the jumma, (revenue,) and he could not obtain it unless by force of arms; and even here he was frequently defeated by their combining their forces against him. Mr. Mead has fully shown in his work—"The Sepoy Revolt"—how truly Oude had been for generations the paradise of adventurers, the Alsatia of India, the nursing-place and sanctuary of scoundrelism, almost beyond a parallel on earth. Sir William Sleeman's work on Oude is probably the most fearful record of aristocratic violence, perfidy, and blood, that has ever been compiled; yet it is written by one who opposed the annexation of the country to the British dominions, and who was regarded by the natives as their true friend. When I entered Oude there were known to be then standing two hundred and forty-six forts, with over eight thousand gunners to work the artillery on their walls, and connected with them were little armies, or bands of fighting men, to whom they were continually a place of shelter and defense. Annexation involved the razing of these forts, and the incorporation of a large amount of those blood-thirsty freebooters, and of the King's troops, into the Sepoy Army—for Lord Dalhousie, the Governor-General, did not know what else to do with them—but what elements of fierceness and lawlessness were thus added to the prejudice and fanaticism of the high caste Brahminical army can be well imagined. Thousands of these mercenaries who could not be employed, and who, with arms in their hands, were sent adrift to seek their fortunes, became the ready instruments of the Talookdars' tyranny and power, when His Excellency announced to them his intention of introducing the British system of land revenue into their country, for they well knew that these public improvements could be established only at the cost of their personal prerogatives and opportunities. The result is before the world.

Yet it was in such a country and among such a people, after months of careful inquiry and inspection of unoccupied fields, that

I concluded the Mission of the Methodist Episcopal Church should be established. We, with our gospel of peace and purity, had evidently found "those who needed us most;" and I had faith to believe that this warlike race, with all their force of character, could be redeemed, and would yet become good soldiers of Jesus Christ. Long after the hand which traces these lines shall have crumbled into the dust will the wide range of that beautiful valley, dotted with Christian churches, and cultivated by Christian hands, be bearing the rich fruition of these hopes.

Satisfied of the suitability of Lucknow to become the head-quarters of our new Mission, I sought from a member of the Government (not Sir Henry Lawrence, however) some statistics of the kingdom, to be incorporated in my Report to the Board at New York. I shall long remember his surprise when he found that we seriously contemplated planting the standard of the cross *there*. He asked me to look at the people, to consider their inveterate prejudices, and the venerable character of their systems, and say if I thought any thing could ever be done there? So far was he from so believing that he considered it was madness for us to try, nor would our life be safe in attempting it. His mind was so made up on that question that he could lend no countenance to such an effort: in fact, he was no friend to Christian missions, and he intimated pretty plainly that he considered I would manifest more good sense were I retrace my steps to Calcutta, and take the first ship that left for America! I received no better encouragement when I afterward called on Sir James Outram—a good man, and one of the bravest generals that ever commanded an army. He could lead the advance that so gallantly captured that city; but to stand up for Jesus alone and unprotected, exposed to the rage of the Mohammedan and the Hindoo in their bazaars, seemed to the military hero something that ought not to be attempted in such a country as Oude. He shrugged his shoulders when I reminded him that, as to our safety, Christ our Master, whose commission we obeyed, would look to that; while our success was in the hands of the Holy Spirit, and duty alone was ours. But he could not see it, and we parted never to meet again. The gallant man, sc justly designated "The Bayard of India," sleeps to-day in Westminster Abbey, among the illustrious dead whom England delights to honor.

Satisfied that we should end our wanderings, and regard Oude and Rohilcund as our mission-field, we sought for a house in Lucknow, but none could be found—all spare accommodation of the kind had been engaged by the officers connected with the increased civil and military establishments of the Government. So we were necessitated, as the next best thing, to go on to Bareilly, where a residence could be obtained, and wait for the future to open our way into Lucknow. We thus escaped the honor and risk of being numbered with those whom the relieving General, speaking for a sympathizing world, was pleased to designate "the more than illustrious garrison of Lucknow," who for one hundred and forty-two days were shut up and besieged within the walls of the Residency and the adjacent buildings, and whose story we shall illustrate in its place.

With many of the survivors, male and female, I was intimately acquainted for years afterward, while my home subsequently was within fifteen minutes' walk of the ruins of the Residency itself.

After full examination and inquiry, I had chosen this Kingdom of Oude and Province of Rohilcund (with the hill territory of Kumaon subsequently added) as our parish in India. In a full report to the Board in New York our reasons for the preference were fully given, and the fact was noted in the correspondence that the field chosen was one of those commended to my attention, before leaving America, by the Rev. Dr. Durbin, as one that might probably, on examination, be found pre-eminently suitable. His opinion and sagacity have been fully justified by the unqualified satisfaction of all concerned with the choice thus made. Our field, then, is the Valley of the Ganges, with the adjacent hill range bounded by the river Ganges on the west and south, and the great Himalaya Mountains on the north—a tract of India nearly as large as England without Scotland, being nearly four hundred and fifty miles long, and an average breadth of say one hundred and twenty miles, containing more than eighteen millions of people, who are thus left in our hands by the well-understood courtesy of the other Missionary Societies in Europe and America, who respect our occupation, and consider us pledged to bring the means of grace and salvation within the reach of these dying millions. (The reader's attention is asked to the Map which is at the beginning of the volume for the localities intimated within or near the scenes of the Ramayana and Mahabarata, and its central position, in the very "throne land of Rama," amid the most important of India's "holy shrines," and where our Christianity can tell so powerfully upon the entire country.)

On my way to Bareilly I called to see the Missionaries of the American Presbyterian Church at Allahabad; and, after explaining my plans and our proposed field, I stated to them how much I felt the need of some native young man who knew a little English—one whom I could fully trust, and by whose aid I might do something while awaiting the arrival of the brethren to be sent to me from America. They had one such whom they thought, under the circumstances, they might spare for such a purpose, though he was very dear to them. His name was Joel. They kindly introduced me to him, and at once my heart went out toward him as just the person I needed. I introduce him here to my readers—my faithful helper, destined to become the first native minister of the Methodist Episcopal Church in India.

Joel had been taken when an orphan boy by the missionaries, and by them was educated and trained. He was at this time about twenty-two years of age, married to Emma, a lovely, gentle girl, four years younger than her husband. They had one little babe, and lived with Emma's widowed mother, a good Christian woman called "Peggy," who doted upon her daughter, all the more, I suppose, because she was so fair and delicate. I remember them distinctly, because they were the first Christianized Hindoo household beneath whose roof I had yet sat down, and they seemed such a happy family. Joel had then gained so much of the English language that, by speaking slowly and using simple words, I could

Joel. From a Photograph.

make him understand me with tolerable clearness. He seemed just the kind of native assistant that I needed, if I could but obtain him. But I was going three hundred miles farther into an unexplored region, in the heart of the country, and where all was new and untried. The proposition to take him away from the friends of his youth, and from Christian services, among utter strangers and heathens, did seem rather trying, particularly in view of the general native timidity to go far from home—for that distance, and into another kingdom, seems to them almost equal to changing their nationality.

The case was laid before God, and his direction sought. It was then intimated to Joel himself, and, to my encouragement, he said he would be willing, but that he did not know how Emma would feel about it, or—which seemed to him a greater difficulty—what Emma's mother would say to the proposal. I feared that the mother's objection would be insuperable. However, I sent Joel to consult Emma first, and the faithful, brave little wife at once consented to go where he would go. Then came the test on which all depended for success. I resolved to accompany Joel to Peggy's residence, to be present when the proposal was made through Brother Owen, who interpreted for me.

When we entered her humble home and sat down, she greeted us with her sweet smile, and there was a pause. Joel looked at me and I at him, but for a few minutes I could not begin. The lonely widow would be so much more lonely when the dutiful and affectionate daughter who sat there would be far away. This, with the possibility that she should see her no more, and that the sacrifice was almost too much to ask, seeming as it did, in some humble sense, to rank with the class of self-sacrifices which required him of old to take his son, his "only son Isaac," whom he loved, to give him up to duty and to God, made my task a painful one. The hesitation to speak was embarrassing, but it had to be done; so, with an anxious heart and some serious doubts, I began and told her where I was going; that I had no aid of any kind with which to begin God's work in the great Valley of the Ganges, and what a treasure and help some suitable young man would be to me, enabling me to speak to the people at once about Christ, and aiding me to gain the language, and assisting in every way. Then, her attention and interest being fixed, I ventured to make the proposal which was to lacerate her feelings and to try her faith; and I said to her, "Joel is my choice; I have met no one who can help me as he can ; he is willing to go with me, and so is Emma, if you can only give your consent."

Woman has made many and great sacrifices for Jesus, and largely by such sacrifices has the cause of truth and purity been advanced among men. Since holy Simeon said to the mother of the Lord's Christ, "Yea, a sword shall pierce through thine own soul also," how many mothers, especially in resigning their children for the service of God at home or in distant lands, or those again in parting with their little ones that they might go there, or stay there—how many such in these Christian sacrifices have felt this anguish pierce their maternal sympathies when, as true followers of the Divine Father, "who spared not his own Son, but freely delivered him up for us all," they have surrendered their loved ones to the Lord's work, enduring their pungent sorrows, and trying to say, "My Saviour, I do this for thee!"

Compared with such offerings, how poor and small, and easily parted with, were the sacrifices of Jewish saints! They had only to surrender their corn, or wine, or oil, the best of their barn-yards or their flocks, or a money equivalent, for their first-born. None of these, save in such a case as Hannah's, went deeper than the purse. They were only property; they left the heart unscathed; they cost no tears, and inflicted no anguish. But it is different with Christian saints, who follow a self-denying Saviour, and who for his sake are willing to bear this peculiar cross. How amply compensated will such mothers feel when, in the presence of Him for whom they made these sacrifices, they shall see the sons or daughters whom they resigned to the work of God, after having turned many to righteousness, "shine as the stars for ever and ever!"

A spark of this Christ-like grace in the soul of a humble woman, once a heathen, can produce the same blessed spirit of self-sacrifice as that which animates the breasts of the most cultured ladies of Christendom; while her prompt and noble reply puts to the blush the selfishness of some mothers in this land, who have dared to stand between their children and convictions of duty to God and a dying world.

Peggy. From a Photograph.

When the painful question was presented to Peggy, after a momentary natural struggle, showing how conscious she was of the sacrifice, she answered me with tears—and I would write the poor widow's words in letters of gold if I could: "Sahib, (Sir, a title of respect,) the Saviour came down from heaven to give himself for me, and why should not I give my daughter to his work?"

It is a pleasure to introduce here the likeness of the devoted woman whose words I have quoted, and whose conduct so encouraged my heart that day.

Joel and Emma and their babe accompanied me to Rohilcund. As we were starting, the good missionaries by whom he had been educated, and who appreciated the gift they were conferring, playfully intimated that Joel had been trained a Presbyterian, knew the Westminster Catechism, and was sound on the Five Points of Calvinism, and that they would naturally expect him to continue in the faith, even though he was going with a Methodist missionary! In reply, I told them that I was more concerned for his religious welfare than for his special theological opinions—a clear conversion was of more moment to me than a creed; but that his views I would not, under the circumstances, interfere with in any way. Nor did I ever do so. I felt assured these things would regulate themselves thereafter.

On our arrival at Bareilly I commenced a little class-meeting, but soon found that Joel did not seem quite at home, and had but little to say in the exercise. So I drew him into private conversation, explained what we meant by the witness of the Holy Spirit, and put into his hands the "Memoir of William Carvosso," telling him that it was composed in very easy English, and was regarded by us as one of the best books ever written to illustrate the faith that saves, advising him to read it through twice, and then tell me what he thought of it. He did so; but before he finished the second reading told me there was something described there which he had not experienced. He had feared God from his youth, respected the Christian religion, attended the means of grace, was moral and upright, and would stand up for Christ and advocate his cause, but to say that he knew God as his reconciled Father was what he had never been able to profess. He now saw its necessity, and began to seek it with all earnestness. Before long he found it, and was enabled to testify that the "Spirit witnessed with his spirit that he was a child of God." Of course the class-meeting was now appreciated, and from that hour to the present, firm and faithful has been the character which he has borne among his brethren. Called by God to preach his Gospel, he has done so in its own spirit. I have often seen him antagonized by bitter-minded Brahmins and Moonshees, using harsh and vexatious language toward him and his cause, but never ruffled or thrown off his guard. "The meekness and gentleness of Christ" has been his protection on these occasions, while, with his Bible in his hand—just as represented in the picture—he is ready for all comers; and in the battles of the Lord with the enemies of the truth he has never turned his back or sounded a retreat—"a good soldier of Jesus Christ" truly.

As to his Calvinism, Joel had read Watson on "General Redemption," and sustained his Conference examination upon the theme, and when Bishop Thomson laid his hand upon his head he ordained a true preacher of the Gospel, who believed as cordially as did the Bishop himself that the Lord Jesus, in the same sense and with the same intention, died for every human being. His fidelity and his progress must be an occasion of gratitude to those who gave him his early training, and toward whom he will ever entertain the gratitude that is justly due.

CHAPTER V.

"IN PERILS BY THE HEATHEN, IN PERILS IN THE WILDERNESS."

ON our arrival at Bareilly in January, 1857, we were most kindly received by the Judge—Mr. Robertson—a member of the Free Church of Scotland. He took us into his home, and entertained us until we could obtain a house and furnish it. He was greatly delighted at our coming, for he believed in Missions, and in the power of the Gospel to reach the hearts of the heathen. For more than thirty years he had been in the civil service, knew the people well, and spoke their language with great fluency. His advice and opinions on our work were freely given and gratefully accepted, and it was evident that we might ever count him among the truest friends of our Mission.

We entered our own home just ten weeks before the Rebellion occurred; settled all things for our work, put up my valued library in its place, and began to study the language, little dreaming that so soon our comfortable arrangements would be consigned to the flames, and we be homeless and hunted for our lives on the adjoining mountains!

Yet, we might have been awakened from our sense of security by many events around us. In particular, one day a native gentleman called at our house and held a conversation, Joel interpreting, in which I was given to understand that my coming among them was regarded by the people of Bareilly with considerable anxiety; that for some time they had been led to believe the English Government had hostile intentions toward their faith, and really intended, by force or fraud, to break their caste and destroy their religion; and the supposition was, that I had been brought there by the Government to be ready, when their caste was broken, to baptize them, and so complete their Christianization!

My earnest denial of any connection with the Government was received with a look of suspicion, for they confounded every white man (then few and far between in India) with the Government; and when I proceeded to assure him that I was not even an Englishman, the Hindoo looked at me and exclaimed, "Why, Sahib, your face is white, you talk the English language, and are by religion a Christian; what else can you be but an Englishman?" I told him I was an American; but, more confused still, he asked, "A what?" "Why, an American." He had never heard the word before, nor perhaps one in ten thousand of his race, and he inquired what "an American" meant. He had no idea there was any other nation than England talking the same language and as white as they, and who were also Christians. This was generally true of his countrymen then. But when, five years after, "the cotton famine" raised so wonderfully the value of their staple, and the Hindoo farmer began to receive two, and even three, rupees for the same quantity of cotton for which he obtained only one the year before, men opened their eyes and began to study geography, to find out that there was a nation, and a great one, beyond England, whose faces were white and who spoke the English language, and were Christians too. So that our civil war in this country woke up the dormant intellect of ten thousand homes in the depths of India, and led men to inquire and study, and so far stimulated education, and showed its value, as no foreign event for hundreds of years previously had done.

But in 1857 the cotton famine had not occurred, and my Hindoo visitor was perplexed. Notwithstanding the general confidence they have in the truthfulness of the white faces, I have reason to think that this man left my dwelling under the conviction that I had tried to deceive him; that I was what he supposed, and had denied it to screen myself and my purpose. It is probable that that interview and its impressions exposed my family and myself to their more special vengeance when the day came.

With Joel's aid I commenced the work, hoping to have something done by the time the first party of our brethren should reach us from America. On the Sabbath we had two services—at eleven o'clock in the Hindustanee language, conducted by Joel, at which our family and a few natives attended; after this service we had our class-meeting, led by myself, six persons (Mrs. B., Joel and his wife, Ann, and Isaac, and Maria) being present, Joel translating for me what had to be said in Hindustanee. In the afternoon I held a little English service, at which a few of the officers and civilians attended. On Tuesday evening, also, we had an Hindustanee service, and an English one on Thursday. Thus our work opened, but it was truly "the day of small things."

The year in which I arrived in India saw the introduction of new arrangements for arming the Sepoy army. Instead of the old "Brown Bess," or regulation musket, with which they had hitherto fought the battles of the British, the rulers of India concluded to arm their Sepoys with the new Enfield rifle. For this weapon a peculiar cartridge had to be prepared, samples of which had been sent out from England to be manufactured at the arsenal of Dum Dum, eight miles from Calcutta. The rifles were distributed to the forces, and the wily Fakirs, ever on the look-out for something new to foment disaffection and distrust, at once declared that these, too, were a part of the insidious plan to injure their faith. The Sepoys received them with suspicion. Lock, stock, and barrel were taken asunder and carefully scrutinized, but nothing dangerous to their faith could be discovered. Yet the Fakirs had assured them there was danger, and that settled the matter.

Then came the intense excitement about the "greased cartridges" for these guns, the purpose being, I suppose, to lubricate the bore of the rifle. It was given out that this grease was "a compound of hogs' lard and bullocks' fat." Only those who have lived among these people, and realized what a horror the Mohammedan has of the hog, and what a reverence the Hindoo has for the cow, can appreciate the storm of excitement and frenzy this simple announcement caused through the whole Bengal army. The Fakirs exultantly pointed to the alleged fact as corroborating all they had asserted of the designs of the English against their religions.

It has never been definitely settled whether the charge as to the composition of the unguent was correct or not. The Government did what it could to allay the excitement and fears of the Sepoys, even to the withdrawal of the obnoxious cartridges, offering the men the right to make them up themselves with such grease as was not offensive to them. But it was all too late; midnight meetings now began to be held and plans of resistance discussed, and immediate and open mutiny was proposed.

General Hearsey at Barrackpore, by a well-timed and judicious address to the Sepoys of his command, in which he showed them the folly of supposing the Government inclined to attempt their forcible conversion, and the Governor General by proclamation to the whole army, tried to arrest the fearful tendency of affairs, and tranquilize the troops; but the effect was temporary. The lull was only the prelude to the storm. The General's manly and straightforward address to the men, with whom he had served nearly forty years, ought, if any thing could have done so then, to have satisfied and appeased them. He told them, among other things, that "the English are Christians of the Book, (that is, Protestants,) and Christians of the Book admit no proselytes, and baptize none, except those who fully understand and believe in the tenets therein inculcated."

But rebellion was a foregone conclusion with these infatuated men; so they dissembled and professed to be "koosh" (pleased) with his address, yet they only awaited their hour. Twenty days after this, on that same parade ground, a Brahmin Sepoy named Mungul Pandy turned out armed, and in the presence of his regiment, not a man of whom interfered to save their officers or to arrest the Sepoy, shed the first blood of the Rebellion by firing on and wounding Adjutant Baugh and Sergeant-Major Hewson. The firing drew General Hearsey and his son to the spot. Mungul took aim at the General, who drew his sword, and with the words, "John, if I fall, rush upon him and put him to death," spurred his horse forward. The man was overpowered, and after attempting suicide was tried and executed, and died refusing to make any statement to implicate his comrades, who were known to sympathize with him.

We heard all this, and as the toils closed around us, began fully to realize how helpless we were, and how entirely in the power of those people and their instruments. In addition to the officials connected with the public offices already mentioned, there were any number of Moulvies and Moonshees, connected with the mosques and with tuition, available for their purposes. These men could control the consciences of the Moslem servants in our families—the servants, of course, had eyes and ears—so that, while we lived in entire ignorance of what they said, or did, or purposed, our whole life lay open to our enemies, and our domestic conversations could be reported to them daily. The influence of the Nana Sahib, and other Hindoo authorities, could equally operate through their Pundits and Priests, and we were helpless between the two, as the full glare of observation and suspicion fell upon us, while those who watched every movement, and waited for our lives, could stand back in the shade and work in darkness.

One of the methods employed was the fabrication and diffusion of false news and prophecies. All that they required was temporary effect to rouse the fanaticism of the fighting class to a white heat of fury, until they committed themselves. As the Sepoys were utterly ignorant, and their minds entirely under the influence of their Fakirs, whom they believed implicitly, nothing promulgated by them was too monstrous for belief. For instance, it was asserted that "the English had imported several cargoes of flour mixed with bones, which had been ground fine, and one morsel of which would destroy the caste of any man;" that "this flour had been covertly introduced, and was then on sale in all the leading bazaars, but so well disguised that even those who bought and sold it could not discover the difference!" All this was believed. It was no use denying it, or asking them to trace it, or name the ship that brought it, or who had landed it; it was enough that the Fakirs had said it; it was certainly so. Thus Brahmin and Sepoy bought their food with suspicion, and eat it with fear. Another report was, that there was a plan for transporting to India the numerous widows of the Englishmen slain in the Crimea. The principal zemindars (landholders) of the country were to be compelled to marry them, and their children, who would not of course be Hindoos, were to be declared the heirs of the estates; and thus the territorial rights of the people of India, as well as their religion, were to be annihilated! With much more of the same sort.

Prophecies were invented, and arrangements made to fulfill them. The leading one was, that "the power which rose on the battle-field of Plassey should fall on the centennial anniversary of that great day." Another form of it, that better suited the Mohammedan mind, was, that "on the hundredth anniversary of Plassey the power that rose should fall, and the power that fell should rise." The meaning of all this is clear enough.

Allegorical expressions in letters and remarks were much used, such as "Pearls (that is, white-faces) are quoted as low in the market; Red Wheat (that is, colored-faces) is looking up." Then in February came that singular movement, the circulation of the "Chupatties," (small unleavened cakes,) the full significance of which has never been explained. Each recipient of two cakes was to make ten others, and transmit them in couples to the Chokeydars (constables) of the nearest village, and they to others, so that in a few days the little cakes were distributed all over the country, causing amazing excitement. It was known that sugar had been used as a signal for the Vellore mutiny, (July, 1806.) And the idea of thus conveying a warning to be in readiness for a preconcerted rising, had precedent enough in the "Feast of the Moon Loaves," still held in commemoration of a similar device, in the conspiracy by which the Mogul dynasty was overthrown five hundred years ago in China, as the reader will find narrated in Gabet and Huq's "Travels in Tartary," chapter iii. No other explanation has ever been given of this singular transaction.

Every supernatural means to which they looked for aid and direction were invoked and propitiated to lend their help in the coming struggle. Hunooman's assistance was confidently expected to render them invincible when they should cross bayonets with the dreaded white-faces. So they sharpened their weapons, lawful and unlawful, and awaited the day

Meanwhile the more intelligent and elevated of the conspirators cautiously sounded the native princes of the semi-independent States, to enable them to understand what part they would probably take in the great effort. Suitable motives were carefully held out to them, and also to the nobles and military classes, founded upon freedom from annexation, restoration of ancient dynasties, the bitter payment of old grievances, with patronage and rank when the Mogul should have "his own again," and be once more paramount in India. The Sepoys were promised promotion, higher pay, and better times generally; the Priests were assured of a deliverance forever from the growing power of Christianity, or even its presence, with a swift reversal of those enactments which had so seriously curtailed their dignity and perquisites, in usages and rites which humanity had swept away. The loose and vagabond classes (called "Budmashes") were linked in with the enterprise by promises of license and plunder; and it was not a secret that they disputed together in advance as to the particular shares to which they should become entitled. Even the criminals in the jails were to become personally interested in the results. In Bareilly, where we lived, was the great central jail, containing nearly three thousand, the convicts of the province of Rohilcund, with its eight millions of people. These wretches, confined there for all crimes, from murder downward, understood that their time would come to be avenged upon the Government and the race that were punishing them. None can say now how we gained the information, only that "a bird of the air" would carry such a matter; but weeks in advance of our flight from Bareilly, the English ladies had heard that those wretched criminals, in their chains and cells, understood that they were to be let loose upon the day of the mutiny, receiving their liberty on condition of consummating the atrocities which the high caste of the Sepoys prohibited them from perpetrating. And, accordingly, let loose they were on that dreadful

31st of May; but, thank Heaven! we had been led by a merciful Providence to anticipate the infernal intention, and removed to a place of safety nearly all of those whom they intended to victimize. Alas! for the few women and children who, tardy in their flight, did fall into their fiendish hands on that ever memorable afternoon.

Incendiary fires in the officers' quarters, which Sepoys refused to aid in extinguishing, now became matters of nightly occurrence in different stations. Partial mutinies took place at Fort William, Berhampore, and Lucknow, until, on the 10th of May the three regiments stationed at Meerut (near our position at Bareilly) rose and set fire to the houses, shot some of their officers, and then ruthlessly murdered all the Europeans on whom they could lay their cruel hands, men, women, and children, over forty in number. All this was done in a station where there were European troops within one mile of this scene of blood, and yet the miserable old General who commanded was so stupefied that he would not permit his men either to attack or pursue them! So the Sepoys hurried up their work undisturbed, and marched off to Delhi. They reached that city the next day. Here the other Sepoy troops, five thousand in number, joined them, and, taking their artillery, they proceeded to the palace of the Emperor, where they hauled down the old flag of England, ran up the green standard of the Moslem, and fired a royal salute in honor of the resumption of Mohammedan sovereignty in India. They then began one of the most ruthless and fiendish massacres of the Europeans which even Delhi (the city of cruelty) had ever witnessed. The Shazadahs were foremost in this devilish work, which was done chiefly in public, before thousands of raging foes, at the Kotwallee (Police Station) of the city. All the Europeans within the palace were slaughtered, with the concurrence, if not by the orders, of the Emperor, including the English Embassador, the Chaplain, Mr Jennings and his daughter, and Miss Clifford—the latter said to be one of the most beautiful English ladies then in the East.

Amid the record of these horrors, it makes one feel proud of his Anglo-Saxon blood to think of some of the daring deeds which were done against such fearful odds, and in the face of almost certain death. One of the most notable of these was Lieutenant Willoughby's defense of the Delhi magazine on that dreadful day. I know the place, and enjoy the honor of a personal acquaintance with some of the brave men whom he commanded then. I have also had the privilege, in company with one of the survivors, to wander over the ruins into which he blew the whole structure when he found he could not save it for his country.

There were no European troops in Delhi to oppose the entrance of the red-handed Sepoys that day; none, except the nine men in charge of the magazine, and which it was of the first moment to Sepoy success that they should seize. In the Lieutenant's judgment it was of equal importance to his nation that they should never have it, and his resolution was promptly taken, that, if it cost his life and the lives of those under his orders, it never should be surrendered. The names of the eight heroes whom he commanded were Lieutenants Forrest and Raynor; Conductors Buckley, Shaw, Scully, and Crow; Sergeants Edwards and Stewart. He first put his guns and howitzers in position for the defense of the place, and then, so as to be prepared for the worst, laid his trains to connect all parts of the magazine. A handful of native assistants happened then to be with them in the magazine, whom they could not open the gates to turn out, for they soon discovered that they were playing them false; so they had to watch them also. The firing and yells resounded all over the city, coming nearer and nearer to them. But there these men stood, with one hope in their hearts, that the European troops whom they knew to be at Meerut would follow up the mutineers, and that they might be able to hold out till they arrived, and so save the magazine and Delhi too. Vain hope--they came not. Soon the Palace Guards were thundering at the gates, and, in the name of the Emperor, demanded the surrender of the magazine. No reply was given. The mutineers then brought scaling ladders from the Palace, and the Sepoys swarmed up upon the high walls all around them.

One of the bastions commanded a view of the country toward

Meerut—a long reach of the road could be seen from it. There Willoughby took his position. Conductor Scully had volunteered to fire the train, should the last emergency come. There he stood, with his lighted port-fire in his hand, watching every movement of his chief. Seeing all was lost, and chafing with impatience, in presence of the raging foes around upon the walls, he would now and then cry out, "Shall I fire her, sir?" But the Lieutenant, who still hoped for the sight of help from Meerut, would reply, "Not yet, Scully—not yet." The despairing but brave man would again look along the road and sigh, while Scully watched for the signal.

Lieutenant Forrest, with the other six men, worked the guns. The gallant little band never once thought of betraying their trust by capitulation. The escalade from without was the signal for a similar movement from the traitorous natives within. In the confusion they managed to hide the priming pouches; they then deserted the Europeans, climbing up the sloped sheds on the inside of the magazine, and descending by the ladders without. The insurgents had by this time swelled into multitudes upon the walls, pouring a deadly musketry discharge upon them at less than fifty yards, but the brave besieged kept up an incessant fire of grape, which told well. At length Conductor Buckley—who had been loading and firing with the same steadiness as if on parade—received a ball in his arm; and Lieutenant Forrest was at the same time struck by two balls. Further defense was hopeless. No help from Meerut. Lieutenant Willoughby saw that the supreme moment had arrived. He lifted his hat, which was the signal, and Conductor Scully instantly fired the trains, and with an explosion that shook all Delhi, up went the magazine into the air, and its vast resources were annihilated. From five hundred to one thousand Sepoys on the walls were killed, and every thing around destroyed. Willoughby, Forrest, and Buckley, though wounded, actually escaped death, and managed to crawl from beneath the smoking ruins under cover of night, and retreated through the sally-port on the river-face, and Forrest and Buckley lived to tell the story of their great deed. Lieutenant Willoughby himself was killed in a village close to Delhi. No trace of Scully or the rest was ever found.

This was a great service for the English cause, but could not turn the tide for them. Unfortunately, there was an arsenal and an immense park of artillery in another part of the city, both which fell into the hands of the mutineers; while the sixty thousand Sepoys who soon found their way to Delhi brought with them from other cities abundant munitions for its defense.

After the destruction of the magazine, the murder of the officers and missionaries and other Europeans, the violation of their wives and daughters, and the spoliation and burning of their homes, was proceeded with. Then followed the demolition of the courts of law, the church, the college, and the printing-office, and deeds were done that day which devils themselves might blush to own. It was an unutterable woe; yet it was not without its great compensation.

There is a permissive providence of our God which sometimes allows a limited calamity to fall upon individuals and communities in order to preserve them from a sorrow that would be overwhelming and unmitigated: in the sense of Caiaphas's words, "It is expedient that one man die for the people," etc. But in such cases, and indeed in general, it requires that we patiently wait until time gives the Almighty the requisite opportunity to be his own interpreter. We could not then understand God. In the midst of these agonies it seemed as if he had "forgotten to be gracious, and in anger had shut up his tender mercies." But what light the succeeding events, and the history of the last dozen years, have shed upon his overruling providence and his wise designs!

Two facts of this class belong just here: one general, and one particular to ourselves. But for the anticipation on the part of the Meerut mutineers of the contemplated universal rising, it seems to me that not a Christian life could have been preserved in all India. Had they patiently waited till the 31st of May, and all had risen, as was intended, so that on the same day and hour, in every place, they had commenced their work of blood, not a lady nor a babe could have been saved. All must have been overwhelmed in one common ruin, and none left to tell the tale.

But those demented Sepoys of Meerut struck twenty-one days too soon, thus throwing the whole country into such an excitement and effort to meet the hour, which was then manifestly inevitable, that every expedient that men could adopt, to remove the ladies, children, and non-combatants to some, to any, place of safety, and the best possible measures for their defense and preservation, were taken. So that to that three weeks of opportunity each lady owes her life, and the world was saved the agony of a tale of horror that would have been even a hundred fold greater than the terrible tragedy which horrified them in 1857–8.

The other fact was personal to ourselves, yet having a kindred significance in its results. Our commanding General in Bareilly was a gentleman of the name of Sibbald. Like many other old officers, he had an infatuated confidence in his Sepoy troops. If he had been at home when the news of the Meerut massacre reached us, the probability is that not a soul of us would have escaped. But, just before the event took place, he was led to proceed upon a tour of military inspection of the province under his authority, and was most providentially away in the mountain district when the news arrived.

He left in command our brave friend, Colonel Troup—a man who knew the Sepoys well, and who did not trust them. Acting on his own judgment and discretion, though he knew the old General would probably disapprove his action, he took that course, in the hour and opportunity afforded him by his temporary command, which proved the salvation of all those under his care who obeyed his orders.

In our flight to Nynee Tal, myself and family brought up the rear. I met General Sibbald half-way down, at Bahari Dak Bungalow, and he was wild with excitement, declaring that Colonel Troup's head was turned to do such a thing as to send away the ladies and children out of Bareilly, and he swore that if he had been at home not one of them should have left. He knew, he said, that his Sepoys were staunch and true, and could be depended upon to defend them! I looked after the old man as he hurried away from me, with the sad presentiment that he was mistaken. He "blew up" Troup, and was so firm in his reliance on the Sepoys that, had it not been for the influence of his officers, he would, in order to show his confidence in his troops, have yielded to their request to order back the ladies to Bareilly. On such a thread as this our fate hung. Yet this very man, to whom his Sepoys swore such fidelity and made such promises, was the first person whom they shot on that Sabbath morning, May 31st. In his dying hour, if he thought of them, he must have felt that the safety of his own wife and daughters was due to the precaution of the officer he had blamed! But we are anticipating what follows.

Forty-eight hours after the Meerut massacre (and three days before the account of that of Delhi reached us) a mounted horseman entered Bareilly, with a letter from the English Governor of the North-west, Mr. Colvin, to the commanding officer, narrating the terrible deeds done at Meerut, and suggesting that every precaution should be taken to provide for the safety of the ladies and children. Colonel Troup, being in command, received the letter and acted as we have stated. The telegraphs had been cut all over the country, and the mails on the Delhi side stopped; so that had it not been for the precaution of Mr. Colvin in sending a message direct, we should have been in ignorance of what had been done, and of our own fearful danger. Many such facts might be given to show the merciful Providence which watched over us to save us. But these may suffice here.

I now turn to our personal narrative, and, in presenting it, have carefully looked over the letters addressed to the Corresponding Secretary of our Missionary Society, in various dates from May 26 to July 10, 1857, when I gave the facts as they occurred; and in the light of the explanations which subsequent years have developed, I find only a few words that I need at all to qualify; so that the facts and impressions are given in the form in which they came from an anxious heart, which, in the midst of danger and in the face of death, tried to trust in God for all events, and yet looked for a happy issue out of these afflictions, and for the life and extension of the mission which we had begun.

On Thursday, May 14, the commanding officer kindly sent his Adjutant over to our house with a serious message. Not knowing what he specially wanted, we engaged for nearly an hour in religious conversation. But I thought from his manner that he looked anxious. With gentlemanly delicacy he was unwilling to mention his message before Mrs. Butler, lest it might injuriously affect her, as she was in circumstances where any shock was undesirable. He, accordingly, asked to see me alone, and then communicated the intelligence of the mutiny at Meerut, stating that word had arrived from the Governor that the insurrection was spreading to Delhi and other places, and that fears were entertained as to the intention of the Sepoys at Bareilly. Under those circumstances, the commanding officer felt it his duty to request that all ladies and children should be sent off quietly, but at *once*, to the hills, and also that he considered it prudent, from the reports in circulation concerning us and our objects, that I also should accompany Mrs. B. and the children, as he considered me in rather special danger in the event of a mutiny. I promised the Adjutant that I would prayerfully consider the message, and let my conclusion be known to the commanding officer that evening. As soon as the Adjutant had gone, I communicated the message to Mrs. Butler. She received it with calmness, and we retired to our room to pray together for divine direction. After I had concluded my prayer, she began, and I may be excused in saying that such a prayer I think I never heard; a martyr might worthily have uttered it, it was so full of trust in God and calm submission to his will. But when she came to plead for the preservation of "these innocent little ones," she broke down completely. We both felt we could die, if such were the will of God; but it seemed too hard for poor human nature to leave these little ones in such dreadful hands, or perhaps to see them butchered before our eyes! We knew that all this had been done on Sunday last in Meerut, and we had no reason to expect more mercy from those in whose power we were, should they rise and mutiny. But we tried hard to place them and ourselves, and the mission of our beloved Church, in the hands of God ; and he did calm our minds, and enable us to confide in him. On rising from our knees I asked her what she thought we ought to do? Her reply was that she could *not* see our way clear to leave our post ; she thought our going would concede too much to Satan and to these wretched men ; that it would rather increase the panic, that it might be difficult to collect again our little congregation if we suspended our services, and, in fact, that we ought to remain and trust in God. I immediately concurred, and wrote word to the commanding officer. He was not pleased at all with our decision. The evening wore on, and we held our usual weekly English service. I tried to preach from Deut. xxxiii, 25, "As thy days, so shall thy strength be," and administered the holy Sacrament. The commanding officer was present. I felt much for him. His responsibility was great, for on his discretion and judgment our entire safety, under God, depended. We passed a restless night, startled at every sound, feeling that we slept over a volcano that might burst forth at any moment, and scatter death and destruction on every side.

Before going to bed we arranged our clothes for a hasty flight, should an alarm be given. But we beheld the morning light in safety, and the mail brought me the *Christian Advocate* of March 19, and one of the first things I saw was the little paragraph which was headed with the words "Pray for your lonely William Butler!" How much I needed to be prayed for! Before that simple sentence my heart gave way, and I could not resist the tears that came. The past and the present were such contrasts! But God graciously soothed my feelings, till I wondered why I had ever doubted for a moment, or failed to see that God, who had brought us hitherto, would not now forsake us, or allow our mission to be broken up. I felt assured that thousands in this happy land did pray for their "lonely William Butler." Three times between that and Saturday evening did my kind friend send to warn me to leave, as did also other friends among the military. By that time nearly all the ladies and children had left. The place looked very desolate, and I began to question whether I was right in resisting advice any longer. My *Moonshee* told me candidly he thought I "ought to go." Being a Mohammedan, and having a pecuniary loss in the suspension of my lessons in the language, his warning had much weight with me. I had then to settle the question, raised by the commanding officer, whether our resistance to going, under those circumstances, was not more a tempting of, rather than a trusting in, Providence? I hated to leave my post, even for a limited time. Yet to remain looked, as he argued, should an insurrection occur, and I become a victim, like throwing away my life without being able to do any good by it; and the Missionary Board would probably have blamed me for not taking advice, and acting on the prudence which "foreseeth the evil," and takes refuge "till the indignation is overpast." Still, had I been *alone*, or could I have induced Mrs. B. to take the children and go without me, (a proposition she met by declaring she would never consent to it, but would cling to her husband and cheerfully share his fate, whatever it might be,) I would have remained. But when to all the preceding reasons, the reflection was added that Mrs. B.'s situation required that, if moved at all, it must be *then*, as a little later flight would be impossible, and she and the children and myself must remain and take whatever doom the mutineers chose to give us, I consulted Joel, and asked his advice as to what had better be done. He thought it safest that we should go, say for three or four weeks, to Nynee Tal, and, if all remained quiet, we could then return. Meanwhile he promised to sustain our humble service, and keep every thing in order. How little he or I then imagined that he himself, or any native Christian, would be in peril, or that before we again stood together on that spot, events would transpire around him that would fill the civilized world with horror!

I, therefore, arranged to suspend my English service, (indeed most of those who attended were already gone,) hoping soon to return and resume it. Saturday night we lay down to rest, not to sleep. The mounted patrols that went round every fifteen minutes would call out to the watchman attached to each house in such boisterous tones that sleep was impossible; and it almost became distracting, from the manner in which it made the poor children startle and cry until daylight broke. It was a solemn Sabbath. We had but ten persons at the native service, and less at the English one; people seemed afraid to come out. A rumor got afloat that Sunday was to be our last day; that the Sepoys intended to murder the Europeans on that Sabbath.

Our class-meeting was a solemn, but profitable, time. We used it as if it were our last. Had it been, I think each of that little band (seven in number) would have been found of God in peace. We lay down again to seek rest, but it was short and disturbed repose. Monday morning came; I tried to find palankeens for our journey, but all were away; so I obtained some bamboos and rope, and took three charpoys, (an article like what our Lord referred to when he bid the man "take up his *bed* and walk,") turned the feet uppermost, put on the bamboos, and threw a quilt on each, and we were equipped. I left three native Christians in the house with Joel, besides two watchmen for night. That evening, at six o'clock, the news arrived that the Sepoys had risen in Delhi, murdered the Europeans, and proclaimed the Emperor. The details were frightful. Just then Judge Robertson appeared upon the scene, and inquired if I too was yielding to the panic? I told him all. He was incredulous. I asked him why he thought so confidently that there would be no rising? He told me he was so advised by Khan Bahadur, the native judge, who assured him there was no cause for alarm, and guaranteed him personal protection under the hospitality of his own roof. Judge R. expostulated with me for leaving, and had not my arrangements been made for going, the influence of his words might have prevailed to lead me to put it off, and we should have shared his sad fate. We were ready when our bearers came at nine o'clock, and I went into my study once more. I looked at my books, etc., and the thought flashed across my mind that perhaps, after all my pains in collecting them, I should never see them again! I took up my Hindustanee Grammar, two volumes of manuscript Theological Lectures, a couple of works on India, my Passport, my Commission, and Letter of Instructions, with my Bible, Hymn Book, and a copy of the Discipline, and sorrowfully turned away, leaving the remainder to their fate. The children, poor little fellows, were lifted out of their beds and placed in the dooley.

Quietly, and under cover of the night, we started, leaving the keys of our house and all things in Joel's charge. Shaking hands with him and the others, we moved off by the light of the Mussalchee's torch, crossed the Bazaar, but no one molested us; they simply asked the men, "Whom have you?" The reply was, "The Padre Sahib," (the missionary,) and we passed through the crowd unmolested. We moved on in the silent darkness, having seventy-four miles to go. About midnight I happened to be awake, and saw we were passing a gig with two ladies in it, and a native leading the horse. It seemed hazardous to stop, but I became so uneasy that I did, and walked back. The ladies knew my voice. There I found them, on that wretched road, twenty miles from Bareilly, in the middle of the night; the ladies, scantily dressed, and crowded, with an Ayah, (a native nurse,) into a small gig, one of them holding up (for there was no room for it to lie down) a poor little sick child. In that posture they had been for nearly eight hours. They were just sitting down to dinner when the news of the massacre of Delhi arrived, and such was the panic produced that the gig was instantly brought to the door, and they put into it and sent off. They must go *alone*, for their husbands were military officers and must remain. I have witnessed desolate scenes, but never saw any thing so desolate looking as those two ladies and that child on that road that night. I took the lady with the child out of the gig and put them into my dooley, and it did my heart good to see them lying down. I then sent them on and took charge of the other lady and the gig. We overtook them, and about five ladies more, next morning, at the travelers' bungalow at Behari. There they remained, as directed, until dooleys overtook them next evening. Here I met General Sibbald, as already stated, hurrying down in a fury; too late, thank God! to carry out his purpose to prevent the departure. We rested till the heat of the day subsided, and then I started with my family again. We reached the first Chowkee safely, changed bearers, and then entered the *Terai*—a belt of deep jungle, about twenty miles wide, around the Himalayas, reeking with malaria, and the haunt of tigers and elephants. The rank vegetation stood in places like high walls on either side. At midnight we reached that part of it where the bearers are changed. The other palankeens had their full complement of men; but, of the twenty-nine bearers for whom I paid, I could only find nine men and one torch-bearer; and this, too, in such a place! Darkness and tigers were around us; the other palankeens were starting one after another, each with its torch to frighten away the beasts, the bearers taking advantage of the rush to extort heavy "bucksheesh." All but two had gone off, and there we were with three dooleys and only men enough for *one*, and no village where we could obtain them nearer than twelve miles. What to do I knew not. I shall never forget that hour. At length I saw there was but one thing to be done; I took the two children and put them into the dooley with Mrs. Butler; a bullock-hackrey, laden with furniture, was about a quarter of a mile ahead, with its light fading in the distance; desperation made me energetic; at the risk of being pounced upon, I ran after the hackrey, and by main force drove round the four bullocks and led them back, sorely against the will of the five men in charge of it. But I insisted that they must take Ann (our servant) and me, with what little baggage we had with us. I put her and the luggage up, the driver grumbling all the while about his heavy load and the delay. I then turned around to see Mrs. Butler off, but her bearers did not stir. I feared they were about to spoil all. They were exhausted by extra work, and might have even fairly refused to carry two children with a lady; and to have taken either of them on the hackrey was impossible. I dreaded the bearers would not go. Delay seemed ruinous to the only plan by which I could get them on at all. If the men refused the burden and left, they would take with them, for their own protection, the only torch there was, which belonged to them, and we should have been left in darkness, exposed to the tigers and the deadly malaria. Mrs. C. and Miss Y.'s bearers had laid them down, and were clamoring for larger "bucksheesh." My ten men looked on. The hackrey-driver turned his bullocks around, and, out of all patience, was actually putting his team in motion. But, in spite of urging, there stood my men. It was an awful moment. For a few minutes my agony was unutterable; I thought I had done all I could, and now every thing was on the brink of failure. I saw how "vain" was "the help of man," and I turned aside into the dark jungle, took off my hat, and lifted my heart to God. If ever I prayed, I prayed then. I besought God in mercy to influence the hearts of these men, and decide for me in that solemn hour. I reminded him of the mercies that had hitherto followed us, and implored his interference in this emergency. My prayer did not last two minutes, but how much I prayed in that time! I put on my hat, returned to the light, and looked. I spoke not; I saw my men at once bend to the dooley; it rose, and off they went instantly, and they never stopped a moment, except kindly to push little Eddie in, when in his sleep he rolled so that his feet hung out.

Having seen them off, I turned around, and there were our two dooleys. I could do nothing with them, so left them for the tigers to amuse themselves with, if they chose, as soon as the light was withdrawn. I ran after the hackrey and climbed up on the top of the load, and gave way to my own reflections. I had known what it was to be "in perils by the heathen," and now I had had an idea of what it was to be "in perils in the wilderness." But the feeling of divine mercy and care rose above all. The road was straight, and what a joy it was to see the dooley-light grow dim in the distance, as the bearers hurried forward with their precious burden.

We moved on slowly after them, owing to the rugged road, the swaying furniture, and the wretched vehicle; but we were too grateful for having escaped passing the night in the miasma and danger of the jungle to complain, though every movement swung us about till our bones ached.

We were ten hours going those fifteen miles. At last day broke, and our torch-bearer was dismissed. "Hungry and thirsty, our souls fainted in us" indeed. But at last we reached Katgodan, and found the mother and babes all safe. They had slept soundly the whole distance, and at daybreak were laid safely down at the door of the travelers' bungalow. It was twenty-two hours of traveling and exposure since we had tasted food, and when it was served up it was indeed welcome.

Mrs. C. and Miss Y. did not arrive for some hours after my wife, having lost the difference of time on the road in contentions with their bearers, and extra bribing to induce them to go on. On my arrival, one of the first remarks I met was from Miss Y.: "Why, what could have happened to Mrs. Butler's bearers, that they started so cheerfully and arrived here so soon, without giving her the least trouble!" Ah! she knew not, but I knew, there is a God who heareth and answereth prayer! O for a heart to trust him as I ought! The divine interposition in the case will appear all the more manifest when I add that even the "bucksheesh" for which the bearers were at first contending, (and which I was only too willing to pay them,) they started off without staying to ask for or receive; nor did they even require it from Mrs. B., when they safely laid her down at the end of their run. I shall never forget the experience and the mercy of that night in the Terai!

We stopped all night at the bungalow, which was crowded, and the heat was beyond any thing I ever felt before. Major T. had kindly sent down jampans (a kind of arm-chair with a pole on each side, carried by four men) to bring us up the mountain. We began the ascent at three o'clock next morning, having eleven miles to go to reach Nynee Tal. As soon as day broke the view was sublime—something of the Swiss scenery in its appearance, but more majestic. The road (a narrow path) wound round and up one mountain after another, by the brink of precipices and land-slips. As we rose the cold increased, till we came to a region where trees and shrubs of European growth were flourishing, bilberries and raspberries made their appearance, and the cuckoo was heard. The last two miles was up the face of a mountain as nearly perpendicular as was possible and yet permit a very zigzag path to be cut on it. At length, after seven hours' toiling, we gained the summit, 7,000 feet above the plains below. What a prospect! In the bosom of those cool mountains lay the sanitarium of Nynee Tal, with its beautiful lake, while behind it rose up the "snowy range," 21,000 feet higher still.

Those who may visit the place for health or pleasure in the days to come can have little idea with what feelings the panting fugitives of 1857 caught this first glimpse of it on that morning.

Nynee Tal occupies a high upland valley or gorge in the Gaghur range, south and east of the point where that range attains its highest elevation at Cheenur Peak, 8,732 feet above the sea. This peak sends off a spur to the south and south-east, called Deoputta and Ayár Páta, and the hollow between the spur and the main range of the Gaghur—here called Shere ke Danda and Luria—is occupied by the flat portion of the station, by the bazaar, and by the lake which gives its name to the place, and which forms the principal feeder of the Bulleah River.

The valley is half land and half water, the lower end being occupied by the lake, and it is only open to the south-east, where the outlet for the water is situated. The length of the whole hollow is a mile and a half, and its average breadth is under half a mile. The length of the lake is a few yards less than one mile. The water is at all times beautifully clear and transparent, and in calm weather reflects the surrounding scenery like a mirror.

The place is approached by two narrow paths from the foot of the hills on the Moradabad and Bareilly sides. The ascent is in places very steep and on the verge of fearful precipices. It had been used for a few years past as a sanitarium by the English residents, and was chosen now for us because the military men believed that it could be easily defended.

All looked so peaceful and felt so delightfully cool! After some

Nynee Tal, as you enter it.

searching, I was fortunate enough to find a little furnished house of four rooms still unengaged, which I gladly hired for $225 for "the season." A bachelor Captain was in it as a day tenant, but he most kindly turned out and let us in at once, and within five hours of our arrival we laid our weary little ones to rest in our new and strange home, not knowing for how long a time we should be able to occupy it. Yet we were even then deeply impressed with the value of such a place for a sanitarium for our mission in the better days of the future, when the brethren and sisters, whose health would require the change, would feel thankful to have within their reach such a refuge from the heat. But under what different feelings and circumstances is it now visited by them from those with which their fugitive superintendent first entered it!

Immediately on reaching Nynee Tal I wrote a few words to Dr. Durbin, and as they express the feelings of the hour, and an unshaken faith in God in the future of our mission, they may be quoted here: "I had hoped by this mail (which closes here to-day) to have sent you a full account of our situation; but this is impracticable until the next mail. We have only just arrived here, and are all in confusion. I can, therefore, only write a few lines. The commanding officer required all non-combatants to leave Bareilly and take refuge here until the Government has put down this insurrection We delayed till the last moment, but had to leave. Our experiences on the way up were, in many respects, trying enough, but God preserved us in safety, so we

"'—praise him for all that is past,
And trust him for all that 's to come.'

"What awaits us we know not; but should any thing happen to us, tell our beloved Church that we had prepared ourselves through grace for all results, and that our last thoughts were given to our mission in the confident hope that the Methodist Episcopal Church would do her part faithfully in redeeming India. Beyond this we had no anxiety except for our poor children. Doctor, you will think of them if I fall! We need now, O how much! the prayers of God's people."

This note worked its way through all the dangers to which the mails, then rapidly breaking up, were exposed, and managed to reach the seaside, and so on to its destination; a better fate than many of its successors had.

For more than ten days all moved on as usual; the mails came and went; Joel wrote and kept me informed how matters progressed till, seeing no further sign of danger, some of our party became impatient, asking ourselves why did we leave at all, and even proposing to return to Bareilly. It was, however, only the lull before the storm.

On the 25th we heard of the mutiny at Allyghur. Sabbath, the 31st of May, I preached twice (the first Methodist sermons ever uttered on the Himalaya mountains) from Acts xx, 21, and Rom. viii, 16. I tried to preach as "a dying man to dying men." At the same hour in Bareilly Joel was conducting the service. He preached—for he had already begun to take a text—the very morning of the mutiny from the words, "Fear not, little flock, for it is your Father's good pleasure to give you the kingdom," when, in the midst of his closing prayer, the guns opened fire, and the slaughter of the Europeans commenced. But we knew it not. Our Sabbath passed peacefully over, while many of the ladies of our party were widows, and the mangled bodies of their husbands were then lying exposed to every form of insult in the streets of Bareilly.

Monday came, and no mail from Bareilly. We feared something must be wrong, and our fears were all verified by the arrival of the first of the fugitives in the evening, bearing the terrible news that at eleven o'clock on Sunday morning the Sepoys had risen and commenced shooting their officers. An understanding had existed among the officers that, in case of a rising, the rendezvous should be the cavalry lines; so, as soon as the firing began, each officer that could do so jumped on his horse and galloped to where the cavalry were drawn up, Brigadier-General Sibbald being killed on the way there. As Lieutenant Tucker, of the Sixty-eighth Native Infantry, was flying on horseback, he saw the Sepoys firing into the houses of the English sergeants; and calling out to one of them, "Jennings, jump up behind me," he was shot dead by the Sepoys, and fell from his horse. Jennings mounted it. They shot the horse under him. He jumped off, ran for his life, and escaped. Captain Patterson, with other officers, was fired on in the orderly room. They escaped by the opposite door, ran to their stables, got their horses, and fled. Colonel Troup heard the firing, and was leaving his house when his own orderlies tried to stop him. He got out by another door, and escaped on foot, but was followed by his *syce* (groom) with his horse. Dr. Bowhill, of the Eighteenth, was in his bath when he heard the firing. He jumped out, drew on his clothes, got out his watch and one hundred rupees, ran to the stable to order his horse, returned, and found that his rascally bearer had made off with money and watch too. I have only heard of one who had time to save a single thing except the clothes they had on them. Captain Gibbs had to ride across the parade ground through a volley of musketry, and the artillery men fired on him with grape. He escaped unhurt. All was so sudden, so unexpected, there was no time for preparation—nothing but to mount and fly. Two minutes after Colonel Troup left his house he saw it in flames; and before ten minutes every bungalow in the cantonments seemed on fire. The road to Nynee Tal was direct through the city. A band of officers and gentlemen, about forty in number, evaded the city, took a by-road for a couple of miles, and escaped. Those who tried the city I believe all perished. Of Lieutenant Gowan (our good friend of the Eighteenth Native Infantry) we could hear nothing; but he was saved by his own Sepoys, who liked him. Under cover of night, when it came, they took him out of a house where they had concealed him, and escorted him, with their Sergeant-Major Belsham and his wife and five children, and conducted them two miles beyond Bareilly to the south, giving the sad party what money they could spare, and their good wishes for their escape. They were joined during the night by four officers that had escaped the massacre, and they resolved to keep together for mutual protection; but the slow pace at which the poor woman and her infants could move soon irritated the officers, and they resolved to leave them behind. Lieutenant Gowan would not listen to the proposal. His humanity saved his life. The four officers pushed on and were murdered, while the little party with the Lieutenant were all saved by the wonderful generosity of a Hindoo farmer, who found them concealed in his field, and who hid them for seven months within his own house at the risk of his life. This was at Khaira Bajera, a place now on our Minutes, and where good Lieutenant (now Colonel) Gowan has built and endowed Christian schools as a memorial of his gratitude to the Thakoor who sheltered him, and to God who inclined him to do so. They are under the charge of our mission.

When the firing first began, at eleven o'clock, some of the officers when they reached the lines of the native cavalry suggested a charge on the artillery and infantry, hoping the cavalry would prove true, as they all professed great loyalty. It was attempted, but the rascals, after going a few paces, hoisted the "green flag" and deliberately rode over to the infantry, leaving the officers in a body, with about twenty-five of the cavalry, who stood faithful. The artillery then opened upon them with grape, and they had to fly. Poor fellows! they rode the seventy-four miles without refreshment or a change of horses; and when they came up the hill to us next morning they were all sun-burned and ready to drop from sheer exhaustion. Some of them had nothing on but shirt and trousers; few of them were completely dressed, as the hour of mutiny was the general hour for bath and breakfast, and they had to spring to their horses without losing a moment to look for any. Fully one half of our little English congregation were murdered. Two of the sergeants who used to attend escaped, and got half way to Nynee Tal, but were attacked by the people of Bahary. One of them, who had become very serious, was there murdered; he fell with his hands clasped and calling upon the Lord. The other was left for dead, but managed to crawl to the foot of our hill, and recovered from his wounds. Mr. Raikes, the chief magistrate, Mr. Orr, and Mr. Wyatt, were all murdered, and Dr. Hansbrow, the Governor of the jail, was killed by the convicts, the native jailer helping them. Mr. Laurance, a widower with four children, was made to sit in a chair while his children were executed before his eyes, and then he was killed. Mrs. Aspinall, who lived next to us, with her son and his wife and child were murdered in their garden. It is said the murderers flung the baby, five weeks old, into the air, and cut at it with their swords as it fell. Some of the accounts are too dreadful to repeat. We cannot but hope that many of them were exaggerated. In all they killed forty-seven Christian people, men, women, and children, in Bareilly that day.

As soon as the officers fled, the Sepoys fired their houses, after which they broke open the treasury and took the money; and then, as if possessed with the demon of madness, they went to the *jail*, broke open the gates, and let loose the criminals. These wretches completed what the Sepoys had begun. The homes of the civilians were sacked and burned. All the gentlemen that had not fled, or were overtaken, were either killed or taken prisoners. The Sepoys then proclaimed the Emperor of Delhi; elected as Nawab *Khan Bahadur Khan*, who had held the office of Deputy Judge under our friend Judge Robertson, and who so deceived him, as already noticed. It is understood that the prisoners were all brought before the new Nawab next morning, (Judge Robertson, Dr. Hay, and Mr. Raikes being of the number,) and this wretch deliberately condemned them to death by the law of the Koran: "They were infidels, and they must die!" He ordered them to be publicly hanged in front of the jail.

The rebels went to my house, and expressed great regret at not finding me. They are said to have declared they specially wanted me. They then destroyed our little place of worship, and burned my house with its contents. All was lost, save life and the grace of God; but the sympathy and prayers of our beloved Church were still our own, so the loss was not so great after all.

It would be affectation if I were to profess that I was unmoved at my loss. So far from it, I felt overwhelmed by it. Every thing was so complete and well arranged for my work. But all was destroyed, and some things gone that could never be restored. All my manuscripts; my library, (about one thousand volumes, the collection of my life, and which, perhaps, I loved too well,) so complete in its Methodistic and theological and missionary departments; my globe, maps, microscope; our clothes, furniture, melodeon, buggy, stock of provisions—every thing, gone; and here we were, like shipwrecked mariners, grateful to have escaped with life. But we tried to say, "The Lord gave, and the Lord hath taken away; blessed be the name of the Lord." I had the consolation to know that my goods had been sacrificed for Christ's sake. When we looked around us and saw the anguish that wrung the hearts of the bereaved of our number, we felt that our loss was light, and could be easily borne. So we were "cast down, but not destroyed."

When the Sepoys had thus slaughtered all the Europeans on whom they could lay their hands, they remembered that there were a few native Christians, and they eagerly sought them out, resolved not to leave a single representative of the religion of Jesus in Bareilly when the sun of that day should set. Their full purpose thus became apparent, and God alone could prevent them from consummating it.

We had in all six Christians, of whom two or three were then regarded as converted, the rest were seekers; but all were equally exposed to the dreadful rage which that noon burst so unexpectedly upon them. In the cloud of darkness and terror which settled over them they were at once hidden from my view. Where they were, or whether alive or dead, I could not find out. Those Europeans who escaped and joined us could tell me nothing at all about them, though I anxiously questioned all who might by any possibility know. I also succeeded in bribing two natives, who remained faithful to us and came up with the ladies, to venture down and seek for Joel and the rest, promising a large reward for any intelligence of him or them; but the messengers did not return to us, and we were left to suppose that they—our Christians—were nowhere to be found in or around Bareilly. Of the death of any of them we received no information; so we kept on hoping that heathen rage had confined itself to the Europeans, and that the others, though scattered, were uninjured. How little we knew what they had suffered!

Though at the risk of anticipating events which date further on, I must here give the facts as I was enabled to ascertain them. As soon as any communication was established between Calcutta and the Upper Provinces on the south side of the Ganges—for all north of that river was still held by the Sepoys—I sent off letters to every place to which I thought it likely Joel could have escaped. He also was trying to reach me by letters, but could not. One of my communications at last found him, as I had hoped, in Allahabad, and, in response to my request, he gave me a narrative of what befell him and the rest on that dreadful day. All his statements we afterward confirmed together on the spot in every particular.

Instead of giving the facts myself, I prefer to present his deeply interesting letter, assured that the reader will kindly excuse its occasional imperfect English and Hindustanee idioms, rendering some words in a few places when it is necessary to give his meaning. I had told him that we had heard of the arrival at Calcutta of the first party of our missionaries, and that if he were outside the circle of danger and at Allahabad, and could communicate with Calcutta, to try and have them come where he was, as the seat of the Northwest Government had been fixed at Allahabad, and all was safe there then; also, that I felt assured, as the armies were rapidly breaking up the Sepoy forces, we at Nynee Tal who were still preserved, though besieged, would soon be relieved, and our mission be once more established at Bareilly. I tried to cheer him, and sustain his faith in God. My letter took twelve days to reach him having to go out through the mountains behind us, and then along their crest till it could reach the Ganges, and get beyond the range of the rebels in Rohilcund. In reply he writes:

"ALLAHABAD, *February* 4, 1858.

"MY DEAR SIR,—Your long-expected letter, dated the 18th January, reached me on the 1st instant. Though the interval is very long, still it was a source of very great consolation to me. It has given fresh vigor and courage. I became happy, exceedingly happy, from its perusal. And nothing could exceed my joy then to hear of the safety and welfare of self and Mrs. Butler, and the little bachchas, (children ;) increased more by the joyous news that another precious little darling [our daughter Julia, born after our flight] has been added to the number of the family, for which I must congratulate you. You ask in your letter why I did not write to you? True, I knew you were in Nynee Tal ; but I could see no way of safety for months and months. I could not know whether communication with Nynee Tal was open or not. The whole country was in such a dreadful disorder I was conscious that it would never reach you ; but the moment that I was assured communication was open, and my letter would fall in your hands, I immediately addressed you two letters in succession, but I am sorry to see it did not reach you. According to your request, I sit down with the greatest pleasure to give you an account of how I escaped. It was on the memorable 31st of May, on Sunday, that the mutiny of the Bareilly troops took place. I was busy with prayers with the other Christians after a sermon on 'Fear not, little flock,' etc., and about the middle of the closing prayer I was informed of the outbreak. I instantly closed, and began to look out for the safety of my wife and child. The Chowkeydar (watchman) aided me in getting the Christian women concealed. I then returned to the Bungalow, (my residence.) By this time it was partly looted and in flame. Seeing it on fire, I threw down the keys, thinking no use to keep keys now, [a very innocent and just conclusion of poor Joel's.] Palwansing and Isaac [two of the native Christians] disguised themselves as gardeners. I went to see if the women were safe, and returned, when I saw Tuggu and another man attacking Isaac with a tulwar to rob him. Palwansing signaled me not to come near, as Tuggu had just said they were searching for me to kill me. They went off, and I came forward, and then I saw Maria [our first female member in Bareilly, and a good Christian girl] coming, running through the trees, but before any of us could reach her a Sowar [mounted Sepoy] caught sight of her and turned, and with his tulwar he struck her head off.

"Seeing all was over, Isaac fled toward Budaon. I heard he was killed on the road. How providential that Emma was a brand plucked out from burning, for in the house where she was going afterward to hide herself a good many Europeans were concealed, and not long after the house was burned by the Sowars, when, with a few exceptions—who were afterward killed—all perished. Emma escaped. Your Dhobin (washerwoman) caught her hand as she was entering, and said, 'You must not go in there.' Again, as Emma was sitting with these women, disguised as one of them, she was remarked by a Sepoy to be a Christian woman, [her bright, intelligent face might well betray her,] and here again the Dhobin's intercession saved her. [This faithful creature also buried Maria's body under the rose hedge. I had the gratification afterward of meeting her on the spot, and rewarding her for the humanity she showed our Christian people.] As soon as it was dark I went to the store-room, where I had, on the first alarm, hidden my Bible, and money, and clothes, under the charcoal, but they were all gone; so we started on foot, and, not knowing where to go, directed our steps toward Allahabad. The Chowkeydar came with us. We did not arrive here till after various wanderings and troubles, tasting the bitterness of death as it were at every step—night and day walking—with my wife, who before could not rough it for half a mile, [she was delicate and weak,] doing some twenty-four or twenty-six miles a day, suffering the pangs of hunger, thirst, and fatigue, and pressed with dangers and difficulties; in perils often, Budmashes [thieves and ruffians] scattered every place. I carried the child, but after the first twelve miles Emma gave out, said she could go no farther, so we had to stop and rest her, resuming our walk at three o'clock in the morning, and going on till nine. Fearing the Budmashes, we left the road and took side paths, which brought us to a village. We had nothing to eat since Sunday morning, but could get nothing there except parched gram, (pulse for horses.) Eat a little and pushed on again.

"By this time Emma's poor feet gave out with soreness, so we bound them up with soft rags to make it easier to walk. We reached Mohumdee, which was infested, and were soon surrounded; but the Hindoo Jamedar (police officer) rescued us out of their hands, and asked who we were. I told him, 'Give food and shelter, for we are strangers, and I will tell you who we are, and where going.' He did, and then asked, 'Are you Hindoos or Mohammedans?' I said, 'Neither; we are Christians.' He advised us not to stop there, but to push on at once. We did, and on nearing Shahjehanpore I saw a Hindoo that I knew. Took him aside, and asked him if any Europeans in S. The man said, 'Not one; all killed.' So we turned off and made for Seetapore. Seeing a man watering fields I asked him if any Sahib logs [white gentlemen] at Seetapore. He said he 'had heard that they were all killed or gone.' We entered and passed through, and rested under a tamarind-tree beyond. Two Hindoos came by, and told of their own accord how the Sahibs were killed there, and added, 'We are hunting for a native Christian.' I asked why they should search for him. They replied, 'He has defiled himself by eating with Christians.' I said, 'Nothing that a man eats can defile him.' Then they asked, 'Who are you?' The Chowkeydar was afraid, and tried to put off the question. But I replied, 'I am a Christian.' They were not pleased, but went on. Soon meeting with two other men they pointed back to our party. For fear of mischief we rose and went on our way, and escaped them. My crying toward God was, 'O that my head were waters, and mine eyes fountains of tears, that I might weep day and night for the slain of the people of the Almighty!' At length we reached Lucknow, which had not yet fallen, and there saw Sir Henry Lawrence and other Englishmen. One of them asked me all about Bareilly. After resting we went on toward Allahabad. In two days reached

Cawnpore. Stopped on the east bank of the Ganges to find out what was the state of C. Found it surrounded on all sides by the rebels under Nana Sahib, and the bridge guarded by two cannon; so we kept on the east bank two days' journey more, till we saw a boat, and the man took us over for a rupee.

"Nearing Futtehpore we met crowds of people hurrying away, and asked, 'What is the matter?' They said, 'O the English are coming and sweeping all before them!' They were in great terror, but we rejoiced now, though we did not tell them so. Not fearing the English, we went on through the flying crowd to meet them. Just then came to the Ten Commandments and Mr. Tucker's house at F. [Mr. T. was a noble Christian—a magistrate—who had had the Commandments cut on two large stone slabs in the native language, and set up by the road-side near his gate, that all persons passing by might read them. They were very large and prominent.] I stood near and read them to our party, then went into Mr. T.'s fine house and took possession, for all was empty. Mr. T. was killed the day of the mutiny. Found good mangoes in the garden and eat them. Started next morning. The villages were deserted. In the evening we lay down in a serai all alone, and slept comfortably, knowing the English must be near. Next morning we were rejoiced to see a white man's face—a man with a party repairing the telegraph. We told him all, and he told us about Allahabad, and that Mr. Owen and all were in the fort there.

"We soon met the army; they did us no harm; my health and spirits revived; we slept near them that night. It was either Neil or Havelock. [It was probably General Neil, with the vanguard of Havelock's force.] Reached Allahabad next day, so happy to find my friends again. God had heard and saved us, though we had been robbed of every thing except a single covering for our bodies; yet here we are at last, joined to our people once more. Thanked and praised be God's holy name, who not only supported and gave us strength, but enabled us to endure all the changes of nature, and safely brought us thus far; and now additional joy has been afforded us by the receipt of your letter, to find you all in health and comfort. How I long to see you, and wish I was with you!

"The fatigue and trouble so overtook Emma, that even up to this time she is in very delicate health. [No wonder. It makes me now shudder to imagine what such a gentle and tender creature must have endured in that dreadful walk of three hundred and forty miles, in the raging heat of an India June, without nourishment, and exposed to insult and even death all the time.] The Allahabad Mission is a heap of ruins. Mr. Owen's bungalow was burned to ashes, and all the furniture and books of the mission and the college destroyed; the church sadly mutilated, though, thank God! no serious damage done to it that cannot be restored with a little outlay; the press, too, and every thing connected with it, all ruined. Mr. Munniss and Mr. Owen had both to escape to Calcutta. But Mr. Owen has now returned. You must have heard of the deaths of the Futtyghur missionaries. They were murdered either at Bithoor or at Cawnpore. [And it occurred about the very time that Joel passed in the vicinity of these places on his way down. How little he imagined that those he knew and loved so well were there, within probably a mile of where he passed, enduring the agonies of Christian martyrdom!] All the houses of the native Christians here were burned and destroyed.

"You write wishing Messrs. Pierce and Humphrey, with their wives, to join me; but I think it impossible. The ladies at any rate cannot go up with them, at least for some months hence, and it is not the orders of the Commander-in-Chief that ladies may go to the upper provinces. I have written to Messrs. Pierce and Humphrey to come here and learn something of the language till the time when Bareilly is retaken.

"I am really very much obliged to you for your kind care of me during these troublesome times; but as I am at present working on the railway here, and earn something to support myself and family, I do not see any necessity of your taking any further trouble about me in regard to money, until such time as I shall be with you again. But whenever, if I will require, I will tell you; and, over and above, I think you can hardly spare any thing, yourself being in trouble.

"I am not at all discouraged with this trouble; on the contrary, I hope it has been sanctified to my good. God forbid that I may be discouraged! but may he grant me that grace which may make my hope strong and my faith firm; and would to God that new vigor should be afforded me in the path of duty! My wife joins with me in sending her remembrance and regards to Mrs. Butler, Mr. Gowan, [whom he supposed to be with our party,] and to all others acquainted with me, and in prayers for our speedy restoration in the field of our labor. My mother-in-law and Jonas and wife offered their best regards to you both. Emma says, 'Give my salaam [the prayer for peace and blessing] to my mother;' that is to say, to Mrs. Butler.

"Believe me to be your most obedient servant,

"JOEL T. JANVIER."

I communicated again with Joel, sending money, and requested him to stand ready to release himself from his situation, and join me as soon as I should call him to his higher work. I knew his heart and could rely upon him. General Havelock's progress was necessarily slow, the fall of Delhi was delayed; but the hour of relief, on the south-west of our position, came at length, and I was enabled to reach the plains on the Dehra Doon side, and have him join me once more.

Every thing English in Bareilly—people, houses, furniture—was ruthlessly destroyed, all save the house which the English officers had used as a Freemasons' Lodge. The poor superstitious Sepoys understood that there was something *mysterious* transacted there, and it might not be safe or lucky to interfere with it in any way. So there it stood in its integrity, when we returned to Bareilly, alone and unharmed amid the ruins of the English station.

After their carnival of blood and ruin had been consummated in Bareilly the Sepoys began the work of dividing the plunder, and strange and fantastic were the scenes as they were afterward described to us. The newly-elected Sepoy officers, who were now to fill the places of their superiors, were decked out, according to their new rank, in the clothes and equipments of the murdered officers, strolling about or riding in their carriages, and doing what they could to enforce the same salutes and honors that were formerly paid to the English officers. Their fellows would grin and ridicule their demands, so that the prospects of discipline or subordination were very poor, and from the first intimated that defect which was one of the causes of their failure.

How strange it seems now to remember that, on that very Sabbath-day, and at the very hours when these deeds were done, and hell seemed to run riot in Bareilly, in the city of Boston there was being held one of the most holy and impressive services ever witnessed there. Bromfield-street Methodist Church was crowded that day to witness the consecration of Messrs. Pierce and Humphrey to the missionary work—*Bareilly* being their destination! God never looked down at the same hour upon two greater contrasts than he gazed upon that day and night—the one worthy of heaven and its joy, the other—but we forbear. How would ten minutes' service of the telegraph (had it been then in use as it is to-day) have changed that holy, joyous scene in Bromfield-street into mourning and woe! But the friends dreamed not of our sorrows, and God honored their faith and devotion, notwithstanding our sufferings and the suspension of our work.

This dreadful 31st of May was, with few exceptions, the general day for rising all over the land. The scenes of Bareilly were repeated in all the cities of Rohilcund, Oude, the Doab, and the North-west Provinces. Volumes might be filled with the sad recitals. But we have no heart for their repetition. One alone, till we come to speak of Cawnpore and Lucknow, must suffice; and we give it because it was the station next our own—Shahjehanpore—forty-three miles east of Bareilly. The atrocities committed there were so cruel and complete that no Europeans escaped; so we rely for our account of their sad fate upon the testimony of the natives themselves, as drawn out by subsequent Government inquiry.

With well-dissembled enmity, the Sepoys at Shahjehanpore went through their duties until the morning of the rising. They waited until their officers and their families had gone to church. This was the opportunity which they preferred. They rose *en masse*, and, having armed themselves fully—though those whom they were to overcome were entirely unarmed and defenseless worshipers in the house of God—stealthily proceeded in a body to the church. They must have taken their measures very quietly and quickly, for they entered while the congregation knelt in prayer, without causing the least alarm, and in some instances dealt their deadly blows on the prostrate suppliants before their presence was known or their purpose feared. Young Spens was on his knees in prayer when his shoulder was laid open by the savage lunge of a tulwar wielded by one of the murderous mutineers. The attack being simultaneous, the people were instantly on their feet, struggling in mortal combat with their assailants. The heart-rending scene that ensued I cannot describe. Words seem too feeble to convey its horrors. It is believed that not one of the number of men, women, and children in that sanctuary ultimately escaped.

Particulars have been ascertained concerning the sad fate of twenty-six of their number. These succeeded, by some means, in getting out of the furious fray and reaching the doors of the church, and, befriended by their syces, or coachmen, reached their carriages and drove off, scarcely knowing or caring whither. They only drew up at a place called Mohumdy, after a drive of many miles. Here they were well received by the Theeselder, or local officer, who seemed sincerely disposed to shield and serve them. The strongest defense at his disposal was a mud fort, and there he placed the fugitives, who began to breathe in hope. It was only for a brief interval. A part of the Forty-first Sepoy Cavalry suddenly appeared, and, having discovered the refugees, demanded their surrender. The remonstrances and resistance of the friendly Theeselder were in vain.

On being given up they were put into their own carriages and driven off under the escort of their captors. Before starting, however, the disabled and bandaged condition of young Spens, who was one of the party, excited the notice of one of the troopers, who stepped up and cleft him in pieces, coolly remarking that it was useless taking a wounded man with them to cumber them.

Whether they had any specific intention concerning their captives on starting it is impossible to say; but it is certain that, after proceeding for some time, they halted, as if in accordance with a pre-arranged purpose. Opening the carriages, they ordered the ladies and children to step out. The unhappy husbands and fathers entreated to be taken in their stead. Impatient of the slightest resistance, they dragged the babes and their mothers to the ground, and, with a refinement of cruelty, dismembered and mutilated them in the presence of their powerless protectors. Having finished with them, they fell upon the men and butchered them also, and then drove off with the empty carriages, leaving the mangled bodies dishonored and exposed upon the road, to be devoured by the jackals and birds of prey. Some friendly villagers, however, soon after they had gone, dug a pit near the spot and buried the outraged remains.

A leading American journal very justly remarked at the time: "Horrible are the atrocities which mark the progress of the present rebellion. The North American savage need no longer be considered the monster of human cruelty, as the red man has found his match in the Sepoys, who cut off women's ears, eyes, and noses, destroying them by tortures worthy of the diabolical rage and malignity of Satan himself." Indeed, one may venture to go further, and say that history may be searched in vain to find a parallel to the riot, plunder, and murder of those dreadful days. The number of the slain and mutilated will probably never be known. Inquiry has ascertained, however, that, apart from the relieving army, not less than fifteen hundred Englishmen and Englishwomen must have perished, not half of whom probably found the rest of the grave: their bodies lay upon the waste, or were dragged out of the bazaars, or left amid the wreck of their own homes, to lie neglected and become the food of dogs and jackals, or the foul birds of prey. How sad were the cases of which I had personal knowledge, as well as the histories to which I have listened during the subsequent years, particularly of the trials and tortures to which ladies were subjected! Volumes might be filled with the dreadful details of these shameful atrocities: we can, however, name a few of the sufferers.

Of the Missionaries of the various societies within the circle around our position, the following suffered a cruel death at the hands of the Sepoys in the cities named:

Rev. W. H. and Mrs. Haycock, and Rev. H. and Mrs. Cockey, at Cawnpore, of the English Gospel Propagation Society.

Rev. J. E. and Mrs. Freeman, Rev. D. E. and Mrs. Campbell, Rev. A. O. and Mrs. Johnson, and Rev. R. and Mrs. Macmullin, at Futtyghur, of the American Presbyterian Mission.

Rev. T. Mackay, at Delhi, Baptist Missionary Society.

Rev. A. R. Hubbard and Rev. D. Sandys, at Delhi, English Gospel Propagation Society.

Rev. R. and Mrs. Hunter, at Sealcote, Scotch Kirk.

Rev. J. Maccallum, at Shahjehanpore, Addit. Clergy. Society.

Some of these had children, who suffered with them.

Several Chaplains also were killed: Mr. Jennings in Delhi, Mr. Polehampton in Lucknow, Mr. Moncrieff at Cawnpore, and Mr. Copeland.

The mission property destroyed was estimated at the value of $344,400. Of this heavy loss, by far the greater portion fell upon the English Church Missionary Society, and the American Presbyterian Missions. The former lost $160,000, and the latter about $130,000.

Thus the mission of the Methodist Episcopal Church to India was, in the first year of its establishment, covered with a cloud, and the faith and patience of our Church was severely tested. It became a solemn question, *how* the Church would take this dispensation of Providence. Will she recede at the first difficulty? Will she give way because earth and hell have roused themselves up to resist her? Nay, "Greater is He that is for us than all that can be against us." Besides, our experience is not singular. Many missions that have been eminently successful have had very unpropitious beginnings; and God eminently honored the faith that did not shrink from difficulties. We recollect with what interest the Church of Scotland sent forth her first missionary, Dr. Duff, to lay the foundation of her mission in India. But seldom has a voyage been more protracted or disastrous than Dr. Duff's first voyage to India in 1830. His ship went down off the coast of Africa, and he lost all he possessed in the world, (including a valuable library, too,) except one copy of the word of God, he and his devoted wife barely escaping with their lives. They made their way to the Cape of Good Hope, and sailed again; but, off the Mauritius, came near foundering, and actually were a second time shipwrecked in the Bay of Bengal: so that their disastrous voyage lasted eight months from the time they left England till they reached Calcutta. But what a glorious work of God has sprung from that perilous and untoward commencement! God grant that the Methodist Mission to North India, notwithstanding "the fight of afflictions" in which it was begun, may find its sufferings, and its faith and patience, honored by similar success! And why not? I thank God *we* were not discouraged. Notwithstanding all we had passed through, or might pass through, we lost neither heart nor hope; we still held on to the expectation that India had a bright future before it, and that our mission would live, and "triumph in Christ," among the very people at whose hands we had suffered.

The refugees from Moradabad reached us by the southern pass within a couple of hours of those from Bareilly. We went to meet them; and how hearty was each congratulation upon their escape and safe arrival! Each man, too, added to the force for our defense, and so strengthened *us*. One officer, as he came over the brow of the hill, and caught his first view of Nynee Tal, looked delighted, as he rested his loaded rifle by his side, till a sudden thought flushed his face with anxiety, and, turning to us, he asked, "But are we *safe* here?" We dared not answer; for we had been asking that question of our own fears for many previous hours, as the fearful emergency in its character and extent opened out so seriously before our view.

A wonderful circumstance occurred in connection with the flight of these people from Moradabad, which illustrates the idea so often expressed of that tender mercy which

"Tempers the wind to the shorn lamb."

The English Government requires a constant supply of elephants for carrying forage, drawing and handling cannon and timber, and other heavy work for the army and commissariat. As these huge creatures do not breed in captivity, the required supply can only be kept up by constant additions from the herds of wild elephants which roam the great Terai forest surrounding the Himalaya Mountains. To accomplish this a regular department is organized, which trains the more docile of the female elephants to aid in capturing the wild ones in the Terai, and they lend themselves to the work with a sagacity and a fidelity that is truly wonderful. At the head of this "Elephant Department" was a Major Baugh, whose residence was at Moradabad. On the very morning of the mutiny his lady was confined, and in less than four hours after that event the Sepoys rose. The Major's feelings may be imagined when he rushed into his home and broke the dreadful news to his wife as she lay in her chamber with her baby by her side. The agonized husband looked at them, and was almost speechless with horror in anticipation of the destruction that would be at their door in a few moments. But the heroic lady, notwithstanding her situation, was equal to the emergency. With a word of cheer to the sad husband, she made the astounding proposal to him to bring the buggy at once to the door. It was done. She then told him to take a bed and put it in the buggy, and to lift her up and carry her and her baby out, and lay them on the bed, and try to escape. Then commending themselves to Heaven's help, the husband, having his sword in one hand and the horse's bridle in the other, they commenced the dreadful and uncertain march for the foot of the mountains, fifty miles distant, over a rough road, crossed by numerous rivers, not one of which was then bridged. Twenty miles of the road lay through the malarious Terai; while they were liable at any hour to be overtaken and cut to pieces, yet not daring to go faster than a walk, for the poor lady's life could not bear more than the strain it was at that rate enduring—and all this beneath that blazing sun of May!

I leave it to those who may read these facts to imagine, if they can, what must have been that husband's feelings during those thirty-six hours of sympathy and fear! But the dear lady went through it all, reached the foot of the hills, was carried up the remaining eleven miles in a jampan, and was received and welcomed by us with the tender commiseration and respect that were due to one who had gone through such an experience. We hardly dared to hope that she could really survive it, but thought it must kill her and her babe too. But no! a merciful Providence carried her safely through. Her recovery was rapid, and in three weeks after her escape she made her appearance upon the Mall which runs around the lake, looking, though pale, so cheery and grateful as each gentleman she met lifted his hat in homage to one who had drawn so deeply upon our sympathies, and whose appearance again gave us as much pleasure as if she had been a personal friend or a sister of ours.

Had our enemies only followed us up at once, instead of waiting to burn, and plunder, and dispute about rank and methods of action, they could most certainly have been upon us before we were prepared for resistance. But we made good use of the forty-eight hours which their wrangling allowed; and when they reached the foot of the hills our measures were taken, and we stood ready for them—so far as a handful could be ready for a host of Sepoys and Budmashes. With a good glass, from certain points we could catch a glimpse of their out-lying pickets when they pushed up to Julee

As soon as the last refugee had reached us we held a "council of war," to see what could be done. The first thing was to ascertain our numbers; so we counted heads, and found that we were eighty-seven gentlemen, with one hundred and thirteen ladies and children to protect. By general consent Major Ramsay, the Commissioner, was elected Commandant. We voted ourselves a sort of militia in her Majesty's service, and pledged the Major our full duty and obedience to defend the place to the last extremity. Somehow or other all of us were supplied with arms ; those who had more than enough divided with those who had none. Here was a case where "he who had no sword" would willingly "sell his garment and buy one," for "the days of vengeance" were upon us, and we had a duty to fulfill on behalf of ladies and little ones that admitted of no hesitation, in view of the relentless enemy who now hemmed us in on every side.

Having elected our Commandant and distributed our arms, the worthy Major asked us to stand up in line, that he might address us a few words. Each shouldered his weapon, and the line was formed. The Commandant looked at his little force. He could not help smiling, serious as he and we felt, for a more "awkward squad" than we appeared no commandant ever inspected. Among the eighty-seven, as they then stood, each "a high private," were three generals, grayheaded and bent with years ; a number of colonels, majors, and captains ; some doctors, judges, and magistrates ; a few Indigo planters, merchants, and shopkeepers ; two English chaplains, and myself, the only American in the party—from the man of fourscore down to the boy of seventeen : yet half of the number had probably never fired a shot in anger, if at all, and had to learn every thing in their new profession.

Our commander's speech was a very brief one. Its burden was the duty that we owed to the ladies and children, with the assurance that, far-off and isolated as we were, England would find us out and rescue us if we could only hold on till her forces arrived ; that, whatever came, the last man must fall at his post ere one of those wretches should cross our defenses. Our hearts were sad enough, but we cheered the speech. We were, to a man, willing to fight, and, if necessary, to die to defend the ladies.

I walked home with my musket on my shoulder and my pockets

full of ball cartridges and caps, greatly to my wife's surprise, who met me at the door and declared there must be some mistake: she had "married a Methodist preacher, and not a soldier." But I took that gun as a religious duty, and intended to use it, too, if I had a chance; for surely these were circumstances in which a Christian could pray God to "teach his hands to war and his fingers to fight." Before one of those bloody men below should burst our bounds, or lay a finger on one of the ladies who relied upon our protection, as, under God, their only hope, I should certainly have fired my last charge, and then laid around me with the butt-end, and, having done all, have "died at my post." So would every man of our number.

But the rascals below were not very anxious to give us a chance to show how valiant we were, so we rested on our arms and awaited their pleasure.

The twenty-five faithful Sowars who had stood firm and come up with their officers were quite a help to us; but in spite of what the brave fellows had risked for their fidelity, (for word had reached them that their fellow-Sepoys would kill their children, whom they had to leave behind in Bareilly, if they did not forsake us,) yet we secretly dreaded to trust them fully, so they were placed down the hill a mile or two to guard that pass, and our "munition of rocks" was defended by our own right arms alone. The hill men, called Paharees, being probably aborigines, hate the plains' men, and the dislike is returned with equal cordiality. We made no effort to heal this breach, but rather fomented it. The Commandant hired and trained as many of these Paharees as he could. We had thus done all we could for our own preservation—placed a small force at the bottom of the hill, then posts every mile or two, which could fall back on each other if overpowered. Half-way we had a small cannon planted, the grape of which would mow down any advancing party; then on convenient turns and narrow places great heaps of stone and trees, denuded of their branches, were ready to be rolled down upon any foe that would venture to come up these passes; then the road had been cut so narrow in places that only two men could walk abreast on the verge of the precipice; we had also undermined the road in several places, so that an invading party could be so isolated that they could neither go back nor forward. In addition, we were well armed, and ready, by day or night, when the signal gun was fired, to rush to the top of the pass, and die there sooner than the enemy should force it, or that a single one of those one hundred and thirteen ladies and children should fall into the hands of those vile wretches. We felt assured, as we looked at our work, that a handful could hold the place against multitudes if their ammunition only held out and their provisions lasted; but that was the question just then.

Our congregation was a sad one. With the exception of my wife and another person, every lady of the party wore some badge of mourning, showing that either relatives or near friends had been killed. Of course house and property were utterly destroyed in every case, while the enemies of our Lord and Saviour were raging and blaspheming below, thirsting for our blood, and vowing, by all their gods, that they would soon have it, and thus finish up their fiendish work. In such circumstances what a significance many parts of the word of God had for us! "The denunciatory Psalms," which in a calm and quiet civilization seem sometimes to read harshly, were in our case so apposite and so consistent that we felt their adaptation and propriety against these enemies of God as though they had been actually composed for our special case. How we used to read them with the new light of our position, and how they drew out our confidence in God for the final issue!

Khan Bahadur, the new Nawab of Rohilcund, strengthened his force to hem us in, and issued his list of prices for our heads, beginning with Mr. Alexander, the Commissioner. Five hundred rupees was, if I recollect rightly, the price he put upon my poor head. Every expedient was used to urge his men to storm our position; but their spies (for they had such) considerably cooled their ardor by the representation of our resolution and preparations; so they came to the conclusion that if they could not get up to kill us, they would do the next best thing for them, by starving us out, which would answer about as well. But we as decidedly resolved that we would not be starved, so we set to work to make the best commissariat arrangements of which the case admitted.

There was a very sparse population of the Paharees sprinkled about in the valleys between us and the higher Himalayas, and every thing these people had to spare we bought up ; the lake furnished some fish, and the forest around had game. The latter, however, was not much aid to us, as it was not prudent to waste our ammunition, nor, in view of our signals, was it desirable to have much firing in our neighborhood. We did as well as we could ; but as week after week went over we felt the pressure more sensibly. Money grew scarce, and clothing, shoes, and other necessities, became harder to obtain.

In about two weeks after our flight the terrible jungle fever, which we hoped we had escaped the night when we were detained in the Terai, began to develop itself, (taking about that time to do so,) and soon our little home was a scene of sickness, while help and medicine were so very scarce. Every one of us had to go through it, four out of the five being down with it at the same time. In the midst of this scene of weakness and sorrow our daughter Julia was born. The day she came was the darkest we had ever seen. Illness, tropical rains, want of help, a scarcity of proper nourishment for the poor mother, with the uncertainty as to the moment when we might be assailed, and my liability to have to leave the sick household to go to my post at the pass, all constituted a strain upon the soul of one anxious mortal that I feel thankful does not often fall to the lot of a husband to endure.

But, notwithstanding, the dear babe brought the light with her. A father's heart may be allowed to say that her presence helped to disperse some of the gloom of the dark days that followed, and added a new motive for vigilance and courage. Yes, let the 30th of June stand as "a red-letter day" in the life of one so deeply indebted as I am to the ruling providence of my God! Our "partners in distress" were pleased to designate her "The Mutiny Baby,' and many a kind word and act were lavished upon her.

Of course our mails were cut off—we were completely isolated from all the world. We could stand on our magnificent elevation and look out upon the plains of India, the horizon stretching for a hundred miles from east to west—could trace the courses of the rivers, and see the forests and towns in the dim distance—but could only imagine what was being done down there. The handful of villagers around us told us that we were the last of Christian life left in India; that from where we stood to the sea, nearly a thousand miles on each side, every white man had been murdered, and the last vestige of our religion swept away. We well knew if this were so our fate was but a question of time; yet "against hope" I "believed in hope." I felt that this could not be true, for Jesus Christ was still on the throne which governs this world, and he would not thus allow the clock of progress to be put back for centuries, nor yield to earth or hell the conquests won on the oriental hemisphere.

Our "raging foes" kept up their alarms, but we estimated them at their worth, and stood on our guard day and night with unrelaxed vigilance. How we longed for news! A letter or a newspaper would have been more precious than rubies; but we were destined to know for weary months what "hunger for news" meant. Our food was often scanty; but we would willingly have done without it, even for days, to have received instead a feast of information, more particularly about those whom we left below, and of whose fate we were so uncertain.

We tried hard to establish some means of communication, but they were all failures. The few natives that remained faithful were offered the largest bribes which our means afforded, to go down and bring us news of how matters stood—whether any of our friends survived, and if there was any prospect of relief. Four or five were induced to go, but only one returned, and he was mutilated. The rebels cut off his nose and ears, and the poor man was a frightful spectacle. Government afterward liberally pensioned him. We were indeed "shut up;" life hung in uncertainty, and we "stood in jeopardy every hour." The outside world lost sight of us, and some of our number were published as among the dead.

In the midst of these vicissitudes the question was discussed whether we had not better, for the ladies' sake, try to cross the Himalayas and strike the Brahmapootra behind them, and so make our way by that river to Burmah ; a proposition that would have been madness to have attempted, situated as we were, without resources, and which would have involved our destruction. The fact of the proposition, however, shows the extremity to which we were reduced when intelligent men could seriously propose such a mode of escape.

The English judge at Budaon, near Bareilly, was a pious gentleman of the name of Edwards. Before the rebellion I had gone, at his earnest request, to visit that place and hold divine service with his family on a Sabbath day. Two or three natives had been led to embrace Christianity, one of whom, named Wuzeer Singh, had resigned his position in a Sepoy regiment to join the little band whom Mr. E. cared for. The "mutiny" broke out soon after. Judge Edwards had sent his wife and child to Nynee Tal, but resolved, to use his own words, "to stick to the ship as long as she floated," and he remained, the only European officer in charge of his district, with 800,000 people within its bounds. "I went," he says, "into my room and prayed earnestly that God would protect and guide me, and enable me to do my duty."

At six o'clock on Monday morning the Sepoys broke into open mutiny. . . . Mr. Edwards, revolver in hand, forced his way through the crowd, and approached a "fine, powerful Patan, about fifty years of age," named Moottan Khan, one of the leaders. Mr. E. rode up to him, and putting his hand on his shoulder, said, "Have you a family and little children?" The Patan nodded "Are they not dependent on you for bread?" "Yes," was the answer. "Well, so have I," said Mr. E., "and I am confident you are not the man to take my life, and destroy their means of support." Moottan Khan hesitated a moment, then said, "I will save your life ; follow me ;" and he escorted him out of the city.

Mr. E. reached a place of safety, a village owned by Hurdeo Buksh, a Talookdar, a man of wealth and influence, near Futtyghur, one hundred and forty miles from Nynee Tal. For many months this noble, friendly Hindoo, at great peril, sheltered him, though constantly threatened by the rebels of Futtyghur. Mr. E. after some time succeeded in finding a man who, by the promise of a large reward, was induced to venture to carry a message to Mrs. Edwards, in Nynee Tal.

She, poor lady, was mourning for her husband in the bitterness of uncertainty and woe unspeakable, supposing that, like the rest, he had been murdered.

Judge E. procured a small piece of paper, and wrote on it that he was still alive, and even well, and in a village named ——. Here he wrote the name of the village in Greek, lest the note should be discovered. He then, with a small knife, slit a bamboo walking stick, inserted the tiny missive, and withdrew the knife. The slit closed so completely as to defy the skill of any seeker, though the messenger was often searched by the rebel police, but they never imagined that there was a letter in the walking-stick. The faithful native reached our position after a variety of adventures, and when challenged by our guards, declared he was a friend, and that he had a letter for delivery to Mem Sahib (Lady) Edwards. They conducted him to her. He found her dressed in mourning, supposing herself a widow. He told her his bamboo stick had a letter in it from her husband. He broke it, and there it verily was, in his own handwriting. In addition to expressing her own joy at the discovery, she knew the native mind and character well, and how to impress it, and that it was necessary that her action now should be significant, as she feared her reply might be lost, or would have to be destroyed by the messenger to save his life, and she must do something which would show him the joy which she felt ; so, telling him to wait, she retired, and soon came back again, and stood before him arrayed from head to foot in *white clothing*. He understood her perfectly, and started back by night on his dangerous journey to Judge Edwards.

"Did you see the Mem Sahib?"

"Yes, Sahib," said the good fellow, "I saw herself in person."

"Well, and how did she look, and what had she to say to you?"

In his estimation, how she looked, and what she said, were all summed up in one fact.

"Sahib, when I gave her your chittee (letter) she was clothed in black, but when she read the chittee she immediately went into another room, and soon came back to me dressed all in *white.*"

The affectionate wife and husband fully comprehended each other's feelings in that action, and we at Nynee Tal rejoiced with her that day that so providentially gave her "the oil of joy for mourning and the *garment of praise* for the spirit of heaviness." It was six months and more before they were able to meet, but they could henceforward live in the hope of being again united in life and love together. There was one less on our mall from that day forward who wore mourning.

Coming down the hill from our Thursday afternoon prayer-meeting one day, a military officer who had been present sought the opportunity of a private interview, and with much feeling he said to me:

"O, sir, permit me to thank you from my heart for the earnest prayers which you put up to God this afternoon for the victory of my country's arms!"

I looked at the man and smiled; asked him if we were not in "the same boat" just then, or whether he thought it likely that those wretches down there would pay more respect to my Stars and Stripes than to his English ensign?

So we lived, and watched, and prayed. Meanwhile the terrible news of the Sepoy Rebellion had reached the shores of Europe and America. England was nerving her energies for our relief. Troops and munitions of war were being prepared as fast as possible. A General, supposed equal to the emergency, was found in Sir Colin Campbell, for two Commanders-in-Chief had already fallen, (Generals Anson and Barnard,) and the little English army in India was without a head. The Queen telegraphed to Sir Colin, after his acceptance of the position, requesting to be informed *when* he could be ready to leave England for the East? His prompt and Spartan reply was telegraphed back, "To-morrow!" The old chief's promptitude reminds one of another "to-morrow" in India's history. At the battle-field of Bidera, when Lord Clive, who founded the British Empire in the East, was Governor-General, Forde, who commanded, applied for written authority to begin the attack. His note reached Clive as he was playing cards with his company, and without quitting his seat, he took a pencil and wrote—

"DEAR FORDE: Fight them immediately, and I will send you the order in council to-morrow!"

Sir Colin, of course, outran his army, for they could not, like him, start "to-morrow." But a merciful Providence had provided a vanguard of help in the army from Persia, (with which peace had just been concluded,) on their return to India. With this little force was that great and good man, General Havelock, whose promptitude and wonderful valor did so much to turn the dreadful tide, and rescue the besieged long months ere Sir Colin Campbel or his troops could reach India. General Havelock, returning victorious from Persia, landed at Bombay with his Highlanders on the very day before the massacre at Bareilly. Unable to cross the country, he went around by sea to Calcutta as rapidly as possible, reaching there June 17, having been delayed on the way by the total shipwreck of the vessel which carried him. His troops followed, and all that could be done to prepare for pushing up the country was accomplished by this indefatigable man, whom God had brought so opportunely to our aid.

Not a day too soon did his succor come. Up to that hour the Sepoys had it all their own way; one post after another had fallen before them; they were gaining ground every week, and the horrors of the situation for the English were deepening daily. Sepoy success was followed by more desperate resolutions and more terrible measures, falsehood and blasphemy being added in any quantity for their purpose. The measures and spirit of these men may be judged from a sample of their public proclamations, issued from Delhi and Cawnpore to the whole Sepoy army, and the officials and people.

The first proclamation was issued in the name of the Emperor's army defending Delhi, which the little English army was then trying to besiege; and the Mogul Court desired to draw the whole Sepoy force in that direction to annihilate them. The glaring falsehoods in the following proclamation are manifest enough:

"*To all Hindoos and Mussulmans, Citizens and Servants of Hindustan, the Officers of the Army now at Delhi send greeting:*

"It is well known that in these days all the English have entertained these evil designs—first to destroy the religion of the whole Hindustanee army, and then to make the people Christians by compulsion. Therefore we, solely on account of our religion, have combined with the people, and have not spared alive one infidel, and have re-established the Delhi dynasty on these terms, and thus act in obedience to orders, and receive double pay. Hundreds of guns and a large amount of treasure have fallen into our hands; therefore it is fitting that whoever of the soldiers and the people dislike turning Christians should unite with one heart and act courageously, not leaving the seed of these infidels remaining. Whoever shall in these times exhibit cowardice or credulity by believing the promises of those impostors, the English, shall very shortly be put to shame for such a deed; and, rubbing the hands of sorrow, shall receive for their fidelity the reward the ruler of Lucknow got. It is further necessary that all Hindoos and Mussulmans unite in this struggle, and that all, so far as it is possible, copy this proclamation, and dispatch it every-where, so that all true Hindoos and Mussulmans may be alive and watchful, and fix it in some conspicuous place, (but prudently, to avoid detection,) and strike a blow with a sword before giving circulation to it. The first pay of the soldiers at Delhi will be thirty rupees per month for a trooper, and ten rupees for a footman, [a large advance on the English allowance.] Nearly one hundred thousand men are ready; and there are thirteen flags of the English regiments, and about fourteen standards from different parts, now raised aloft for our religion, for God, and the conqueror; and it is the intention of Cawnpore to root out the seed of the devil. This is what we of the army here wish."

But this was mildness compared to the following blasphemous proclamation next issued from Cawnpore by the Nana Sahib:

"As by the kindness of God, and the good fortune of the Emperor, all the Christians who were at Delhi, Poonah, Sattara, and other places, and even those five thousand European soldiers who went in disguise into the former city and were discovered, are destroyed and sent to hell by the pious and sagacious troops who are firm to their religion; and as they have all been conquered by the present Government; and as no trace of them is left in these places—it is the duty of all the subjects and servants of the Government to rejoice at the delightful intelligence, and carry on their respective work with comfort and ease.

"As by the bounty of the glorious Almighty and the enemy-destroying fortune of the Emperor, the yellow-faced and narrow-minded people have been sent to hell, and Cawnpore has been conquered, it is necessary that all the subjects, and land-owners, and Government servants should be as obedient to the present Government as they have been to the former one; that it is the incumbent duty of all the peasants and landed proprietors of every district to rejoice at the thought that the Christians have been sent to hell, and both the Hindoo and Mohammedan religions have been confirmed; and that they should as usual be obedient to the authorities of the Government, and never suffer any complaint against themselves to reach to the ears of the higher authority."

But even this is exceeded by the outrageous falsehoods of the proclamation with which he further imposed upon their credulity, and tried to rouse them to greater efforts. It finished up with what he deemed to be a suitable quotation from one of the Persian poets, and ran thus:

THE PROCLAMATION OF THE NANA SAHIB.

"A traveler just arrived at Cawnpore from Allahabad states that just before the cartridges were distributed, a Council (of the Governor-General at Calcutta) was held for the purpose of taking away the religion and rights of the people of Hindustan. The Members of Council came to the conclusion that, as the matter was one affecting religion, seven or eight thousand Europeans would be required, and it would cost the lives of fifty thousand Hindoos, but at this price the natives of Hindustan would become Christians. The matter was therefore represented in a dispatch to Queen Victoria, who gave her consent. A second Council was then held, at which the English merchants were present. It was then resolved to ask for the assistance of a body of European troops, equal in number to the native army, so as to insure success. When the dispatch containing this application was read in England, thirty-five thousand Europeans were very rapidly embarked on ships, and started for Hindustan. Then the English in Calcutta issued the order for the distribution of the cartridges, the object of which was to make Hindustan Christian. The cartridges were smeared with hog and cow's fat. One man who let out the secret was hung, and one imprisoned.

"Meantime the embassador of the Sultan of Roum (Turkey) in London sent word to his sovereign that thirty-five thousand Europeans had been dispatched to Hindustan to make all the natives Christians. The Sultan (may Allah perpetuate his kingdom!) issued a firman to the Pasha of Egypt, the contents of which are as follows: 'You are conspiring with Queen Victoria. If you are guilty of neglect in this matter, what kind of face will you be able to show to God?'

"When this firman of the Sultan of Roum reached the Pasha of Egypt, the Lord of Egypt assembled his army in the city of Alexandria, which is on the road to India, before the Europeans arrived. As soon as the European troops arrived the troops of the Pasha of Egypt began to fire into them with guns on all sides, and sunk all their ships, so that not even a single European escaped. The English in Calcutta, after issuing orders for biting the cartridges, and when these disturbances had reached their height, were looking for the assistance of the army from London. But the Almighty, by the exercise of his power, made an end of them at the very outset. When intelligence of the destruction of the army from London arrived, the Governor-General was much grieved and distressed, and beat his head.

> "'At eventide he intended murder and plunder;
> At noon neither had his body a head nor his head a cover.
> In one revolution of the blue heavens
> Neither Nadir remained, nor a follower of Nadir.'

"Done by the order of his Grace the Peishwa, 1273 of the Hegira."

Of course every word of this was believed by the Sepoys, for they not only had the proclamations of their Emperor and the Peishwa, but their Fakirs stood sponsors to the hideous falsehoods.

How appropriate is all this to the spirit of the Moslem creed—a Government communicating to its subjects "the delightful intelligence," not that its enemies were defeated or slain, but that they were damned—"sent to hell!" Worthy indeed to be the successors of Tamerlane, who, after proving his claim to the title of "the scourge of God," and marking his long track with massacre and desolation, coolly and complacently wrote with his own hand in his memoir that he felt it to be "a pious duty to assist God in filling hell chock-full of men and genii."

When, in 1856, Sir Culling Eardly, the President of the Evangelical Alliance, wrote to Dr. Duff, of Calcutta, to ascertain the real sentiment of Mohammedans in India on a question in which the British people felt interested, (as their Government were then pressing certain reforms on the Sultan of Turkey, involving the principles of religious liberty for his subjects,) the world were somewhat surprised at Dr. Duff's reply. His inquiries led him to the conviction that Mohammedanism (like Popery) is *unchangeable;* that, where it has the power, it would not only enforce its claims and creed, but would do so at the sword's point. Individual Mohammedans may, like individual Romanists, be and are exceptions to this statement, and better than their training; but I speak of the system and of the general action—and here are its terrible illustrations in the hour of its opportunity.

Our fate evidently hung upon that of Delhi. If that city fell, we should probably be saved; if not, we must expect the worst, and that soon. But what could less than seven thousand soldiers and a few Sikh and Ghoorka allies do, and that in the open air and in the hottest season of the India year, against a strongly-fortified city, behind whose walls from forty to sixty thousand Sepoys fought! The Commander-in-chief of the Sepoys was Bukt Khan, an acquaintance of my own, for he was from Bareilly, and was Subadar of Artillery under our friend Major Kirby. When I have sat with the Major in the cool of the evening, and seen this sleek Sepoy come in, with such profound courtesy to us both, to deliver his daily report, how little I could have imagined the part he would yet, and so soon, play behind the walls of Delhi, with the Major's coat and cocked hat upon him, and his sword by his side!

Even though that handful of Englishmen could not take the city till they obtained more assistance, it was of immense benefit to us and to India that they held so many Sepoys fast there. The rebels came out in force on the 23d of June, and fought for thirteen hours. Their "astrologers" had declared that "unless they should beat the English army *on that day*" (the anniversary and centenary of the battle of Plassey, the most important action of the English in India) "the British would hold the country *forever*." Hence the force and numbers with which they attacked, and the perseverance with which they kept up the contest. They were repulsed, however, leaving, as usual, the English masters of the field. They were much discouraged at their failure. Their loss on that day was, after all, but small—not over 500; their mode of fighting accounts for this. When they can choose their own ground and method they are very averse to any thing like "close quarters," and much like the long-shot mode of warfare. This, and lurking under the shelter of the garden walls that surround Delhi, was the leading reason why the English could not manage them. Had they come out and fought in the open field, the General would gladly have met them, even with his so much smaller force, and a single day would probably have decided the whole contest. Besides, they found it made a great difference to them whether they were led by English officers or by officers of their own race.

Our provisions were now becoming more and more scarce and dear. Instead of one hundred eggs for sixty-two and a half cents, as it used to be, we had now to pay five cents for a single egg, and all other things rose in value about in the same proportion. Just in our extremity, and quite unexpectedly to us, the Nawab of Rampore, a territory in the plains on the south of our position, sent up a confidential messenger to inquire what he could do for us? This was a great surprise, as he was a Mohammedan and governed a Mohammedan State, and we supposed that he would have gone with the Delhi conspirators. But, in the hour of decision, he remembered that he owed his throne to the justice of the English Government, which refused to carry out the will of the former sovereign of Rampore, one of whose wives induced him to arrange so as to cut off the rightful heir in favor of her little son. The English declined to commit this wrong, but, instead, confirmed the present Nawab; and now, when he was appealed to by the Delhi faction to join them, he declared that, come what might, he would never draw his sword against a people whose justice had defended his rights. He quietly withstood all their persuasions and threats, even at personal hazard, and was faithfully sustained in his resolution by his Minister and the Commander-in-chief of his little army—two men whom I had afterward the satisfaction of seeing publicly rewarded for their fidelity.

This was a great providence for us. Had the Nawab proved hostile, especially as our south pass touched his territory, our position would have been probably untenable for a single week. But he quietly covered our danger on that side, and left our defenders more free to watch our Bareilly foes on the east pass. What he did in our favor, however, he had to do quietly, so as not to rouse the fanaticism of his own population, or the hostility of Khan Bahadur Khan.

On ascertaining our extremity he sent us rice, sugar, flour, etc., with some medicine and money—what he could spare and safely remit to us. We were certainly very much obliged to "his Highness" for these unlooked-for succors. But even his messengers could not restrain their bigotry: they duly informed our few Ghoorkas (hill soldiers) that "the 'King of Rohilcund' had raised an army of twenty thousand, and was casting cannon, etc.; also, that the Emperor of Delhi had taken the Fort of Calcutta, and his victorious armies were spreading all over the country!" So that even this help brought its own danger with it, and increased our anxiety.

The road to the Punjab through Kurnal was most providentially kept open. The Punjab was the only source from which a man, or a barrel of flour, or a case of medicine, could reach the English army before Delhi. Had that road been closed upon them, their condition must soon have become desperate. But the circumstances that retained that key of their position in friendly hands was as providential as the good will of the Rampore Nawab toward us at Nynee Tal. Mr. Le Bas, the Judge of Delhi, owed his life on the day of the slaughter to the speed of his horse. He reached Kurnal, about forty miles to the north-west, and sought an interview with the Nawab. It was the hour of England's deepest humiliation, and Le Bas trembled for the loyalty of the Nawab. But early the following morning he came to Mr. Le Bas and said: "I have spent a sleepless night in meditating on the state of affairs. I have decided to throw in my lot with yours. My sword, my purse, and my followers are at your disposal."

Faithfully did the brave Nawab redeem his promise, and at the head of his little force he saved many a European life, several ladies among them, and kept the road to the Punjab open till Delhi fell, and the English Empire was restored.

It is also a pleasure to record another instance of wonderful humanity from a very unexpected quarter. In the month of July a Fakir named Himam Bhartee found his way to Meerut, and presented himself before Mr. Greathead, the Commissioner, with a little European baby in his arms, which he had found deserted and alone near the Jumna River. He had taken care of it, and even defended its life at great risk to himself, and delivered it up safe and sound. Mr. Greathead was delighted, and pressed the Fakir to receive a reward; but he would accept none, and only expressed a desire that a Well might be made to bear his name and commemorate the act. The Commissioner promised it should be done, and the Fakir departed well pleased. Let the name of this humane creature live here, and my readers remember Himam Bhartee, of Dhunoura. The parents of the little one were never discovered; but good Samaritans were found to adopt and love it.

The sad monotony of our life was suddenly disturbed early on Sunday morning, August 4th, by an imperative message from our Commander, ordering all the ladies and children, with three or four gentlemen in charge of them, away at once that day from Nynee Tal to Almorah, thirty miles farther into the mountains. Information that he had received required this movement as a matter of precaution to them, while it would leave their husbands more free and unshackled to meet the emergencies that were expected to arise.

Several reasons had concurred to lead to this measure. First of all, our provisions were becoming exhausted, and our supplies from below being (except from the Rampore side) cut off, the Commissioner felt himself quite puzzled to sustain our market.

In the next place, the delay of the fall of Delhi was rendering our enemies more rampant, in the expectation that they would soon weary out and destroy the little English army (now reduced, besides Ghoorkas and Sikhs, to twenty-five hundred European bayonets) before its walls; and then they hoped to make short work in other parts of the country.

Another reason was, that our friend the Nawab of Rampore was considered to be exposed to peculiar danger at the approaching Eyde, (an annual festival of the Mohammedans, during which they are peculiarly excitable.) The Nawab's refusal to join the Bareilly rebels, and his kindness in sending us supplies and money, had rendered him very unpopular with the Mohammedan fanatics among his people, and it was feared that, during the Eyde, he might be assassinated, in which case his successor would probably have been elected with the express understanding that he should do what he could to aid the rebel interests, and, likely, to begin by an attempt to cut us off, as we were close at hand.

The next and chief reason for our removal was, that Khan Bahadar Khan, the new "King of Rohilcund," had actually dispatched an increased force from Bareilly to Nynee Tal, in order to destroy us; and the Commissioner had certain information on Saturday morning that they had not only started, but were encamped at Bahari, mid-way between Nynee Tal and Bareilly. Still, even this alone would not have caused us to leave, for "his army" were not likely to look our three hundred Ghoorka troops in the face, much less to have gone near the cannon and the body of English gentlemen with which we had fortified the head of the pass. But our anxiety was, that inasmuch as preparation to meet them involved the withdrawal of all the troops and the gentlemen from Nynee Tal, this would necessarily leave our ladies and children unprotected against any attempt that such an hour of opportunity would present to the Mohammedans in the Nynee Tal Bazaar. Were they to rise while we were below, they might slaughter every soul of them in a single hour, and the more easily, should the rebels below agree, as they likely would, to attack us at both passes at once, so as to divide our little force.

The distance from Nynee Tal to Almorah is thirty miles over the mountains, by a path which varies from four to six feet in width. It runs in some places on the very verge of precipices that are as nearly perpendicular as possible, while the depths below are sometimes frightful to look at. It requires great steadiness and care, from the rough and narrow path to be traversed, to go without danger, while in some places a single false step, especially at night, is instant destruction.

Ladies are carried in a little chair-like vehicle by four men, with four to relieve. Gentlemen generally ride one of the hill ponies, which are very sure-footed. The journey occupies three days, ten miles being as much as can be comfortably accomplished in one day.

When our sudden order of departure came I arranged everything for the ladies intrusted to my charge, and sent them on, expecting to follow and overtake them in a short time; but such was the demand, I could not obtain coolies enough to take their luggage (including food and bedding, which travelers must always carry with them) till four o'clock in the afternoon. I then started, but the lateness of the hour entailed on me a great deal of toil and suffering. Indeed, I never had such a journey in all my life as that was. For an hour or two I made my way tolerably well. The sunset was brilliant, and among other objects of interest were immense lizards (some of them full fourteen inches long) which were darting across my path and over the verges. My way lay over and around a succession of mountains—so it was constantly up and down—the valleys between varying from a quarter of a mile to a mile in width. The little torrents had torn the path here and there, and in some places it was so rocky and rough that it was very hard work to pick one's way over it. Going down the hill was, from the precipitous and stony condition of the narrow path, something like going down an irregular flight of stairs a mile or more in length.

The daylight began to decline, and my little pony showed symptoms of unsteadiness. The heavy rains had softened the edge of the path, and rendered it liable to give way under very moderate pressure, so that caution was doubly necessary. At one place that looked doubtful I dismounted, and had not gone many yards when one of the hind feet of the pony sank, which caused him to stagger, and in a moment he went hastily over the precipice. The jerk on the reins caused one of the bit buckles to give way, which was a great mercy, as it gave me an instant in which to turn round and lay some pressure on the reins as they flew through my hand,

and I was thus enabled in some degree to arrest his downward progress before he went too far to be recovered.

There he clung, the poor brute, with merely his nose above the edge of the precipice, and he eagerly holding on to the bank like a man standing on a ladder. Beneath him sloped down the decliv-ity for several hundred feet, till the mist terminated the view; what was beyond that limit I could only infer by the roar of the river beneath, which sounded very deep indeed, so that had the poor fellow missed his hold, or taken one roll, his doom was cer-tain. In an emergency how rapidly one can think! There was no help within many miles, and a very few minutes would decide his fate. I had sold his worthy predecessor, when rather hard pressed for cash, and had paid only forty dollars for him; but he looked very valuable as he hung on that precipice, and I imagined to myself what could I do without him there in that wilderness, with such a journey before me, and I alone; the night, too, falling fast. I felt for the poor creature, and I pitied myself, for I could ill afford to lose him, particularly there and then. To get him straight up would have required twenty men's strength. No time was to be lost. I feared every moment that he would begin to struggle, and then I must be prepared to know how long I dare hold on, and what instant I must let him go, lest he should jerk me over along with himself, and both be lost. A thought struck me. I got his head round on one side; he seemed to understand my object, and slightly shifted one foot, while I held him as fast as I dared by the rein. He then dug the other foot into the ground, and soon I had the gratification of having him right across the hill, and then by a little maneuvering I moved him, step by step, till I got him up. He was not much hurt, and after a little while I mounted, but had not proceeded half a mile when he trod on another soft edge. I felt him stagger, and had just time to free my right foot from the stirrup, and pitch off into the mud of the road, as he went over the bank. There I hung, half-way on the path, my legs dangling over the margin. Having scrambled up, I saw that he had dropped down about twelve feet, on a heap of sharp stones, and on going down to him I found his hind shoes torn off, and he lamed and much injured. I managed to get him up again to the path ; but, alas ! he was now worse than no horse at all. Seven long miles of that narrow and dangerous road lay between me and the dak Bungalow, and he could not walk a step only as I dragged him along. The night soon fled, and he failed fast. Never in all my life have I felt any thing so lonely as was that weary walk through those dark woods and over those high mountains. The keen remembrance of it will go with me to the grave. The poor animal had some of the stumps of the nails in his hoofs, which every step seemed to drive higher as he trod on the stony path, until at last it was real misery to look at him as he slowly and painfully limped along. What to do I could not tell ; he was getting worse every step. To abandon him seemed cruel, and yet to stay with him, without even the means of lighting a fire, was to expose myself to equal danger. I had no alternative but to bring him along as well as I could ; so I pulled him on over the rocks and streams, and up the hills, till I became utterly spent. The solitude around was something dreadful — no sound save the occasional yells of the wild animals—and I was obliged to keep a sharp look-out lest we should be pounced upon by a tiger. I had my gun on my shoulder, but the only charge I had with me was in it, so that one shot was my whole dependence in that line. Another element of anxiety was the fact that at the cross paths there were no sign-boards, and painful indeed was the suspense sometimes felt as to which road to take, or whether I was on the right path at all. Many an earnest prayer I put up to God at some of these doubtful points that He would in mercy guide me aright. The heat in the woods and valleys was great, and this, added to my exertions, caused so much perspiration that it fast exhausted my remaining strength, till at last I had to sit down and calculate what was to be done. I was also faint from hunger, having only had a light and very early breakfast, and neither dinner nor supper. My tongue swelled, and seemed to fill my mouth. As I sat there and thought of all I had given up for India, perhaps it was pardonable that, for a moment, I indulged a longing for the peace and privileges of the happy land I had left; but it was only for a moment, and all was right again. I felt I was just where I would like best to be, though for the present these trials seemed hard to bear. It was an hour of unusual experience, and the depression was correspondent to it. The hunger, the darkness, the surrounding danger, the heat and laborious exertion, with the uncertainty of my whereabouts, and the probable distance of any help, all together constituted such a drain on my strength, and hope, and fortitude, as I never before endured. To complete my calamities, both my boots had given way on the stony paths, and my feet were wet as well as sore.

As I was looking round for a tree in which I might spend the night, out of the reach of the animals, (for I felt as if I could go no farther,) I recollected Brother Stevens and "Old Jeddy," and the "rest at home" that cheered him on that eventful night in the wilderness. I lifted up my heart to God and asked for strength for body and for soul; and there, in the midst of my gloom and solitude, I was cheered by the presence of my heavenly Father. A train of delightful reflections set in. I thought of my own deep indebtedness to the Divine mercy; I thought of our Church, and the glorious work that God had spread before her; and I thought of my own mission, and of that future day when it would spread among these degraded multitudes, and when they would love the Redeemer as I loved him then! How these thoughts and feelings braced up my soul for life and duty! Exhaustion was forgotten, and my full heart gushed out in strong affection toward the blessed Jesus, until I felt ready to bear any thing for his dear sake. I felt it easy to come to the conclusion that my state, with all its weariness, was one that I would not exchange with any of the votaries of this world's pleasure or ease. I rose to my feet, and these words came from the depths of my heart, and went up on the night air to heaven:

"In a dry land, behold I place
My whole desire on thee, O Lord;
And more I joy to gain thy grace
Than all earth's treasures can afford."

Shortly after, when climbing round the spur of one of the mountains, the dense clouds separated and exposed to view right before me the "Snowy Range" towering up so majestically to the skies! The full moon was shining upon it, and imparting to it that purple tint which makes it look so lovely and so unearthly! It was the grandest natural sight I ever beheld, and to me was brilliantly suggestive of that "land of rest," where the sun shall no more go down, neither shall the moon withdraw itself; but the Lord shall be unto us an everlasting light, and the days of our mourning shall be ended!

I resumed my weary way, our pace being now about one mile an hour, and at nearly eleven o'clock came to the summit of a high mountain, where there seemed to be two paths, which increased my perplexity; but on looking off to the right I could make out that the hills rounded into a crescent, on the far point of which I discovered a light, which I knew must be from the window of the dak Bungalow! After all my anxiety I had been guided in safety by a way I knew not. On reaching the Bungalow, I found that neither bed nor food was to be had. However, I was too tired to care much for food, so the privation was little felt. I could have relished a comfortable bed had it been available, but the floor and shelter of a roof were mercies. The ladies had safely and duly arrived, and were stretched, some on the ground and others on charpoys, and thus the night wore over.

Next morning there was no sign of the coolies, so we resumed our march, my poor horse being obliged to remain where he was, and by evening we were overtaken at the next Bungalow by our bedding and food, both of which were very welcome indeed. We arrived at Almorah next day, tired enough, and were accommodated with a couple of rooms in a little house near the fort. Some of our friends would smile could they see the humble accommodations, for which we felt no small amount of gratitude. The floor was of clay; we had two camp tables, three chairs, and two charpoys—that was the extent of our furniture! But "necessity is the mother of invention," and we soon found out that a trunk lid could be made into a table, and that a child can sleep as well in a basket or in an old box as on a mahogany bedstead. So our "picnic" fashion of life in Almorah gave us little concern, any inconveniences being amply balanced by the reflection that thirty miles more of mountains lay between our precious charge and danger.

Our worthy Commissioner, after a time, unable to endure longer this "hunger for news" that was consuming us, organized a post department of his own, and by relays of Paharees, stretching along the crest of the Himalayas, for what is usually seventeen days' journey to Mussoorie, above Dehra Doon, managed to reach on to beyond the immediate circle of Sepoy power and establish communication with the Europeans there, who were able to correspond with the Punjab, and obtain such news as was available from that quarter.

Information of our whereabouts and safety now got abroad, and worked its way around by the sea-coast to Calcutta. The 13th of August was *a joyful day.* To our delight and astonishment, the Paharee postman that morning brought us three numbers of the *Christian Advocate*, and three of *Zion's Herald*, for the month of April! The postmaster at Bombay had found us out, and commenced sending us a mail whenever he had the chance, *via* Kurrachee, Lahore, and Mussoorie. So we now began to receive papers and letters with more or less regularity. Only those who have been, as we were, shut up for three months and a half without a letter or a paper or a word from home, can imagine the joy with which we grasped the precious documents, and sat down to devour their contents. It was almost like life from the dead!

But, while grateful for news at last, what horrible accounts of massacre and pillage poured in upon us—frightful details of what had occurred! How truly we realized, as we heard or read them, the reality of the lines—

> "My ear is pained,
> My soul is sick, with every day's report
> Of wrong and outrage."

At our family altar, and in our closet, our cry was, "O Lord, how long" Nor was the suffering and wretchedness limited to the

Europeans. The feuds between the Hindoos and Mohammedans were revived, and conflicts between them increased in bitterness and cruelty, until the country became one scene of anarchy. Trade, agriculture, and industry in general were all but suspended; any one that had a rupee to lose lost it; riot and bloodshed became the order of the day, while rapine and murder were openly carried on by the Goojurs, a Gipsy-like class of vagabonds, whom the miserable Mohammedan Government was unable to put down.

Short as our time was in Bareilly, I have the satisfaction of knowing that our labors were not altogether fruitless. Several of the Europeans who attended our little English service had spoken in grateful terms of the benefits received under the preaching. Among these was the excellent Dr. Bowhill, Surgeon of the Sixty-eighth Native Infantry. This gentleman had a very narrow escape for his life on the day of the massacre. His horse carried him only about twenty miles, and then fell dead lame. The remainder of the seventy-four miles he had to walk (with a very occasional lift on the horses of others of the party) under a broiling sun. I went to meet and congratulate him on his escape. We kneeled down together, and never shall I forget his emotions while I offered up to the service of the Holy Trinity the life that had been so mercifully preserved! It was a privilege to have made the friendship of such a man; and not only so, but also to have had that friendship cemented by the holiest ties. His sense of duty led him, as soon as the Commissioner arranged the letter post along the Himalayas, to venture to cross to Mussoorie and thence to Kurnal, and then join any passing column, so as to reach the little English army before Delhi, where his professional services were so much required. The brave man made his perilous way in safety, and we heard occasionally from him. In reply to a letter which I had written, expressing my gratitude for great professional kindness, especially at Nynee Tal, and adding a word or two to "strengthen his hands in God," he says: "I do not feel that I am in any way entitled to the thanks you give for my attendance on your family. Inasmuch as the soul is more worthy than the body, so much the more are my thanks due to you; for, under Providence, I have to thank you for teaching me to love God. I feared him before I knew you, and that fear restrained me. Now I feel that, through your means, I love my Saviour and Redeemer, and try to obey because I love him." What must have been then the condition of things before Delhi may be understood by the Doctor's statement, when he adds in this communication, that "Such is the amount of sickness which prevails, that twenty-five hundred of our men are in hospital, two hundred and forty-one of whom entered in one day. In my own regiment of five hundred men two hundred and forty-seven are lying sick! I fear that if the assault does not take place *soon* we shall not have men enough in health to attempt it. May God save us from a reverse before Delhi! The effect of a repulse here might be ruinous throughout the whole country." How earnestly we prayed for the brave men in that little army who were thus suffering and fighting for us there!

Just then we had a little battle of our own to go through. On the Thursday after the receipt of this letter from Delhi, Khan Bahadur ordered his forces to assault our position. They moved up nearer to our defenses and encamped for the night, perhaps not realizing, being all "plains men," how chilly they would feel the next morning in the cold hill air. Our Commandant saw his advantage, and very early next morning dropped down into the little valley where they were encamped, with thirty gentlemen and the twenty-five faithful Sowars, making a little body of cavalry; these, with the two hundred and fifty of our Ghoorka (hill) troops, came quietly upon them before they had unrolled themselves out of their blankets, and a fearful carnage ensued. In an hour all was over. The Sepoys fled in every direction, leaving one hundred and fourteen of their number dead, besides what wounded they managed to carry off.

After counting the enemy's dead, our men turned to ascertain their own loss, and, to their surprise and gratitude, found that they had only one man—a Sowar (native horseman)—killed, and two Ghoorkas wounded. One officer, Captain Gibbency, was slightly touched by a pistol ball, and this was all. The effect of this contest was of great importance. It struck some terror into the Sepoy mind, and they refused ever after to come up into our glens again; it raised our spirits, and had an immense effect upon the hill people, who of course flattered themselves that the victory was due to their own prowess. It also deepened their hatred of the Mohammedan party; while below, the Hindoo villagers took courage to help the Commandant, and actually captured nine rebels, stragglers who had turned to the work of plundering the villagers and abusing their women. They were brought up to Nynee Tal, tried, and executed at once. I was informed that they met their doom with the indifference that characterizes Mohammedan fatalists.

After this event some of the villagers and Hindoo Zemindars (landholders) of the plains around our hills sent up deputations to our Commandant, requesting him to assist them against the Mohammedans, and offering to pay their jumma (revenue) to him if he would only sustain them (as they thought him now able to do) against the rebel Government. But Major Ramsay was too prudent to go beyond his safe line, especially as he well knew he was still closely watched by a powerful and wily foe, and must risk nothing while he had ladies to protect. That foe, however, was beginning to feel certain qualms of anxiety, for already Havelock's name and the story of his victories were flying over the land, and they felt that he, or some other English General, might ere long give them a better opportunity to prove their courage than what they had when they so leisurely and safely cut down and butchered unarmed men and defenseless women and children.

It was "a day of rebuke and blasphemy," but I still believed that our redemption was drawing nigh, and that all would be overruled for good. How grateful I feel that my letter to the Corresponding Secretary, written at this time, closes with the following words, now measurably in process of fulfillment:

"One sentence in closing. Believe me, this is one of the last terrible efforts of hell to retain its relaxing grasp on beautiful India, and the issue will be salvation for her millions . . .

Don't be discouraged for us. If the sufferings abound, so do the consolations. But if I am cut off, (which is not improbable,) *remember my mission and sustain it.* Farewell, Doctor. Again let me beseech you, whether I live or die, remember my mission and sustain it. FOR INDIA IS TO BE REDEEMED!"

CHAPTER VI.

THE CAWNPORE MASSACRE AND THE RELIEF OF LUCKNOW.

WHILE we were thus maintaining, as best we could, our position against fearful odds, and hoping for that relief which had yet, for the reasons following, to be so much longer delayed, our fellow Christians down in the plains below us were passing through sorrows and agonies in the presence of which our trials were not worthy to be mentioned, and the accounts of which were about to fill the civilized world with horror.

With a sad heart we tell the story of Cawnpore—the "city of melancholy fame"—and present to our readers that wonderful record of fruitless valor and unutterable woe which was there exhibited. Fourteen years have passed over since these deeds were done, but the fearful record of them will be read with deepest interest by Christian men and women long after the present generation has passed away. This story can never die. Wherever and whenever read, it should be remembered that England alone did not suffer there. The dire agony of Cawnpore was shared by American gentlemen and ladies ; indeed, they took precedence in these sorrows, for the group first "led as sheep to the slaughter," before the murder of those from the intrenchment was perpetrated, included the Rev. Messrs. Freeman, Johnson, M'Mullin, and Campbell, with their dear wives and children, from Futtyghur—the very next station to the one then occupied by the writer, who, with his family, had to conclude whether to accept the invitation to join this party, and attempt escape by the Ganges, or else "flee to the mountains" on the north. He decided for the latter, and thus narrowly escaped the fate which befell these brethren and sisters, whom he had already learned to esteem so highly for their own and for their work's sake.

Of few of "the martyrs of Jesus" in any age may it more truly be said than of them, "These are they which came out of *great tribulation*." The sharp agony of that hour is ended, and they have met again where He who loved them has long since wiped away all tears from their eyes. The American Presbyterian Church, to which they belonged, should nobly press on the work for which they died, and be earnest to reap the harvest made so fertile with their blood.

"The massacre of Cawnpore" has been truly called "the blackest crime in human history." Every element of perfidy and cruelty was concentrated in it. No act ever carried to so many hearts such a thrill of horror as did the deed that was done there on the 15th of July, 1857. Yet no complete account of it has been laid before the American public. To supply this deficiency, so far as our space allows, is the aim of these pages. Our authorities are the best: Trevelyan, (of whose excellent work we make free use,) with Thomson, Bourchier, *The Friend of India*, and the *Calcutta Quarterly Review*, together with the personal communications of Havelock's soldiers; while photographs, taken on the spot, enable us accurately to present "the Well" into which the ladies were thrown, and the beautiful monument which a weeping country has placed over their remains.

The city of Cawnpore is situated on the banks of the Ganges, six hundred and twenty-eight miles from Calcutta, and two hundred and sixty-six miles from Delhi. At the time of the great Rebellion, the English general commanding the station was Sir Hugh Wheeler. He had under his command four Sepoy regiments, and about three hundred English soldiers. In addition to these, there were the wives and children of the English officers and of his own force, and of the force at Lucknow. Oude having been but recently annexed, the families of the officers in Lucknow could not yet obtain houses there, and so were left for the present under the care of Sir Hugh Wheeler at Cawnpore. When the alarm began to extend, the ladies and children of the stations around also went to him for protection, so that, before the rebellion broke out, the

General found himself responsible for the care of over five hundred and sixty women and children, with only three hundred English soldiers and about one hundred and forty other Europeans, for their protection.

Sir Hugh had been over fifty years in India. His age and his confidence in the loyalty of the Sepoys under his command ill-fitted him for the position he then held. He would not credit the imminence of the danger, nor make that provision against it which some of those under his orders believed to be urgently necessary. He still trusted the loyalty of the Nana Sahib, and placed the Government treasure—an immense sum of money—under his care; and there was even a proposal to send the ladies and children off to the Bithoor palace for safe-keeping. There was a strong magazine on the banks of the Ganges, well provided with munitions of war and with suitable shelter, to which Sir Hugh might have taken his charge, and where, it is believed, he could have held out till relief reached him; but unfortunately he thought otherwise, believing himself not strong enough to hold it. So he crossed the canal and took a position on the open plain, in two large, one-story barracks, and threw up a low earth-work around it, and thought himself secure till assistance could reach him from Calcutta. He did not take the precaution to provision even this place properly or in time, and also left the strong intrenchment on the Ganges stored with artillery of all sizes, and with shot and shell to match, with thirty boats full of ammunition moored at the landing-place—left all to fall into the hands of his enemies; and it was actually used, profusely used, against himself in the terrible days that followed. The few cannon which he took with him were no match for those he left behind, and which he had afterward to fight so fiercely and at such disadvantage.

On the 14th of May intelligence reached them of the fearful massacres of Meerut and Delhi. On the 5th of June the Cawnpore Sepoys broke into open mutiny, having been joined by other regiments from Oude. The Nana Sahib had been in intimate communication with the ringleaders; yet for some reason or other, probably a disinclination to murder their officers or to face the few English soldiers there, the Sepoys seemed more inclined to leave the station and march for Delhi than to remain and attack the English They actually started, performed the first stage, and encamped at a place called Kullianpore. The wily Azeemoolah and his master now saw that their hour had come. Arriving in the camp, they persuaded the Sepoy host to return to Cawnpore and put all the English to the sword before they left the place. Their unwillingness was overcome by the promise of unlimited pillage, and the offer by the Maharajah of a gold anklet to each Sepoy. They retraced their steps. That night the English officers were, some of them, sleeping in their own houses, imagining that they had seen the last of that Sepoy army. But early the next morning the Nana announced his intention to commence the attack at once, and there was barely time to summon the officers and families outside ere it began. Every thing of value, clothing and stores of all kinds, had to be suddenly abandoned. He who in that close and sultry night of midsummer had sought a little air and sleep on his house-top might not stay "to take any thing out of his house;" he who had been on early service in the field might not "turn back to take his clothes." Few and happy were they who had time to snatch a single change of raiment. Some lost their lives by waiting to dress. So that, half-clad, confused, and breathless, the devoted band rushed into the breastwork, which they entered only to suffer, and left only to die.

Within this miserable inclosure, containing two barracks designed for only one hundred men each, and surrounded by a mud wall only four feet high, three feet in thickness at the base, and but twelve inches at the top—where the batteries were constructed by the simple expedient of leaving an aperture for each gun, so that the artillery-men served their pieces as in the field, with their persons entirely exposed to the fire of the enemy—within this inclosure were huddled together a thousand people, only four hundred and forty of whom were men, the rest being women and children. Here, without any thing that could be called shelter, without proper provisions for a single week, exposed to the raging sun by day and to the iron hail of death by day and night, these Christian people had to endure for twenty-two days the pitiless bombardment, the rifle-shots, and storming-parties, launched at them from a well-appointed army of nearly ten thousand men.

How well those four hundred and forty men must have fought, when, with closed teeth and bated breath, the Brahmin and the Saxon thus closed for their death grapple, where no quarter was asked or received, may be imagined. But who can imagine the terror and the sufferings of that crowd of five hundred and sixty ladies and children, not one of whom could be saved, even by all the valor of those brave men who fought so hard and died so rapidly to protect them! Of the whole number, only *three* men escaped—Captain Delafosse, Major Thompson, and Private Murphy.

America and Europe have ever forbidden their warriors to point the sword at a female breast. But Asiatics have no such scruples. The Hindoos, who allow their women few or no personal rights, and the Mohammedans, who doubt if they have souls, have no tenderness for the position or treatment of the weaker sex. The sharp-shooters and gunners of the Nana Sahib were true to their heathenism. They gave no rest, and showed no mercy. Some ladies were slain outright by grape or round shot, others by the bullet: many were crushed by the splinters or the falling walls. At first every projectile that struck the barracks, where they were crowded together, was the signal for heart-rending shrieks, and low wailing, more heart-rending still; but ere long time and habit had taught them to suffer and to fear in silence. The unequal contest could not last long. By the end of the first week every one of the professional artillery-men had been killed or wounded, besides those who had fallen all around the position. Sun-stroke had dazed and killed several. Their only howitzer was knocked clear off its carriage, and the other cannon disabled, save two pieces which were withdrawn under cover, loaded with grape, and reserved for the purpose of repelling an assault. Even the bore of these had been injured so that a canister could not be driven home, and the poor ladies gave up their stockings to supply the case for a novel, but not unserviceable, cartridge. As their fire became more faint, that of the enemy augmented in volume, rapidity, and precision—casualties mounted up fearfully, and at length their misfortunes culminated in a wholesale disaster. One of the two barracks had a thatched roof. In this, as more roomy, were collected the sick, and wounded, and women. On the evening of the eighth day of the bombardment the enemy succeeded in lodging a lighted "carcase" on the roof, and the whole building was speedily in a blaze. No effort was spared or risk shunned to rescue the helpless inmates; but, in spite of all, two brave men were burned to death. During that night of horror the artillery and marksmen of the enemy, aided by the light of the burning building, poured their cruel fire on the busy men who were trying to save the provisions and ammunition, and living burdens more precious still, out of the fire, while the guards, crouching silent and watchful, finger on trigger, each at his station behind the outer wall, could see the countless foes, revealed now and again by the glare, prowling and yelling around the outer gloom like so many demons eager for their prey.

The misery fell chiefly on the ladies: they were now obliged to pass their days and nights in a temperature varying from one hundred and twenty to one hundred and thirty-eight degrees, cowering beneath such shelter as the low earth-work could give—and all this to women who had been brought up in the lap of luxury, and who had never till now known a moment of physical privation. There were but two wells within reach; one of these had been used to receive their dead—for they could not bury them—the other was so trained upon day and night by the shell of the enemy that at last it became the certain risk of death to remain long enough to draw up, from a depth of over sixty feet, a bucket of water for the parched women and children. Yet necessity compelled that risk, while it made the sip of water rare and priceless, but left none to wash their persons or their wounds. A short gill of flour and a handful of split peas was now their daily sustenance. The medical stores had been all destroyed in the conflagration—there remained no drugs, or cordials, or opiates to cure or alleviate. The bandages for the newly wounded were supplied off the persons of the ladies, who nobly parted with their clothing for this purpose, till many of them had barely enough left to screen their persons. And to this condition were these once beautiful women reduced—herded together in fetid misery, where delicacy and modesty were hourly shocked, though never for a moment impaired. Bare-footed and ragged, haggard and emaciated, parched with drought and faint with hunger, they sat watching to hear that they were widows. Each morning deepened the hollow in the youngest cheek, and added a new furrow to the fairest brow. Want, exposure, and depression speedily decimated that hapless company, while a hideous train of diseases—fever, apoplexy, insanity, cholera, and dysentery—began to add their horrors to the dreadful and unparalleled scene. Alas! even this does not by any means exhaust the list of terrors, but we can go no further. American ladies will add their generous tears to those which have been flowing for their sorrows in many an English home during the past few years.

They tried hard to communicate with the outside world—with Lucknow or Allahabad—for they had a few faithful natives who ventured forth for them; but so close were the cavalry pickets around their position that only one person ever returned to them. These spies were barbarously used. The writer saw some of them after the Rebellion in their mutilated state—their hands cut off, or their noses split open; and one poor fellow had lost hands, nose, and ears. The native mode of mutilation was horribly painful, the limb being sometimes chopped off with a tulwar—a coarse sword—and the stump dipped in boiling oil to arrest the bleeding.

Events had now reached their dire extremity. The sweetness of existence had vanished, and the last flicker of hope had died away. Yet, moved by a generous despair and an invincible self-respect, they still fought on for dear life, and for lives dearer than their own. By daring, and vigilance, and unparalleled endurance, these brave and suffering men staved off ruin for another day, and yet another. Long had their eyes and ears strained in the direction of Allahabad, hoping for the succor that was never to reach them, The 23d of June dawned—the anniversary of the battle of Plassey. The Nana Sahib had vowed to celebrate that centenary of the rise of the English power in its utter overthrow; the Sepoys had sworn by the most solemn oath of their religion to conquer or perish on that day. Early in the morning the whole force was moved to the assault; the guns were brought up within a few hundred yards of the wall; the infantry in dense array advanced, their skirmishers rolling before them great bales of cotton, proof against the bullets of the besieged, while the cavalry charged at a gallop in another quarter. It was all in vain. The contest was short but sharp. The teams which drew the artillery were shot down, the bales were fired, the sharp-shooters driven back on their columns, and the saddles of the cavalry were emptied as they came on. The Sepoy host reeled before the dreadful resistance and fell back discouraged—nor could they be induced to renew the effort. That evening a party of them drew near the position, made obeisance after their fashion, and asked leave to remove their dead. This acknowledgment of an empty triumph was a poor consolation to these gaunt and starving Englishmen, under the shadow of the impending doom of themselves and those whom they so well defended.

The result of this day's conflict produced a sudden change in the plans of the Nana Sahib. He began to despair of taking the position by storm, and events were forbidding him to wait for the slower process of starvation. The Sepoys were already grumbling, and another repulse would set them conspiring. The usurper saw he must bring matters to a speedy conclusion; for, in addition to Sepoy discontent, rumors had already reached him of an avenging force having left Benares to save those whom he had resolved to destroy. He had not a day to lose. It behooved the monster to bring the matter to a speedy conclusion by any means, even the very foulest, as all others had failed. He therefore resolved to insnare where he could not vanquish—to lure those Christians from the shelter of that wall within which no intruder had set his foot and lived. He suspended the bombardment and opened negotiations. The world had never yet heard of treachery so hellish as what he meditated then. Though some of the ladies had their fears, yet none imagined the purpose which was in the depths of the dark hearts of this man and his minion Azeemoolah. Admiration of the defense was expressed, and sympathy for the condition of the ladies still living, with the offer of boats provisioned, and a safe conduct under the Nana's hand to take them to Allahabad. The terms of the conference were committed to paper, and borne, by Azeemoolah, to the Nana for his signature; all was made seemingly right and safe for the capitulation. The boats were actually moored at the landing-place and provisions put on board, and the whole shown to the committee of English officers. That night they could obtain water, and deep were the draughts of the blessed beverage which they imbibed; they could also sleep, for the bombardment had ceased, though a cloud of cavalry held watch around their position. They slept sounder the next night, as the Nana intended that they should.

Some criticisms have been made upon their agreement to surrender at all. It may be answered, that had that garrison consisted only of fighting men, no one would have dreamed of surrender. But what could be done when more than half their number, male and female, had already been killed, and the balance was a mixed multitude, in which there was a woman and child to each man, while every other man was incapacitated by wounds or disease, with only four days more of half rations of their miserable subsistence, and the monsoon — the tropical rains — hourly expected to open upon them in all its violence? The only choice was between death and capitulation; and if the latter was resolved on it was well that the offer came from the enemy.

Eleven o'clock next morning, June 27th, came. Every thing was ready; all Cawnpore was astir, crowding by thousands to the landing-place. The doomed garrison had taken their last look at their premises and at the well, into which so many of their number had been lowered during the past three weeks. The writer has walked over the same ground, between their intrenchment and the landing-place, wondering with what feelings that ragged and spiritless cavalcade must have passed over that space that day. But they had at least this consolation—they thought that their miseries were ending, and that they were going toward home, with all its blessed associations. They moved on, reached the wooden bridge, and turned into the fatal ravine which led to the water's edge. Two dozen large boats, each covered with a frame and heavy thatch, to screen the sun, were ready; but it was observed that, instead of floating, they had been drawn into the shallows, and were resting on the sand. The vast multitude, speechless and motionless as specters, watched their descent into that "valley of the shadow of death." The men in front began to lift the wounded and the ladies into the boats, and prepared for shoving them off, when, amid that sinister silence, the blast of a bugle at the other end of the ravine, as the last straggler entered within the fatal trap, gave the Nana Sahib's signal, and the masked battery, which Azeemoolah had spent his night preparing, opened with grape upon the confused mass. The boatmen who were to row them thrust the ready burning charcoal into the thatch, plunged overboard, and made for the shore, and, almost in a moment, the entire fleet was in a blaze of fire. Five hundred marksmen sprang up among the trees and temples, and began to pour their deadly bullets in upon them, while the cavalry along the river brink were ready for any who attempted to swim the Ganges. Only four men made good their escape—two officers and two privates, one of whom soon afterward sank under his sufferings—and they owed their lives to their ability in swimming and diving, and were indebted for their ultimate safety to the humanity of a noble Hindoo, Dirigbijah Singh, of Oude. The Nana Sahib was pacing before his tent, waiting for the news. A trooper was dispatched to inform him that all was going on well, and that the Peishwa would soon have ample vengeance for his ancient wrong. He bade the courier return to the scene of action, bearing the verbal order to "keep the women alive, and kill all the males." Accordingly the

"The House of Massacre."

women and children whom the shot had missed and the flames spared, were collected and brought to land. Many of them were dragged from under the charred woodwork, or out of the water beside the boats. Some of the ladies were roughly handled by the troopers, who, while collecting them, tore away such ornaments as caught their fancy, with little consideration for ear or finger. Their defenders were all soon murdered, and lay in mutilation on the banks or in the boats, or floated away with the stream. The ladies were taken back along the road, through a surging crowd of Sepoys and towns-people, till the procession halted opposite the pavilion of the Maharajah, who, after receiving his wretched captives, ordered them removed to a small building north of the canal, which was to be the scene of their final sufferings on the 15th of the following month. We present a sketch of this place, known afterward as the "House of the Massacre."

It comprised two principal rooms, each twenty feet by ten, with three or four windowless closets, and behind the building was an open court, about fifteen yards square, surrounded by a high wall. Guarded by Sepoys, within these limits, during nineteen days of tropical heat, were penned up together these two hundred and one ladies and children and five men—two hundred and six persons in all—awaiting their doom from the lips of a monster. Their food during those terrible days was very coarse and scanty indeed; and, to add to it the keenest indignity that an Oriental could give, it was cooked for them by the Methers, (scavengers.) They lay on the bare ground, and were closely watched day and night. "The Well," into which he had their mangled bodies thrown, is shown on the left side of the picture.

That evening the Nana Sahib held a State review in honor of his "victory," ordered a general illumination of the city of Cawnpore, and posted the Proclamation already quoted, in which he called upon the people to "rejoice at the delightful intelligence that Cawnpore has been conquered, and the Christians have been sent to hell, and both the Hindoo and Mohammedan religions have been confirmed."

The Maharajah at length enjoyed the compliment he had so long coveted, and was so long denied—at the review he was greeted with the full sum of twenty-one guns, his nephew and two brothers receiving seventeen each. He wore his royal honors for seventeen days and no more. Distributing $50,000 among the mutineers, he returned in state to his Cawnpore residence. This was a hotel kept by a Mohammedan, and in which the writer slept when in the place a few months previously. The Nana took possession of these premises, which were about seventy-five paces from the house here shown, where the poor ladies were confined. Here he lived from day to day in a perpetual round of sensuality, amid a choice coterie of priests, panderers, ministers, and minions. The reigning beauty of the fortnight was one Oula or Adala. She was the Thais on whose breast sank the vanquished victor, oppressed with brandy and such love as animates a middle-aged Eastern debauchee. She is said to have counted by hundreds of thousands the rupees which were lavished upon her by the affection or vanity of her Alexander.

Every night there was an entertainment of music, dancing, and pantomime, the latter being some caricature of English habits. The noise of this revelry was plainly audible to the captives in the adjoining house; and as they crowded round the windows to catch a breath of the cool night air, the glare of the torches and the strains of the barbarous melody might remind them of the period when he who was now the center of that noisy throng thought himself privileged if he could induce them to honor him with their acceptance of the hospitality of Bithoor. To such reality of woe were they reduced! Heat, hardship, wounds, and want of space and proper nourishment were beginning to release some from their bondage before the season marked out by Azeemoolah for a jail delivery such as the world never witnessed before. A sentence of relief may be added here, as rumors contrary to the fact have been circulated: Trevelyan, whom we have so freely copied, declares that the evidence shows that these ladies died without mention, and we may hope without apprehension, of dishonor.

The hour of retribution dawned at length! Outraged civilization was coming with a vengeance to punish the guilty, and to save this remnant if it were possible. General Havelock and his brave little brigade were on their way, making forced marches daily. The Nana roused himself to meet the danger. He had forwarded armies to resist their approach, but twice his forces were hurled back, bringing to him the news of their disaster. Reserving his own sacred person for the supreme venture, he now ordered his whole army to be got ready. But before setting out he took advice as to what was best to be done with the captives. It was seen that dead men or women tell no tales and give no evidence, and this was important in case of a reverse; while he also reasoned that, as the British were approaching solely for the purpose of releasing their friends, they would not risk another battle for the purpose merely of burying them, but would be only too glad of an excuse to avoid meeting the Peishwa in the field. So he and his council concluded. Their decision was that the ladies should die, and that, too, without further delay, as the army must march in the morning.

We purposely omit many of the details of the horrors of that dreadful evening, as we have read them or heard them described by Havelock's men, and will try to give the result in brief terms. About half past four o'clock that afternoon—the 15th—the woman called "The Begum" informed the ladies that they were to be killed. But the Sepoys refused to execute the order, and there was a pause. Nana Sahib was not thus to be balked, even though the widows of Bajee Rao, his step-mothers by adoption, most earnestly remonstrated against the act. It was all in vain. The Nana found his agents. Five men—some of whom were butchers by profession—undertook the work for him. With their knives and swords they entered, and the door was fastened behind them. The shrieks and scuffling within told those without that these journeymen were executing their master's will. The evidence shows that it took them exactly an hour and a half to finish it; they then came out again, having earned their hire. They were paid, it is said, one rupee (fifty cents) for each lady, or one hundred and three dollars for the whole, and were dismissed. Then a number of Methers (scavengers) were called, and by the heels, or hair of their head, these once beautiful women and children were dragged out of the house and dropped down into the open well—shown on the left of the picture—the dying with the dead, and the children over all! The well had been used for purposes of irrigation, and was some fifty feet deep. Next morning, when the army marched, no .iving European remained in Cawnpore.

Commanding in person, the Nana Sahib went forth that day to meet General Havelock, bent on doing something great in defense of his tottering throne. But, notwithstanding the disparity of their numbers, he soon realized the difference between them and the group of invalids and civilians, whom he had brought to bay behind that deserted rampart, or a front rank of seated ladies and children and a rear rank of gentlemen, all with their hands strapped behind their backs, as in his first "victory." Now he saw before him, extending from left to right, the line of white faces, of red cloth, and of sparkling steel. With set teeth and flashing eyes, and rifles tightly grasped, closer and closer drew the measured tramp of feet, and the heart of the foe died within him; his fire grew hasty and ill-directed, and, as the last volley cut the air overhead, the English, with a shout, rushed forward at their foes Then each rebel thought only of himself. The terrible shrapnel and canister tore through their ranks, and they broke ere the bayonet could touch them. Squadron after squadron, and battalion after battalion, these humbled Brahmins dropped their weapons, threw off their packs, and spurred and ran in wild confusion, pursued for miles by the British cavalry and artillery. At nightfall the Nana Sahib entered Cawnpore upon a chestnut horse drenched in perspiration and with bleeding flanks. On he sped toward Bithoor, sore and weary, his head swimming and his chest heaving. He had never ridden so far and fast before. It was the just earnest of that hardship which was henceforth to be his portion. Far otherwise had he been wont to return to that palace after a visit of state to the English: lolling, *vinaigrette* in hand, beneath the breath of fans, amid the cushions of a luxurious carriage, surrounded by a moving hedge of outriders and running footmen. Placing his harem on steeds, with some treasure and provisions, and with his brothers and such as chose to follow his fortunes, he accompanied his forces to resist General Havelock's advance on Lucknow. When again defeated, for the fifth time, he fled to the congenial society of Khan Bahadar at Bareilly, where he made his last stand; and he then, having filled to overflowing the measure of his guilt, passed away like a thief in the night, and left his wealth to the spoiler. Accompanied by his evil spirit, Azeemoolah, he and his followers entered the jungles of Oude and penetrated deep into desolate wilds, where the malarious fever soon thinned off his company, and reduced the remnant to the final distress. For the last that is known of this man's doom we have to depend upon the reports of two native spies who followed him, and two of his servants who subsequently found their way out of those Himalayan solitudes. Wasted and worn at last by fever and starvation to utter desperation, they are reported to have held a council, and concluded to put their swords each through his own women, and then to separate and die alone. Certainly a remnant of any of them has never since been seen. The Nana Sahib wore that great ruby which was so celebrated for its size and brilliancy. His priests had told him that it was an amulet which secured to him a charmed life. He trusted in it, no doubt, to the very last. It was probably in his turban when he wandered up that deep ravine to die alone; and if so, there it lies to-day, for no human hand will ever penetrate those pestilential jungles to gather it. The eagles of the Himalayas alone, as they look down from their lofty height for their prey, are the only creatures that will ever see the burning rays of that ruby, as it shines amid the rags of the vagrant who perished there long years ago!

On the 17th of July at daybreak the English army reached Cawnpore; they passed the walls of the roofless barracks, pitted with shot and blackened with flames, and then came to "the Ladies' House," and, as they stood sobbing at the door, they saw what it were well could the outraged earth have hidden—the inner apartment was almost ankle deep in blood! The plaster all around was scored with sword-cuts, not high up, as where men had fought, but *low down*, and *around the corners*, as if a creature had crouched there to avoid the blow. Fragments of dresses, large locks of hair, broken combs, with three or four Bibles and Prayer Books, and children's little shoes, were scattered around. Alas! it was thirty-six hours too late! The Well beside the House held what they had marched and fought so hard to save, and marched and fought in vain. They had to leave them as they found them; so they filled up the well and leveled the earth about it. Over that well a weeping country has erected a graceful shrine, and has turned the ground around it into a fair garden, and made the whole forever sacred to their memory. We present views of the outside and inside of the shrine, engraved from photographs taken on the spot.

Around the rim of the stone covering the well's mouth is this inscription:

> "SACRED TO THE PERPETUAL MEMORY OF A GREAT COMPANY OF CHRISTIAN PEOPLE, CHIEFLY WOMEN AND CHILDREN, CRUELLY MASSACRED NEAR THIS SPOT BY THE REBEL NANA SAHIB, AND THROWN, THE DYING WITH THE DEAD, INTO THE WELL BENEATH ON THE XVTH DAY OF JULY, MDCCCLVII."

Over the door outside are the words of the one hundred and forty-first Psalm, "Our bones are scattered at the grave's mouth, as when one cutteth and cleaveth wood upon the earth."

The garden, inclosed, planted, and made so lovely, with the monument in the center, is now such a contrast in its peace and beauty to the sorrows once endured within its limits, that one is reminded of the words which Havelock's men cut on the temporary monument of wood which they placed over the well: "I believe in the resurrection of the body." The entire premises have been placed by Government under the appropriate guardianship of Private Murphy—one of the three survivors of that fearful siege—and here he may be seen daily, accompanying visitors from many lands, who with sad thoughts and respectful steps approach the Ladies' Monument in the Memorial Garden of Cawnpore.

"The Well"—inside view.

"The Shrine"—outside view.

It may be well here to consider for a moment the alleged severities which some of the English soldiers and commanders inflicted upon those red-handed Sepoys. Who will wonder, as he thinks of the men that stood around the door of that "Slaughter House," (as it was long after called,) and who gazed upon a sight that no other men had ever seen, and who, as they reflected upon all they had themselves so vainly endured to save those whose gory mementoes lay before them, causing these sun-burned soldiers to sob and weep like children, that such soldiers, in such circumstances, should have vowed vengeance against the perpetrators of this matchless cruelty? Does not even humanity, in advance, require a gentle judgment upon their feelings and resolutions, or the retributions which they afterward administered?

One of them told me that, as they stood around the door and looked in, a tuft of hair, from a lady's head, floated on the congealed mass; a comrade went in, walking on his heels to keep his shoes above the gore, and snatching up the handful of hair, he returned to them and proposed they should share it among them. They stood around in a circle, and divided it, taking an oath that they would have a Sepoy life for each hair they held! This dreadful resolution may be forgiven. General Havelock was a man of mercy as well as of valor, and impressed his authority upon them, so as to keep them from exercising this vengeance upon any save resisting rebels and convicted criminals. Two of his Aids, Generals Neill and Renaud, were more severe; they felt it their duty to break the caste, as well as to take the life, of the more prominent murderers who fell into their hands, by requiring these Brahmin Sepoys to wipe up the blood which their leader had caused to be shed; reminding one of the punishment inflicted by Ulysses in the palace of Ithaca, as related by Homer, only that the provocation was so much greater at Cawnpore. Under any other civilization than Christianity, in its hour of triumph, retaliation would have been general and undiscriminating. The citizens of Cawnpore well knew that a Hindoo or Moslem army, in such an opportunity, and with such a deed to revenge, would have given them and their city to fire and sword, and have left only a ruin behind.

The practice of "blowing men from guns" in India during the Rebellion also needs a few words of explanation. The act has been much misunderstood, especially in this country. I have met with strange assertions upon this matter, some of which assumed that the Sepoys were actually rammed *into* the guns, and then fired out! and too often has it been said or supposed that the act was perpetrated as a refinement of cruelty. Both of these opinions are mistaken. The mode of death in this case was, usually, to sink a stake in the ground, and tie the man to it; the gun was behind him, from six to eight feet distant, loaded with blank cartridge, and, when discharged, it dissipated the man's remains. It was a quick and painless mode of death, for the man was annihilated, as it were, ere he knew that he was struck. But what the Sepoys objected to in it was, the dishonor done to the body, its integrity being destroyed, so that the *Shraad* could not be performed for them. [The Shraad is a funeral ceremony, which all caste Hindoos invest with the highest significance, as essential to their having a happy transmigration; the dissipation of the mortal remains of a man thus executed would necessarily render its importance impossible, and so expose the disembodied ghost, in their opinion, to a wandering, indefinite condition in the other world, which they regard as dreadful; and, to avoid this liability, when condemned to die they would plead, as a mercy, to be hung or shot with the musket—any mode —but not to be blown away.

Knowing that this was the only procedure of which their wretched consciences were afraid, two of the English officers—one of them being General Corbett, at Lahore—threatened this mode of punishment upon Sepoy troops whom they could not otherwise restrain from rebelling. Corbett did, at last, execute it upon twelve of the ringleaders of a Sepoy regiment which, during the height of his anxiety for the safety of the Punjab, rose one morning and shot their officers, and marched for Delhi. He took two Sikh regiments and pursued and scattered them, bringing back these leaders for trial and execution. The court resolved death should be inflicted in this mode, as a last resort to strike terror into the other two Sepoy regiments, so as to restrain them from rising. And it certainly had that effect. From the hour of that execution till Delhi fell, not a single Sepoy hand was raised against an officer's life or the Government. They saw that the man at their head would not shrink from violating their prejudices, even as to their Shraad, if they committed mutiny and murder, and they would not face that danger. So the Punjab was kept quiet, and we at Nynee Tal, and they at Simla and Delhi, (including hundreds of ladies,) were saved, more probably by *that* act of stern discipline than by any other event during those seven months.

Every generous and candid heart will judge the General's action by his motive and the circumstances around him, as well as the minds on which he had to operate. He was far, as was his noble Governor, Sir John Lawrence, from any wish to perpetrate an undue severity or refinement of cruelty. He was in circumstances where he had reason to believe that this was the only way to arrest murder and mutiny, and save thousands of lives whose fate hung on the position of the Punjab and his measures to preserve it. This was equally the motive of the other General, who employed it as a measure of restraint as well as punishment. The act itself was analogous to the policy of Christian States one hundred years ago, in refusing what was called "The Benefit of Clergy" to certain notorious criminals. Lord Canning, the Governor-General, as soon as he heard of it, however, believing that it infringed too much upon the conscience of the Hindoos, forbade its repetition by any Commander, and it was therefore entirely abandoned. As a mode of punishment it was introduced into India by the French during their brief rule in the South. Wilkes's "History of the Mysore" relates its infliction, by Count Lally, in 1758, upon six Brahmins.

The consideration of Lord Canning, however, was not reciprocated by the Sepoy power itself, for in the hour of their opportunity they made no scruple whatever to employ this mode of execution upon other people. We have testimony that several of the Europeans who fell into the hands of the Nawab of Futtyghur and the Nana Sahib, were executed by being blown from guns; and even the greased cartridges, to which they at first objected, when their own time came, they are said to have readily used to murder the Europeans who fell into their hands.

Though, unhappily, too late to save those who suffered at Cawnpore, the relieving army were destined, after endurance and valor which received the admiration of all who ever heard of it, to reach and rescue the larger garrison of Lucknow, which, as the reader will see on the map, lies forty-three miles beyond Cawnpore.

The Mission of the Queen of Oude in 1856 had failed, the decree had gone forth and was unalterable, and an English Governor ruled the kingdom, which became a part of British India. His official residence—ere long to become so famous—is shown in the picture on the opposite page. This building, before the annexation, was the home of "the Resident," or English Embassador, at the Court of Oude, and afterward became the house of "the Chief Commissioner," or Governor, of the kingdom, and was therefore called "The Residency."

No record of human endurance exceeds that which was here exhibited from June to November, 1857. "The Story of Cawnpore" is, alas! more tragical; but for the great qualities of the heroic and the enduring, Lucknow may well challenge human history to furnish a higher example, especially when we remember the number of women who were here shut up, and how nobly they bore themselves amid risks and sufferings which only Christian women of our Anglo-Saxon race could bear to the bitter end, and yet emerge from them all in moral triumph. Nearly a dozen volumes, by different hands—three of them from the pens of ladies—have presented the facts to the world. They abundantly show how nobly woman can illustrate the virtue inculcated by Virgil:

> "Do not yield to misfortunes,
> But advance to meet them with greater fortitude."

Probably there never was such a siege as that of Lucknow. History seems to have no parallel to it in its extraordinary circum-

"The Residency," Lucknow, India.

stances, the bravery of its garrison, the privations, risks, and horrors to which the women were subjected, while hope was deferred, and England gave them up as dead, and they themselves at length, "not expecting deliverance," resolved to die, if die they must, with their face to their bloody and relentless foe. The women of Carthage are celebrated for having cut off their hair to make bow-strings for their husbands, but the resolute and enduring courage of these daughters of Britain make them worthy of higher fame. Englishmen may well feel proud of their countrywomen.

Two great and good men are the central figures of this siege and relief, Sir Henry Lawrence and Sir Henry Havelock—the former an Episcopalian and the latter a Baptist—both men who honored and loved God, and who were greatly honored by God, the first in defending, the latter in rescuing, against fearful odds, the gallant men and women of the Lucknow Residency.

Sir Henry Lawrence, after spending more than thirty years in the military and civil service in India, was appointed Governor of the Kingdom of Oude. He reached Lucknow, the capital, and entered upon his duties early in 1857, fully impressed by the dangerous condition of things at that time. Though in very feeble health, he set himself vigorously at work to prepare for the coming storm, which at length broke over India on the memorable 31st of May. Every city in Oude, save Lucknow, was seized that day by the Sepoys, and deeds of cruelty and blood perpetrated which shocked the whole civilized world. Lucknow alone, where Sir Henry dwelt in the Residency, was held, and even his vigor and ability could not have suspended its fall had he not had a handful of English soldiers to rely upon. He at once collected all the civilians and Christian residents of Lucknow, with a few native troops whose fidelity he thought he could trust, and over whom he exerted a wonderful influence, into the Residency, and some other houses close to it, and began to fortify them in the best manner that the time and means at his command would allow. Provisions were collected rapidly, and ammunition stored and prepared, guns put in position, and his people organized. In addition to the

Residency, he also occupied an old fort called the "Muchee Bhawun," about one third of a mile west of the Residency, and close to which are our mission premises. Dividing his force, he fondly hoped to be strong enough to hold both positions till re-enforcements should reach him, and enable him to restore law and order at the capital, and throughout the kingdom. How little he foreboded the fearful odds against which his feeble garrison would soon have to contend! Meanwhile the reports of the fiendish atrocities of Delhi, Meerut, Shahjehanpore, Bareilly, and other places reached Lucknow, and its few hundred anxious Christian people began to realize more fully how completely they were cut off from all human assistance, and how dark their own future was becoming.

The natives in the city had become so persuaded of the overthrow of the English power that the Government securities, which a few days before were selling at a premium, had fallen from over one hundred to thirty-seven. Fanatics paraded the city—some of them haranguing the crowds of people, and exhibiting pictures of Europeans maimed and mutilated by Sepoys; others had a show of dolls dressed as European children, which ended by striking off their heads, to the great delight of the mobs, who looked on and applauded; while the blasphemy of Mohammedan Fakirs became bold and frightful, as they exulted in the overthrow of Christianity, and demanded the blood of "the Kaffirs" in the Fort and Residency, as the consummation of their efforts. These wretched men imagined that the whole of Hindustan had fallen, that the few of our faith around Sir Henry Lawrence were all of the Christian life left in India; and for many long and weary months the Christians generally, like those at Nynee Tal, did not know but that this was the terrible truth.

While busy preparing the defenses with which they were surrounding the Residency and the other houses near it, so as to form intrenchments, and make the best of their position, Sir Henry was joined by the few Europeans who had escaped from the massacres at Secrora and other stations in Oude. The news they brought deepened the gloom of the situation. Reports of the dead bodies of Europeans, among them three women, lying by the road side a few miles out, were brought to them, and the fiendish cruelty to which they were exposed received a fearful illustration when, one day, some natives brought to the Residency the body of an English lady, which they had found lying by the road side cut up into quarters! These unfortunate people were evidently making for the Residency when they were overtaken and thus cruelly murdered and mutilated by the Sepoys.

Sir Henry now redoubled his efforts to complete the batteries, stockades, and trenches around his position, and prepare for whatever might occur. Hearing, on the 29th of June, that the insurgents were approaching Lucknow, he concluded to march out with a part of his little force, hoping to defeat them before they reached the city, and so save himself from investment and the city from being taken; but, unfortunately, his information of the strength of the foe was defective, and in the moment of emergency, when he suddenly came upon them at Chinhut, seven miles from Lucknow, he found his little force of six hundred and thirty-six men and eleven guns in front of an enemy fifteen thousand strong, with six batteries of guns of various caliber, all ready to receive him. Before his force could recover their surprise the foe opened upon them, their cavalry quickly outflanking them, and it seemed for a while as though not a man could escape to tell the tale. But the brave handful of troops showed a bold front, charging with the bayonet when the enemy came near enough, yet unable to follow up their advantages. The native drivers of the British guns fled in terror, and their artillery was rendered nearly useless, and most of it fell into the hands of the foe. Colonel Case, at the head of his men, was struck by a bullet and dropped. Captain Bassano, seeing him fall, turned to assist him, but the dying hero waved him off, saying, "Captain Bassano, leave me to die here; your place is at the head of your company. I have no need of assistance."

They now tried to return to Lucknow, but only about two hundred and thirty-four of their number reached the Residency; they saved only sixty-five of their wounded—the rest were all cut up.

The wonder is, that any one escaped. Had the rebel cavalry used its opportunity not a single man of Sir Henry Lawrence's force, or of the faithful natives he had with him, could ever have returned to the Residency.

This sad event of Chinhut caused Sir Henry Lawrence the deepest anguish, and it is thought tended to shorten his life. His face, already careworn enough to be remarkable, assumed a sad aspect that it was painful to contemplate. But he nerved himself to meet the stern realities of the position, and all allow that it was, under God, to his foresight and efforts that the Lucknow garrison held out to be at last relieved by Havelock. Those who had till this day remained outside the intrenchments had now to fly to the Residency, leaving houses and property unprotected, sacrificing every thing, and thinking only of saving their lives. The Residency became one scene of confusion—the women and children rushing to find a place of refuge from the relentless foe, who, flushed with victory, were approaching with flying colors and drums beating, confident of an easy triumph over the remnant that remained.

Men, covered with blood, some with mangled limbs, their muscles contracted with agony, their faces pale, and bodies almost cold, others with the death-rattle in their throat, were brought in by their comrades and laid in rows in the banqueting hall, now turned into a hospital. The ladies crowded around them, fanned them, supplied temporary bandages, and showed as much solicitude for them as though they had been their own relatives, which was probably the case as to some of them. The surgeons were soon busy enough, cutting, probing, amputating, and bandaging. All the horrors of war were at once laid bare before the anxious crowd.

Every man, including the civilians—some of whom had never handled a musket before, but whom Sir Henry had armed—were now called out to defend the position, for the exultant enemy were pouring over the two bridges and up the streets to the very gates of the Residency, and getting their guns into position. The people of the city within range were flying, with their goods, out of the way of the expected bombardment, while both sides prepared for the terrible and unequal conflict. The defenses of the Residency were hastily completed. Barricades were formed in all exposed situations, and it is marvelous to read the elements of which some of them were composed—mahogany tables and valuable furniture of all kinds, carriages and carts, the records of Government officers in large chests, boxes of stationery, and whatever could be laid hold of and piled up, to cover from the enemy's fire or stop a bullet. Even Captain Hayes's famous library, consisting of invaluable Oriental manuscripts, the standard literary and scientific works of European nations, and dictionaries of almost every language, were, for the nonce, converted into barricades.

These, with the other defenses which they had already prepared, were by no means strong, though the best they could extemporize. Their chief reliance was on the number of their guns, the quantity of their ammunition, and their own courage, which they hoped the God of Hosts would crown with his blessing, till relief could reach them from Calcutta or from England.

Their enemies had taken possession of the houses deserted by the citizens, and were filling them with sharp-shooters, loop-holing the walls, and putting their numerous cannon in position all around the Residency, as near as they could come, a few of them being so close that they were not more than forty or fifty yards from the intrenchments around the buildings occupied by the Christians. This seems almost incredible, but I can vouch for its truthfulness from personal knowledge before the siege, and personal examination after it, while the battered and torn Residency is to-day its standing memorial. Each party spent a busy night, and next morning the iron messengers of death were flying back and forth in increasing numbers.

Let us pause here and note the respective strength of the parties in this fearfully unequal conflict, and the object for which each was about to fight. On the one side were part of an English regiment, one company of British artillery, a few hundred faithful Sepoys, with some English and European civilians ; on the other, the whole army of Oude. But this fact is worthy of more detail.

The entire number now inside the Residency, including those holding the fort of the Muchee Bawun, near by, was as follows:

Men: European soldiers	629
" civilians	298
Native soldiers	765
Total bearing arms	1,692
Women	240
Children	310
Total inside the Residency	2,242

This includes the sick and wounded after the disastrous defeat at Chinhut.

Outside, their enemies swarmed around their position in such numbers that they have been variously computed at from 30,000 to 100,000 strong at different periods during the siege, with about one hundred guns bearing on the devoted Residency and its defenders.

But mere numbers do not give a sufficient idea of this dreadful contest. Many of those now within the Residency had fled there in such panic as to leave behind in their homes their provisions, money, and furniture, and were literally without a change of clothing, or a bed to lie down upon, or a knife and spoon with which to eat their scanty food. The hottest time of the year was upon them, with not the first of the appliances by which they had been accustomed to mitigate its rigor. Crowded into the narrowest space, most of them had to lie down on the ground, the heat, mosquitoes and effluvia being almost intolerable: the shot of the enemy, too, often came crashing through the walls, sprinkling them with the dust and mortar as it passed over them, while sometimes a fearful shell would explode in their midst, and kill or wound two or three or more of them. Alas! one hundred and forty-three days of such suffering lay before them now, during which time two fifths of their number were to die, and more than a thousand brave men would have to perish in order to save the remnant that was left!

The Residency itself, and a few houses around it—the homes of the officers in the suite of the Governor—occupied an elevated plateau, with the city on three sides of it and the river Goomtee on the north. From the roof of the Residency the view was beautiful, extending over the city and surrounding country. The number and variety of the buildings, the gilded domes and cupolas, the elegant outlines of the palaces, all set in the deep green of the surrounding trees and gardens, together made up a scene of surpassing beauty; but no building could have been less calculated for purposes of defense. Its lofty windows, which had not been walled up, offered unopposed entrance to every bullet that came. The roof was wholly exposed. Below its ground floor the Residency had a spacious "Tyekhana"—underground rooms, used by people in India as a retreat from the heat and glare of the mid-day sun in the hot season, and as soon as the siege commenced the ladies and children were crowded into this splendid cellar, and had to remain there. The Banqueting Hall was turned into a hospital, and the upper rooms occupied by the soldiers. Altogether, in this one building there were from 800 to 1,000 persons. The remainder were placed in the houses around, or at the batteries, or where any shelter could be found.

Meanwhile the siege went on, and increased in its fierceness; closer and closer still was drawn the circle of guns around the position, and they were served with great ability. Every loop-hole made in the walls of the houses around had a sharp-shooter at it day and night, and the moment a head was exposed the rifle sent forth a leaden messenger of death. Sir Henry soon became convinced that he was too weak in numbers to think any longer of holding both the Muchee Bawun and the Residency. He saw that he would be overwhelmed in the assault which would probably follow this fierce bombardment, so he resolved to give up the Muchee Bawun and concentrate his whole force within the Residency. But how to effect the junction now, when the river side of the road the whole way to the Muchee Bawun was lined with the batteries and troops of the enemy, was a difficulty before which most men would have shrunk. Sir Henry, however, saw it must be attempted, and every thing was done to carry it out. By telegraphic signals from the tower, shown in the picture, communications were at length established, and the order was transmitted to the commanding officer, "*Blow up the fort and come to the Residency at twelve o'clock to-night. Bring your treasure and guns, and destroy the remainder.*"

That night was anxiously looked for, and many an earnest prayer went up to God that every movement might be made safely and well, so that the retreat of the retiring force might not be intercepted. To distract the attention of the enemy the batteries opened fire, especially toward the iron bridge, by which the column must pass. The movement was most successfully accomplished, and so noiseless was the march, favòred by the darkness, that the head of the column was at the Residency gate at fifteen minutes after twelve. There was a little delay here, as, not being so quickly expected, the gate had not been made ready. It was dark, and a very serious accident had almost occurred, for the leading men finding the gates closed, cried out, "Open the gates." This the artillerists at the guns above, which covered the entrance, mistook for "open with grape." They flew to their guns and rammed in the grape, when an officer rushed up and set them right. The whole force came in without a shot being fired by them or at them. The distance is fully one third of a mile, and the enemy was on their left hand, within fifty or sixty yards of them most of the way. The explosion had not yet occurred, the fuses having been left extra long to give time for the rear to be quite clear of danger; but soon a shake of the earth, a volume of fire, a terrific report, and an immense column of black smoke shooting high into the air, announced to Lucknow that the Muchee Bawun was no more. All the ammunition that they could not remove—two hundred and fifty barrels of powder and several millions of ball cartridge—was destroyed, together with the buildings and their contents. The shock resembled an earthquake.

How gladly the garrison greeted their comrades as they entered! The junction of the two forces was an incalculable gain, for the additional men were actually required to man the defenses, and their safe arrival greatly cheered every person in the Residency. Strange things will occur in the most solemn circumstances. On calling their muster-roll they found one man was missing—an Irish soldier. He was given up as lost. The unfortunate fellow had been left behind in a state of intoxication. He was thrown into the air and returned again to mother earth unhurt, continued his drunken sleep, and awoke early next morning to find, to his astonishment, the fort all in ruins around him. He deliberately walked to the Residency, unmolested by any one. The men inside the Residency gate, just as day was breaking, were not a little surprised to hear a man outside sing out to them, with a rich Irish brogue, "Arrah, thin, open your gates!" Convulsed with laughter, they opened and let the poor fellow in. He was asked why he had left the fort, and with a look of wonder and simplicity answered, "Sure, an' I didn't see e'er a man in the place."

Every one seemed to catch the spirit of the noble chief—Sir Henry's presence anywhere was like a re-enforcement. Day and night he was inspecting and encouraging the various posts, exposed to imminent danger all the while. From twelve to forty men were at each point or battery, with thousands of the bloodthirsty and blaspheming fanatics opposed to each set; but these outposts must be maintained, for if once in, the enemy never could have been turned out; every man, woman, and child would have been ruthlessly butchered; yet each party fought under the apprehension that others might be more hardly pressed than themselves, and occasionally the cry would be heard, "More men this way!" and off would run two or three, all that could be spared, till a similar cry was heard from another direction, when others would rush to that point to give assistance.

On July 4 the heaviest trial that could befall them occurred—their trusted and heroic commander was struck down. The Sepoys had found out what room Sir Henry Lawrence occupied—the one shown on the lower floor, right-hand side, in the picture, and they began to send shells into it. One of these entered and exploded close to Sir Henry, tearing the thigh from his body, and mortally wounding him. He lingered for two days, and then departed as noble a spirit as ever animated human clay. He spent the conscious moments of these two days in directing and advising what should be done in carrying on the defense till succor should arrive. Frequently he would arouse himself, and exclaim to the mourning group around him, "Save the ladies!" and for their sakes he enjoined upon them, in view of what had been done at Delhi and Cawnpore, *never to surrender!* His last thoughts were given to those he loved so well, and to the Redeemer whom he had served for many years. He expressed his anxiety for the welfare of the "Lawrence Asylum"—a school which he had founded for the children of soldiers in India; sent affectionate messages to his children and to his brother, late Viceroy of India, and to his sisters; and spoke most affectionately of his wife, Lady Lawrence, who had died four years previously. He then earnestly pointed out to those around him the worthlessness of all human distinctions, recommending them to fix their thoughts upon a better world and try to gain it. He was prayed with, and received the holy sacrament, praising God, and expressing his perfect faith and reliance on his divine Saviour, and in this state of mind he passed out of that scene of conflict and confusion to that blessed clime where

> "No rude alarm of raging foes,
> No fears, shall break his long repose."

Military honors marked not their respect for his remains. The times were too stern for such demonstrations. "By dead of night" a hurried prayer, amid the booming of the enemy's cannon and the fire of their musketry, was read over his corpse, and he was lowered into a pit, with several other, though lowlier, companions in arms, and there he sleeps behind the Residency, awaiting the resurrection of the just.

A feeling of despair for a few hours seemed to take possession of every man and woman, but they had to rouse themselves to meet the stern realities of their position. Darker and more dreadful the days came on; yet still they fought and suffered. Their hopes of relief were still deferred, and their hearts were sick, while their foes grew stronger in numbers and determination to destroy them, and would frequently yell out, with fearful imprecations—for they were near enough to be heard—what they would do with them when they did get in. But the garrison were determined there should not be another Cawnpore. Sir Henry's injunction "never to surrender" was fully accepted. It is fearful to read their resolves should the worst come, and to find the ladies acquiescing; and even, in some cases, requiring an engagement from their husbands to fulfill those wishes rather than that they should fall into the hands of the Sepoys.

This awful alternative was actually taken by some of those who fell at Jansee. One lady in particular is mentioned, who pledged her husband, an English officer, that when death became inevitable, he was not to allow her to fall alive into the power of the Sepoys, but she was to die by a pistol-ball from his own hand. Sadly and reluctantly he gave the promise; and when the fearful hour came, and the enemy broke in upon them, she sprang to his side, and, with a last caress exclaimed, "Now, Charley, now—your promise!" He kissed her, put the pistol to her head, and then turned and sold his own life dearly to the wretches around him.

Such cases cannot be judged by ordinary rules. Those who entertained such thoughts were confronted by an Oriental foe, whose fiendish malice and cruelty to women and children are not known in civilized warfare. It is a matter of devout thankfulness that the Lucknow garrison were not reduced to this dreadful extremity. It would have clouded the bright record of their heroic endurance.

Space would fail to give even a brief outline of their sorrows during the next three months. Reduced to starvation allowances of the coarsest food, many of them clad in rags, and all crowded into the narrowest quarters, so that Mrs. Harris's Diary speaks of the ladies lying on the floor, "fitting into each other like bits in a puzzle, until the whole floor was full," they still courageously endured.

And if this was the condition of those in health, what must have been the state of the sick and wounded! Small-pox, cholera, boils, dysentery, and malarious fever added their horrors to the situation, while the iron hail of death, mingling with the drenching rain of the monsoon, dropped upon them, so that by the first of August the deaths sometimes rose to twenty in a single day. During this period, and amid all this turmoil and sorrow, eight or ten little ones were born; and most of these "siege babies," as they were called, actually lived through it all, and still survive, while many of the poor mothers sank under their privations. But the bereaved babies were cared for by the noble women around them. Daily the men fell in the presence of the enemy; and it is described as truly affecting to see how the list of newly-made widows increased in its number and sadness.

Food and clothing became painfully scarce, and now "money was despised for bread." The effects, or little stores, of the officers killed were at once sold by auction to the survivors, and it is curious now to read the prices that were eagerly paid. A bottle of wine brought 70 rupees, (the rupee is 50 cents in gold;) a ham, 75 rupees; a bottle of honey, 45 rupees; a cake of chocolate, 30 rupees; a bottle of brandy, 140 rupees; a small fowl, bought by an officer for his sick wife, 20 rupees; two pounds of sugar brought 16 rupees, and other things in proportion. An old flannel shirt, that had seen hard service in the mines—which they had to dig to countermine the enemy—brought 45 rupees. The single suit with which many of them had to hurry into the Residency was being fast worn out, and the officers might have been seen wearing the most extraordinary costumes. Few had any semblance of a military uniform, and many were in shirts, trousers, and slippers only. One gallant civilian, having found an old billiard-table cloth, had contrived to make himself a kind of loose coat out of it. All carried muskets, and were accoutered like the soldiers.

While the feeble garrison were thus decreasing in numbers, their foes were augmenting their strength. The Talookdars (Barons) of Oude were sending their armed retainers to aid the Sepoys, till it was thought that by the end of August there must have been as many as one hundred thousand men around the Residency. Their leaders were maddened by the continued and successful resistance of the English; and all that they could do to inspire their men, by fanaticism, bhang, (an intoxicating liquor,) and brave leading, were done to capture the position. They attempted to *storm* it several times. Three of these occasions are specially memorable; and it is perfectly amazing to read the stern, unconquerable resistance with which this handful of heroic men, behind their intrenchments, met and dashed back again that raging tide of fierce and blaspheming assailants. They would begin by exploding the mines which they had driven close up to or under the defenses, open with a fearful cannonade, and then swarm up to the breaches made. On July 20th the fight lasted from 9 A. M. to 4 P. M., with the broiling sun up to 140 degrees. At what cost these repulses must have been received may be understood by the fact, that the native report of the attempt to storm on the 10th of August admits a loss on their side of four hundred and seventy men killed and wounded on that day alone.

Lady Inglis, wife of the Commander, in her journal of this terrible day, while the poor ladies down in the Tyekhana trembled for the result, refers to the soothing influence of *prayer*, as she tried it there with that excited and terrified crowd of women. The effect, she says, was amazing; each of them seemed to rise above herself, and with calmness and true courage they awaited the result, realizing that, though the enemy was near, God himself was nearer still, and could preserve them. And he did preserve them.

It is described as one of the most affecting sights that ever was witnessed in a scene of battle to see how the wounded men acted on that day. Knowing the danger, and how their comrades were pressed, they insisted on leaving their beds in the hospital and being helped to the front. The poor fellows came staggering along to the scene of action, trembling with weakness and pale as death, some of them bleeding from their wounds, which reopened by the exertions they made. Those whose limbs were injured laid aside their crutches and *kneeled* down, and fired as fast as they could out of the loop-holes; while others, who could not do this much, lay on their backs on the ground and loaded for those who were firing. With such endurance as this the fierce enemy was beaten back; and Asiatics were taught how Christian soldiers could fight and die when defending the lives and honor of Christian women. The storming over, the usual cannonade and musketry were resumed; but the garrison had become so used to danger and death, that by this time the balls would fall at their feet, or whiz past and graze their hair, frequently without causing any remark about their escapes —they were so common, yet so narrow. The very children began to act like soldiers, playing the mimic "game of war." One urchin of five years was heard saying to another, "*You* fire round shot, and I'll return shell from my battery." Another, getting into a rage with his playmates, exclaimed, "I hope you may be shot by the enemy!" Others, playing with grape instead of marbles, would say, "That's clean through his lungs," or, "That wants *more elevation.*" These young scamps picked up all the expressions of the artillery, and made use of them at their games.

The peacock abounds in India, wild and "in all his glory." On the 30th of June, during a lull in the firing, one of these magnificent birds flew near the Residency, perched on the ramparts, and there quietly plumed his feathers. The hungry men looked at him for awhile, and all felt what a welcome addition he would be to their scanty fare. They could easily have shot him, but they refrained; the beautiful creature seemed like an omen of coming liberty and peace, and he was allowed to remain unmolested as long as he liked.

To insult the garrison, the Sepoys would frequently send the regimental bands to the opposite banks of the river Goomtee, and have them perform the popular English airs that they used to play there for their officers in other days. With any thing but pleasant feelings, the garrison would have to listen to "The Standard Bearer's March," "The Girl I Left Behind Me," "See, the Conquering Hero Comes," etc. The disloyal rascals had the

Henry Havelock.

By permission of Bryan, Taylor & Co.

impudence always to finish the concert with the loyal air, "God Save the Queen."

We pause here to consider what was being done, meanwhile, hundreds of miles away for their relief. The English authorities at Calcutta had become ere this fully aware of their danger, and were straining every nerve to send them assistance. But what could they do without men? Delhi had not a soldier to spare, nor had other points throughout the land where a few English troops were found. Relief must come from without, until the four tedious months rolled over that would bring it from England, twelve thousand miles away.

It was this terrible emergency that made the little force from the Persian Gulf so opportune in its arrival in June. Its saintly and gallant commander was General Havelock, whose portrait we here present.

No account of the Sepoy Rebellion would be just or adequate that would fail to give him that prominence in its overthrow which Almighty God, in his wonderful providence, awarded him.

About a month after the battle of Waterloo Henry Havelock entered the English army as Second Lieutenant in the Rifle Brigade. In 1823 he was ordered to India, and it was while on his way there, on board the "General Kyd," and chiefly through the instrumentality of Lieutenant James Gardner, that he was led to that full surrender of his heart and life to the Lord Jesus which he so consistently sustained through the evil and good report of the following forty-three years of his eventful military career. His consecration to God was so complete that a brother officer has testified of him that "he invariably secured two hours in the morning for reading the Scriptures and private prayer." He did this even when campaigning; so that "if the march began at six o'clock, he rose at four; if at four, he rose at two." He recognized the claims of God upon his money as well as his time, and from his conversion to the close of his career he devoted regularly one tenth of his income to the cause of God; so that he might be truly described, in the words applied to the Centurion of the Italian band at Cesarea, as "a devout man, and one who prayed to God alway." His talents were equally at the Lord's service, so that he was ever ready to visit the sick, to hold a prayer-meeting, to address an audience at a missionary or Bible meeting, while his efforts to lead the men whom he commanded to Christ, and to promote temperance and virtue among them, are well known to have been continued to the last, and to have been greatly owned of God.

Havelock was a Baptist by profession, but he would not be a close communionist. He loved all good men, and delighted to join with them in celebrating his Lord's death. In all his public acts, when he rose to eminence and command, his dispatches and orders acknowledged God, and he delighted to ascribe to him the victories that he was enabled to achieve. How touching are these, especially in his last campaign!

His life was one of continued exposure and hard service. In 1824 he fought under Sir Archibald Campbell in Burmah, where he had the satisfaction of assisting at the liberation of Dr and Mrs. Judson from the Emperor's cruel tyranny. It was then, in the midst of a serious military move, and when the corps ordered to occupy a most important point were found utterly incapable, from intoxication, to fulfill their duty, that his commander-in-chief paid him and his men that rough compliment—"Call out Havelock's saints; they are never drunk, and Havelock is always ready!" The "saints" and their leader promptly responded, the position was saved, and the enemy repulsed.

How he was esteemed by his men, for whose highest good he labored so earnestly, may be seen in the fact that when, in 1836, his house was accidentally burned with all its contents, the men of his regiment came in a body to him, begging him to allow each of them to devote one month's pay to help him to sustain the loss. He gratefully declined the aid pressed upon him, but what a satisfaction must it have been in showing the estimation in which these men held him. He might well offset any petty High Church *hauteur* which certain parties might affect toward him because he was a "Dissenter," with this noble instance of the value in which his character and services were held by those who best knew in what his Christianity consisted.

If the consideration intimated had any thing to do with the fact that he was allowed to serve his country twenty-three years as a subaltern before he was promoted to a captaincy, the narrow-minded bigots who did him the injustice are not to be envied now. When they shall have been long forgotten, the good soldier of Jesus Christ, whose advance they retarded, will be remembered and honored by gallant men and true women on both Continents.

In 1838 he took part in the invasion of Afghanistan, was at the storming of Ghuznee, at the forcing of the Khoord Cabool Pass, and aided in the memorable defense of Jellalabad, where he won his majority, and received the Cross of the Bath for conspicuous bravery. He took part in the forcing of the Khyber Pass, in the invasion of Kohistan, and in the battle of Muherajpore. He wrote the military memoirs of some of these great events, and was Persian interpreter to the Commander-in-chief. At Moodkee, in 1845, he had two horses shot under him, and another at the battle of Sabraon; became Military Secretary to the Commander-in-chief and Colonel; till at length, after twenty-six years of hard service, which bore heavily on a constitution not naturally strong, he was permitted to visit England to recruit that energy which would soon be required in circumstances of greater emergency than he or his country had ever seen in the East.

Divine Providence had thus trained him for the supreme duty of his life. In 1855 he was back in India, appointed Adjutant-General, and just entering his sixtieth year, and in January, 1857, was nominated in orders to command the second division of the army employed against Persia, under Lieutenant-General Sir James Outram, from whence he returned victorious. In the heart of Persia we find him writing to his beloved wife, (the daughter of Dr. Marshman, the well-known missionary:) "I have good troops and cannon under my command, but my trust is in the Lord Jesus, my tried and merciful friend! To him all power is intrusted in heaven and on earth" He had to pass a fort here, his steamer being crowded with his Highlanders, whom he made to lie down, while, Farragut-like, he took his station on the paddle-box, to aid as the emergency required. Though the bullets whizzed all around him he was untouched. After the victory was won, he writes: "I felt throughout that the Lord Jesus was at my side."

The sympathy of this noble man with "the common people" is beautifully illustrated just here, when we find him engaged in writing a long letter to a Christian soldier then in London, named Godfrey, who had formerly served under him, a letter from whom found him in Persia.

But now came the days when we needed him and his brave men, and a merciful Providence causes war to cease in Mohummera, and returns him to India on the very day before the Bareilly massacre. He is delayed by shipwreck, and by having to wait for his troops at Calcutta. The 78th Highlanders, 84th and 64th Queens', reach him at last, and, as no more can then be spared, save a few Sikhs, and notwithstanding that he must know that he had probably a heavier duty on his hands than any soldier of his race ever undertook, he shrinks not—but with the words to his wife, "May God give me wisdom and strength to fulfill the expectations of the Government, and restore tranquillity in the disturbed provinces," he sets out on his last eventful campaign, to find a grave at its close, but realizing all through it, ay, and at the end as well, that "the Lord Jesus was at his side!"

With only fourteen hundred British bayonets and eight guns, united to less than three hundred Sikhs and thirty irregular cavalry, he sublimely writes in starting: "I march to-morrow to endeavor to retake Cawnpore and rescue Lucknow!" He was to do this through a country swarming with Sepoy troops, who had been well disciplined and armed by Englishmen, and to do it, too, at that season of the year when the rains fall fast and frequently, and the flat country is inundated, and the sun pours down its rays like fire, till the thermometer stands at one hundred and thirty-eight degrees—to do it all with a poorly-supplied commissariat, with few tents, and little shelter. Were ever such results sought by such means under such circumstances? But they were the best the times admitted, and knowing the danger of delay for the precious lives at Cawnpore and Lucknow, he would take them, and trust Him for the results who can save by few as by many.

At Futtypore he was confronted by thirty-five hundred rebels—two regiments being cavalry and three infantry—with twelve guns His men had just finished their march under a broiling sun that forenoon, when the Sepoys bore down upon him, confident of an easy triumph. But in four hours Havelock had his victory, with eleven of the rebel guns, their ammunition and baggage, as the trophies of it in his hands. In his General Order he ascribes his triumph "to the power of the Enfield rifle in British hands, to British pluck, and to the blessing of Almighty God on a most righteous cause—the cause of justice, humanity, truth, and good government in India." This conflict occurred on the 12th of July—the anniversary of the battle of the Boyne, as noticed by the General. He also notes that one of the infantry regiments opposed to him was the 56th, the very regiment which he himself led at the battle of Maharajpore a few years previously! He challenged them in particular, and was exultant over their defeat; yet adds in his letter, "But away with vain-glory! Thanks to Almighty God, who gave me the victory!" Such was the man, and such the heroes whom he led, who were thus fighting their way up to our relief against such fearful odds.

It was near Futtypore, and about one day before the battle, that Joel met this force. His party had slept the night before in Judge Tucker's house, as narrated in his letter. That gentleman's death was avenged before the General left Futtypore. On the day of the rising in May, Judge Tucker refused to desert his post, hoping to preserve the peace by the assistance of his subordinate, Hikrimtoolah Khan, the Deputy Collector. But, like Khan Bahadar, this man proved a cruel traitor. He himself led on the mob which surrounded the Judge's house. Hikrimtoolah proposed to try him, but the stern Judge would not surrender. Sixteen of his assailants fell by his hand ere this brave man was overpowered. At length

Hikrimtoolah had him at his disposal, and, taking off his hands, feet, and head, he held them up before the mob as trophies. All this was known; for evidence of native Christians, and others who fled, was taken on oath, and was already on file in Havelock's hands. Instead of keeping out of the way, Hikrimtoolah, with consummate hypocrisy, supposing his deed unknown to the General, came out to congratulate Havelock on his victory. He was at once arrested, the evidence of his guilt was found to be conclusive, and he was executed on the spot.

At Aong and Pandoo Nuddee Havelock was again victorious. This latter action brought him within a few miles of Cawnpore. Intelligence of the defeat of his Sepoy forces reached the Nana Sahib on the night of the 15th of July, and was immediately followed by the massacre of the ladies, already described.

The weary soldiers were aroused by the bugle-blast long before daylight on the morning of the 16th. They had that day to meet the sternest resistance they had ever yet encountered, for the whole force of the Nana Sahib, who commanded in person, lay between them and Cawnpore, where they hoped to find alive, and still holding out, the noble men they were marching and fighting so hard to save. The foe was met strongly intrenched at Ahirwa, and they fought like furies for two hours and twenty minutes, with every advantage in their favor. The British charge that day is described by those who witnessed it as one of the most sublime illustrations of the power of discipline that was ever witnessed. That little force of thirteen hundred men moved up, steady and silent as a wall, to conquer or to die, amid those crashing shells and volleys of musketry; and the heart of the foe died within him, and his fire became hasty and ill-directed, as the sheen of the British bayonets became ominously distinct, till, within one hundred yards, they delivered their fire, and with a cheer dashed through their own smoke at the enemy. Then each rebel thought only of himself. These humbled Brahmins dropped their weapons, stripped off their packs, and spurred and ran for dear life back to the city of their hideous crime, leaving all their guns in Havelock's hands. He lost one hundred of his small force in this fierce contest. It is believed that "in no action ever fought was the superior power of arrangement, moral force, personal daring, and physical strength of the European over the Asiatic more apparent" than in this case, for the rebels fought hard and well, but they had met far more than their match, and were terribly beaten. Thus, between the 7th and 16th of July, Havelock's men had marched one hundred and twenty-six miles, under an Indian sun, alternated with tropical rains; had fought four battles, and captured forty-four guns; yet their labors and sufferings were only beginning. Still their General trusted in God, and held that his soldiers' discipline was equal to their valor, and he resolved to push on and finish the work that was given them to do.

The wounded are gathered and cared for, the dead buried, and the weary heroes lie down on the soaking earth to rest and dream of the deliverance they will surely bring to-morrow to their beleaguered friends in Cawnpore. In the middle of the night a crash that shook the ground beneath awoke them—Nana Sahib had blown up the Cawnpore magazine. On the morning of the 17th the British marched into Cawnpore. A Eurasian with whom I am well acquainted, a Mr. Shepherd—the only living Christian in the district, and who escaped as by a miracle—rushed out from his hiding-place and joined them; he told them all, and led them to the house of blood! These men, who had charged to the cannon's mouth on the preceding day, sank down on the ground and wept like children at this spectacle of crime and suffering. Havelock's feelings of grief were inexpressible. Nana Sahib's butcheries were evidently a defiant challenge to a conflict of absolute extermination on the one side or the other: none could misunderstand his purpose.

Resting his weary and sorrowful troops for that day, on the 19th Havelock marched against Bithoor. But Nana Sahib had fled and crossed the Ganges, to get between Havelock and Lucknow, so as at least to delay his march till the Sepoys there could have time to copy the hideous infamy of which he had given them the example.

On the 20th General Neill, at Havelock's urgent request, had joined him from Allahabad with every available man—only two hundred and seventy of the Fusileers in all. Leaving Neill at Cawnpore with a few soldiers, Havelock, strong in hope that he should yet be in time to save the Lucknow garrison, crossed the Ganges on the 21st with his gallant fifteen hundred men, and began his first march for their relief. He fought two battles and gained two victories at Onao and Busserut Gunge in one day. But at this season the rains deluge the whole face of the country, which is quite flat between the two cities. There is only one road for that forty-three miles, and his foes, recruited from Lucknow, were swelled to ten or fifteen thousand men, with ample artillery and cavalry. Havelock had lost many of his officers and men. The gallant Renaud was killed; Beatson had died of cholera; disease and sun-stroke were busy in his ranks; and the great and good man was compelled, with a sad heart, to come to the conclusion that he must return nearer to Cawnpore, and wait for reinforcements, ere he could venture to resume his march. To persevere now would be certain destruction. So he returned to Munghowur, sent his sick and wounded to Cawnpore, and corresponded with Calcutta and Allahabad, entreating for help.

All this time he was trying to communicate with Lucknow, by hiring faithful natives to venture to carry letters to the garrison. Three of his missives did reach them—short, written in Greek, and inclosed in a quill, which the messenger could conceal in his mouth when liable to be searched by the rebel police and others. He had the satisfaction of receiving two replies from them, telling him of their condition and how they looked for his arrival. They little imagined with how small a force, and under what disadvantages, he was trying to reach them, for he made light of his obstacles, and wrote cheerfully of his hopes.

Neill sent out to him every available soldier that could then be obtained; and with fourteen hundred healthy men Havelock commenced his second march to relieve Lucknow on the 4th of August. The enemy had taken up a strong position on their old ground, at Busserut Gunge. The Sepoys, in great force and well posted, had the town for their second line of defense. The country on either side of the road was little better than a lake; so, as it was impossible for Havelock to turn the position, he had to advance along the road which they so completely commanded, to drive them from their position. But he did this, and gained the town, and drove the rebels through and beyond it. He had only a handful of cavalry to follow up his advantage. This was his seventh victory.

But now appeared an invisible foe whom he could not conquer. The terrible Asiatic cholera broke out among his men, and he was in the field, exposed to the elements, and surrounded by swamps and malaria. He had, therefore, to retreat again, not from the face of man, but from the fearful pestilence. He retired upon Mung-howur, which was on rising ground, and here he wrote one of his last letters to Mrs. Havelock, evidently fully conscious of the emergencies of his position, and says: "I have every-where beaten my foes, but things are in a most perilous state. If we succeed in restoring any thing, it will be by God's especial and extraordinary mercy. I must now write as one whom you may see no more, for the chances of war are heavy at this crisis. Thank God for my hope in the Saviour! We shall meet in heaven."

What the Duke of Wellington said of a soldier whom he saw turn *pale* as he looked at the fearful breach which he was mounting up to storm—"There is a brave man; he sees his danger, and yet he faces it"—might with every propriety be said of this warrior and his men. They were fully sensible of their risks, and yet they gallantly faced them. What would four or five thousand men have been to Havelock then! But help was far away. A few hundreds were struggling up to him from Calcutta, but the forces he needed were tossing on the billows off the Cape of Good Hope, while twenty thousand Sepoys, well provisioned, and in splendid condition, lay extended across the road by which he wanted to march to the relief of the beleaguered garrison in the Residency. He had lost one hundred and forty men out of a thousand, and was but ten miles on his road to Lucknow. He evidently had no alternative but to go back to Cawnpore and wait for help. On the thirteenth he recrossed the Ganges, and here the additional danger of his position broke upon him. Nana Sahib had recrossed the river before him and was threatening Cawnpore, and also his communications with Allahabad, while Neill and his little force were on the brink of destruction. He soon retrieved the state of affairs, fighting another well-contested battle, and scattering the rebel hosts to the winds.

Himself and men were now doomed to a brief term of enforced rest, which they greatly needed ere they entered upon their last great struggle. On the 15th of September came some of the help for which he had so longed, for Lieutenant-General Sir James Outram, with two thousand men, reached Cawnpore that day. General Outram could, in view of his superior rank, have at once assumed command; but, with a magnanimity as rare as it was generous, he waived his right, that he might gratify and honor the noble man whose devotion and gallantry he so highly appreciated. He therefore issued his divisional order on the night of the 16th, saying, "The important duty of first relieving Lucknow has been intrusted to Major-General Havelock, and General Outram feels that it is due to this distinguished officer, and the strenuous and noble exertions which he has already made to effect that object, that to him should accrue the honor of the achievement. General Outram is confident that the great end for which General Havelock and his brave troops have so long and gloriously fought will now, under the blessing of Providence, be accomplished. The General, therefore, in gratitude for, and admiration of, the brilliant deeds in arms achieved by General Havelock and his gallant troops, will cheerfully waive his rank on the occasion, and will accompany the force to Lucknow in his civil capacity as Chief Commissioner of Oude, tendering his military services to General Havelock as a volunteer."

Havelock gratefully and publicly acknowledged this generous and noble conduct of his chief, and, with renewed hope, prepared for the great task before him. The first letter of Havelock's that the garrison in the Residency received was on the 24th of July, promising, as the writer fondly hoped, relief in a few days; but it was not till the 29th of August that they understood the reasons of his delay, and now, nearly a month later still, he was at length to inform them in person what he had endured in order to reach them, and why he could not do so at an earlier day.

On the 20th of September Havelock again crossed the Ganges with 3,179 men, composed of the 78th and 91st Highlanders, the 64th and 84th, and the 1st and 5th Fusileers, a regiment of Sikhs, and 168 volunteer cavalry. No greater work was ever accomplished by military skill and daring than the relief of the Lucknow garrison by this handful of men.

The faithful native messenger, Ungud, again reached his camp, and was at once dispatched to give the final assurance to the garrison that he was at last really coming, and that, God helping him, they should be relieved within three or four days. This glad news reached them on the 22d of September, and raised the drooping spirits of all. How fervently they prayed, and how anxiously they watched, during the three following days, trembling to think how many precious lives of their approaching friends would have to be sacrificed in order to rescue them!

General Havelock had to fight two battles more between Cawnpore and Lucknow, but these he fought and won. Within five miles of the city they could hear the artillery booming around the Residency of Lucknow, and the General ordered a royal salute to be fired from his heaviest guns, in the hope that his beleaguered friends might hear the report and understand its import—that deliverance was drawing nigh.

Their beaten foes fell back on their strong city, about two miles of which Havelock's men must fight their way through, ere they could reach the Residency. Every inch of ground was disputed; palisades and barricades had to be taken at the point of the bayonet. The flat-roofed houses had been furnished with mud-walls on the top, on the street side, pierced for musketry, where the Sepoys could fire on the men in the narrow streets without exposing their own persons, thus doing dreadful execution. No words can do justice to that march of fire and death. "Broad, deep trenches had been cut across the road, fitted with every kind of obstruction. Each inch of the way was covered point-blank by unseen marksmen ; at every turn heavy artillery belched forth its fiery breath of grape and canister. Above, below, on all sides, crowds of human tigers glared from housetop and loop-holed casement upon the intrepid band, while, as they turned the corners which open upon the squares of the palace, surrounded by high walls, they had to encounter from many thousand rifles an iron hurricane of destruction and death." A bullet here strikes General Neill, and he falls to rise no more. But the brave men and their gallant leaders move steadily on, capturing guns and positions, till they reach the Kaiser Bagh—the King's Palace Garden—which they also capture. And here they try to collect and secure their wounded, and rest for the night, for they can go no farther. Alas! many of their wounded, about whom they are so anxious, fell into the hands of the cruel enemy, the fate of some of whom was dreadful. They were collected early in the night by these barbarians into one of the squares, and were there actually burned to death in the doolies, or hospital litters, in which they lay.

Early the next day the troops resumed their terrible task. A long reach of the city still separated them from the Residency. Strong positions and lengthy streets must be won ere they are heard or seen by their anxious friends there. The distance has often been walked over in twenty minutes by the writer, but it took these brave men more than twelve hours of the fiercest fighting to accomplish it that day. This was the 25th of September. One of the staff thus describes what followed: "About eleven o'clock A. M. the people in the Residency could distinctly perceive an increased agitation in the center of the city, with the sound of musketry and the smoke of guns. All the garrison was upon the alert, and the excitement among many of the officers and soldiers was quite painful to witness. About half past one P. M. they could see many of the people of the city leaving it on the north side across the bridges, with bundles of clothes, etc., on their heads.

The Relief of Lucknow by General Havelock.

Still their deliverers were not yet visible. At four P. M. a report spread that some of them could be seen, but for a full hour later nothing definite could be made out. At five o'clock volleys of musketry, rapidly growing louder and nearer, were heard, and soon the peculiar ring of a Minié ball over their heads told them their friends could be only a gun-shot from them now. They could see the Sepoys firing heavily on them from the tops of the houses, but the smoke concealed them. Five minutes later and the English troops emerged where they could actually be seen, fighting their way up the street, and though some fell at every step, yet nothing could withstand the headlong gallantry of the men. The 78th Highlanders were in front, led in person by General Havelock. Once fairly *seen*, all doubts and fears regarding them were ended, and then the garrison's long pent-up feeling of anxiety and suspense burst forth in a succession of deafening cheers. From every pit, trench, and battery—from behind the sand-bags piled on shattered houses—from every post still held by a few gallant spirits—rose cheer on cheer, even from the hospital. Many of the wounded crawled forth to join in the glad shout of welcome to those who had so bravely come to their assistance. It was a moment never to be forgotten."

The shouting made the ladies rush out from the Tyekanahs, just in time to witness the Highlanders and Havelock, having borne down all before them, reach the Residency. The enthusiasm with which they were greeted baffles all description—tears, hurrahs, every evidence of relief and joy, as they welcomed Havelock and the gallant men who had come in time to save them. Our picture but feebly depicts this thrilling scene, yet the heart of every humane person will easily imagine all that pen or pencil fails to portray.

Soon the whole place was filled, the Highlanders shaking hands frantically with every body, and then these great, big, rough-bearded men, black with powder and mud, seized the little children out of the ladies' arms, and were kissing them, and passing them from one to another, with tears rolling down their cheeks, thanking God that they had come in time to save *them* from the fate of those at Cawnpore.

For eighty-seven days the Lucknow garrison had lived in utter ignorance of all that had taken place outside. Wives, who had long mourned their husbands as dead, were now suddenly restored to them—some of them had come as volunteer cavalry with Havelock—and others, looking fondly forward to glad meetings with those near and dear to them, now for the first time learned that they were alone in the world. On all sides eager inquiries for relations and friends were made. Alas! in too many instances the answer was a painful one. Sleep was out of the question, and the morning dawned upon the inquirers still asking for more information.

It is excusable that you find them recording now, amid this joy of their rescue, as they realized the success of their protracted struggle, the proud consciousness of the defense that they had made against such fearful odds, in preserving not only their own lives, but the honor and lives of the ladies and children intrusted to their keeping. Now they learned at last that they had not been forgotten. They were told what sympathy their fearful position had awakened in all noble hearts in England and America, and throughout the civilized world. The general order issued next day, in eloquent and beautiful terms, gave them official assurance of all this.

"Havelock's hundred days" were ended in success, and that brave heart glowed with gratitude for the wonderful mercy that had helped him thus to struggle on to the end through the terrible tide of battle, disease, and death, to insure their safety. Now that it was accomplished, he acknowledged the divine help in the words of the Hebrew warrior: "Not unto us, O Lord, not unto us, but unto thy name give glory."

His gallant friend General Outram here assumed command, and in his dispatch he refers specially to a fact which shows that a delay of forty-eight hours more might have involved the destruction of all in the Residency. He writes: "We found that they (the Sepoys) had completed six mines in the most artistic manner —one of them from a distance of two hundred feet under our principal defensive works, which were ready for loading, and the firing of which must have placed the garrison entirely at their mercy. The delay of another day, therefore, might have sealed their fate." So near, apparently, did they come to being made another "Cawnpore."

The few native troops that had nobly and faithfully stood by them were well honored and rewarded. Ungud, their valiant messenger, received five hundred rupees for each letter he carried, quite a fortune for the worthy native. The spirit of these brave Sepoys, who had so long resisted unto blood, "faithful among the faithless," may be illustrated by a sad but touching incident, related by Mr. Rees, and which occurred at the entrance of the 78th Highlanders on the day of the relief. Coming with a rush on the Bailey Guard outposts, defended by the faithful Sepoys, and not knowing it to be within the Residency inclosure, or that these Sepoys were faithful, the Highlanders stormed it, and bayoneted three of the men, whom they mistook for rebels. The men never resisted, and when explanations ensued, and regret was expressed, one of them waved his hand, and crying, "Kootch purwanni—Never mind—it is all for the good cause; welcome, friends!" he fell and expired.

General Havelock was too weak in men to attempt to bring out the garrison; he had to remain shut up with them till the Commander-in-chief, Sir Colin Campbell, came to their assistance on the 22d of November. The Sepoys still kept up their cannonade, but at a more respectful distance, and the ladies no longer feared either storm or capture. But Havelock's vigor was now unmistakably on the wane. Symptoms of serious illness were developing. By the effort of a strong will he tried to think lightly of them, and was still actively engaged day and night; but a "reduced ration of artillery bullock beef, chuppaties and rice" was poor nourishment for an invalid who had not even a change of clothing for the following forty days, the baggage being four miles off at the

Alumbagh. Bread, tea, coffee, sugar, soap, and all such articles, were then unknown luxuries there. The wretches outside still sustained their incessant din of shells and bullets, and raged in tens of thousands in the streets and occupied the buildings which all around commanded the Residency. They were as resolved as ever to destroy the garrison, while they must have been well aware that it could never escape from that position unless relieved by a powerful English army.

But that army, though not large in numbers, was now on its way. Sir Colin Campbell had landed at Calcutta, and with the first five thousand men that arrived he started for Lucknow.

On the 16th of November Sir Colin approached the city. Avoiding the crowded and barricaded streets, he took a course around by the Royal Park on the east, and, being on rising ground, his force, as they fought the enemy, could be seen from the Residency. They were sternly resisted the whole day. The garrison eagerly watched the conflict. One person was most conspicuous; he was mounted on a white horse, and seemed to be everywhere. They all felt very anxious for this person, for they guessed, and rightly too, that he was the Commander-in-chief. He advanced upon the Residency by the Dilkoosha and Martiniere and the line of palaces; but it required three days of fighting for him to accomplish his purpose. How fierce that fighting was may be imagined from a single item in the Commander-in-chief's dispatch, wherein he says that within the limits of a single building, the Secunderbagh, and its garden, the bodies of two thousand Sepoys were counted.

As soon as they left the Park and entered the city they were of course hidden from view, and terrible was the anxiety within the Residency for their success, and even their fate, as hour after hour went over, and the second, and even the third, day came and yet they could not see them. Nothing was known of them but the noise of the firing, the shouting, and the smoke of battle; still they felt that they must be coming nearer to them, for these sounds gradually became more distinct. This was the moment chosen for that imposition upon the sympathies of the world, the story of "*Jessie Brown*" and her "Dinna ye hear the slogan?" The heroine and the incident are alike fictitious; but what a wide currency the story obtained! Martin ascertained that it was originally a little romance, written by a French governess for the use of her pupils, which found its way into the Paris papers, thence to the Jersey *Times*, thence to the London *Times*, (December 12, 1857,) and afterward appeared in many of the English and American papers, and is to this day quoted as authentic. Yet the incident had some foundation in fact, though not in the form in which the poet has presented it. The bagpipes were heard certainly, but not till the Highlander who played them had got into the Residency; he was in among the first. The inspiration of the welcome set him going. As each party of the brave deliverers poured in they were greeted with loud hurrahs, which each garrison in the intrenchments would catch up, and so the cheers ran the rounds, and rose one wondrous shout to heaven. He who bore the bagpipes worked his way into this exulting mass of men, women, and children, and as he strode up and down and around the Residency he gave forth pæns of triumph in the shrill and joyous notes of his instrument, adding, of course, to the enthusiasm, and calling forth ardent repetitions of the wild delight of the occasion. Music never did more for the anxious human heart than was effected in that hour by those simple bagpipes. The sorrowful sighing of these prisoners of hope was suddenly turned into the joyous sense of deliverance; and it was fitting that Scotland's music should first thrill those hearts that Scotland's sons had been foremost to save.

On the evening of the 17th the army of the Commander-in-chief had fought their way near enough for the garrison to co-operate with his fire and attempt a junction. Notwithstanding the balls were still flying, Havelock and Outram rode forth to meet their deliverer. And what a meeting was that! The Scottish Chief, Sir Colin, grim with the smoke and dust of battle, "the good Sir James," as Outram was called, and the dying Havelock, with their respective staffs around them, met opposite the king's palace gate, about four hundred yards in front of the battered Residency, and there stood, hand grasped in hand, amid the roar of the cannon and the loud, glad cheers of their troops! Mansfield was there, and Hope Grant, and gallant Peel, with Norman, Ewart, Greathed, Sir David Baird, Adrian Hope, Gough, the Allisons, and scores of others, who had fought and suffered bravely to see that hour. All were in a tumult of joyous excitement. England has tried to do justice to that great meeting by a magnificent picture of the scene. But how significant of their toils and dangers is the reflection that of the names I have mentioned all but about two of this group of Christian knights are in their graves to-day! Campbell and Outram rest in Westminster Abbey, Havelock lies in the lonely Alumbagh, (he ought to sleep with his illustrious comrades,) and half the others repose beneath India's soil, on subsequent battle-fields, which had to be fought ere complete peace was conquered.

The relief of the Residency was at once followed by its evacuation. The women and children required to be promptly removed from danger to a place of safety; and, as this must be accomplished without risk to any of them, the intention had to be entirely disguised from the enemy, fifty thousand strong around them. The Commander-in-chief considerately intrusted the arrangement of this honorable duty to General Havelock; it was the last service he would ever render, and most efficiently was it performed. The whole force was admirably handled, the fire of the Residency being sustained, and even their lights left burning till sunrise. At midnight of the 22d all was ready, and along a narrow, tortuous lane, (the only possible path,) protected on both sides by the outposts, which, as the last of the column passed, were quietly withdrawn, "the pickets fell back through the supports; the supports glided away through the intervals of the reserve; the reserve, including the Commander-in-chief, silently defiled into the lane; while the enemy, seeing the lights and fires burning, thought the Residency still occupied, and kept up on the south and west sides their usually desultory night-firing." Not a single mishap occurred, and, to the delight of their deliverers, not one soul that had left the Residency that dark night was missing, as the garrison, with the four hundred and seventy-nine ladies and children, found themselves at sunrise on the morning of the 23d safe in the center of the whole English force, camped in the Dilkoosha Park, while the Residency, five miles away, the prison of their long agony, could be seen in the distance, swarming all over with the enraged Sepoys, who had just discovered, with the daylight, how completely they had been out-generaled!

The fresh air and green fields, the bread, butter, and milk, and clean table-cloths, and other comforts, which for many months they had not seen or tasted, are described as almost bewildering to the poor ladies and children, while the grateful hearts and tearful eyes of the officers who waited upon them so tenderly was a homage to their worth and sufferings which must have been very cheering to them. They were safe and well protected now.

But, in a tent near by, the noble man who had so uncomplainingly endured more than his enfeebled health could bear, was sinking, now that his great work for them was done. He had been helped off his horse and laid in a dooley. General Havelock was seriously unwell. His gallant son, with one wounded arm hung in a sling, was sitting by his cot, reading the Holy Scriptures and praying with his father. He was full of gratitude for the rescue so gloriously accomplished, and had accepted with becoming modesty the marked attention paid to him on all sides. He had also just heard of the gratitude of his country, the thanks of his Queen, for his noble services, and the fact that she had made him a Baronet, with a pension of £1,000 per year. But he had higher honor and reward than this awaiting him, and in a few hours was to pass away to its enjoyment. His disease was dysentery, which had been for several days aggravated by the "bread want," so severely felt at the Residency. Every thing that medical science and human sympathy could effect was now done, but all in vain; there was no remnant of strength to fall back upon, and the complaint had assumed its malignant form. He realized that his hour had come, and his work was done, and that now he had nothing more to do but to die. For that, too, he was ready. "The Resurrection and the Life" was beside him in that little tent, ready to pass with him through the valley and shadow of death. He feared no evil. Messages to his dear ones were delivered, and his last thoughts were given to the Redeemer, whom he had served and loved so long. He would say, and repeat it, "I die happy and contented!" To his eldest son, who waited upon him with such tenderness and loving attention, (though himself a wounded man and needing care,) he exclaimed, "My son, see how a Christian can die!"

General Outram, his illustrious comrade, asked to be permitted to see him. They had confronted danger together on many a hard-fought field, and death in all its reality was to be faced now. The Christian warrior looked up into the kindly, sympathetic countenance of his visitor, and said to him, "Sir James, for more than forty years I have so ruled my life that when death came I might face it without fear." Then pausing, as he realized that death had come, he added: "So be it. I am not in the least afraid. To die is *gain!*"

On the evening of the 24th he "departed to be with Christ," realizing the literal truthfulness of the favorite lines,

> "My body with my charge lay down,
> And cease at once to work and live."

He was buried amid the tears of those he saved, and his companions in arms, on the following day, in the Alumbagh, five miles on the Cawnpore side of Lucknow.

> "There rest thee, Christian warrior, rest from the twofold strife:
> The battle-field of India, the battle-field of life!
> * * * * * * *
> Victorious first at Futtypore, victorious at Lucknow,
> The gallant chief of gallant men is more than conqueror now."

We cannot conclude without referring to the loss of the garrison and the cost of their rescue. Of the 1,692 fighting men in the Residency on the 29th of June, the loss was 713—including 49 officers—when they were finally relieved. To these are to be added 19 ladies and 53 children killed, besides those wounded. Of General Havelock's force of 3,179 men, the total killed and wounded, besides 76 officers, was 966, nearly a third of his force. The Commander-in-chief had 45 officers and 536 men killed and wounded; so that the total casualties to rescue the Lucknow garrison amount to 121 officers and 1,490 men. Adding the loss of the garrison, the entire number of killed and wounded was 170 officers, and 2,203 men.

The ladies and children were safely escorted to Cawnpore, and thence to Allahabad. Word had been telegraphed in advance of their coming, and the whole city seemed to turn out and welcome them. Government officials, troops, natives, every body wanted to see and greet the ladies of the Lucknow garrison, for whose safety they had so long trembled.

At length the train rolled into the station, and the thundering cheers that greeted them, and were over and over again repeated, was a welcome that few have ever received. They stepped out of the carriages, and the haggard, pale faces of many of them, with their evidence of suffering and their scanty raiment, all told a tale that brought the tears to many an eye. As the last of these brave women passed out of the station, and the sympathizing crowd dried their tears and looked after them, their pent-up feelings found expression in response to an English soldier, who was holding on to a lamp-post, as, flinging his cap into the air, he sung out at the top of his voice, "One cheer more for our women, boys!" On the following day they went in a body to the church in Allahabad, and there returned thanks publicly to Almighty God for their most merciful preservation and rescue.

CHAPTER VII.

THE CAUSES AND FAILURE OF THE SEPOY REBELLION.

THE hate and cruelty of these fearful scenes have now to be accounted for. To what cause are we to ascribe them? Next to the facts of the great Rebellion, men have sought for the explanation of its origin.

I. The earliest reason to account for it was that put forward by certain members of the British civil service—venerable men, who had long administered the rule of the East India Company, and reflected so exclusively its merely commercial and worldly spirit that they seemed to forget they were Christians, or from a Christian land. They so fully vindicated and illustrated their master's doctrine of "neutrality," as in effect to discountenance Christianity and favor idolatry. Of such men the slang used to be that they "had left their religion at the Cape of Good Hope, to be resumed there on their return to England."

Such men had become *Hindooized* from long contact with idolatrous usages and ceremonies, almost verifying in regard to heathenism the reality of the lines,

> "Vice is a monster of such frightful mien,
> That to be hated, needs but to be seen;
> But seen too oft, familiar with her face,
> We first endure, then pity, then embrace."

They paid a certain deference to idol shrines, to caste prejudices, and heathenish customs; and very decidedly discountenanced all attempts at Bible or tract distribution, or legislation which aimed at abolishing even the cruel rites of Hindooism. They discouraged the incoming of missionaries or their preaching, and, if public sentiment would have permitted it, they would have persecuted and expelled them, as they once actually expelled Judson, and tried to drive away Carey, Marshman, and Ward. Even their own countrymen were not welcome to enter India as traders or merchants. Up to the time when I reached it their ready nickname for all such persons was, "Interlopers."

Long had they threatened that ruin would come if all such people as these were not kept out, and the inhabitants of India reserved for the exclusive manipulation of the East India Company and its servants. No one else was needed or desired there. These were the men who, thirty years ago, led the heathen to believe that "the English had really no religion." Well might they think so. As the mutiny developed, these conservatives looked round for some specific act to which they could triumphantly point the people of England as a verification of their predictions, and an adequate and valid reason for the Sepoy Rebellion. They found it in the fact that the Governor General, Lord Canning, (fresh from home and not yet tainted with their Christless "neutrality,") had so far forgotten the obligations of his high position before the people of India, that he had actually contributed money in aid of a Missionary Society!

By an American reader this statement must be thought simply ridiculous, and the writer be deemed trifling. But no, far from it; we are in sober earnest. This was, in all seriousness, solemnly put forward before the British people and Parliament as the cause of the Rebellion by these "most potent, wise, and reverend seigneurs" of the East India Company! They found a mouth-piece even in the House of Lords, in the person of one of their former associates, Lord Ellenborough, who rose in his place, and lifted his hands in horror as he announced the fact, and declared that nothing less than Lord Canning's recall could be considered an adequate penalty for so great a violation of the rules and traditions of the Honorable Court!

This "old Indian," who thus made a fool of himself, and slurred the Christianity of the very crown before him in the presence of what has been called "the most venerable legislative assembly in Christendom," was answered "according to his folly," not so much by his brother Peers, or by Christian clergymen, as by a man who is no Christian at all. God stirred up the spirit of a Hindoo in India to reply to it, and that far more effectually than any one else could have done it.

I have genuine pleasure in quoting this man's glowing words, and, from personal knowledge of him, I believe his utterance was the profound conviction of his heart. I commend the last paragraph of his speech to those who wish to know how one of the most intelligent men in India, speaking for himself and his fellows, regards Christian Missionaries.

This enlightened native is a gentleman by the name of Baboo Duckinarunjun Mookerjee, Secretary of the British Indian Association, a native club of considerable influence, with head-quarters in Calcutta. In regard to those mistaken views put forward in the House of Lords, the Baboo, at the next meeting of the association in Calcutta, repudiated any such idea, as a reflection upon the people of India, who, he alleges, can discriminate as well as other men between a personal and an official act. He said, "Lord Ellenborough, on the 9th of June last, in the House of Lords, was pleased to observe that the recent mutinies here are attributable to an apprehension on the part of the natives that the Government would interfere with their religion; that the fact of Lord Canning's rendering pecuniary aid to societies which have for their object the conversion of the natives, operates detrimentally to the security of the British Indian Government, which must be maintained on the principles of Akbar, [a tolerant ruler,] but never could be maintained on those of Aurungzebe, [an intolerant one,] and if it be a fact that the Governor General has subscribed to such societies, his removal from office would obviate the danger arising from the error. If the premises laid down by Lord Ellenborough be correct, there could be no two opinions as to the unfitness of Lord Canning to fill the vice-regal chair, and the urgent necessity of his Lordship's immediate dismissal from office; but in considering so momentous a question, it is requisite that the facts upon which Lord Ellenborough grounds his premises should be fairly inquired into, and no place is more appropriate to institute that inquiry than Hindustan, nor any assembly more competent to decide upon that subject than the one I have the honor to address. First, let us then inquire whether the present rebellion has arisen from any attacks, made or intended, against the religious feelings of the people by the administration of Lord Canning? Secondly, What are the real circumstances that have caused this rebellion?

"Speaking, as I am, from the place which is the center of the scenes of those mutinies that have drawn forth the remarks of Lord Ellenborough, and possessing, as we do, the advantages of being identified in race, language, manners, customs, and religion with the majority of those misguided wretches who have taken part in this rebellion, and thereby disgraced their manhood by drawing their arms against the very dynasty whose salt they have eaten, to whose paternal rule they and their ancestors have, for the last one hundred years, owed the security of their lives and properties, and which is the best ruling power that we had the good fortune to have within the last ten centuries—and addressing, as I am, a society, the individual members of which are fully familiar with the thoughts and sentiments of their countrymen, and who represent the feelings and interests of the great bulk of her Majesty's native subjects—I but give utterance to a fact patent to us all, that the Government have done nothing to interfere with our religion, and thereby to afford argument to its enemies to weaken their allegiance.

"The abolition of the diabolical practice of infanticide by drowning children in the Ganges, by the Marquis of Hastings, of the criminal rite of Suttee suicide, by Lord Bentinck, and the passing of other laws for the discontinuance of similar cruel and barbarous usages, equally called for by justice and humanity, by Governors General, (though they existed among us for ages,) never for a moment led us to suspect that our British rulers would interfere with our religion, or weaken the allegiance of any class of subjects in India. And is it to be supposed that Lord Canning's subscription to the Missionary Societies has ignited and fanned the awful fire, the flame of which now surrounds the fair provinces of Hindustan, and has changed the obedient and faithful native soldiers of the State into fiends who delight in plunder, massacre, and destruction? No, certainly not; our countrymen are perfectly able to make a distinction between the acts of Lord Canning as a private individual, and his Lordship's doings as the Viceroy of her gracious majesty Queen Victoria.

"Chiefs of all denominations, both Hindoo and Mohammedan, as well as the merchants and soldiers of both these races, possess enough of intelligence and shrewdness to know that what a person does in his *Zaut Khass* is quite a different thing to what he does in his *wohdah;* and Lord Ellenborough must have been misinformed as to the impression the Governor General's subscription to the Missionary Societies has produced in this country, when he surmised that that had occasioned the rebellion.

"Aware of the weight that would be attached by the British public to the views expressed by that personage, I feel it incumbent on me to point out his Lordship's mistake. Then, as to the Missionaries, a man must be a total stranger to the thoughts, habits, and character of the Hindoo population who could fancy that because the missionaries are the apostles of another religion, the Hindoos entertain an inveterate hatred toward them. Akbar of blessed memory, whose policy Lord Ellenborough pronounces as peculiarly adapted to the government of these dominions, (and which, no doubt, is so,) gave encouragement to the followers of all sects, religions, and modes of worship. *Jaugeers* and *Altumghas* bearing his imperial seal are yet extant, to show that he endowed lands and buildings for the Mohammedan musjids, Christian churches, and Hindoo devasloys. The Hindoos are essentially a tolerant people; a fact which that sagacious prince did fully comprehend, appreciate, and act upon: and the remarks of Lord Ellenborough that Akbar's policy should be the invariable rule of guidance for British Indian Governors, is most correct—but in the sense I have just explained—and should be recorded in golden characters on the walls of the Council Chamber. When discussing an Indian subject, it should always be remembered that this country is not inhabited by savages and barbarians, but by those whose language and literature are the oldest in the world, and whose progenitors were engaged in the contemplation of the sublimest doctrines of religion and philosophy at a time when their Anglo-Saxon and Gallic contemporaries were deeply immersed in darkness and ignorance. And if, owing to eight hundred years of Mohammedan tyranny and misrule, this great nation has sunk into sloth and lethargy, it has, thank God! not lost its reason, and is able to make a difference between the followers of a religion which inculcates the doctrine that should be propagated at the point of the sword, and that which offers compulsion to none, but simply invites inquiry. However we may differ with the Christian Missionaries in religion, I speak the minds of this Society, and generally of those of the people, when I say that, as regards their learning, purity of morals, and disinterestedness of intention to promote our weal, no doubt is entertained throughout the land, nay, they are held by us in the highest esteem. European history does not bear on its record the mention of a class of men who suffered so many sacrifices in the cause of humanity and education as the Christian Missionaries in India; and though the native community differ with them in the opinion that Hindustan will one day be included in Christendom, (for the worship of Almighty God in his Unity, as laid down in the Holy Vedas, is, and has been, our religion for thousands of years, and is enough to satisfy all our spiritual wants,) yet we cannot forbear doing justice to the venerable ministers of a religion who, I do here most solemnly *asseverate*, in piety and righteousness alone are fit to be classed with those Rishees and Mohatmas of antiquity, who derived their support and those of their charitable boarding-schools from voluntary subscriptions, and consecrated their lives to the cause of God and knowledge.

"It is not, therefore, likely that any little monetary aid that may have been rendered by the Governor General, in his private capacity, to Missionary Societies, should have sown the germ of that recent disaffection in the native army which has introduced so much anarchy and confusion in these dominions."

That will suffice. The East India Company is well, and forever, answered by one of its own Hindoo subjects.

II. Men outside of India, imperfectly acquainted with its people and the condition of the English administration there, had their theory to account for the rebellion, and supposed that it was owing to causes, among which was the preference of the natives for some other rule—say that of the Russians, whose incoming would be hailed by them as a deliverance from a yoke which galled them, and the misrule of which was crushing them down.

Here, too, let the natives speak for themselves. They know their own grievances best, and have no restraint upon their utterance. The few educated men among them have spoken. Any quantity of testimony might be given, but two or three will suffice. These men understand the difference of things; know what good government, and personal security, and equal rights mean; they appreciate fine roads, arrangements for irrigation, and provision for public instruction; they value peace, and law, and progress; and are well enough acquainted with their country's history to know that their land never had so much of all these as it has to-day. They know this, also, notwithstanding that they are equally alive to what they regard as the defects of the English rule, yet they have patience, and are aware that that too is fast improving in their interest.

One hundred and seventy years ago France contended with England for commercial and military supremacy in Southern India, but England won the rich prize then, as she did at the beginning of this century, when she destroyed the embryo French State which Perron was erecting in North India, on the banks of the Jumna. The Marquis of Wellesley smoked the French out of India by a vigorous use of his artillery, and the Land of the Veda was saved, in the mercy of Heaven, from becoming a French colony, from which freedom, and the Bible, and the missionary would have been excluded for ages, while the wealth of the conquered people might have been employed to inflate French vanity and extend her bigoted misrule over Europe and the world.

One of India's most intelligent sons, Baboo Bholanauth Chunder, remarks upon this escape of his country from French domination: "It is well that an end was put to this French State in embryo. The fickle and freakish Frenchman has no genius for consolidating an empire which India wants. If he had stepped into the shoes of the Great Mogul, India would have been brought up in *sans-culottism,* under a galling chain of gilded despotism. Under French rule the staid Hindoo would have been a strange animal, with many a vagary in his head. How little could their own distractions have allowed Frenchmen the time to look after the welfare of two hundred millions of human beings. Doubtless the French acknowledge, but fail to act up to, the necessity of accommodating the institutions of government to the progress of information."

He adds, as to the comparative value of the two civilizations which contended for supremacy in his country, "It may be questioned whether there is not more tyranny in France than in India. The conquered Indian is happy to have no bit in his mouth—to speak out his grievances. It is necessary for us to appreciate correctly the character either of the French or of the Russian. If it be the will of Providence to have a yoke upon the neck of our nation, our nation should, in the ripened maturity of its judgment, discriminate, and prefer the yoke of the English to be the least galling. Nothing less than British phlegm, and imperturbability, and constancy, and untiring energy, could have steadily prosecuted the task of consolidating the disjointed masses of India, and casting her into the mold of one compact nation. They want but 'the high thoughts seated in a heart of courtesy' to attach us to their rule with a feeling of loyalty that, not merely 'playing around the head, should come near the heart.'"

What the Hindoo mind thinks of its present masters, and of that possible Russian rule of which people outside of India sometimes prognosticate, may be understood from the utterance of such a native journal as "*The Som Prukash,*" which, in its issue for December, 1870, in an article on Russia and England, remarks: "Other nations seem to think that the Indians are disaffected toward England, but there can be no greater mistake than this. That there is dissatisfaction is true, but that the rule of Britain should pass away is not the desire of any. It is the dissatisfaction that seeks to prevent arbitrary measures, and to establish a more large-hearted policy. If Russia or Germany depend at all upon our dissatisfaction, they will soon find proof to the contrary. Should there be war with Russia, all the inhabitants of India would zealously come forward to support the Government."

Their preference for English rule, and their appreciation of its advantages, is equally if not more fully entertained on the western coast. Mr. Satyendra Nath Tagore, a cultivated Parsee of Bombay, speaks for his class of the population in the following enlightened language:

"It is not for nothing that India has been placed under the British rule. It is impossible to think that her destinies have been ruled by blind, unsparing Fate, or that it is for the glory and power of England alone that such a wonderful bond of connection has been established by an inscrutable Providence between the two countries. There is one hope, one intense conviction from which no true patriot can escape; that is, that England and India are to be a mutual blessing; that our country, once famous in the world's history, is destined to be helped out of her present degeneracy and utter stagnation. And is there no reason for this hope? and are there no data to base this conviction upon? What was India a few years ago, and what do we now see around us? We see a marked progress, brought about by Western civilization. We see a nation domineered over by caste and idolatry—a nation of which the men are completely enslaved to custom, and the women kept down and tyrannized over by the men, by dint of sheer physical strength, which they cannot resist—a nation which has long ceased to be progressive, and of which inertia and stationariness is the natural condition. Even this nation, opening its eyes to the enormous evils around it, is gradually awakening to the influences of the bright light of thought and knowledge, before which millions of false stars are fading away. India sank down under the weight of the accumulated corruption of ages; foreign influences were requisite to arouse her. These are being felt throughout her length and breadth. A steady, though slow, progress is perceptible. The tyranny of society is slowly succumbing to the gaining force of individuality and intellect. Superstition is losing its strongholds one after another. Ceremonial observances are being replaced by true principles of morality. There are many things still wanting, hideous defects to be remedied; but let us work and hope for a brighter future. May India be grateful to England for the blessing she has been enjoying under her benign rule! May England feel that India is a sacred trust and responsibility, which cannot be thrown away!"

In the same spirit, but with even a wider and more candid range of moral vision, (all the more remarkable from such a source,) Baboo Keshub Chunder Sen of Calcutta tells the world what he and his Brahmo Somaj think of English rule, and the Christian missions which it protects. The Baboo says, (and I would commend his words to the consideration of some of his Christian (?) and clerical admirers in New York and Boston, as a lesson which they certainly much need to learn :)

"It cannot be said that we in India have nothing to do with Christ or Christianity. Have the natives of this country altogether escaped the influence of Christianity, and do they owe nothing to Christ? Shall I be told by my educated countrymen that they can feel nothing but a mere remote historic interest in the grand movement I have described? You have already seen how, in the gradual extension of the Church of Christ, Christian missions came to be established in this distant land, and what results these missions have achieved. The many noble deeds of philanthropy and self-denying benevolence which Christian missionaries have performed in India, and the various intellectual, social, and moral improvements which they have effected, need no flattering comment; they are treasured in the gratitude of the nation, and can never be forgotten or denied. That India is highly indebted to these disinterested and large-hearted followers of Christ for her present prosperity, I have no doubt the entire nation will gratefully acknowledge. Fortunately for India, she was not forgotten by the Christian missionaries when they went out to preach the Gospel. While, through missionary agency, our country has thus been connected with the enlightened nations of the West politically, an all-wise and all-merciful Providence has intrusted its interests to the hands of a Christian sovereign. In this significant event worldly men can see nothing but an ordinary political phenomenon; but those of you who can discern the finger of Providence in individual and national history will doubtless see here a wise and merciful interposition. I cannot but reflect with grateful interest on the day when the British nation first planted their feet on the plains of India, and on the successive steps by which the British empire has been established and consolidated in this country. It is to the British Government that we owe our deliverance from oppression and misrule, from darkness and distress, from ignorance and superstition. Those enlightened ideas which have changed the very life of the nation, and have gradually brought about such wondrous improvement in native society, are the gifts of that Government; and so, likewise, the inestimable boon of freedom of thought and action, which we so justly prize. Are not such considerations calculated to rouse our deepest gratitude and loyalty to the British nation, and her Majesty Queen Victoria? Her beneficent Christian administration has proved to us not only a political, but a social and moral blessing, and laid the foundation of our national prosperity and greatness, and it is but natural that we should cherish toward her no other feeling except that of devoted loyalty."—*Carpenter's Six Months in India*, Vol. II, p. 73.

Such men, of course, deprecated the Sepoy Rebellion, and lament it to-day as the greatest mistake that their ignorant and fanatical countrymen could have made, and the success of which would have been the doom of India for ages. Bholanauth Chunder speaks the mind of every enlightened Bengalee Baboo when he says:

"In their infatuation they entered upon a bubble scheme, the bursting of which no sane man could doubt. They raised the standard for national independence, and anticipated that event at least two centuries before its time. We have to learn much before we ought to hazard such a leap. India can no longer be expected to relapse into the days of a Brahmin ascendency or a Mahratta government. The advent of the Anglo-Saxon race was not merely fortuitous, but had been fore-ordained in the wisdom of Providence. First of all, our efforts should be to shake off the fetters which a past age has forged for us; to effect our freedom from moral disabilities; and not to stake the well-being of the country on the result of a contest with veteran soldiers who have marched triumphant into Paris, Canton, and Candahar."

Another Hindoo testimony is to the same effect, only stronger in its satisfaction with the results:

"The mutiny was a fatal error; it once more plunged the country into the misrule of past ages. It jeopardized the vital interest of India, and was to have proved suicidal of her fate. The exit of the English would have undone all the good that is slowly paving the way to her regeneration. Rightly understood, to own the government of the English is not so much to own the government of that nation, as to own the government of an enlightened legislation, of the science and civilization of the nineteenth century, of superior intelligence and genius, of knowledge itself. Under this view, no right-minded Hindoo ought to feel his national instinct offended, and his self-respect diminished by allegiance to a foreign rule. The regeneration of his country must be the dearest object to the heart of every enlightened Hindoo; and it must be perfectly evident to him that the best mode of attaining this end is by striving to raise himself to the level of his rulers. What can the most patriotic Hindoo wish for better than that his country should, until its education as a nation is further advanced, continue part of the greatest and most glorious of empires, under a sovereign of the purest Aryan blood?"

Baboo Chunder, in the first volume of his *Travels of a Hindoo*, having twice lately gone over the extent of Hindustan Proper, gratefully contrasts the present with the past in the peace, security, and prosperity of the people of the great Gangetic Valley, and ascribes it all to the beneficence of English rule. This impartial witness says:

"The public works of Hindoos were for the comfort only of the physical man. The Mohammedans exhibit but the same care for the material well-being, without any progress made by humanity toward the amelioration of its moral condition. Far otherwise are the public works of the English. Their schools and colleges, literary institutions, public libraries, museums, botanic gardens, are proofs of a greater intellectual state of the world than in any preceding age. Supposing the English were to quit India, the beneficence of their rule ought not to be judged of by the external memorials of stone and masonry left behind them, but by the emancipation of our nation from prejudices and superstitions of long standing, and by the enlightened state in which they shall leave India. In the words of De Quincey, 'higher by far than the Mogul gift of limestone, or traveling stations, or even roads and tanks, were the gifts of security, of peace, of law, and settled order.'

"Nothing afforded me so great a pleasure as to pass through a country of one wide and uninterrupted cultivation, in which paddy-fields, that have justly made our country to be called *the granary of the world*, extended for miles in every direction. No such prospect greeted the eyes of a traveler in 1758. Then the annual inroads of the Mahrattas, the troubles following the overthrow of the Mohammedan dynasty, frequent and severe famines, and virulent pestilences, had thinned the population, and reduced fertile districts to wastes and jungles. It is on record that previous to 1793, the year of the English Permanent Settlement, one third of Lower Bengal lay waste and uncultivated. Never, perhaps, has Bengal enjoyed such a long period of peace without interruption as under British rule. From the day of the battle of Plassey no enemy has left a footprint upon her soil, no peasant has lost a sheaf of grain, and no man a single drop of blood. Under security against an enemy from abroad, population has increased, cultivation has been extended, the country has become a great garden, and landed property has risen in value more than forty-fold in one province, nineteen-fold in another, and more than ten-fold throughout all Lower Bengal.

"The Mahratta freebooter, the murderous Patan, and the Jaut bandit, have settled down to an agricultural life, and honest labor has superseded lawless rapine as an occupation."—Vol. I, p. 421, etc.

I can add my personal testimony to this general peace and security. Traveling for nearly ten years in a palankeen, alone and unprotected in the hands of the natives, I have slept in their serais and under their trees, often fifty miles from any white man, yet I moved in perfect security, was never molested, and never lost the value of a cent in all my peregrinations. So profound is the confidence in the power of law and the care of the Government, that ladies travel alone in this way every night in the year without hesitation or anxiety. Such is the security of person and property under English rule in India. It never was so before; and every honest and candid mind should give them credit for what they have there accomplished. The Hindoos do so frankly, and have even tried to make capital out of the wonderful fact, to the credit of their own system of idolatry, in the following singular fashion, as related by General Sleeman in his "Recollections." He says:

"A very learned Hindoo told me in Central India that the oracle of Mahadeva (the Great God) had been at the same time consulted at three of his greatest temples—one in the Deccan, one in Rajpootana, and one in Bengal—as to the result of the government of India by Europeans. A day was appointed for the answer, and when the priest came to receive it, they found Mahadeva (Shiva) himself, with a European complexion, and dressed in European clothes. He told them 'that their European government was in reality nothing more than a multiplied incarnation of himself, and that he had come among them in this shape to prevent their cutting each other's throats, as they had been doing for some centuries past; that these, his incarnations, appeared to have no religion themselves, in order that they might be the more impartial arbitrators between the people of so many different creeds and sects who now inhabited the country; that they must be aware that they never had before been so impartially governed, and that they must continue to obey these governors, without attempting to pry further into futurity or the will of their gods.'"—Vol. II, p. 241.

Thus Brahmos, Bengalees, Parsees, and Hindoos, the educated, the agriculturists, and even the idolaters themselves, admit the mighty change, and rejoice in it. Instances are even found where candid men among them, and even Brahmins, will go further than all these have gone, as in the recent case at Arcot and its medical mission.

A reading-room had been opened at Madnapilly. At the dedication, the Rev. Jacob Chamberlain delivered an address, at the close of which a Brahmin requested permission to make some remarks. Without the least conjecture of what he was going to say, he was allowed to commence, when he proceeded to deliver a remarkable eulogy on the missionaries. He compared them to the mango tree, which, however beaten, and wounded, and stripped of its fruit, still goes on, year by year, to yield its wholesome fruit. He dwelt with enlargement and unction on this subject, and then added as follows:

"Now what is it makes him do all this for us? *It is his Bible.* I've looked into it a good deal at one time and another in the different languages I chance to know. It is just the same in all languages. The Bible—there is nothing to compare with it in all our sacred books for goodness, and purity, and holiness, and love, and for motives of action. Where did the English-speaking people get all their intelligence, and energy, and cleverness, and power? It is their Bible that gives it to them. And now they bring it to us and say, 'This is what raised us; take it and raise yourselves.' They do not force it upon us, as the Mohammedans used to their Koran; but they bring it in love, and translate it into our languages, and lay it before us, and say, 'Look at it, read it, examine it, and see if it is not good.' Of one thing I am convinced: do what we will, oppose it as we may, it is the Christian's Bible that will, sooner or later, work the regeneration of this land."

The missionary adds, "I could not but be surprised at this testimony thus borne. How far the speaker was sincere I cannot tell; but he had the appearance of a man speaking his earnest convictions. Some three years ago I had attended, in his zenana, his second wife, a beautiful girl, through a dangerous attack, and I knew that he felt very grateful; but I was not prepared to see him come out, before such an audience, with such testimony to the power and excellence of the Bible. My earnest prayer is, that not only his intellect may be convinced, but that his heart may be reached by the Holy Spirit, and that he may soon become an earnest follower of Jesus."

These quotations, which are rather lengthy, are of high significance, as showing what is the condition of multitudes of the thinking classes of India, and what changes are imminent in that magnificent land, when leading men can be found thus to stand forth before their countrymen and utter such words. To all this can be added that England has given India the printing press, the telegraph, the iron horse, the Ganges canal, (which irrigates 3,380,000 acres of land, and makes famine impossible in the Doab,) and that these improvements are constantly on the increase. Allowing for her time and the circumstances, she has done wonders for the land she rules, and the immense majority of the people knew this well, and had no sympathy for, and lent no aid to, the Sepoy Rebellion, for they did not desire a change.

But England had her enemies. The Mohammedans generally, the Fakirs, most of the Brahmins, the Thugs, and the lawless and criminal classes, to a man hate her. These together amounted to millions. Circumstances gave them an imperial name for a rallying cry, a Peishwa's influence and a Sepoy instrumentality for the working power, and they made wonderful use of the peculiar combination. But why did they single themselves out, and in the name of the people of India, which the immense majority never gave them the slightest authority to use, commence the work of extermination? We have already given the reasons which influenced the Mogul Court, the Nana Sahib, the Mohammedans, and the Fakirs. But there were other reasons which account for the Brahminical interest in the matter, as well as that of the Thugs and the lawless classes, which have not yet been presented, and a knowledge of which is essential to a full and complete view of the motives which originated the fearful combination against Christianity, and the English power which protected it.

Slowly, but surely, the better portion of the British administrators were urging on reforms and legislation in the interests of humanity. They had much to contend with in their noble aims between, on the one hand, the old civilians of the Company, who were still in the higher posts of the service, and on the other, from the men whose power and emoluments were derived from usages and institutions which they were striking down one by one. The abolition of female infanticide was allowed to pass with little resistance, because it brought no profit to priest or Fakir. But it was different with the far greater crime of deliberately roasting alive the beautiful and wealthy ladies of the land who had the misfortune to become widows, for there the ceremonies were splendid, the Brahmin exercised the height of awful power, and his perquisites were larger than in any other ceremony of his faith.

This extraordinary and (save in India) unparalleled crime, reduced to a system, sanctioned by their religion, and practiced for ages, is so wonderful in itself and its circumstances that the Western reader will desire to be more fully informed of its character, and the motives under which it was inflicted and endured, than he could be by a mere passing allusion, so we pause here to illustrate and describe it.

The suttee commemorated in this steel engraving took place in the neighborhood of Baroda, in the dominions of the Guicowar, during the period that Sir James Carnac was English Resident (Embassador) at that Court. The sketch was made and the whole

Preparing for the Immolation of a Hindoo Widow.

circumstance described, by Captain Grindley, as it was one of unusual interest. The suttee was a young Brahmanee woman. On her intention becoming known to the Resident, he went at once to her house with the humane intention of persuading her to abandon her purpose. Failing to produce any impression, the Resident waited on the ruling Prince, who kindly undertook to add his persuasion, but he was equally unsuccessful. Determined to prevent her burning herself, he surrounded her premises with his troops. He offered her the means of subsistence, and urged the duties she owed her family. The widow remained unmoved and unconvinced. On being told she would not be allowed to ascend the funeral pile, she drew a dagger from the folds of her dress, and, with all the vehemence that passion could add to fanaticism, declared that her blood—the blood of a Brahmin woman—should be upon the soul of him who offered to prevent her performing her duty to her husband. Intimidated, the Guicowar with his retinue withdrew. The unhappy woman rushed away to the river brink, and there, aided by her friends and the Brahmins, she quickly went through the ablutions and prescribed ceremonies, and ascended the steps to the fatal spot—immediately behind the domed arch in the engraving—and threw herself into the midst of the flames.

Christian women will wish to understand the reasons that could thus so strangely and determinately overcome, in one of their sex—a young and beautiful woman—the love of life, of friends, and of children, and lead her to dare death in one of its most awful forms, in obedience to what she regarded as a supreme duty.

Of suttee, or widow burning, the origin is unknown. But it must be very ancient, for it is alluded to by Diodorus Siculus as being then an established custom. Such a horrid rite should certainly be able to show the highest authority for itself. Accordingly, the Brahmins of India have asserted that the Vedas, which they hold to be their most ancient and divine writings, have expressly required this last evidence of a wife's devotion to her deceased lord. So long as these writings were unknown to the outside world, they might make their assertion with safety. But of late years Christian men have mastered the ancient Sanscrit, and have read the Vedas, and demanded from the Brahmins the proof of a statement under which millions of women have been foully murdered during the past twenty-five hundred years. The depth of their villainy has been revealed by the appeal made to the highest authority of their own religion. The honor of demolishing the last Brahminical pretext for regarding suttee as an orthodox Hindoo practice belongs to Horace Hayman Wilson. In a paper read by the learned professor before the Royal Asiatic Society on February 4, 1854, he proved that the passage—and it was the solitary text from all the Vedas that the Brahmins could bring forward in its defense—the passage quoted had actually been corrupted by the substitution of a single letter, which changed the whole sense, *agneh* for *agreh*, the meaning being thereby perverted from, "let them [the widows] go up into the *dwelling*," to "let them go up into the *fire*"—the *r* changed to *n* made this difference; and these cruel men were responsible for the flagrant corruption! Professor Wilson added, that he was supported in his opinion by Dr. Max Müller, and that Aswalayana, the author of the Grihya Sutras—a work little inferior in authority to the Vedas themselves—actually designates the proper person to lead the widow away at the conclusion of the funeral rites; so that so far from demanding her immolation, the text inferentially enjoins the widow's preservation. Suttee, therefore, with all its antiquity, is proved by the Vedas to be, like female infanticide, an accursed invention of modern Hindooism.

Next to the Vedas, the "Institutes of Menu" are the highest authority to a Hindoo conscience. I have carefully read this entire code of laws; but not one obligation to such a rite as suttee is to be found in it. The Brahmins have not dared to reply to the learned professor. They assert, of course, that it is recommended in the Shasters and Puranas; but these are all of more recent origin, and are far below the paramount authority of the Vedas, and no serious doctrine can be built on them alone; so that they stand convicted of teaching for doctrines novelties which are only "the commandments of men," like the Jews of old, or the Romanists of our own day. Exactly as the present Pope has done, when, eighteen hundred years after the canon of Scripture was closed, he dared to invent a new doctrine — that of the Immaculate Conception of the Virgin Mary—and would fain make its belief binding on the consciences of Catholics, even so have these Brahmins acted at distances almost as great from the date of their own Vedas.

Every suttee, therefore, has been without what even they regard as the divine sanction, which alone could ordain it. Christian Orientalists and missionaries have pressed this position, to the utter discomfiture and confusion of these guilty Brahmins.

But while the Vedas and the Code are thus entirely silent, and even lay down the laws by which a widow's life is to be guided, the inferior authority of modern Hindooism—and any thing is "modern" in their view which dates within two thousand years of this time—are particular and definite enough, in prescribing the barbarous rites under which she is urged to yield her delicate body to the devouring flames ; so that upon this fraud on the faith of India has been built up the greatest victory that priestcraft has ever achieved over the natural feelings and instincts of mankind in any age or nation.

The words of the Puranas, which commend this dreadful rite, are as follows : " The wife who commits herself to the flames with her husband's corpse shall equal Arundhoti, [the exalted wife of Vashista,] and dwell in Swarga, [heavenly bliss.] As many hairs as are on the human body, multiplied by threescore and fifty lakhs [each lakh, 100,000] of years, so many years shall she live with him in Swarga. As the snake-catcher forcibly draws the serpent from his hole in the earth, so, bearing her husband from hell, she shall with him enjoy happiness. Dying with her husband, she purifies three generations—her father and mother's side and husband's side. Such a wife, adoring her husband, enters into celestial felicity with him—greatest and most admired ; lauded by the choirs of heaven, with him she shall enjoy the delights of heaven while fourteen Indras reign."

In the event of her husband dying while absent from her, provision is made for her suttee in the following words of the Brahma-Purana: "If the husband be out of the country when he dies, let the virtuous wife take his slippers, or any thing else that belongs to his dress, and, binding them or it upon her breast, after purification, enter a separate fire." The same Purana adds: "While the pile is preparing, tell the faithful wife of the greatest duty of woman. She is alone loyal and pure who burns herself with her husband's corpse. Having thus fortified her resolution, and full of affection, she completes the Pragashita, and ascends to Swarga."

The circumstances are defined in which widows are excused from the obligation of suttee. For example, if a woman has recently become a mother, or expects soon to be, she may hold herself exempted; yet even she is at liberty, thirty days after childbirth, to assert her fidelity by dying amid the flames.

In case a Hindoo widow decides not to burn, then these priestly law-makers have prescribed her future condition under degrading obligations, that often prove but a little less terrible than death itself; but of this we shall speak more fully when we come to describe the condition to which Hindoo law reduces the afflicted widows of that land. Before considering the motives of this fearful sacrifice, and the extent to which it has prevailed, we will place before our readers a description of the rite of suttee as it is usually performed.

The husband is dead. In India the body must be disposed of within twelve hours. In the tumult of her grief, the Brahmins and friends wait upon the distracted widow to learn her intentions. There is no time for reflection or second thought. Within an hour it is usually settled. She agrees to mingle her ashes with her lord's. Opium or strong liquor is given to sustain her courage. Before the word is spoken the decision is with herself; but, once consenting to die, she may not recall her words. Millions, of course, have expressed a trembling preference for life, even with all its future gloom to them; but multitudes have consented at once to burn, and, even in advance of being asked, they have, in the first spasm of their bereavement, uttered the fatal and irrevocable cry, "*Suth! suth!*" Orders are at once issued for the erection of the fatal pile, and the accustomed ceremonies; the widow, too, has to be prepared. Friends sometimes, with more or less sincerity, try to dissuade her from her purpose; but all her religious convictions and priestly advisers urge on the poor, infatuated —perhaps intoxicated—woman to her doom. On the banks of the sacred river, while she bathes in the Ganges, a Brahmin is coolly reading the usual forms. She is now arrayed in bridal costume, but her face is unvailed, and her hair unbound and saturated with oil, and her whole body is perfumed. Her jewels are now added, and she is adorned with garlands of flowers. Thus prepared, she is conducted to the pile, which is an oblong square, formed of four stout bamboos or branches fixed in the earth at each corner. Within those supports the dry logs are laid from three to four feet high, with cotton rope and other combustibles interlaced. Chips of odoriferous wood, butter, and oil are plentifully added, to give force and fragrance to the flames. The ends above are interwoven to form a bower, and this is sometimes decked with flowers. The husband's body has been already laid upon it. In the south of India the fire is first applied, and the widow throws herself into the burning mass; but the more general way is not to apply the fire till she has taken her position. The size of the pile is regulated by the number of widows who are to be burned with the body. Cases are well known, like the one at Sookachura, near Calcutta, where the pile was nearly twelve yards long, and on it eighteen wives, leaving in all over forty children, burned themselves with the body of their husband.

When the widow, thus prepared, reaches the pile, she walks around it, supported if necessary by a Brahmin. She then distributes her gifts, including her jewels, to the Brahmins and her friends, but retains her garlands. She now approaches the steps by which she is to mount the pile, and there repeats the *Sancalpa*, thus: "On this month so named—that I may enjoy with my husband the felicity of heaven, and sanctify my paternal and maternal progenitors, and the ancestry of my husband's father—that expiation may be made for my husband's offenses—thus I ascend my husband's pile. I call on you, ye guardians of the eight regions of the world, sun and moon, air, fire, ether, earth, and water, my own soul, Yama, [god of the dead,] day, night, and twilight! And thou, conscience, bear witness, I follow my husband's corpse on the funeral pile!"

She then moves around the pile three times more, while the Brahmins repeat the *Muntras*—the texts on burning already quoted, and others—and then ascends to the corpse, and either lies down by its side, or takes its head in her lap. In some places ropes are thrown over to bind the living to the dead, or long bamboos are bent down upon them both, and the ends held firm by attending Brahmins. Sometimes she is left untied and loose. All is now ready: her eldest son, if she have one—if not, the nearest male relative—stands ready to discharge the cruel office of executioner by igniting the pile at the four corners quickly. The whole structure instantly blazes up, and the poor lady is at once enveloped in a sheet of flame. Musical instruments strike up, the Brahmins vociferously chant, the crowd shout "Hari-bal! Hari-bal!" [call on Hari—a name of the god Vishnu,] so that her moans or shrieks are drowned in the infernal din raised around her.

Just at this period of the proceedings is the dreadful moment when woman's courage has so often failed her, and nature has proved too strong for fanaticism. If not at once overwhelmed or suffocated, even though she knows that her attempt to escape will be resisted as a duty by her own friends, who would regard her as an outcast, the victim not unfrequently, when left untied, springs off the burning mass among the spectators and piteously pleads for life. Alas! it is too late; there is no mercy for her now! She is at once struck down by a sword or a billet of wood, and flung back again on the pile, her own son having been known to be one of the most forward to tie her hands and feet for this purpose.

The writer remembers to have heard of a case at Benares, where the poor woman was actually saved by a sudden and singular thought of the English magistrate, a young gentleman of the name of Harding. On the death of the Brahmin, Mr. Harding was successful in persuading the widow not to burn; but twelve months after she was goaded by her family into the expression of a wish to burn with some relic of her husband preserved for the purpose. The pile was prepared for her at Ramnugger, two miles above Benares, on the other side of the Ganges. She was not well secured on the pile, and as soon as she felt the fire she jumped off and plunged into the river. The people ran after her along the bank; but the current carried her toward Benares, where a police boat put off and took her in. Her oiled garments had kept her afloat. The police took her to the magistrate, but the whole city of Benares was in an uproar at the rescue of a Brahmin's widow from the funeral pile. Thousands surrounded Mr. Harding's house, and the principal men of the city implored him to surrender the woman; among the rest was her own *father*, who declared that *he* could not support his daughter, and that she had, therefore, better be burned, as her husband's family would not receive her. The uproar was quite alarming to a young man, who felt all the responsibility upon himself in such a fanatical city as Benares, with a population of three hundred thousand people. He long argued the point with the crowd, urging the time that had elapsed, and the unwillingness of the woman, but in vain; until at length the thought struck him suddenly, and he said that the sacrifice was manifestly unacceptable to their god—that the sacred river itself had rejected her, as she had, without being able to swim, floated down two miles upon its bosom, in the presence of them all; and it was, therefore, clear that she had been rejected! Had she been an acceptable sacrifice, after the fire had touched her the river would have received her! This Hindoo reason satisfied the whole crowd. The father said, after this unanswerable argument, he would receive his daughter. So the poor woman was saved.

The question has been raised, To what *extent* has suttee prevailed? It is very difficult to reach even an approximate reply to this inquiry. Lord Bentinck's efforts for the abolition of the rite led to the possession of the only reliable statistics that we have upon the subject. From these the rest must be inferred. The cruel custom has been almost restricted to the affluent and higher orders, as the poor are unable to bear the expense; so that it has been the most exalted, wealthy, and beautiful ladies of the land who have thus been immolated.

From statistics obtained by the magistrates of the district around Calcutta prior to 1829, a published list gives fifty-four cases in the months of May and June, 1812, where sixty-nine women, of ages from sixteen to sixty, were burned with these fifty-four dead bodies; leaving altogether one hundred and eighty-one children, who were, as in all such cases, thus deprived of both parents at once. Another list for the region within thirty miles of Calcutta, gives two hundred and seventy-five known cases for the year 1803. In the Bengal presidency, in the year 1817, there were seven hundred and six cases recorded—nearly two each day for that part of India alone. In ten years, from 1815 to 1825, these lists, for the localities where English magistrates took note of suttees, show that five thousand nine hundred and ninety-seven widows were thus immolated. These are only the more public instances coming to the knowledge of the magistrates within the limited portion of India then directly ruled by England. But what of those of all the rest of the country, from the Himalayas to Cape Comorin? And, if they could be numbered and known, then, to obtain the sum total, you have to multiply them by the two thousand five hundred years during which these unwarranted and fiendish cruelties have been practiced on gentle women before the face of heaven in India! The blood of these millions of women has been crying to God from the ground all that time, against the Brahmins of Hindustan.

The *origin* of suttee, some have supposed, might be found in the cruel jealousy of husbands, reaching thus beyond the grave; while others refer it to the tradition that it was adopted as an expedient for the preservation of men's lives. Doctor Chever, in his recent work on Indian Medical Jurisprudence, traces the custom to this origin. He brings forward authorities to show that the Brahmins themselves invented the law as a means of self-protection against their wives. Before its introduction, the wives were in the habit of avenging themselves on their husbands for neglect and cruelty by mixing poison with their food; and at last things came to such a height that the least matrimonial quarrel resulted in the husband's death. An easier remedy for the evil might have been found in compelling the wife to eat out of the same dish as the husband, but this would have involved too wide a departure from the customs of society; and it must be admitted that there is a peculiar refinement of cruelty in the expedient adopted, which would commend itself to the Asiatic mind. The Brahmins thus gave the matron an interest in the preservation of her lord's life, by decreeing that her ashes should mingle with his. If this were its origin, then the deepest insult was added to the most cruel wrong of which woman can be made the victim, when thus surrendered to a false religion, and into the hands of men as oppressive as their faith.

The *motives* which have perpetuated the rite are more easily found. So far as the priestly Brahmin is concerned, he has a direct pecuniary interest in the existence and increase of the cruel custom. Brahmins officiating at suttees are always well rewarded, both by fees and gifts; and quarrels among themselves about their earnings are no novelty. The family of the immolated woman are taught that to them belong the invisible and spiritual blessings of the suttee—that this doomed widow's agonies are to expiate the foulest sins of them and of her husband, and lift them all to heavenly bliss. The reader will remember the Puranas already quoted, where this is expressly taught. Hence the eagerness with which her consent to become a suttee is sought, and the barbarity which helps on, and even enforces, her destruction when her resolution has failed. The motives of the poor lady herself are still more manifest. There is, first of all, her obedience to her religious obligations. Her faith, like that of the Romanist, must be an unquestioning faith. Woman in India seems never to have thought of looking behind this Brahminical teaching, and demanding a "Thus saith the Lord" for the peculiar woes to which she submits.

Then there is the appeal to her love as well as her duty. She is told, and her uninstructed soul believes the lie, that her husband needs the attendance and care in the other world which she lavished upon him here; nay, more, that he is actually suffering for want of it. Her terrified imagination is appealed to, and he is pictured in a fearful intermediate hell—the counterpart of the Romish doctrine of Purgatory—out of which her merits alone can lift him; and her loving heart urges her to the great effort, which is to save and bless him, and herself with him. Again, there is the motive of fame. By it she can demonstrate the perfection of her conjugal devotion; she rises from obscurity, before her friends and the world, to the eminence of a heroine, a saint, a savior; she avoids a life of insult and misery, and the splendid monument on the spot where she suffers will keep her name and memory before her people in future ages.

I was intimate with a family in India, the head of which, a physician, gave the following description of a suttee at which he was actually present. It was in the city of Lahore, in June 1839, and was witnessed by this gentleman and some other Europeans. The occasion was the burning of the body of the Maharajah Runjeet Singh—he who was commonly called the "Lion of the Punjab," and who was the last Oriental sovereign that wore the great Koh-i-noor diamond. (The father of the Prince represented on page 47.) On account of his special orders, the funeral pile was composed of an unusual quantity of the precious sandal-wood. It was also made large enough for his eleven wives to burn with his body. Early in the morning, an immense concourse attending to witness the ceremony, the body of the Maharajah, decorated and wrapped in Cashmere shawls, was brought out from the palace and the procession formed, the four Ranees (Queens) in order, unvailed, sitting in open palanquins, followed by the seven other wives on foot, barefooted—some of them, the doctor declared, being not more than fourteen or fifteen years old. Then came the court, the officials, the military, and the crowd. The ceremonies performed, the body was lifted to the top of the great pile; then the four Ranees ascended in the order of their rank, seating themselves at the head; the other seven placed themselves around the feet. The chief widow, now sitting on the funeral pile, apparently as calm as any American mother on her dying bed, called to her Khuruk Singh, the son, and Dhian Singh, the favorite minister, of the Maharajah, and, placing the dead king's hand first in the hand of the royal heir, and then in the hand of the powerful minister, made them swear to be mutually faithful. They then retired, and a strong, thick mat of reeds was placed around and over the ladies, and oil plentifully poured upon it. There they cowered in silent expectation of the fatal moment. The brand was applied quickly, and the roaring flames leaped up and enveloped them, and in fifteen minutes nothing remained of the eleven beautiful women but a heap of bones and ashes. Preparation was now made to convey part of their remains to the Ganges. Some of the bones and ashes of each were placed in urns; these were put in separate palanquins richly decorated, and attended with the same pomp and splendor as if the Maharajah and his wives were still alive. Surrounded by guards and attendants, and accompanied by costly presents, such as shawls, decorated elephants and horses, with money, etc., for the Brahmins, the procession passed through the Delhi gate, amid the last royal salute from the fort and ramparts of the city. Here the minister and chiefs returned, leaving the remains and presents to proceed under the care of the military. The Brahmins received the whole on its arrival at the Ganges. The bones and ashes they put into the river, the valuables they divided among themselves, and the guard returned. The whole ceremony was one of the most extravagant ever seen in India, and must, Dr. Honiberger thinks, have cost several millions of rupees.

That the subject may be fully understood, I will add two cases of suttee where the victims were more than usually willing, and exhibited a resolution that will surprise the reader. The first is described by an intelligent young native, who was the nephew of the lady burned. He gives the facts from his Hindoo stand-point, yet with much simplicity and candor.

He says: "Fearing intervention from the British authorities, it was decided that this solemn rite, contrary to the usual practice, should be performed at a distance from the river-side. The margin of the consecrated tank was selected for the purpose. After ceremonies of purification had been performed upon the spot, strong stakes of bamboo were driven into the ground, inclosing an oblong space about seven feet in length and six in breadth. Within this inclosure the pile was built of straw, boughs, and logs of wood; upon the top a small arbor was constructed of wreathed bamboos, and this was hung with flowers within and without. About an hour after the sun had risen, prayers and ablutions having been carefully performed by all, more especially by the Brahmins and Lall Radha, the widow, who was also otherwise purified and fitted for the sacrifice, the corpse of the husband was brought from the house, attended by the administering Brahmins, and surrounded by the silent and weeping friends and relations of the family. Immediately following the corpse came Lall Radha, enveloped in a scarlet vail, which completely hid her beautiful form from view. When the body was placed upon the pile, the feet being toward the west, the Brahmins took the vail from Lall Radha, and, for the first time, the glaring multitude were suffered to gaze upon that lovely face and form; but the holy woman was too deeply engaged in solemn prayer and converse with Brahma to be sensible of their presence, or of the murmur of admiration that ran through the crowd. Then, turning with a steady look and solemn demeanor to her relations, she took from her person, one by one, all her ornaments, and distributed them as tokens of her love. One jewel only she retained, the tali, or amulet, placed around her neck by her deceased husband on the nuptial day; this she silently pressed to her lips. Then, separately embracing each of her female relatives, and bestowing a farewell look upon the rest, she unbound her hair, which flowed in thick and shining ringlets almost to her feet, gave her right hand to the principal Brahmin, who led her with ceremony around the pile, and then stopped, with her face toward it, on the side where she was to ascend. Having mounted two or three steps, the beautiful woman stood still, and, pressing both her hands upon the cold feet of her lifeless husband, she raised them to her forehead, in token of cheerful submission ; she then ascended and crept within the little arbor, seating herself at the head of her lord, her right hand resting upon his head. The torch was placed in my hand, and, overwhelmed with commingled emotions, I fired the pile. Smoke and flame in an instant enveloped the scene, and amid the deafening shouts of the multitude, I sank senseless upon the earth. I was quickly restored to consciousness, but already the devouring element had reduced the funeral pile to a heap of charred and smoldering timber. The Brahmins strewed the ashes around, and with a trembling hand I assisted my father to gather the blackened bones of my beloved uncle and aunt, when, having placed them in an earthen vessel, we carried them to the Ganges, and with prayer and reverence committed them to the sacred stream."

The other, and the most determined instance of suttee, in view of her age, etc., that is on record, is described by an English gentleman who was governor of that part of the country, and in whose presence it took place. He says : "On receiving charge of the District of Jubbulpore in 1828, I issued a proclamation prohibiting any one from assisting in suttee. On Tuesday, November 24, 1829, I had an application from the heads of the most respectable family of Brahmins in the place to suffer an old lady, aged sixty-five years, to burn herself with the body of her husband, Omed Sing Opuddea, who had died that morning. I threatened to enforce my order and punish severely any man who assisted, and placed a police guard to see that no one did so. She remained sitting by the edge of the river with the body, without eating or drinking. The next day the body of her husband was burned to ashes in a small pit, about eight feet square and four deep, before thousands of people who had assembled to see the suttee. All strangers dispersed before evening, as there seemed no prospects of my yielding to the urgent solicitations of her family, who, according to the rules of their faith, dared not touch food till she had burned herself, or declared herself willing to return to them. Her sons and grandsons and some other relatives remained with her, urging her to desist; the rest surrounded my house, urging me to allow her to burn. She remained sitting upon a bare rock in the bed of the Nerbudda, refusing any subsistence, and exposed to the intense heat of the sun by day, and the cold of the night, with only a thin sheet thrown over her shoulders. On Thursday, to cut off all hope of her being moved from her purpose, she put on the *dhujja*, or coarse red turban, and broke her bracelets in pieces, by which she became dead in law, and forever excluded from caste. Should she choose to live after this, she could never return to her family. Her children and grandchildren were still with her, but all their entreaties were unavailing. I became satisfied that she would starve herself to death if not allowed to burn, by which her family would be disgraced, her miseries prolonged, and I rendered liable to be charged with a wanton abuse of authority, for no prohibition of the kind I had issued had as yet received the formal sanction of the Government. Early on Saturday morning I rode out ten miles to the spot, and found the poor old widow still sitting with the dhujja around her head. She talked very collectedly, telling me that 'she had determined to mix her ashes with those of her departed husband, and she would patiently wait my permission to do so, assured that God would enable her to sustain life till that was given, though she dared not eat or drink.' Looking at the sun, then rising before her over a long and beautiful reach of the Nerbudda River, she said calmly, 'My soul has been for five days with my husband's near that sun; nothing but my earthly frame is left, and this I know you will in time suffer to be mixed with the ashes of his in yonder pit, because it is not in your nature or your usage wantonly to prolong the miseries of a poor old woman.' I replied, 'Indeed it is not; my object and duty is to save and preserve them, and I am come to dissuade you from this idle purpose, to urge you to live and keep your family from being thought your murderers.' She said, 'I am not afraid of their ever being so thought; they have all, like good children, done every thing in their power to induce me to live among them, and if I had done so, I know they would have loved me and honored me, but my duties to them have now ceased. Our intercourse and communion here end. I go to attend my husband, Omed Sing Opuddea, with whose ashes on the funeral pile mine have been already three times mixed.'

"This was the first time in her long life that she had ever pronounced the name of her husband; for in India no woman, high or low, pronounces her husband's name. She would consider it disrespectful toward him to do so. When the old lady named her husband, as she did with strong emphasis, and in a very deliberate manner, every one present was satisfied she had resolved to die. Again looking at the sun, she said with a tone and countenance that affected me a good deal, 'I see them together under the bridal canopy!' alluding to the ceremonies of marriage; and I am satisfied that she at that moment really believed that she saw her own spirit and that of her husband under the bridal canopy in paradise, and equally believed that she had been, in three previous births, three times married to him on earth, and as often had died with him, and must repeat it now again. I asked the old lady when she had first resolved to become a suttee? She told me that about thirteen years before, while bathing near the spot where she then sat, the resolution had fixed itself in her mind, as she looked at the splendid temples on the bank of the river erected by the different branches of the family, over the ashes of her female relatives, who had at different times become suttees. Two were over her aunts, and another over her husband's mother. They were very beautiful buildings, erected at great cost. She said she had never mentioned her resolution to any one, till she called out *Suth! suth! suth!* when her husband breathed his last, with his head in her lap, on the bank of the Nerbudda, to which he had been taken, when no hopes remained of his surviving the fever of which he died.

"I tried to work upon her pride and her fears—told her that it was probable that the rent-free lands, by which her family had been so long supported, might be resumed by the Government, as a mark of displeasure against the children for not dissuading her from the sacrifice; that the temples over her ancestors on the bank might be leveled with the ground, in order to prevent their operating to induce others to make similar sacrifices; and, lastly, that not a single brick or stone should ever mark the place where she burned, if she persisted in her resolution; but that, if she consented to live, a splendid habitation should be built for her among these temples; a handsome provision assigned for her support out of these rent-free lands; her children should daily visit her, and I should frequently do the same. She smiled, held out her arm, and said: 'My pulse has long ceased to beat, my spirit has departed, and I have nothing left but a little earth that I wish to mix with the ashes of my husband. I shall suffer nothing in burning; if you wish proof, order some fire, and you will see this arm consumed without giving me any pain.'

"Satisfied that it would be unavailing to save her life, I sent for all the principal members of her family, and consented that she should be suffered to burn herself if they would enter into engagements that no other member of their family should ever do the same. This they all agreed to; and the papers having been drawn out in due form, about mid-day I sent down notice to the old lady, who seemed extremely pleased and thankful. The ceremonies of bathing were gone through with, the wood and other materials for a strong fire collected and put into the pit. She then rose up, and, with one arm on the shoulder of her eldest son, and the other on her nephew, she approached the fire. I had sentries placed all around, and no one else was allowed to go within five paces of it. As she rose up fire was set to the pile, and it was instantly in a blaze. The distance was about one hundred and fifty yards. She came on with a calm and cheerful countenance, stopped once, and, casting her eyes upward, said: 'Why have they kept me five days from thee, my husband?' On reaching the sentries her supporters stopped; she advanced, walked once round the pit, paused, and, while muttering a prayer, threw some flowers into the fire. She then walked deliberately and steadily to the brink, stepped into the center of the flame, sat down, and leaning back in the midst, as if reposing upon a couch, was consumed, without uttering a shriek or betraying one sign of agony!"

In another part of the country a most affecting instance occurred. A young princess named Mutcha Bae lost first her son and then her husband. She resolved upon being burned with the corpse of the latter, and met the remonstrance of her own mother, the excellent Alia Bae, who begged that she might not be left thus alone and desolate in the world, by saying, "You are old, mother, and a few years will terminate your pious life. My husband and my only child are gone, and when you follow, life, I feel, will be insupportable, and the opportunity of closing it with honor will then have passed." Nothing could alter her purpose; and the royal mother, finding she could not prevail on her child to consent to live, resolved to witness her beloved daughter's suttee. She joined the cruel procession and stood close to the pile: two Brahmins held her by the arms. She bore it all till the flames rose round her beautiful child, when she lost all her self-control; she shrieked with anguish, while the crowd shouted; and her hands, which she could not liberate, she actually gnawed in agony. By great effort she so far regained her self-possession as, after the bodies were consumed, to join in the ceremony of bathing in the Nerbudda. Then she retired to her palace, and for three days she fasted in her deep grief, never uttering a word. She subsequently sought relief in erecting a beautiful monument to the memory of the dear departed. Such monuments, the tombs of suttees, varying in size and form, yet generally pyramidal, are seen along the banks of the different sacred rivers.

At length this terrible crime, which the edicts and energy of such emperors as Akbar and Aurungzebe could not restrain, trembled before the cross of Christ. The Protestant missionary entered India, and stood up to "plead for the widow." Before the blessed Name which he invoked, the demon of suttee feared and fled from British India. What Veda, and Shaster, and Menu, Mohammedan Emperor and European governor, all failed to prevent or terminate, in the long experience of twenty-five centuries, was effected by the beneficent religion of Him who, in every age and in every land, has proved himself to be woman's greatest and truest friend.

The honored man who signed the prohibitory edict which ended this awful crime was Lord William Bentinck. He bore unappalled the brunt of native and European opposition. The highest English functionaries expressed their forebodings of *danger* from its forcible suppression, and the Brahmins protested and defended it, as a religious rite that must not be meddled with. Amid this storm of opposition and fears, and sustained by the sympathy and prayers of the missionaries and other good men, his Lordship, on the 4th of December, 1829, signed the act which ended this outrage on human nature and the laws of God. Widow-burning prevails still, to some extent, in those provinces of India not under the direct government of England. Two notable cases were recorded while I was in India—one in March, 1858, in the city of Aurungabad, in the dominions of the Nizam, and the other in August, 1859, at Koonghur. But the flag of Britain no longer waves over a suttee, and the governors are doing what they can to induce the native Princes to complete its suppression.

Lord Bentinck visited Behrole in 1832, in company with General Sleeman, and, pointing to some magnificent tombs of suttees, asked what they were. When told, he remained silent; but he must have felt at the moment the proud consciousness of the debt of gratitude which India and India's daughters owe to the statesman who had the Christian courage to put a stop to the great evil in spite of the fearful obstacles that opposed him.

O, Christian women of America! amid your happy homes, and the exalted privileges and honor with which the Cross has surrounded you, remember your sisters who are still in the bonds of this cruel idolatry! Urge on and extend the missions that are toiling there, until they penetrate to the very last of "the dark places" of India, where "the habitations of cruelty" still erect the suttee; and there

A Group of Thugs. From a Photograph.

let them, in Jesus's name, "relieve the oppressed, judge the fatherless, and plead for the widow."

Meanwhile, let us bless God for that wonderful victory of Christian civilization in 1857–58 over Brahminical rebels, who, had they triumphed, would most surely have rekindled the fires in which, as in former days, the daughters of India would again have had to mount their chariots of flame, to be borne, not to their Vedic heaven, but before the tribunal of Him who has forbidden self-murder, because he "will have mercy and not sacrifice," and who declares to the deluded suttee, as to the wayward sinner, "I have no pleasure in the death of him that dieth."

In all lands, but especially in a country like India, with the millions utterly uneducated, and debased in conscience and morals, there are "dangerous classes," who live by fraud and violence, and who are ever ready for any opportunity of plunder and crime that may occur.

But in India there exists what is not found elsewhere on earth, a class of men whose trade is blood, who follow murder as a profession, and even perform it as a religious duty! The *Thugs* for centuries have

"Laughed at human nature and compassion."

Their organization was complete; they were bound to each other by oaths and engagements as relentless as death and as heartless as hell. Their accessions were from the worst of all classes; the perfection of villainy became a Thug.

I present here seven members of this infernal association, whom I have seen in India. Every man of the group is a murderer, and a murderer, not by the heat of passion, or revenge, or the stimulus of strong drink, but a cool, sober, unexcited trader in human life, whose conscience knows no remorse, because he regards himself as rendering in the act the highest service to his chosen deity!

One day, at Agra, I had the opportunity of seeing these monsters. The English Government have a special police and staff—one of the most perfect detective systems in the world—for the capture of these wretches. At the head of this "Thuggee Department" was Colonel Williams—he whom Government employed to take the evidence of the Cawnpore Massacre. A number of ladies, among whom was Mrs. Havelock, the General's sister-in-law, expressed a desire to visit the Taj that afternoon. The courteous Colonel offered to escort us, and on our return casually remarked, as we crossed the road from the Taj, "Come, and I will show you something else." So he turned down an ominous-looking portal, and we followed him through the guarded gate into a square with high walls, and thence by a gloomy passage into another inclosed court, where were a group of some of the most awful-looking men that I had ever seen. The Colonel coolly remarked, "These are some of my pets." In a moment we realized where we were standing, three gentlemen and a party of ladies unguarded, in the very presence of nearly two hundred Thugs! It made one's flesh creep. The feeling was dreadful, and the situation was not at all relieved, when, in retiring again through the long, dark passage, a number of these wretches came clanking close after us, to plead in the outer court for some concession from the Colonel. The ladies of the party could hardly forgive our gallant escort for the trick he played upon them in leading them into such a presence, and that, too, after coming out of the Taj. It seemed like leaving paradise and descending into hell among those who, in chains and darkness, await the judgment of the great day!

The Colonel permitted a photograph to be taken of some of the most notorious of his collection. They were unshackled, and brought into the parlor of the prison for the purpose. He pointed out one man (the one in front, on the left hand in the picture) who had confessed to having committed *thirty* murders, and who had given him the details of each! And yet every one of these heartless villains were let loose upon society when the Sepoys rose, and since the suppression of the Rebellion the Thuggee Department has had a busy time in ferreting them out and recapturing them.

Sixty years ago these men plied their dreadful trade almost unmolested. The native Governments could not cope with them.

They infested the public roads disguised as merchants, travelers, and Fakirs, but always in gangs, each man knowing his part of the service when the moment came for action.

If any thing further were possible to add a more damning character to these deeds of blood it is found in the fact that Hindoo Thuggeeism has dared to add a *divine* acquiescence to these practices; for their abominable creed has furnished a suitable patron to accept and delight in the groans and dying agonies of their wretched victims.

The consort of Shiva—the third member of the Hindoo Trimurti—the female Moloch, to whose horrid appetite for blood, and hunger for the human lives on which she is represented as feeding, with a desire that is insatiate, is the being to appease and gratify whom the benighted mothers of India have for ages sacrificed their daughters' lives, and her adorers, these Thugs, have strangled the thousands whom they have immolated. Her name is *Kalee.* She is the most popular deity of Bengal—the etymology of the name of the metropolis of India being derived from her designation and shrine—Kalee, and Ghat, a place of ablution—Kalee's-ghat—hence Calcutta.

Of this abominable idol the *Kalika Purana* declares, in describing her appetite for blood and carnage: "If a devotee should scorch some member of his body by applying a burning lamp, the act would be very acceptable to the goddess; if he should draw some of his blood and present it, it would be still more delectable; if he should cut off some portion of his own flesh and present it as a burnt-offering, that would be most grateful of all. But if the worshiper should present her a whole burnt-offering, it would prove acceptable to her in proportion to the supposed importance of the animated beings thus immolated—that, for instance, by the blood of fishes or tortoises, the goddess is gratified for a whole month after; a crocodile's blood will please her three months; that of certain wild animals nine months; a guana's, a year; an antelope's, twelve years; a rhinoceros's, or tiger's blood, for a hundred years; but the blood of a lion, or a *man*, will delight her appetite for a thousand years! while by the blood of three men, slain in sacrifice, she is pleased a hundred thousand years!"

This is the patroness of these Thugs, these professional murderers, who, when their victim is in the agonies of strangulation beneath their knees, on the ground, are engaging in acts of prayer—offering to Kalee the life that is passing away—and to this abomination, thus said to feed on the human soul, have the mothers of India for ages immolated their daughters!

So popular is she and her worship, that even the English Government cannot keep the public offices open during the term of the "Durga-Poojah" holy days, from the first to the thirteenth of October, for all Calcutta then runs mad upon this idolatry. I have seen her image, larger than the human form, painted blue, with her tongue represented as dripping with gore upon her chin, her bosom covered with a necklace of human skulls, and her many arms each bearing a murderous weapon, carried in proud procession through the streets of Calcutta during those holidays, accompanied by bands of music and tens of thousands of frantic followers.

Of this teaching and worship Thuggeeism was the natural result, combining rapine with religion, the service of their goddess with love of plunder—the life for her, the booty for themselves. It raised ruffianism to the dignity of a fulfillment of duty, and swelled the numbers of these religious murderers to a fearful height, till the public thoroughfares were haunted by these wretches, as well as by the brigands and plunderers who imitated them in their lesser guilt. It was on the discovery of thirty dead bodies in different wells of the Doab, (when these assassins had grown to be so reckless in their work that they were ceasing to act with their usual caution in burying and concealing the bodies of their victims,) that Thuggeeism was first brought to the knowledge of the English Government in 1810; and so determined were the measures taken by them for its suppression, and so faithfully have they since been followed up, that the Thug had to disappear from the roads of British India, and confine his limited depredations within the bounds of native States, where English law cannot penetrate. Hundreds of them were ferreted out, and are now confined for life within the walls of safe jails. The Government presses upon the rulers of native States the necessity of imitating English example in this regard. But, while willing to follow the friendly advice of the paramount power, they have not yet the nerve and energy of the Anglo-Saxon, to accomplish its complete extirpation.

Even as late as the days of Bishop Heber (1825) the common people went to market armed with swords and shields and spears and matchlocks. Just as I have seen the plowman in Oude, at the time of the annexation, with his sword by his side and his friends within view—such was the public apprehension of the lawless and violent, by whom life and property might at any moment be assailed. What a change has the presence of the English magistrate made all over the land, within twenty-five years! Very justly does a native writer remark: "The trader and traveler now pass along the loneliest highway without losing a pin. If a corpse were now discovered in a well, or found by the side of a jungle, it would cause a general uproar in the community, and create a greater sensation than the irruption of a Mahratta horde. The wicked have been weaned from their life of rapine, and taught to subordinate themselves to the authorities of society and the State."

Over and above all these elements of wrath and hatred might be enumerated the "Budmashes," "Dacoits," "Goojurs," and criminal classes generally, with all the disaffected elements of every kind, who only needed the sanction of their Brahmins and Fakirs, and the leading of the Sepoys, to be ready for every evil work against law, reform, and government. The reader, from these conditions of society, can easily divine for himself the causes and motives of the great Sepoy Rebellion. He can see what classes, and how many, regarded it with terror and detestation, and what classes reveled in its developments, and by what purposes they were actuated.

Can any just and adequate interpretation be put upon this terrible conflict, that does not acknowledge that its life and soul was the religious question? The Rebellion was Heathenism—vile, selfish, and cruel—trembling for its very existence and goaded to retaliation, rising up in its hour of opportunity against the Christian civilization, whose increasing reforms and enlightenment manifestly knew no limit save the overthrow of every wrong, and the removal of every error, in India. It was the irrepressible and inevitable conflict of light with darkness; it was the Christian knowledge and saving faith of the nineteenth century mightily wrestling with venerable ignorance and licentious idolatry for the possession of the bright Land of the Veda, and for perpetual supremacy over its 200,000,000 of men! The prize and the agony for its possession were correspondent; and God defended the right.

III. Yes; for God and his providence must be acknowledged here as we search for the causes of this great conflict. On how many of its facts, as well as its precious results, is written, "This is the finger of God!" The permissive providence which allowed this terrible calamity to fall upon the English in India, was, even by their own subsequent, contrite acknowledgment, only what their sins deserved. It is consistent with all that we know of the divine government to suppose that the Almighty must have taken cognizance of their compromises of his truth, of their patronage of idolatry, of their repression of his Christianity, so as to keep it away from a people who needed it so much. He knew that if such a course was to continue unchecked India could not be saved for long centuries to come. He was resolved that caste and idolatry must be overthrown; and if Englishmen dared to prop up the God-dishonoring systems, they must feel the blow which dashed those systems to pieces.

I need not enumerate their national sins in India—they have done so themselves. As I write, the pamphlets are before me which contain their petitions to their Queen and Parliament, signed by multitudes of the best men of Britain, acknowledging before God and the world, in the hour of their national agony, how unworthy and responsible they felt themselves to be for the sins and shortcomings of their rule in India, and how earnestly they pleaded with their Government to reform what was wrong in the administration of India, and act henceforth on Christian principles in the rule of that land. Here is what these people said in 1857 in their Memorial to Parliament:

"By professing to be neutral among the various religions of its Indian subjects, the Government has in effect denied the truth, and given a great moral advantage to those foolish, wicked, and degrading systems to which the great bulk of the people adhere. Nor has the advantage thus given been merely moral. Idolatry has formerly been, and to some extent still is, publicly patronized and subsidized. Its immodest and cruel rites have been honored with the attendance of Government officers, and paid for from funds under Government control. The system of Caste, which, in every part of it, contradicts and counteracts the Christian religion, has been recognized in Government arrangements for the administration of justice, as well as in the organization of the army, and selfish humanity and contempt of their fellow-men and subjects, have thus received the highest official sanction. The Government has discouraged the teaching of the Christian religion to certain classes of its subjects, and made the profession of it, in a sense, penal, by placing some who have been turned from idols to serve the living and true God under disabilities to which they were not, before their conversion, liable. And, while allowing the Koran and the Shaster to be freely used, it has forbidden the teaching of the Holy Scriptures, or even the answering of spontaneous inquiries respecting their contents, during school hours, in the educational institutions which it supports. In all these instances the Indian Government, though professing neutrality in matters of religion, has practically countenanced and favored falsehood and wickedness of the most flagitious kind."

They here quote dispatches of the East India Company, who had ruled India for a hundred years, in proof of the foregoing statements, and also refer to facts well known in India—such as Lord Clive personally attending a heathen festival at Conjeveram, and presenting an ornament to the idol worth 1,050 pagodas, ($1,850;) Lord

Auckland, another Governor General, offering 2,000 rupees ($1,000) at the Muttra shrine, and being highly praised in a native newspaper for his piety! Lord Ellenborough, in 1842, ordering the gates of the Temple of Somnath (carried off by a Mohammedan conqueror eight hundred years ago) to be carried back hundreds of miles, with military honors, and his issuing a proclamation, announcing the heathenish act, "to all the Princes, Chiefs, and People of India." They also refer to the conduct of Lord Dalhousie, later still, paying reverence to an idol, by changing his dress on entering the heathen temple of Umritsur, and making an offering to it of 5,000 rupees, ($2,500.) These things were done by Indian Viceroys, while Government servants were required to collect pilgrims' tax, administer the estates of idol temples, and pay allowances to officials connected with heathen shrines; and even military officers had to parade troops and present arms in honor of idol processions!

These things were so. The writer has seen (and could give the name of the place, and of the commanding officer responsible) British cannon loaned, and ammunition supplied, to fire a salute in honor of a heathen idol, and that on the holy Sabbath day! Christian Englishmen in India groaned over these acts, officers in the army threw up their commissions sooner than obey such orders, and men in high positions protested against them as sins of the deepest dye, fearing that God would "visit for these things," and appealed to the British public to stop the madness of the East India Company and their servants in India. When I entered India there was not over one native Christian in Government employ in all the North-west Provinces. While that very year the only Sepoy who, up to that time, had ever become a Christian (save one, mentioned by Heber, who was also dismissed) was, by order of the Governor-General, removed from the army because he had become a Christian, and the commanding officer and the civil judge who attended at the baptism were reproved by his Excellency for doing so! His object, in this mistaken policy, was to prevent the discussion and prejudice which would result, and convince the Sepoy army how fully his administration would sustain the doctrine of "neutrality." But what must Almighty God have thought of such conduct, and that, too, on the part of men who went to Church on Sunday, and professed to be members of a State Establishment of Christianity!

The patience of Him who will "not give his glory to another, nor his praise to graven images," was about exhausted with that proud company and their policy, and the Parliament of England and its Christian people were already preparing the overthrow of both, and deliberately making up their minds to the introduction of a more Christian and manly administration of Indian affairs. The petitioners end their Memorial, earnestly pleading that these Government sins should cease, and India be henceforth ruled in a way more worthy of the duty which Christian England owes to that people.

Their confession and humiliation were candid and sincere, and in the hour of their deep distress God was entreated for the land. Defeat was soon after turned to victory. He saved them from among the heathen. God came to their aid, not in the infidel, Bonapartist sense, in which He is said to be "on the side of the strongest battalions," for here he clearly was on the side of the weaker, and gave the victory to the "few" instead of the "many."

No Government ever committed a greater mistake than the East India Company did when it adopted this "neutrality" policy. The result was, it laid itself open to the charge of underhand designs for the overthrow of the popular faith—for the people could not imagine a Government without a religion—and it was consequently disbelieved and distrusted, while the Christian missionaries, who boldly and openly denounced idolatry, and invited the people kindly and candidly to embrace Christianity, were understood, and even trusted, by the masses. So marked was this fact, that in the panic at Benares, and when the vanguard of Havelock's troops were passing through, and extra supplies were urgently required, the Government officials could not induce the villagers around to bring them in; a very serious condition of things was arising. In the emergency a Christian missionary, Mr. Leupolt, could do what the commissariat officers failed to effect. He went out among the villagers—heathens, to whom he had often preached on the guilt and danger of their idolatry—and told them what the Government needed. The people asked him if he would give his word that they should be justly treated if they furnished what was needed? He said he would. Without more ado they loaded their hackeries, and accompanied him to the city, and furnished all that was required. This I know to be a fact. A similar instance is on record in the experience of Missionary Swartz in the south of India.

Honesty is the best policy. If the India Government had acted on it they would not have exposed themselves to the retort of Rajah Janaryan, of Benares, a liberal and wealthy friend of native education, who, when a Christian physician, who had raised him up from a severe illness, urged the claims of the Gospel upon his mind, the Rajah at first seemed disposed to yield; but presently, on reflection, he stifled his convictions by the remark, "Sir, had the Christian religion been true, the Company Bahadur [the Government] which has, in other respects, benefited my country, would not have withheld from at least commending this religion to our notice!"

Sir John Lawrence was Governor of the Punjab when the Rebellion broke out; the elements around him were as energetic, and some of them as dangerous, as any in India. He had been superior to the policy of his masters, and would insist on favoring Missionaries and the Bible in the schools. What was the result of this open and candid course, even in the hour when all around them had fallen? The missionaries waited upon him to say that, if their public preaching in the streets of Lahore was any embarrassment in the condition of the country, they were ready to pause for a season, if he thought it requisite to do so. His prompt reply, which will be a lasting honor to him, was, "No, gentlemen; prosecute your preaching and missionary enterprises just as usual. Christian things, done in a Christian way, will never alienate the heathen." They acted on his advice, and did not preach a sermon the less for the Rebellion. Though all India around them had "gone," their Punjab stood firm, and even supplied the men and means for sustaining the siege of Delhi, till it fell, and the Government was fully restored. The East India Company was abolished, amid the contempt of all good men, and even of the candid heathen; while this very man, Sir John Lawrence, was chosen by the Queen to be Viceroy of India, to introduce that better and more Christian condition of things which prevails there to-day! What an illustration of the promise, "Them that honor me I will honor, and they that despise me shall be lightly esteemed!"

At the close of September the insurrection between Mooltan and Ferozepore suddenly stopped all mails, and we were left for a time without any further news. Just then our implacable foe, Khan Bahadur, made his last fierce effort for our destruction. For a few days our anxiety was terrible. The force at Bareilly had been augmented by the arrival there of the Nana Sahib, and their rage had risen with the spirit and character of their visitor, and the followers he brought to their aid. Of course he advised our destruction, and it was attempted by the largest force hitherto sent against us, consisting, it was said, of over one thousand cavalry and four thousand infantry. They came to the Huldwanee side of our position for their attack, but our trust was still in the "God of battles;" so there we stood, calmly awaiting the result. Few as we were, we knew that there was succor, in which "they that be with us are more than they that be with them." (2 Kings vi.)

The help of Providence is not less certain or near because it is invisible. It was "a day of trouble, and of rebuke and blasphemy." This modern Sennacherib had come up to cut off "the remnant that are left," full of rage at Christ and his people. His blasphemies against the Lord's Anointed doubtless exceeded in bitterness the reproaches of the Assyrian king, and with similar pride and confidence he said, "With my multitude I am come up to the height of the mountains, to the sides of Lebanon, and I will cut down the tall cedar trees thereof, and the choice fir trees thereof, and I will enter into the lodgings of his borders, and into the forest of his Carmel." (2 Kings xviii, 19.) He would, we knew, if God allowed him, but not otherwise. Yet this haughty spirit was the precursor of his own destruction.

Of course he kept us in distress and excitement, and this was intensified by the cutting off of our mails, so that we could get no information. For a few days we could but fear the worst. How we longed for the news of the fall of Delhi, and for the relief that would come when that was accomplished! But God was working out our salvation in his own way, and in the height of this very emergency one of his most manifest interpositions was developed. A few days after their arrival this powerful force, by some unaccountable influence, suddenly decamped, without doing us the smallest injury. Our spies brought us word that every one of them had fled, and, on some of us going down, we found that they had evidently left, not merely in a hurry, but in a panic, for the heel ropes of the cavalry horses, instead of being untied and taken with them, were all found cut and left fast to the stakes! The only way we could account for it was a report which was said to have reached them that we were going down to surprise them with immensely augmented numbers. Be this as it may, they left suddenly and went back to Bareilly.

The old Nawab was outrageous at their return, and insisted upon a renewal of the effort; but a terror from God seemed to have fallen upon them, and this was immediately followed by the news, so dreadful to them, of the capture of Delhi by the English troops, spreading consternation through their ranks. They received that information some days before we did; but at length it came to us at the close of September.

I was sitting that afternoon, writing in a very pensive mood, when the sudden roar of a cannon, from the little fort near our cottage, brought me to my feet, and a brilliant hope flashed across my heart. I snatched my hat and ran up the hill, while peal after peal thundered out, making the grand Himalayas reverberate. At last I gained the summit, and stood till I counted the "royal" twenty-one. I needed no one to tell me what it meant. Our commanding officer had just received the message which announced that *Delhi had fallen!*

I stood there, wrapt in thoughts never to be forgotten, and a luxury of feeling flowed through my heart, which will make that moment a bright spot in my life and recollection forever.

How often before had the thunder of those British cannon proved the inlet of salvation to the oppressed and persecuted! I was not the first American missionary to whom they had announced "glad tidings of great joy." I thought of Judson and his heroic wife, of Wade and Hough, on whose ears, in their melancholy captivity, those cheerful peals proclaimed approaching liberty.

None but those who, like ourselves, have been practically captive for months, not knowing but that any day our doom might be sealed by the hand of violence, can imagine how every gun seemed to ring the knell of the Moslem city and power, while it proclaimed liberty to the Christian and the missionary of the cross—none but those so situated can appreciate the luxury of an hour like that.

It was impossible, as I returned down the hill, to repress the tears that so freely flowed; yet they were caused by no craven love of life, nor coward fear of death. I had passed through sufficient ordeals to know "in whom I had believed." No, my tears flowed, but they were for India's own sake; shed in joyful hope and largeness of heart, that God was once more setting free those Christian agencies which alone could redeem "her from her sins" and sufferings, and which would lead her to the possession of those untold mercies that even she shall yet enjoy in common with all Christian nations.

If time is to be measured by the magnitude of events that transpire within any given space, how long and how much we seemed to have lived during those past five months!

The capture of Delhi is too well known to the reader to require any thing more than mere references in these pages. It was the event on which our fate, and the fate of British India, seemed to hang during those long months; and its capture by a mere handful of troops was one of the marvels of those stirring times. At length we breathed freely, and the hope of deliverance rose brightly upon our horizon. The scattered Sepoy host had to be followed up through all parts of India, Rohilcund being left until the last. Lucknow could not be reoccupied till March of the following year, (1858,) and it was not till May the 5th that Bareilly was captured, and our way opened to return there.

We were thus free to go out on the north-west side, while we were to be shut up on the south-east for eight months more, so we concluded to leave for the plains, after most of our number had already gone. To remain longer where we were seemed out of the question. No money could reach us; I had exhausted every source, and to borrow any more was impracticable.

Ere the snow closed the road over the Himalayas for the winter, we concluded it was best for us also to go. At Meerut we could obtain the means required, and should also be on the "grand trunk road," and, after the fall of Futtyghur could, if necessary, join the brethren expected at Calcutta, and decide with them what was best to be done for the present. We could also obtain requisites for the mission and for ourselves, and be ready to return with our brethren and sisters as soon as our field was again open.

Before starting, we had the joy of receiving a letter from Brothers Pierce and Humphrey, dated Calcutta, September 30, with the glad news of their safe arrival there in good health. They wrote in their letter: "We knew nothing of the fearful scenes transpiring in India until our pilot came on board on the morning of the 19th instant, bringing files of the latest papers. After we had recovered ourselves a little from the first blow, we turned to the account of the Bareilly tragedy. I read it aloud, trembling almost to read from line to line. Twenty-nine out of eighty-four Europeans escaped, and your name unmentioned! Our worst fears were excited. We saw, however, that only official names were given; but, after resolving the matter, could encourage ourselves but little to hope for your safety. We remained in this state of intense suspense until four P. M. on Monday, the 21st, when we cast anchor at Calcutta. I hastened on shore, called on Mr. Stewart, and learned the joyful tidings of your escape to Nynee Tal. Our interest was all concentrated in the question, 'Are Brother Butler and family safe?' When we learned this, our gratitude and gladness were such that we scarcely thought, for the time, of your losses and sufferings: it seemed enough that you were saved. 'O that men would praise the Lord for his goodness, and for his wonderful works to the children of men!' I returned to the ship; then were we glad, thanked God, and took courage."

It seems a singular coincidence that the English and American Methodist missions to India should both have commenced their labors under afflictive circumstances connected in each case with their superintendent.

On the 3d of May, 1814, the leader of the first band of Wesleyan missionaries, Dr. Coke, suddenly died, almost within sight of India. His brethren, deprived of their zealous and devoted superintendent, landed in grief and sadness.

On the 19th of September, 1857, another ship neared the coast of India, this time bearing, not English, but American, Methodist missionaries. They also are the first band that this Church has sent to India; and they, too, are in anxiety and distress, for they fear that their superintendent has been murdered.

But this is not all. On Dr. Coke's death, the Rev. James Lynch was appointed to the superintendency. He labored nearly thirty years, and then returned to his native land, and was appointed to the Comber Circuit. Being feeble, the writer was sent to assist him. We traveled and labored together; God was with us, and sinners were converted. During the Sepoy Rebellion he was calmly awaiting his departure to a better world, full of years and the grace of God, while the boy preacher, whom he so kindly cherished and prayed for fifteen years before, was in that very India, and superintendent of the first American Methodist Mission established there!

The journey across to Landour was a wonderful one. We climbed mountains, forded rivers, clambered round frightful precipices, often on narrow paths which, in places, were not more than twenty to thirty inches wide. At a gorge in the mountains we crossed the Ganges, there a roaring torrent between walls of rock, on a miserable *rope* bridge, which had been condemned as unsafe, and which swung in the wind, sixty feet above the water that foamed beneath it. It was a journey never to be forgotten for its magnificent views, its tall pine forests, the wildness of the scenery, the beauty and variety of its birds, and the singular sensation that we were moving over mountains and through forests infested by tigers and all sorts of savage animals, against which our only protection was the sunlight by day and the flaming log fire by night. But God guided us in safety. Though, to show how near we were to danger, and how much we required merciful care, I will state that one night we had camped in a lonely valley by a stream, having with us a goat which we had brought along to give milk for the little "Mutiny Baby." The poor goat was left fastened, as usual, to the peg at the tent door, with the fire in front outside, and our lantern lighted within. The fire unfortunately went out, and in the middle of the night we were startled out of our sleep by a roar and a yell of agony, and, jumping up and opening the tent door, I found that the wild beasts had carried off the poor goat bodily, and were already clear out of sight with her!

Occasionally we slept five thousand feet higher, or lower, than where we rested the night before. Our "house and home" was a little tent eight feet square. A day's journey varied from seven to fifteen miles, according to the character of the road. It was generally four or five P. M. by the time we reached the camping-place. The tent was then set up, our dinner cooked, and there, beside our large log fire, sometimes ten or twenty miles from any habitation, we enjoyed the grand solitude. After this we would heap more logs on the fire for protection against the animals, and, commending ourselves to the care of God, would lie down and sleep tranquilly. The wild beasts, by which we were generally surrounded, disturbed us no further. So it went on for sixteen days and nights from the time we started, the whole distance being about one hundred and eighty miles.

The last day, when crossing the highest mountain of the range, the snow began to fall, so that we had to camp that night upon it, with a few boughs under us. But the next morning we crossed it, and began to descend to the plains, and soon were beyond the snow line.

Our last communication from America was dated several months before. How people over there felt about our position and circumstances, and in regard to our mission, we knew not. We could only hope that our beloved Church, far from being daunted or discouraged, was more than ever resolved and prepared to do her duty toward her great work in India.

We reached Dehra Doon December 5th. How calm and beautiful all things in the valley seemed to us, after being shut up so many months upon the mountains! But the Rohilcund rebels were across the Ganges, so we kept off by Saharunpore, and thence to Kurnal and the imperial city. It was two hours after midnight when we passed the outskirts of Delhi. We rolled down the empty street of the Subzee Mundee, rattled on to the bridge over the moat, and hailed the sentry, who, seeing a white face, asked no questions, but opened the ponderous gates, and—ten weeks after its capture—we were *in Delhi!*

There is something very solemn in passing through the deserted streets of a conquered city. We could dimly see that all was desolation and utter confusion. Having reached the lonely house assigned for travelers, and taken a cup of tea, my curiosity was too great for rest or sleep, so I procured a light, and wandered down the Chandnee Chowk, (the Street of Silver.) All was still as death; indeed the silence was dreadful; not a ray of light anywhere, except from the lantern which I carried. Not a human being to be seen. Every door, whether of store or private house, lay open. I entered five or six shops. No words could describe the wreck: even the floors had been torn up by the "loot" seekers. One was a native doctor's shop. The drawers were all out, half the bottles still on the shelves, and the rest overturned and smashed. Every thing valuable in each case had been carried off, and there lay the worthless remnants, knocked to pieces on the floors. In some places a heavy fermentation was going on, causing an insupportable smell. The wretched cats were silently moping about, and the poor dogs howled mournfully in the desolate houses.

And this was Delhi, and this her recompense! Far rather would one see a city knocked down and covered with its own ruins. than to behold a scene like this. A tomb in Herculaneum can be contemplated with interest; but Delhi, that night, was like *an open grave* rifled of its ornaments, and its dishonored, reeking condition lying exposed to the gaze of the lonely visitor. No wonder that its excluded Mohammedan population, as they prowled around its vicinity, said, "This is a worse punishment than that of *Nadir Shah*. He gave up the city to massacre and pillage for a few days, then all was over, and the surviving inhabitants returned to their homes and employments, and every thing went on as before. The English took no such vengeance; but they drove us out, and week after week they kept us excluded, and will not let us return."

No doubt, such language correctly represented their feelings. This decided exclusion of them; this calm and continued investigation by the civil and military authorities; this searching out, and bringing to justice, the perpetrators of the crimes of May and June—giving them the opportunity of proving their innocence, (one trial alone having lasted ten days,) and then their prompt execution when found guilty of murder—all this, together with the disposition of the Government to acknowledge and reward fidelity where they found it, produced an immense impression. It was so contrary to the rash and indiscriminate mode of Oriental despotism.

When I reached the Kotwalie (the Mayor's office) in the square, a horror came over me as I remembered that I was then standing upon the very ground where, on the 12th and 13th of May, Englishwomen

> "Perished
> In unutterable shame;"

where good Rajib Ali, and many others with him, were tortured, not accepting the deliverance urged upon them by the raging crowd on condition of apostasy; and where also the murdered and mutilated bodies of Christian men and women lay exposed and insulted, till at length, when no longer endurable, they were dragged away out of the city and flung to the jackals and the birds of prey; and here I was, standing alone at midnight amid the darkness which my lantern only made visible, in the very center of Delhi, with no sound to be heard save the sighing of the wind in the great, dark peepul trees above my head, till my excited fancy almost imagined that I heard them moan out, "How long, O Lord, how long!" The reminiscences of that moment were enough to chill the blood of the strongest man. They recur to me now like a dream of terror that can never be forgotten.

I walked on to the Emperor's gate, but it was shut; the walls frowned darkly down upon me, and all was silent as death. I turned back by the other side of the street to my lodging, a walk of more than a mile, without meeting a single human being.

As I stood that night in the midst of this stern desolation, I was forcibly reminded of the Lesson in the calendar for the 14th of September, which attracted our attention so much when reading it, and all the more when we heard afterward that it was the Lesson for the day on which *the assault was given.* It was in Nahum iii, and begins, "Woe to the bloody city!" etc.; as applicable to Delhi as ever it was to Nineveh—and here was her "woe." She was "naked," "a gazing stock," and "laid waste;" her "nobles in the dust," her "people scattered;" so that with equal truth it might then be said of her, "There is no healing of thy bruise; thy wound is grievous; all that hear the bruit of thee shall clap their hands over thee, for upon whom hath not thy wickedness passed continually?" (Verse 19.)

I picked up an Hindustanee account book lying at a merchant's door, and returned and went to bed absorbed in the thoughts of a retributive Providence, and the sad miseries of war among which I lay.

Early the next morning I was out again rambling through the streets. The people who had passes were admitted for trade and market. The Chandnee Chowk, with a few of its leading tributaries toward the Palace, (inside the walls of which were the troops and the prisoners,) were the only portions of Delhi where I met any number of people. The rest of the city was a desert, where one might walk half a mile and not meet a human being, even at midday. Coming around to the Kotwalie, an awful sight presented itself. On a high gallows (which the darkness prevented me from seeing when I stood there a few hours before) were hanging by the neck, dead, eighteen of the "Shahzadas"—the king's seed—who had been found guilty of terrible crimes, many of them committed at this very place. They had been hanged at daybreak, and only a few persons were standing around.

I had, of course, heard the report of their fiendish deeds, but to come thus suddenly upon the authors of them, bearing their penalty on the very spot where their crimes were committed, was enough to chill the blood in one's veins. How dreadful is sin! The sight made me sick, and I turned hastily away.

During the day we called upon Lieutenant E., a military friend, who kindly gratified our wishes to be shown "the sights." Mounting us on one of the government elephants, he took us over the battle-field, and described the siege and the assault, and the capture of the city at the different points. We lingered where General Wilson stood when the terrible assault was made, and seemed to realize the whole scene. It is doubtful if any commander in modern times has sustained a weightier responsibility than he did then.

Further delay was impossible; there was no room for any reverse. He *must* succeed or all was lost. A repulse would have involved consequences so terrible that the mind dare hardly contemplate them. If he failed, that little army, without a miracle, must have been annihilated, the wavering Punjab would have "gone," and the undecided princes have been drawn into the current, which would probably, within a few weeks, have swept away every thing British and Christian from the soil of India.

We wandered over the battle-field, by the broad shore of the

Jumna, and saw that, notwithstanding the efforts to clear the ground, the sanguinary character of the contest was still manifest: dead horses and camels, and occasionally human remains, with portions of exploded shells, might be seen. The "Brahminee hawks" and vultures were still hovering around. I took up a human skull; it was that of a Sepoy for the marks of the *pawn* were still on the front teeth. A round shot or sword-cut had taken off the top of the head; death must have been instantaneous. I thought of the lines of the classic poet as I thus looked upon the most vivid realization of them I ever saw, or ever expect to see:

> "The wrath which hurled to Pluto's gloomy reign
> The souls of mighty chiefs untimely slain;
> Whose limbs, unburied on the naked shore,
> Devouring dogs and hungry vultures tore!"

From the battle-field we went in the afternoon to Selim Ghur, and thence along the fortifications by the river. We were fortunate in falling in with Brigadier Jones, who took the Palace on the last day of the assault. He told us that he led 780 men into action, of whom nearly 450 were either killed or wounded, the proportion of officers being very large. This fact shows what a desperate service he had to perform. Personally he escaped untouched. The Brigadier commanded a few months afterward at the battle of Bareilly.

We went next to the magazine, the defense of which has rendered the name of Willoughby so famous. Here we were also favored in having as a guide Lieutenant Forrest, who was one of Willoughby's officers on that occasion. He conducted us over the place, and explained the details of the ever-memorable defense.

We next went to see the beautiful Jain Temple. The outward court reminded me of the description of Solomon's Temple, it was so rich and elegant. In the sanctuary there stood a shrine, which rose tier above tier, till it terminated in a dome on four pillars, the proportions of the whole being exquisite. Each part was richly carved in screen work in white marble, and inlaid with precious stones; but every thing movable had been carried off, including the magnificent curtains, embroidered in gold, which were hung around the court, perhaps twenty in number.

In the sanctuary we found two Parisnaths, (or Parswanaths,) one of them as large as life, in black marble, with a genuine negro type of countenance, high cheek bones, thick lips, and curly hair. On asking the reason, the priest informed us that their god Parisnath was exactly like a negro, an idea which they hold in common with all Buddhists.

Both of the venerable deities had their noses smashed, and looked, in consequence, rather ridiculous. I asked the priest, "Who mutilated them?" He said, "The Mohammedan Sepoys did so, and then the Sikhs came afterward, and robbed us of every thing they could carry off." This temple, for its size, is certainly the most splendid place of worship I ever saw. The Motee Musjid, in Agra, is more chastely elegant; but there was about the structure and appearance of this edifice something which, though "not worthy to be compared," yet helped to a more adequate idea of that matchless "house of God" which the liberality of Jewish piety erected on Mount Zion.

From this we went to see the Jumma Musjid, the greatest Mohammedan "cathedral" of the East, and one of the very largest, if not the largest place of worship, in the world. The view from the top of the minarets was magnificent. These lofty towers were occupied by the leaders of the defense during the siege, and in that vast court below thousands of those blood-thirsty fanatics, from sunrise to sunset, during that long anxiety, implored God, for Mohammed's sake, to aid them in exterminating the followers of the hated Messiah. Here they "raged" and "took counsel together;" but God, instead of answering, rejected their prayers, confounded their devices, and "dashed them" and their government "in pieces like a potter's vessel," and here was the center of the fearful wreck of all their purposes.

The whole place was desecrated. Native soldiers were cooking their food in the cloisters. The high priest's throne was smashed, and every thing valuable carried off. I entered their treasure room, and on the ground, covered with broken boxes and rubbish, I found those marble slabs, (of the existence and use of which I had previously heard,) one professing to bear the impress of Mohammed's hand, and the other of his foot. Notwithstanding the boast of the Mohammedans as iconoclasts, they do pay these relics a certain religious veneration that is idolatrous. I found them where they kept their most venerated things. Those who sought only precious metals and other valuables had not considered them worthy of removal, but to me they were deeply significant, and, as "looting" was the order of the day, I carried them off, to the great amusement of the Beloochee soldiers, who laughed at the idea of the "Sahib" soiling his clothes to carry away "such useless things as those dirty stones." As long as they last they will be an evidence of the debasement of Oriental Mohammedanism, furnished by the treasure room of its greatest mosque.

From the Jumma Musjid we went to the Hindoo Temple of Mahadeva, near the palace gate. Destruction had raged here also. The high priest was very civil, telling us "how thankful he was that our Raj (Government) had returned." They confound all white men with the Government. We entered, and the little knot of priests looked sad and sorrowful enough. Seeing that the idols were all off their pedestals, I inquired where they were. They led us up to the place, and there, on the ground, covered reverently with a cloth, were nearly twenty of their gods, beautifully carved in white marble, about as large as little babies, all in a state of mutilation, not one whole one in the lot. Their legs, and arms, and heads were off, and their noses smashed, while the bright eyes of one and another looked up out of the pile as if they were astonished!

The poor priests looked down, with rueful countenances and heavy sighs, at the wreck and confusion. I had no condolence to offer, for the scene was such an illustration of the folly and impotence of idolatry that I felt like giving way to immoderate laughter, but refrained, as I knew it would annoy them to the last degree. We asked, "Who or what wrought all this destruction?" "Why, Sahib, the Budmash Mohammedans, of course. They came into our temple, and with the butt ends of their muskets they knocked off their legs and arms, and smashed their noses, and flung them on the ground, and desecrated them." I told them we had no pity for them. They had, with their eyes open, joined these "Budmash" Mohammedans, to expel a Government that had never outraged their religion, but always protected them in its exercise, and which they themselves had often declared was the best Government their country ever knew. They admitted the assertion, and when we asked them why they did so, they replied, "Because, Sahib, we were deluded. Those people told us, if we would only join them this once, they would give us perpetual deliverance from all fear of the growing power of Christianity, which, they said, was about to destroy our religion; and that they would also give us equal rights and privileges. Their war cry was, 'Do deen ek zeen men,' (two religions in one saddle;) but they soon gave us to understand that one of the two must ride behind; and when they came to decide which it should be, they settled that after their fashion." He added, "I prayed to God for your return to this city. O, how thankful we are that your Raj has come back again!"

I asked if I might take two or three of the broken idols. They submissively replied, "What you like; you are master here." They lent me a basket, and procured a coolie to carry the three which I picked out. I placed some money in their hands for them. They seemed surprised that I had not acted on my "right of conquest," and taken them without payment. On asking them what they were now engaged in worshiping, as their other gods were destroyed, they seemed afraid to reply. We told them they need not be, and that we had heard of it, and knew what it was, and only wished to see it. After obtaining our promise that we would not demand that too, if they showed it, they led us into the sanctuary, and there it was, nothing more nor less than the upper and hinder part of a bull, (Nundee Davee,) carved and polished in black marble. The flowers and Ganges water were fresh upon it, showing that it had been worshiped that day. And this was Hindoo worship, in one of its chief temples in the imperial city!

Our kind guide now brought us to see the Emperor, Empress, and the Princes, who were awaiting trial; but before doing so, he led us up to that part of the palace where was the suite of apartments which had been occupied by the English Embassador, and into his reception-room, where he and the chaplain, and the two ladies, were murdered.

In the East a violation of hospitality is regarded as a crime of greater magnitude than it is with us. This is fully illustrated in the Scriptures; yet here, under the very roof of the Emperor, the Embassador, Hon. Mr. Fraser, (the second brother killed within those walls,) with the Rev. Mr. Jennings and his daughter, Miss Jennings, with her cousin, Miss Clifford—said to be one of the most beautiful Englishwomen then in the East—were ruthlessly cut to pieces in this very room. Their blood still stained its floor, the marks of the tulwars were in the plaster round about, and on the walls was the impress of some of their gory hands, made as they leaned after receiving their first wounds; while the head of another of the party had fallen back against the wall, and described part of a circle as it sank to the floor, leaving the blood and hair in the track of its passage!

There were bitter feelings expressed against the Empress, especially for these assassinations. It was considered that under her own roof, at all events, it was entirely in her power to have saved these ladies had she chosen to do so; but she made no effort for this purpose, and when her own hour of sorrow came, it was remembered to her disadvantage.

We were obliged to procure a written permission to see the Emperor. There had been no restriction on the public curiosity till a gentleman, who had lost several relatives by the mutiny, went lately to see the Emperor, and, losing control of his feelings, used such language as put the old man in "bodily fear" for his safety. This, with no doubt other reasons, led to his being kept a close prisoner, and interviews permitted only in the presence of the magistrate and the officer of the guard who had him in charge. The place of his residence was a small house of three rooms in his own garden. Accompanied by the officer and Mr. Ommanney, we passed through the guard of the Rifles, and entered the room where the Emperor was sitting cross-legged, after the Oriental fashion, on a charpoy, with cushions on each side to lean upon, engaged in eating his dinner, using his fingers only, without knife or fork.

His dress was rich, his vest being cloth of gold, with a beautiful coat of Cashmere, and a turban of the same material. The figure of the old man was slight; his physiognomy very marked; his face small, with a hooked or aquiline nose; his eyes dark and deeply sunk, with something of the hawk aspect about them; his beard was gray and scanty, running down to a point. Notwithstanding his crimes, it was impossible to look upon this descendant of Tamerlane without emotion. My mind went back two hundred and forty years, to the time when England's Embassador humbly sought, in the splendid city of Jehangeer, a foothold for the East India Company. How different the scene before us from what Tavernier saw when he beheld Shah Jehan in that magnificent court, seated on his jeweled "Peacock Throne!" Here was his lineal descendant a prisoner, while two English soldiers, with fixed bayonets, stood guard over him. It recalled the astonished exclamation of a seraph to another potentate in guilt and captivity,

"If thou beest he; but O, how fallen!"

It was just twelve months that very week since I saw the "Princes of Delhi" at the Benares Durbar, in all their pomp and finery, presented in turn to that kingly-looking man, the late Governor Colvin, himself a sacrifice to this rebellion. What one short year had done! Many of those "Princes" were now filling the graves of traitors and murderers, while others of them were awaiting their trial and doom within a minute's walk of where I was standing. This wretched old man was then surrounded with imperial state, and living on his $900,000 per annum; and now, here he was a guilty, forsaken, penniless king—a gazing stock, awaiting his doom. What a change!

The feelings with which we contemplated him were a strange mixture of interest, pity, and contempt. The reader will remember the reflections of the Countess of Blessington when she met the mother of the fallen Napoleon leaning on the arm of the ex-king of Westphalia, as they wandered pensively amid the ruins of Rome.

This case added another illustration of the poet's thought:

> "He who has worn a crown,
> When less than king is less than other men;
> A fallen star extinguished, leaving blank
> Its place in heaven."

But in the instance before us there seemed a lower depth of degradation than crowned head had ever reached before; a profound of folly and guilt that forbade human sympathy, as was very truly set forth in the speech of the United States Minister at the great meeting in London four months before.

As we entered, the Emperor looked up at us for a moment with a flash in his eye that was easily understood. We belonged to the white-faced race, and were of the religion that he detested; and the man must have keenly felt, as we stood in his presence and looked at him, how fallen he then was. He, before whom and his predecessors multitudes had bowed down in such lowly prostration and homage, had then to realize that there was

> "None so poor to do him reverence."

It was not possible, after all, to look at him without a measure of sympathy: "a star" that had shone for eight hundred years in this political "heaven" had fallen to the earth and was lying at our feet, its light extinguished forever.

I asked the soldiers why the old gentleman was so closely guarded in that inclosed place? They replied, "Sir, it is not for fear of his getting away, but to protect him from harm till he is tried." On expressing my surprise at this explanation, the man added, "Well, you see, sir, people are coming here every day to look at him—wives, whose husbands were killed by his Sepoys, and husbands whose wives were worse than killed. You see, sir, *his* was the name in which every thing was done, and when they look at him and realize it all their feelings get the better of them, and they feel like flying at him and revenging their wrongs upon him, so we have to protect him." Yes, I saw it all; and the bitter remembrance of the cruel deaths of some precious friends of my own at Bareilly, and elsewhere, seven months before, banished all sympathy for this guilty author of their sufferings. In response to some remark which I made to this effect, I saw the blood mount to the cheek of the soldier as, drawing back his hand in which was the bayonet, he said, with deep feeling, "Yes, sir, it would give me the greatest satisfaction to put *this* through the old rascal!" The honest earnestness of the man provoked a smile; and I thought, what would Sir Thomas Roe—England's first Embassador to this Court—say, could he rise from the dead, and, after all the reverence he paid here to "the divinity which hedged" these gorgeous kings, hear a common soldier of his nation express his disgust at having to act the jailer over the Great Mogul!

A day or two previously my friend, Rev. J. S. Woodside, Missionary of the American Presbyterian Church, was here. He went to see the Emperor, and took the opportunity of conversing with him about Christianity. The old man assented to the general excellence of the Gospel, but stoutly declared that it was abrogated by the Koran—as Moses and the law were abolished by Christ and the Gospel—so, he argued, Mohammed and the Koran had superseded Christ and every previous revelation. Brother Woodside calmly, but firmly, told him that, so far from this being the case, Mohammed was an impostor and the Koran a lie; and that unless he repented and believed in Christ, and Christ alone, without doubt he must perish in his sins. He then proceeded to enforce upon his bigoted hearer the only Gospel sermon which he had ever heard. And Brother Woodside was the very man to utter it. Was not his Church entitled to that privilege by the sacrifice of the precious lives of four of their Missionaries at Futtyghur, as mentioned on page 151?

It was a just and significant providence that in such a moment, when this blasphemous usurpation, arrested by the hand of God, and about to be hurled from all its aspirations of supremacy over the mind of India, a Minister of Jesus Christ should, in this presence, ring, as it were, the knell of its hopes, and utter those truths as the last Imperial representative of Oriental Mohammedanism was bidding a "long farewell to all his greatness," and the political power of his system was falling,

> "Like Lucifer,
> Never to hope again !"

My wife went in to see the Empress, and found her, with two of her maids, very plainly dressed and but poorly lodged. When she came out, she was not at all enthusiastic about the Empress's present beauty. Still, competent evidence declares that Zeenat Mahal, as she appeared in 1846, is faithfully represented in the picture presented on page 111 ; but twenty years of such a life as she led in that Zenana, and the apprehension of guilt which she must then have felt, with the doom impending over her husband and house, all must have wrought sad changes in that once fair young face.

From the Emperor we went to the cells where the other prisoners were awaiting their trial. These cells were in a sort of offset from the palace grounds, in which stood the beautiful Dewanee Khass, and had doors of iron railing, through which the prisoners could glance across into the palace gardens beyond. It strikingly suggested the separation, and yet sight, of each other in the parable of the rich man and Lazarus. We walked past some of them, and it was sad to see within these iron doors, awaiting their fate, men like the Rajah of Dadree, the Nawab of Bullubghur, and others of their class. Twelve months before, these captives were occupying thrones, and governing their States in peace, under the protection of the paramount power of England ; and here they were now, awaiting their turn to be tried for treason, and, some of them, for murder as well. They had sided with the Emperor, sending their troops and treasure to Delhi to aid him against the British, and his defeat and fall had dragged them down into the ruin which had overtaken him. A few of them were very gentlemanly-looking men, and courteous, salaaming to us as we passed them. But it was too painful to complete the entire round, so we walked sadly away.

On the 27th of the following month the Emperor was put upon his trial in the Dewanee Khass, having counsel to aid in his defense, and, after a patient investigation lasting nineteen days, was found guilty on all the charges against him, and sentenced to be transported for life. Many thought the sentence too light; but it was probably sufficiently severe thus to pass from a throne to the deck of a convict ship, to end his days among strangers. Zeenat Mahal and one other of his wives shared his exile. He died at Rangoon in 1861. Two years after, when in Burmah for the benefit of my health, I had the opportunity of passing by his lonely grave behind the quarter guard of the English lines. But no Taj or Mausoleum will ever rise over the spot where rests, solitary and alone, on a foreign shore and in a felon's grave, the last descendant of the Great Moguls!

The closing words in the defense of one of his own nobles, the Nawab of Bullubghur, whom I saw tried and sentenced to die in that same Dewanee Khass, might well apply to his Imperial master. The Nawab was a noble-looking man, with dark, lustrous eyes, and fine figure, clad in the usual style of an Oriental prince. There he stood, during those long hours, before that commission of English Officers, making the best defense he could for his life.

He admitted the charge, but pleaded in extenuation, that in sending his wealth and troops to Delhi to help the Emperor he had acted under compulsion. This was known to be untrue, as it was well understood that he had acted freely and promptly, and had even submitted to circumcision, and forsaken his Hindoo faith, to curry favor with the rising Mohammedan power.

He evidently felt, as he closed his address, that he was not believed—that he was a doomed man. With considerable feeling, and in their figurative phraseology, he ended his defense with these words: "Gentlemen, one short year ago I sat on the topmost bough of prosperity and honor; in an evil hour I lent my ear to other counsels—I sawed asunder the branch that sustained me, and *this is the result!*"

On Christmas day, 1857, I attended Christian worship in the Dewanee Khass—the first ever celebrated there. A crowded audience made its walls resound with the unwonted strains of Christian hymns; and there that day the Gospel was preached and prayer was offered in the blessed Name so long blasphemed beneath that roof. As I stood amid that throng, and remembered where I was, and what had there been said and done, and what was then transpiring, I realized that I was beholding one of the most wondrous victories ever consummated by the glorious Son of God over the enemies of himself and his holy religion. They had distinctly joined issue with Him on this very ground; and here he was, in his almighty providence, victorious amid the utter overthrow of the wealthiest, most powerful, and implacable foes of his divinity and atonement; expelling them from the "Paradise" which they had profaned, and asserting his right, ere he consigned it forever to degradation and to ruin, to use even their Dewanee Khass for his own worship, and thus answer, in divine vengeance, the blasphemies against himself inscribed upon its walls. "Just and true are thy ways, thou King of saints!"

The crystal musnud, (throne,) the last remnant of its glorious furniture, was carried away, a present to the Queen of England. All veneration for the place seemed to cease by common consent; the visitors and soldiers dug out the precious stones from the walls and pillars with their knives, and it was soon despoiled. A few weeks after, I saw its crenated arches built up with common sun-dried bricks, and the whole structure whitewashed and turned into a hospital for sick soldiers. Its destruction was at last complete!

The rebels failed, and that failure was both miserable and total. We may endeavor, as has been attempted by various writers, to account for that failure by their want of concert as to the time of commencement; by the escape of nine tenths of those whom they intended to destroy; by their want of leaders of ability, (though the Rebellion developed Tantia Topee and Kooer Singh;) by the fierce contentions of their chiefs for supremacy, rank, and power; by the fact that the Hindoos, disgusted and deceived, deserted the cause; by the perfidy of the Mohammedans in the hour of their triumph; by the heroism and endurance of the British soldiers, invincible not only against overwhelming odds, but over the difficulties of climate, season, sickness, and deficiency of resources of all kinds. Yet, after all, while gratefully and cordially admitting to the full every one of these considerations, and all the aid which they involved in the terrible struggle, even wicked men in India in 1857 and 1858 were constrained to admit, and were prompt to acknowledge, that any or all of these combined could not and did not rescue us;—that our salvation was, without a doubt, entirely due to *the special interposition of Almighty God.* It was the divine help that gave England's cause the victory, and gladly and gratefully did they, saint and sinner together, raise their private and public Ebenezers to Him who alone had saved them!

No attribute of the Almighty could take part with the Sepoy, the Brahmin, or the Mogul. Every hope for India was bound up with the defeat of their cruel, self-interested, and wicked purposes. Grateful India herself will yet place among her highest mercies the mighty overthrow of 1858.

Mr. Rees has truly shown that the merits of this contest, on the part of the natives, was a frantic fear and hatred of the growing influence of Christianity; that it was not a war of the oppressed against the oppressors, of a nation rising against their rulers, or of Hindustanees against Englishmen; on the contrary, that it was a war of fanatical religionists against Christians, of barbarism against civilization, of error and darkness against truth and light. Had it been different—had patriotism prompted the rebellion—had the natives, as one nation, determined to shake off the yoke of the foreigner, and had they conducted their war like soldiers and brave men, instead of acting the part of cowardly assassins, then indeed might they have enlisted sympathy for their cause among the civilized nations of the earth, and found defenders and advocates among the people of England themselves.

It is not easy to impart to an American reader a just idea of how far the people of India—nine hundred and ninety-nine out of every thousand of them—are from the knowledge of freedom, the appreciation of law, or the rights of constitutional government, as we understand such privileges. One of their own educated men speaks but the simple truth of them when he says :

" The Oriental mind is decidedly wanting in the knowledge of the construction of a civil polity. It has never known, nor attempted to know, any other form of government than despotism. Political science and political reform appear, like the oak and the elm, to be the plants of the soil of Europe and America. Never has any effort been made for their introduction to the plains of Persia or the valley of the Ganges. Though the most important of all branches of human knowledge, politics have never engaged the attention of the people of the East. They have never studied the theory and practice of a constitutional government, never conceived any thing like republicanism, never understood emancipation from political servitude, never known a covenant between the subject and the sovereign. They have never had any patriotism or philanthropy, any common spirit and unity for the public weal, or what it is to govern for the good, not of the fewest, but of the greatest, number."—*Travels of a Hindoo,* Vol. II, p. 408.

Progress, preservation of order, the physical and moral well-being of the people, the advance the world has made in humanity—a humanity that is extended even to the inferior animals—they do not understand. They have only just begun to dream about them, and, even for the dream of the blessed day that is dawning, they are (as the evidences which I have furnished show) wholly indebted to the Christianity which has come at last and breathed the thought into their slumbering souls.

CHAPTER VIII.

RESULTS OF THE REBELLION TO CHRISTIANITY AND CIVILIZATION.

FROM Delhi we went on to Meerut, where we remained two months, while the troops were clearing the country of the scattered bands of Sepoys between that point and Cawnpore, and restoring order, so that mails and passengers might once more move up and down to Calcutta. More British troops had arrived, and the Commander-in-chief was directing the movements of the five columns into which the army was divided, our position at Meerut being about central to all the operations, and about forty miles from the nearest of them.

Here I had the joy of again meeting our dear friend Lieutenant (now Colonel) Gowan, who escaped from Bareilly, and had been hidden for so many months in a Hindoo house, as narrated on page 248. He had managed at last to communicate with the English authorities here, and even before a sufficient length of the roads westward was clear, his rescue was attempted. The kind Hindoos who had sheltered him, when all had been arranged, took him by night in a bylee, (a native carriage used by ladies,) with the curtains closed, under pretense of going to the Ganges to bathe. A boat was quietly procured, and they ran him across the river to the other bank, where an elephant and a band of cavalry were awaiting him, and before sunrise he was safe in Meerut. How we rejoiced together! The last time I saw this Christian officer (who used to help us occasionally in conducting our Hindustanee meeting) was in Bareilly on the evening before we left, when I was trying, in our English service, to strengthen our hands in God by preaching from the text, "As thy day, so shall thy strength be." For nearly seven months, though in jeopardy every hour, did God fulfill to him that precious promise, till he saw fit to terminate his captivity and bring him forth in safety, and now here we were again together, consulting about God's precious work.

In the course of conversation I happened to remark that I was *en route* for Calcutta, when he suddenly lifted himself up, and looking me in the face, inquired, "What, are you going to leave the country?" (fearing for the moment that I was discouraged and about to abandon the work.) I looked into his earnest countenance and replied, "Leave the country! No, sir. The devil has done his worst, but he may be assured that we are not going to yield the field to him now that the fight is won. So far from it, I am going down to bring up the first band of my missionary brethren, with whom I expect soon to be preaching Christ through all Rohilcund."

I shall long remember the immediate effect of my reply. He looked at me for a moment, then paused, and

"Delight o'er all his features stole."

His very moustache twitched again with pleasure, and, with a smile covering his entire countenance, he turned away, and said not another word.

He made over to me an orphan boy whom he had rescued from danger and misery, to whom he had given his own name, and promised to be responsible for his support and education from that day.

This was the origin of our Boy's Orphanage, and its first member, thus received, was the son of a Sepoy officer killed in battle, the poor child being found on the back of an elephant, where his father had left him during the fight. In the midst of his sorrow he fell into the hands of Colonel Gowan, who promised to be a father to him, which pledge he has faithfully redeemed, and the orphanage is to-day its result.

This devoted servant of God encouraged and stood by me in all my future plans for the extension of our mission. No other man in the East or in America has given half as much money to develop our work in India as Colonel Gowan has contributed. He aided me in procuring homes for the missionaries, in establishing our Orphanage and Training School, and he built and endowed the schools in Khera Bajhera, (the village where he was so long sheltered,) so that his liberality to our mission work, up to the present, cannot be much less than $15,000, and yet this liberal gentleman was a member of another Church—the Church of England; but he is the type of a large and an increasing class of Christian Englishmen in India who prize our work, and are glad to aid it.

Apropos of leaving the country, while in Meerut I received a letter from Brother Wentworth, in China, inviting me to join them in Foochow. He says: "If British predominance is not soon established, get leave of the Board and come on here, where there is as great need of laborers as in India."

Well, that was all very good; but, on reading further in the Doctor's letter, I was highly amused to find the guarantee of additional security which I was to enjoy by following the course suggested. My good brother added: "Last spring we were fearing the rebels might drive us from this station, and are not now without apprehensions that the war between Canton and England may become a general one, and result in the temporary expulsion of all foreigners from the empire. In case of any sudden outbreak we are in an unfortunate situation for escape, being ten or twelve miles from the foreign shipping, and no vessel of war near. A sudden and decisive outbreak might cost us our lives at any moment." This for me would have been "out of the frying-pan into the fire" with a vengeance. Indeed, I thought my circumstances were every way preferable to his, so far as British predominance and personal security were concerned, and concluded that I might well return the compliment, and invite my good-natured brother, if driven from his post, to come and join me.

However, it is our privilege to live by faith, and as the Doctor observes, to "feel secure in the protection of Him who guides revolutions among the nations as he does tempests in the sky."

I did not proceed to Calcutta, because, from the center which I then occupied, I was soon satisfied that the country was fast quieting down, and that my brethren would be able immediately to join me, when we could afterward proceed to our own field of labor and begin our work.

While at Meerut my aid was requested, as one of "the Rohilcund Refugees," to help the Postmaster in the melancholy task of looking over the bags of letters, directed to gentlemen in that province by their correspondents at home in England, which had accumulated there for months. I could tell who were dead, and, generally, where the others were scattered, so as to intimate how he should direct them. It was a sad sight to see the pile of letters from anxious friends which had to be returned to England, because those addressed were no longer among the living.

Early in March it seemed practicable to have the two missionaries and their wives join me. The only portion of the way where there was any danger was from Cawnpore to within twenty miles of Agra, from parties of Sepoys crossing the Grand Trunk road. The telegraph had been restored, and the mails were coming twice a day. I went on from Meerut to Agra, to get into direct communication with them. Through the kindness of the Postmaster and the use of the telegraph, I kept myself well acquainted with the condition of the road as they advanced. They had directions to call at every telegraph office which they passed, so that if there had been any danger ahead of them I could at once have stopped them at any station, until it had passed away; but, by the "good hand of God upon them," they reached me at Agra in perfect safety on the the 11th of March. The destroyed houses of the English were still in ruins, and the people all in the Fort, which was crowded; so that at first I did not know where or how I could prepare for them a night's lodging, ere they resumed their journey on to Meerut. But in these circumstances I thought the magnificent Taj none too good for them. So I arranged all, and on their arrival had them comfortably lodged in this "Wonder of the World." Ours was a joyful meeting, and the splendid Taj Mahal was worthy to be the scene of it.

Little did Shah Jehan, or his bigoted Moomtaj-i-Mahal, imagine that a day would come when this matchless mausoleum would be occupied by a party of Christian missionaries, at a time, too, when the last Mogul of their line—after an effort to fulfill the carnelian prohibition upon her cenotaph, and carry out Jehan's fierce order, "Expel those idolaters from my dominions!"—would be himself a prisoner awaiting his doom, in the hands of that very "tribe," (see page 147;) or that these missionaries would, as we did, promenade in peace, in the delicious moonlight, through that lovely garden which he planted, and sing our Christian doxology, with unction and glowing hearts, standing over their very dust, and in the presence of that powerless and mistaken prohibition!

We left the Taj the following afternoon, by way of Meerut, for Nynee Tal, as we could there best devote ourselves to the acquisition of the language, and be ready to descend to Bareilly and our other stations when God had prepared our way, after the reoccupation of Rohilcund by the English Government. Joel had been directed to join us on the route. Notwithstanding the distance and danger, all was correctly timed and safely accomplished. The day after I received the Missionaries at the Taj Mahal, I joyfully clasped Joel's hand once more, on the road to Meerut. It was to both of us like life from the dead. His devoted wife remained under the care of her mother till Rohilcund and Oude were cleared of the rebels, when she rejoined us at Lucknow, from which place I afterward moved them to Bareilly, where we were again together on the scene of our former sufferings.

We reached Nynee Tal in safety, and at once entered upon our mission work, and soon had the satisfaction of seeing a little congregation collected. We also commenced a Christian day-school for the native children in the Bazaar.

I present a rough sketch of our first chapel, drawn by Sister Pierce. Our room having become inconveniently small for the number of natives attending the preaching, we greatly needed some larger place for worship. The only building available then was a sheep-house, which stood on the side of a hill. This, we concluded, could be turned into a chapel. It was done in three or four days. We cleared it out; a quantity of clay was thrown in and leveled,

The First House of Worship of the Methodist Episcopal Church in India.

which, beaten down, made a good floor. I whitewashed it, Brothers Pierce and Humphrey made the benches, and Joel saw to the leveling of the ground outside. When it was finished and swept out, though too humble to have a formal or public "dedication" awarded it, yet I resolved that a hearty consecration to God's service it should not lack; so, shutting the door, and all alone, I kneeled down and offered up to the condescending God of mercy this humblest of all the "places where he records his name," and earnestly besought him to make it the birthplace of some of those poor, dark souls that, during the ensuing six months, would come to worship there.

When Sunday arrived, the smiles and congratulations of our ladies were really delightful. They could not imagine how we had made such a commodious-looking affair out of such a place as it had been. "Why, it looks almost like a church!" they said. Even the poor natives caught the spirit of the occasion, and, as they came in and seated themselves, looked around smiling and nodding to each other.

The entire cost of fitting up, including the boards and nails for the seats, was four dollars and thirty-six cents. Only missionaries—and missionaries under such circumstances—could adequately appreciate our joy over this humble commencement.

I also present another sketch, (on the top of the next page,) that will give an idea of the appearance of our congregation inside the "Sheep-House" Chapel.

The reader can imagine that he sees *Joel* preaching, and we sitting around him, the congregation being in front. The women sit on the benches to the right; the men in the center. Two poles. supporting the roof, run up in the center of the house.

We occupied this humble place for some months, when our worthy commandant, Colonel Ramsay, (to whom, next to Colonel Gowan, our mission is most indebted for munificent financial aid,) seeing our earnestness and success, resolved that we should have a house more worthy of our cause. The result was the erection of our Nynee Tal chapel, costing about $2,500, the whole amount

The Sheep-house Congregation.

being subscribed by the Colonel and his acquaintances and friends in Nynee Tal and Almorah.

Lucknow was recaptured, and the English Government restored there, at the close of March. The defeated Sepoys fled into Rohilcund, or across the Grand Trunk Road into Central India, with the columns of British troops in pursuit. Jhansee and Gwalior were recaptured, and Kooer Singh and the Ranee of Jhansee killed. This was followed by the capture and death of Tantia Topee. Most of the other chiefs surrendered, and the columns were at last turned northward for the pacification of Rohilcund. Three of them, including the one led by the Commander-in-chief, were to concentrate on Bareilly, then viewed as "the metropolis of the revolt." On the 5th of May, within a few hours of each other, and from opposite directions, they approached that city. Sir Colin Campbell led his column by the Futtyghur road, General Penny his by the Allyghur road, through Budaon, and General Jones the third, by way of Moradabad. Here was to be the last great effort, and it was fought, the dispatch says, amid "a mass of one-storied houses in front of the British lines," that is, it was fought on the very ground where I had lived, our ruined house and garden being by the road-side, between the cantonments and the city, in the very center of the contest, the walls of the houses giving shelter to the Sepoys as they awaited the onslaught of the Commander-in-chief's forces.

The rebels were headed by the Nana Sahib of Cawnpore, Prince Feroze Shah of Delhi, and Khan Bahadur of Bareilly, and with them was the Begum of Oude and her troops. So here, as it happened, were concentrated for the final effort the living representatives of the four great centers of the Sepoy Rebellion. Their resolve and fighting on that dreadful day were worthy of the desperate cause and the desperate men, who well knew that this was to be their final chance; that here, at last, it was to be for them either death or victory. The 42d and 79th Highlanders bore the brunt of the struggle, which was short and sharp. A body of *Ghazees* (Mohammedan fanatics of the most desperate character) led the Sepoys. These men, sword in hand, with their bossed bucklers on their left arms, and their characteristic green waistbands, rushed out of their concealment to the attack, brandishing their tulwars over their heads, and shrieking out their favorite cry, "Bismillah Allah! deen! deen!" ("Glory to Allah! the faith! the faith!") In the confusion they were not recognized as distinguished from the Sikhs, who were fighting with the British, till they came close on the side of the 42d Highlanders. The Commander-in-chief had just time to cry out, "Steady, men, steady! close up; bayonet them;" when the struggle ensued. Russell, the "special correspondent" of the London *Times*, who was present, gives a vivid picture of this fearful moment. He himself was wounded, as were General Walpole, Colonel Cameron, and others, for the Ghazees seem to have made straight for the officers; but the quick bayonets of the 42d closed around them, and in ten minutes the dead bodies of the devoted band (as their name implies) were lying in the circle. Not a man of the one hundred and thirty-three turned back. They all believed, according to the tenets of their creed, that they were martyrs, and were sure of paradise if they fell.

Nearly twenty of the Highlanders were wounded in the struggle, the Commander-in-chief having had a narrow escape. A Ghazee, with tulwar in hand, was lying, feigning death, in front of him, and as he approached, the fellow sprang to his feet to kill him, when the quick eye of a mounted Sikh soldier saw the move, and (Russell says) "with a whistling stroke of his saber he cut off the Ghazee's head with one blow, as if it had been the bulb of a poppy!" General Penny was killed near Kukrowlee. The Commander-in-chief had only a skeleton staff. He had completely "used up" more than one set of officers, and on this occasion had only his chief of staff, General Mansfield, with Captain Johnson, to aid him. Under such circumstances the battle of Bareilly was fought and won before the sun went down. Early next morning the city was attacked, but it was found that during the night the Sepoys had fled, with Khan Bahadur and the other rebel leaders. The city surrendered at once, save some Ghazees, whose positions had to be stormed. A timely proclamation of amnesty to all save notorious rebels and murderers, with precautions to prevent any plundering, restored confidence to the terrified inhabitants, and they willingly submitted once more to British rule and protection.

It was at this spot that the Nana Sahib last saw the face, and witnessed the prowess, of the white man; and it was from this battle-field he took that departure for the jungles of Oude mentioned on page 309 of this work. It is some satisfaction to have the assurance from good authority that two, at least, of the companions of his flight, the Begum of Oude and Prince Feroze Shah, denounced his cruel treachery at Cawnpore, as having brought the curse of God upon the native cause. The deadly Terai was but forty-eight miles away. It was the only shelter in all India that was open to receive them. He and his companions, and the remnants of the rebel host, entered its malarious inclosures, and, save Khan Bahadur, who lagged behind in its outskirts, and was captured and brought back to Bareilly, the rest of the unhappy crew found sickness, despair, and death within its gloomy shades. Thus, in the providence of God, ended the great Sepoy Rebellion, and the twelve months of its Mohammedan misrule and cruelty closed amid the dying groans of its emissaries at the foot of our hills, and almost within sight of our place of refuge.

Our impatience now to go down to our work in the plains was sorely tried by the refusal of the Commander-in-chief to permit us to do so for some weeks longer—the ladies he would not allow to do so till October, not only because the country needed to be cleared and quieted, but also because houses had first to be built for them. At length the permission came for gentlemen to go down, and taking the road to Moradabad, lest that through the Terai, on the Huldwanee side, might have straggling Sepoys in it, we reached Bareilly on the 28th of August. We found every thing, of course, much changed. The burned houses and bare walls had a look of fearful desolation about them.

On entering Bareilly I went, first of all, to *my own residence*, (which was so, fifteen months before.) Nothing was standing but the bare walls; the floors were all grown over with deep grass. I called a coolie, and dug up the rubbish in my once comfortable study, and we soon came on the charred remains of my precious books. All had been destroyed by fire! I took up a handful of the burnt paper, and of the melted glass of the book-cases, as a memento, and walked away to the spot where Maria lay buried beside the rose hedge, and then on to where Joel's house stood. What a change from the day I last stood there! But no murmuring thought arose. It was all well: "Blessed be the name of the Lord!" We were to begin again, and that, too, under brighter prospects than India ever knew before. I wandered all over Bareilly. The people were very civil. I knew that I loved them then *better* than I had ever done, and felt sure that God would yet have mercy upon them, and that we should soon see days of grace in Bareilly.

I then wandered off toward the encampment of the English troops, and one of the first gentlemen whom I met was our dear, good friend Dr. Bowhill, safe from Delhi, and the rest of his campaigns. The warm-hearted Scotchman hugged me up to his heart, and wept for joy that we should meet again, after all we had gone through, on the same old ground where we first met, and where God had blessed his soul in the dark days before the mutiny.

And then I found kind General Troup, to whose prudence we owed our lives. He was in command of Havelock's Brigade, and worthy of the position. The excellent Magistrate also received us cordially, and advised an immediate commencement of our work, promising to aid us in every way. Before I was twenty-four hours in Bareilly a subscription was started to help us in organizing our missions. That financial liberality has continued, year by year increasing, to this day; those excellent men, in the civil and military service of England, have since furnished the means required to carry on our system of Christian schools and our Orphanages, averaging over $10,000 gold per annum.* We promised, as soon as our Mission in Lucknow was commenced, to begin the work at Bareilly. At the latter we could not yet find shelter, but in Lucknow houses could at once be obtained, by the assistance of Sir Robert Montgomery, the successor of Sir Henry Lawrence in the government of Oude. He was kind enough to write to me and advise our immediate occupancy of that city, and we were now *en route* to do so.

The Sabbath was a blessed day. The troops (two thousand seven hundred men) then stationed in Bareilly were chiefly Scottish regiments. The Chaplain being sick, the General commanding sent tc request that I would undertake the chaplain's duties for the Sabbath. Of course I gladly did so. My opportunity was one I shall never forget. Arriving on the parade-ground, I found the troops drawn up. I took my stand; the men were formed in a "hollow square," the drum of the regiment was placed before me, and a Bible and Psalm Book lay upon it. The General and his officers stood beside me, and the band behind. I gave out the one hundredth Psalm, and the music and voices rose up on the Sabbath air to heaven. I then prayed with an overflowing heart, and stood up to preach "the glorious liberty of the sons of God."

My emotions almost overwhelmed me when I looked at my audience. For *who* were the men that stood around me? These were

Havelock's heroes! the illustrious warriors who first relieved the garrison of Lucknow. Yes, these brave men before me had performed one of the greatest military feats known to history, and did it, too, notwithstanding that they lost nearly one half of their number in its execution. I looked at their sun-browned faces, and thought of the manly tears they shed when, covered with dust and smoke, they rushed through the last street and into the "Residency" among the men and women whom they had suffered so much to rescue, and, snatching up the children in their arms, thanked God "that they were in time to save *them!*"

Noble men! I realized, as I stood before them, that their fame belongs to *our* nation as much as to their own. And I shall ever esteem it one of the highest privileges of my life that I was permitted to preach, and that, too, on the very ground of their last battle-field, to the men that General Havelock led to the relief of Lucknow!

Though it anticipates the time somewhat, I may here mention that Khan Bahadur was captured and brought into Bareilly. He and four or five others were confined in the little fort, awaiting their trial. Wishing to see my old neighbor, and say a word to him before he died, I obtained permission to do so, accompanied by Rev. Mr. Humphrey. There, in his cell, we found Khan Bahadur, his long white beard hanging down nearly to his waist. It was a trying moment for us both. Here was the man who sent to my house to kill me and my family, who expressed his deep disappointment at our having escaped his hands, and who afterward set a price upon my head! This was the man, too, who had deliberately murdered Judge Robertson, Judge Raikes, Dr. Hay, and many more of my acquaintance!

What a curious thing is human nature! Here was a criminal, of whose deep guilt no one that knew him could have the least doubt; and yet an author like Montgomery Martin, who never saw him, and had no adequate knowledge of his desperate wickedness, half undertakes to whitewash his ensanguined fame! But this is consistent with Mr. Martin's course, in his efforts to find cause of commiseration for the Delhi Emperor, while he seems to exhibit but scanty sympathy for the victims of the Delhi court—an author who can indulge in cold-hearted and cynical criticism upon such men as Sir R. Montgomery and Sir Henry Lawrence, who went through fiery trials of responsibility of which he, in his comfortable London home, ten thousand miles away from their danger, could have little idea. I am sorry to write these words. But I was there, he was not; and I know whereof I affirm, and can conscientiously say that I consider some of Mr. Martin's representations in his "Indian Empire" to be unworthy of the confidence of the American public. His slurs and innuendoes caused deep feeling in the minds of some of the best men in India, many of whom were not at all his intellectual inferiors, while they were his superiors in opportunities for forming correct opinions. They had not to depend, as he seems to have done for some of his representations, upon hasty and partial statements, or such writers as "Bull-Run Russell!" His glorification of Sir Colin Campbell and Sir James Outram, to the prejudice of General Havelock and Sir John Lawrence, only shows that he had his favorites, and would belittle other men to make *them* look greater. But we in India knew the difference, and it was the conviction of many there, competent to give an opinion upon such matters, that Sir Colin Campbell was not only slow, but that he did nothing more than what any brave English officer could have done with the same resources. As to Sir James Outram, so far as the establishment of Christianity in the Valley of the Ganges is concerned, I know from my own personal intercourse with both, and their actions, that we may have great reason to be thankful that Sir James Outram was superseded, and the evangelically courageous Sir Robert Montgomery was appointed to be ruler of Oude during the founding of our Mission in that kingdom.

Mr. Martin's peculiar notions on the lawfulness or expediency of capital punishment must have been often offended by the events of the time. It would, however, have been but fair to have extended the benefit of his doctrine as fully to the victims of the Sepoys as to the Sepoys themselves. It may, however, be doubted if his narrative shows this clearly. The consideration he seems so ready to exhibit for the Sepoys is an anomaly not easily accounted for; but he has found few sympathizers. I would not speak too harshly, even of a criminal; yet I will take the responsibility of saying, that I never saw or heard of men to whom, more appropriately or deservedly than to the Sepoys and their chiefs, could be applied the terrible character given by the Holy Spirit, when he so fully describes those whose profanity, crimes, and riot, exhibit them "as natural brute beasts, made to be taken and destroyed." 2 Peter ii, 12. They were men who neither knew nor showed mercy, any more than would be exhibited by the tigers of their own jungles; and toward whom the most just and saintly magistrate on earth would be guilty, before God and human society, if he should not firmly "bear the sword" until he had, at least, controlled their cruelty, and stopped their power for further mischief.

Mr. Martin has not increased his fame by thus obtruding upon his countrymen his mistaken and conceited assumptions of "impartiality" toward bloodthirsty wretches who, as a class, so generally (I might almost say universally) proved themselves ready, from the first hour to the last, to become the destroyers of churches, the murderers of the ministers of God, and the slayers of undefended women and children.

But to return to Khan Bahadur. He asked me how had I escaped? I told him. He seemed uneasy, and evidently thought that my visit was in some way connected with his approaching trial. I assured him that he might dismiss all anxiety upon that point—my testimony was not required. Far worse than I could present had been heaped up by his own fearful actions, and was now ready for his condemnation. I had come, with my brother Missionary, to visit him with a kind intention; that I forgave him all the harm he did me in the destruction of my home and property, and the more serious harm which he intended to do in taking our lives; that our only object in coming was to converse with him about his poor soul, which would so soon have to appear before God, as we felt sure that his days were numbered, and he could not hope for mercy here, in view of the past; and we closed by entreat-

29

ing him to turn to God in penitence, and seek pardon through the Lord Jesus, who died for him and for all sinners. This was done in a very kind manner by Brother Humphrey, and I hoped the old man would have been impressed by it; but his Mohammedan bigotry rose up bitterly against the Saviour's atonement, and he would not admit his necessity of any such help. The Koran was enough; he wanted nothing more, and wished to hear nothing else.

I saw him tried before two judges. He was defended by a native lawyer, who managed the sad case as well as he could. Mr. Moens, an English magistrate, prosecuted. The old Nawab's policy was to deny every charge, but any number of native witnesses were ready to come forward and prove them. On the afternoon of the second or third day the trial was closed in connection with a singular forgetfulness of his. A witness on the stand was testifying to the color of the robes which Khan Bahadur wore on the day when he witnessed the exposure of the bodies of the murdered English people at the Kotwalie. The old man had denied that he was there at all, but, forgetting himself in his rage against the witness, who swore it was a blue dress he had on, Khan Bahadur turned to him and said, "You lie, you rascal! it was not blue, it was a *green* dress that I wore." The look of blank astonishment that came over the face of the native lawyer at his client's acknowledgment was a study, while Mr. Moens turned toward the judges and merely remarked, "Your honors hear the admission of the prisoner." The trial closed that afternoon. He was condemned to be hanged at the Kotwalie. He passed me on his way to execution in a cart, sitting on his coffin, with a guard of the 42d Highlanders around him, lest the Mohammedans should interpose any trouble; but they attempted none; there seemed to be among the natives a general acquiescence in his doom, as one that had been fully deserved.

A medical friend went down to see him executed. On his return he told me what had occurred, remarking, "I had some sympathy for the old man, but his wicked utterance at the close took it all away." The facts were these: when Khan Bahadur mounted the scaffold and stood on the trap, which was about to be drawn from beneath his feet, the rope resting loosely on his shoulders, and the cap ready to be drawn down, Mr. Moens, who had acted as council against him on his trial, and was now acting as sheriff, stepped forward and said, "Khan Bahadur, have you any thing to say before you die?" "Yes," was the prompt reply, "I have two things to say: first, I hate you;" and then added, speaking as an Oriental, and using the certain for the uncertain number, while his face lit up with a glow of awful gratification, "but, Moens, I have had the satisfaction of killing a thousand Christian dogs, and I would kill a thousand *more* now, if I had the power."

Ten minutes after, that man stood in the presence of the Judge of all, and he went into eternity with the Mohammedan conviction that, in killing Christians, he had been doing God service, and consequently his crown of martyrdom would be all the brighter for every life which he had sacrificed; hence his confidence and exultation in that fearful moment.

We left Bareilly for Lucknow, attended to Futtyghur (seventy-four miles) by relays of sowars, (native cavalry,) the General considering the precaution still necessary. On reaching Futtyghur we went to the mission premises. But what a ruin! When I was last there, the beloved brethren and sisters of the Presbyterian mission were surrounded by a happy, native Christian community, engaged in supporting themselves by tent-making and other employment, and in the center of the village stood their nice church; but all was destroyed and desecrated now, and these dear Missionaries and their wives were numbered among "the noble army of martyrs."

We pushed on for Lucknow. It was the month of September. How well we could understand now, what Havelock and his men must have gone through during that month last year! My entry, made at the time, tells of the torrents of rain, of the flooded country, and of having to cross unbridged rivers twenty times in that seventy miles. We were twenty-six hours going about twenty-five of these miles The rain, the mud, and the slippery way were very trying; yet Havelock had to take an army over this very ground, and at the same season. Here he had to fight battles, carry his wounded, and sustain his men. The Ganges had so overflowed its banks that it was nearly five miles wide where we crossed it.

At Cawnpore we visited "the Well" of sad memories, and the Shrine, (then being built) and the Intrenchments, and Ghat, and conversed with Private Murphy, the only survivor in India of the terrible massacre.

On reaching Lucknow we were most kindly received at Government House, no longer the Residency, but a building in another part of the city. Mr. (now Sir Robert) Montgomery welcomed us with the cordiality of a Christian, requesting us to consider his house our home till we could obtain a mission residence, and offering to aid us in every way within his power. He believed in Missions, and in the ability of God's truth to reach the hearts even of the turbulent race whom he ruled.

After breakfast next morning I started off to explore Lucknow. Going out of the door, how well I remembered the last time I went through it, starting from the Residency on the back of an elephant, guarded by a Sepoy all day. But Mr. Montgomery did not offer me an elephant on this occasion, and there were no Sepoys to attend me. So I walked off, quite content to have it so, and was not ten minutes in the Bazaar till it was all explained. The change was amazing, even already. Instead of every man being armed with tulwar and shield, nobody bore a weapon, save the native police. Every person seemed to be minding his own business. The shop-keeper's sword was no longer on his counter, yet his goods seemed safe enough. Mr. Montgomery had disarmed the entire population, and taught them that they must no longer fight and wound each other. If they had a quarrel, they must not take the law into their own hands; the courts were open to them, and they must go there and have the magistrate settle it for them. They submitted, and seemed amazed how well the new arrangement worked. Never before had it been so seen in Lucknow. It was the new and wonderful reign of law and equal justice in the land of the Sepoy.

The public, shameless vice, that so shocked me when I last passed through these streets, was no longer seen. It had been told it must retire, and cease to shock virtue and decency by its hateful presence. The order, the industry, and the propriety of the streets, were to me simply marvelous; and the people were so civil—making their salaam as I passed along, much gratified to find that I returned their courtesy. And this was *Lucknow*, with its hundreds of thousands of people, and I, a white face, alone and unarmed among them! I could hardly believe my own senses. But it was just so; and I felt that we might almost conclude that the city was already about half saved.

Yet there was enough to remind you of the savage and cruel past. The houses were all bullet marked, and some blown to pieces. There still remained the mud walls on the roofs, pierced for musketry, behind which knelt the fierce Sepoy as he so safely poured his deadly bullets on Havelock's men as they fought their way along the streets on which I was then so peacefully walking! I went straight to "The Residency." No words could do justice to the change from what it was when I stood there eighteen months before! Battered out of all recognition, yet still a glorious monument of what brave men can do and endure in a worthy cause.

So here we stand, in the capital of the Sepoy, and on the spot where he did his utmost, and found even that no match for Christian heroism. Now let us, in closing this chapter, take our rapid review of results achieved by the valor so gloriously illustrated on this spot. The former and the present are here, and the future opens, while, before our face, old things are passing away, and all things are becoming new. We recognize the blessed changes; changes for which India herself will yet adore the Providence which refused her victory to her own ruin. God has subjected her "in hope" that she "shall be delivered from the bondage of corruption into the glorious liberty of the children of God."

And, first, as to the great Sepoy Army. This military monster, recruited chiefly from the Brahmin class, had, amid all their ignorance and unreasoning bigotry, grown into a full knowledge of its own power. They well knew that they were united in a common class interest, could dictate their own terms, and had the Government at their mercy. They were pampered to the last degree by their timid and politic rulers. The stronger they grew, the more dangerous they became, and sooner or later a fearful conflict with them was inevitable; and the longer it was deferred, the more destructive it must be to the weaker party. Even now it makes one shudder to remember how completely we were in the power of these cruel and wicked men. All this is now changed. That vast combination of brute force, with its ignorance and fanaticism, has melted away. Only two regiments remain, who, I fear, more from peculiar combinations of circumstances than from any special virtue of their own, remained loyal, and wear to-day the title of "*Wufadars*," (faithful;) all the rest of the mighty host has vanished away.

Nor did they fall alone—they dragged down into their hideous ruin the whole class from which they were recruited. A large portion of the towns and villages of Oude was a mere Sepoy training ground for the East India Company. Here, for generations, the inhabitants contemplated no other employment save service in the Company's army. At twice the compensation of artisans, with easy times, and decked out in the pomp of military array, these men lived in comparative affluence, and on the expiration of their term of service, they were retired on pensions for life equal to about half their pay. So that there were three generations of Sepoys in these villages in 1857, namely, the serving Sepoys, and as pensioners, their fathers and their grandfathers; and when the active force threw off their allegiance to the Government of Great Britain, and lost their cause, the reaction against them was so great, that, at one swoop, the Government which they had outraged cut off them and theirs from the rolls forever. Pay and pensions ceased, and two hundred thousand Sepoys, invalided and active, were thrown upon their own resources, and reduced to hopeless poverty. The old fathers and grandfathers were maddened by the result, and when the defeated Sepoys, those of them who escaped death on the field or in the jungle, came slinking, in disgrace and fear, back to their native villages, they soon realized that their bitterest foes were "they of their own household." They were driven out with taunts and hatred by their own fathers, whom their perfidy had reduced to ruin. The quiet peasantry on whom they had brought the calamities of war had no sympathy to bestow on them. Hooted with curses and contempt from their homes, afraid to associate together save in the jungles, lest the eyes of the Government should see and pursue them, many of these wretched men became fugitives and vagabonds.

Driven to the dire necessity by actual hunger, some of them threw off their lordly Brahminical assumptions, and were glad to go between the handles of a plow, to turn up the soil for an honest living, like common men—a wonderful fact, and one that people did not dream of in 1856. It was one of the most fearful blows that Caste and Brahminism ever received, and has forever lowered the prestige of that proud class in India. A mixed native army, to more limited numbers, formed out of all creeds and parties, has taken their place, while the amount of British soldiers has been more than doubled, and the forts, arsenals, and magazines of India are henceforth in their safe keeping.

Second. Equally marked have been the results of the great Rebellion upon the Mohammedan portion of the population. To conciliate these people is impossible. Nothing less than the conviction and grace that can lead a Romanist to esteem and love evangelical Christians, can ever induce a Mohammedan to become a willing subject of a Christian power. Till then their insolence has to be borne with, and their rage controlled by a firm, but humane, hand. They were in this case the greatest sinners, and they are the greatest sufferers. Their imperial pretensions, with their dynasty, have sunk into the dust forever. Their hopes of supremacy are utterly annihilated; their nobles fill the graves of traitors and murderers. They, themselves, are distrusted by all, and hated with a double intensity by the Hindoo race, whom they first misled and deceived, and then oppressed, during their brief term of power. The worst that they can do is now well known, and they are well aware that they are no longer feared. An amazing submission has been developed, showing how effectually the proud, imperious conceit has been whipped out of them.

In illustration of this fact, I will ask the reader's indulgence while relating an incident, rather "free and easy" in its character, but one which made a lasting impression upon my mind. It will point its own moral much better perhaps than a dozen sober facts could do.

Three weeks after my arrival in Lucknow, as the result of diligent search, we found premises for sale in the Husseinabad Bazaar, which seemed just what we needed for our Mission establishment. They belonged to a relative of the ex-King, a Nawab, or native nobleman, whose reduced circumstances made him glad to dispose of them. All being ready for payment, I went with this gentleman to the English magistrate's Court, to have the deed recorded and the cash paid, and have the signature and seal of the Court added, to render all safe and valid. The Court, for want of a more suitable place, was then held in the splendid Tomb of Asaf-ud-Doulah, second King of Oude. This was situated in the west end of that great Bazaar; the Fort, occupied by English soldiers, being at the other end; and between these two points, at any business hour of the day, you could find eight or ten thousand men lounging about or engaged in trade. Eighteen months before, such was the turbulence there, that a Mohammedan yell of "Deen, deen!" would have brought a mob of probably five thousand men around you in five minutes, every man armed and used to weapons, for many of them had served as Sepoys—all ready for any deed of violence or blood, in which they had the example of the vile Mohammedan Court then in Lucknow. It may be doubted if there was then a more combustible and fanatical scene any where on earth than that Bazaar held. Mr. Mead's description of it, on page 211, will be remembered by the reader.

Passing through the crowds we reached the Court, which was filled, only the aisle in front of the table, down to the door, being unoccupied. Mr. Wood, the magistrate, was in his place, and we took seats on either side of him, and all business was quietly proceeding, when a tumult outside, in the Bazaar, attracted our attention, and in a few moments in rushed a Jamadar (sergeant) of police, followed by six of his men, all in a wonderful hurry and excitement. The Jamadar was a large, heavy man, rigged out with a red pugree (turban) on his head, and a red kummer-bund around his waist, with his tulwar tucked under his arm, his men being similarly decorated and accoutered. His face was flushed, for he had run hard; and, having for the moment lost his breath, when he drew up in front of the magistrate's table, and joined his hands to address him, the man could not say a word for a few seconds. At length he gasped out, "O Sahib, burra tukleef Bazaar men hai!" (O, sir, there is dreadful trouble in the Bazaar!) When the magistrate had succeeded in quieting the perturbation of the poor Jamadar, he was duly informed that "a gora log [a white soldier] had come out of the Fort into the Bazaar, armed with a stout stick, and that the first man he met he stretched him on the ground, and the rest, seeing what he had received, had retreated, jumping off their stalls and leaving money and goods behind them; and," continued the distressed and terrified Jamadar, "Sahib, the gora is cutting capers there in the middle of the Bazaar, swinging his stick, and challenging them to come on, and offering to fight them all; but, of course, they wont go near him. They are all here in a heap at the end of the Bazaar, and, Sahib, what *am* I to do?" "What are you to do! You gudha, (donkey,) why, go and arrest the man. What else would you do?" The astonished police officer looked at his chief as if he could not believe his own ears, and asked, "What did you say, Sahib?" "I said, go and arrest him." He looked at Mr. Wood, and in deep distress at the danger of his disobedience, exclaimed with emphasis, "Sahib, *it cannot be done.* There is not a man in the Bazaar would dare to look him in the face!" Mr. W. insisted that he must "look him in the face," and bring him up before him, adding, "If you are afraid, then take your six men," (who all stood in a row behind their gallant leader, with about as much courage as Falstaff's squad, gazing right into the face of the magistrate;) "surely seven of you, armed with tulwars, are enough to arrest one English soldier with only a stick in his hand."

It was all of no use; go they would not, and much as they loved livery, and power, and pay, they were, to a man, ready to resign the service sooner than execute the commission; so that Mr. W. had no alternative but to write a line to the English sergeant of the guard at the Fort, directing him to send a couple of soldiers to arrest the man and bring him up. A swift messenger, by a back road, soon delivered the chittee, and we sat still to see the result. In a short time a military tread was heard, the road clearing as they came, and the disturber of the peace, with the stick in his hand, was walked in between two of his brethren right up to the magistrate's table. He looked around at the crowd, and at us, and at the magistrate, in astonishment, every glance seeming to say, "What in the world have I been brought here for?"

Mr. W. broke the silence with, "Well, sir, I am given to understand that you have been disturbing my people in the Bazaar." Steadying himself for a reply, (the first word he uttered showing that he was an Irishman, and half drunk at that,) he said, with a significant twirl of the stick, "Yis, yer Honor, I've been stirring them up a little;" looking very merry over it, as if he had been "doing the State some service," which ought to be recognized. It rather sobered him down, however, to hear the magistrate's prompt and stern reply, "Then, sir, I wish you to understand that I don't want them 'stirred up.'" The soldier was incredulous. He evidently thought the magistrate was only joking. "Ah now, yer Honor, you don't mean that at all, at all!" His Honor said he did mean it, and, trying to look as severe as he could, he added, "And more than that, I want to know what brought you into my Bazaar at all?" This question, and its manner, roused the soldier, his rollicking aspect became serious, as, bringing down the end of his stick with a sharp ring on the floor beside him, and the tears springing to his eyes, he stretched out his hand, and for a few moments he seemed to me the most eloquent speaker I had ever heard: "Ah, yer Honor, listen to me. If yer Honor only knew the races I have had after these rascally Pandies, in rain, and hunger, and mud, and how many noble comrades have fallen by this side," (striking his thigh,) "and on this!" (repeating the action there.) Here his feelings seemed to overcome him. He paused, and then added, "Yer Honor, the spirit was up in me a little this mornin' and I thought I'd just come out and have a little bit of a fight on my own private account; but, yer Honor, I could not get a single one of the spalpeens to face me, and what was I to do, yer Honor?" His Honor's calm rejoinder was, "You were to let them alone." But the poor fellow could not see it. A happy thought seemed then to strike him, and the spirit of fun was once more in full possession of him. Stretching out his stick toward Mr. Wood, he exclaimed, "Now, yer Honor, what's the use of talkin'; just do you say the word, and I'll lick out every mother sowl of them for you in five minutes!" By this time he was in an attitude, and looked the fighting Irishman all over.

Mr. Wood, I suppose, made about the best effort of his life to keep his countenance and seem serious; he could not afford to give way before his Court. How he ever did it I cannot imagine. Being under no such restriction, I shook with laughing till I nearly fell off the chair, and all the more, when I saw the effect of the attitude and the stick on the great fat Nawab on the other side of the table. With his hands on his knees, and evidently alarmed, he watched every movement of the soldier, and not knowing a word of English, he seemed to realize the fellow's antics boded no good to *him* personally, and looked as if he was ready to bolt. It was useless for Mr. Wood to rejoin, as he did, that he "did not want them licked out," for the Irishman proceeded, quite in a confidential way, blandly to assure him, "Yer Honor, you wont have *the least trouble;* you will only just have to say the word, and I'll do the business for you!"

Things were going from bad to worse, and the magistrate saw he must lose no time in getting rid of the fellow; so, with a threat that, if ever he found him in his Bazaar again he would hand him up for court martial, he said to the guard, "Take him away!" and off he was walked, to the great relief of the Nawab, and the Jamadar, and all the natives present, and I suppose to Mr. Wood as well. And this was in *Lucknow*, and only ten months after its recapture!

Solomon says, "There is a time to laugh." I have found in my life few occasions more appropriate for that exercise than the one here given, which I have faithfully described as it occurred. It is allowable occasionally to pass

> "From grave to gay,
> From lively to severe."

My book has more than enough of the grave and the sad; let this, then, have a place here, for here it belongs, and has a lesson far beyond what appears on the surface of this ludicrous scene. I have introduced it, not for the sake of its levity, though it was rich and almost inimitable, but for the sake of its lesson. One can read that lesson, and even laugh over it, as I did, near the graves of Havelock and Henry Lawrence. Laughter may be religious. It was so here. To adequately appreciate the enlargement of heart, or even the hilarity of that occasion, one would need to have experimentally known our previous conditions there—to have ridden on an elephant's back, with a Sepoy guard, through those very Bazaars of vice and danger—should have been, as we were, acquainted with those who endured there that long agony of the defense—must have stood with us for seven months on the summit of Nynee Tal, with the fear that you were the last of the Christian life left in India, and that our fate, at the hands of these bloody men, might be but a question of time, while our only hope, under God, were these very red-coated soldiers whom we feared might yet be ten thousand miles away from us. A "dying hope," no relief, and hardly expecting deliverance, and then to drop right out of those circumstances into a scene like *this!* The blessed God himself would sanction laughter here. For, when He "turned again the captivity of Zion, we were like them that dream. Then was our mouth filled with laughter, and our tongue with singing." For, it was literally true in the Bazaars of Lucknow, that "They said among the heathen, God has done great things for them." He did—here was a striking evidence of it—and "we were glad!"

Even as I looked and laughed at this half-drunken creature, how vividly did God's holy Word come to my mind, as I saw him in his whimsical resolution and proposal, exulting in his ability, and so eager for its display, offering to fulfill, to the letter, those words of Holy Writ, so true then to the race whom he, even in his unworthiness and unconsciousness, there represented, that "One should chase a thousand;" nay, even more than that, for he alone offered to do the work of the "two" to whom a covenant God had engaged, that they should "put ten thousand to flight!" And why? Because "their Rock had sold them, and the Lord had shut them up;" while Christendom was, at that very time, mingling their congratulations with England for this wondrous divine deliverance, and obeying the command of the Lord Jehovah, "Rejoice, O ye nations, with his people; for he will avenge the blood of his servants, and will render vengeance to his adversaries, and will be merciful unto his land, and to his people." Deut. xxxii, 43.

Third. The results upon the Hindoo race are equally marked. They, too, have lost their Peishwa and their prestige; they have become deeply convinced of the impotence of their idols to aid them in any great emergency; they have learned an additional lesson of Mohammedan perfidy and bitterness, which can never be forgotten by them, and which forbids the possibility of any future combination with their cruel antagonists. Their most intelligent men are fully satisfied that, till the time comes when they shall be fit for self-government, their best interests are bound up with their allegiance to the English Government. Under the security and peace which it gives them they are now, as never before, devoting their energies to material and educational improvement.

Fourth. The abolition of the East India Company is another of the merciful results of the Rebellion. This proud and powerful body of commercial men rose, in two hundred years, from the humble position of a mere trading company, through a series of events the most wonderful in modern history, till they came at last to sway their scepter over an empire six times more populous than that of their own Queen, and twice as populous as that of Augustan Rome, and separated, till recently, from them by a voyage of four or five months. But this vast opportunity, the greatest that Christian rulers ever possessed, was not improved to the intellectual or moral good of the vast multitudes whom they governed. What they chiefly considered was large dividends, and every thing had to bow to that. As a corporation, they had no soul that would feel for the guilt and danger of perishing men, or make any effort to redeem them, but, on the contrary, they tried to discourage all such efforts. To this unworthy and unchristian policy they held on to the last, and would have held on probably for ages if God and the English public had not abolished their rule on the 1st of November, 1858. Even in the terrible lessons of the first outbreak, instead of relenting and turning from their course, they clung all the more tenaciously to it. In evidence of this, the fact can be referred to, that in the first panic caused by the news which reached England in July, 1857, informing all classes of the terrible events which had taken place on the 31st of May, and that British supremacy seemed to hang in the balance, one of their kind in London, well acquainted with the East, and from whose military character, if nothing more, utterances of another sort would have been consistent—this man, the editor of "*The United Service Magazine*," in his leading article for his August number, was so carried away by his fears and by false and godless theories, that he deliberately proposed to sacrifice the claims of his faith, and the moral hopes of India, and surrender all to heathenism at the first blow, and without a struggle, in language which his descendants can never peruse without a blush for the cowardly "Christian" who wrote it. Speaking of the measures to be henceforth employed in India for the pacification of the country, and the retention of British supremacy, he says: "*Missionaries must be sent away about their business, and the practice of attempting conversions be put immediate stop to.* If a black individual express a sincere desire to become a Christian, by all means let his wishes be instantly attended to by the ministers of the Gospel, [the Episcopalian chaplains of the troops and civilians.] By the substitution of this arrangement we are certain that there would be no material diminution of the number of real converts per annum, for at present the interior of a Cremorne omnibus would afford them ample accommodation."—*United Service Magazine*, 1857, p. 480.

In that "omnibus" I would have claimed at least three seats—one each for Joel and Emma, and one for Peggy, Emma's mother, and would have felt satisfied, as I handed them in, that the youngest and weakest of their number had a courage and constancy for Jesus and his cause which might well put to shame—as it will yet in the presence of "the worthy Judge eternal"—the cowardice and sarcasm of this unworthy Briton, who thus dared to offset the policy and claims of the East India Company against the present and final salvation of two hundred millions of benighted men.

I am thankful that this despicable and wicked utterance expressed the feelings of a very small fraction of English society—smaller to-day than ever, and growing "beautifully less"—while the "Company" whose policy and practices it pronounced, within twelve months of the day when these words were printed, was forever extinguished, as a governing body, by the Parliament of England, which resolved to sustain British Christianity, while they vindicated British supremacy, in India. The clique who could thus insult God and his ministers, and wish to hinder the conversion of India's millions, were regarded as henceforth unworthy to administer the political affairs of that great empire; and this very utterance was the knell of their doom, as it was also of the Sepoy power on which they so vainly and madly leaned for support. Natives and Christians alike celebrated with gladness the day that saw the country pass under the control of the Queen of England, to be henceforth ruled by the Parliamentary Government of Great Britain.

Fifth. The Government of India to-day, in its freedom from the policy and traditions of the Company, its separation from idolatrous administrations, its strength and justice, its outspoken interest in the intellectual and moral well-being of the people, its humane and impartial administration, is a wonderful improvement upon the former things that have passed away. At length the oft-repeated assertion, that "India is the noblest trust ever committed to a Christian nation," seems to have taken possession of the minds who guide her destiny.

The moral impression made by English prowess over Asiatic combination and purpose has been immense, and has affected other lands far beyond the bounds of India. It has convinced the Asiatic nations of the superiority of Christian civilization beyond any other event that has transpired on that hemisphere. The result in India itself is, that England is considered to hold the land by a stronger right than ever; her laws are more respected, her magistrates more implicitly obeyed, her roads are safer, her peace is more profound. What her Government know to be right can now be attempted and carried out free from the temporizing of the past, so that legislation is more decided, and radical, and beneficent. A magnanimity that before was not dreamed of guides British policy. Native gentlemen of education are now invested with Commissions of the Peace. The native element is introduced into legislative halls, and connected with the government of their country. Already they sit on the bench of the High Court, and hold honorary positions in Council, as the colleagues of the Governor General. Public education is encouraged and pushed forward, the admission of ladies into general society commended, female education among all classes encouraged to the utmost, and extravagant costs of weddings and funerals discountenanced. The legislation, the principles, and the personal influence of the Government, are all thus bearing upon the repression of what is wrong in Hindoo society, and the encouragement of all that is right and good.

None but those who have lived in India can adequately appreciate the difficulty or the delicacy of the great task which England is trying to fulfill there to-day. One feature of the structure of society there will sufficiently intimate this fact. There are in all one hundred and fifty-three Hindoo and Mussulman Princes, governing semi-independent States, under the protection of the paramount power. These communities are less affected by intelligence, and more liable to caste notions and time-honored observances, than the territories directly governed by the British, and their influence has to be considered; then there are as many more Princes, (retired from business,) some of them still bearing royal titles, and drawing royal revenues from the treasury—any number of Maharajahs, Nawabs, and Kings—within the British territories. These have courts, ceremonials, and claims, which are all maintained with a tenacity that, to us of the West, seems simply ridiculous, and which are, and must be, to India's rulers, matters of worry and difficulty; but they have to deal gently with them, and work on in hope that, in the progress of the country toward popular government, these "royal" folk (including the Nawab Nazim of Bengal, the King of Oude, and others) or their descendants will become content, in the interest of the unity of their magnificent land, and its preparation for the popular native government which will one day direct its destinies, to sink title and claim, and accept a position in native society analogous to that of the Peerage of England. The day is past for the continued existence of "three hundred and seventy-four States" in a country that can be but one nation. As Noblemen around their strong Government, these representatives of dead or dying dynasties might do much for their country, as well as opening a way for their own children to be trained and educated for employment in positions of trust and usefulness.

These are but a mere intimation of the peculiar circumstances which English administrators in India have to deal with as they try to guide the interests of that country. The rebellion broke down many of these difficulties, and simplified their task to a great extent, making them more fully the masters of the situation; time, education, and Christianity will do the rest.

Meanwhile the country is progressing rapidly in the right

direction, its own people testify to their contentment and hopes of its bright future, while travelers from other lands add their evidence to the peace and prosperity which have followed the sorrowful chapters which we have traced. The appreciatory words lately uttered by the Hon. W. H. Seward, after having traveled through India, will be in the remembrance of the reader. Mr. Seward's opinion is well sustained by another American gentleman, Dr. Prime, of the *Observer*, just returned from a visit to India. With a candid appreciation of the present, as compared with the past, he uses the following language:

"I have spoken of the complete change which has come over the government of India in its being made directly responsible to, and dependent on, the British Crown. A still greater change has taken place in the objects for which the government is administered. For two centuries and a half India was ruled for the benefit of the East India Company. . . .

"But that is all changed, or, if not *all*, the purpose of the Government is changed. It is ruled now for the good of India, for the sake of the people of India. I take the greatest pleasure in bearing testimony to the high character of those who have the administration of affairs in that empire, and to the aspect of the country in its material, educational, social, and religious interests, as being full of promise. I doubt if any country has more conscientious and intelligent public officers controlling its destinies than has India. There are reforms yet to be consummated. The extreme caution of rulers prevents them from entirely giving up a sort of complicity with idolatry; the great work of education which the Government is carrying on, to which I shall again allude, is confined too much to a privileged class; but it has been a great pleasure to me to find this land making such rapid progress in all that is calculated to promote the highest good of the people who dwell in it, to whatever race they belong. Overlooking all the past, I heartily rejoice that India is to-day under British rule. Long may that rule be undisturbed! May it not be broken until the tribes of the land shall be able, intelligently and wisely, to govern themselves. The effect of the present system will be to develop their powers of self-government. In addition to the native princes, who are still recognized as the heads of their limited territories, natives are admitted as members to the Supreme and Provincial Councils. The Government is doing nothing directly to advance the Christian religion, (though as much as our own Government is doing,) and many evils growing out of the peculiarities of the people, the varieties of races, the inveterate nature of hoary prejudices, yet remain to be removed or remedied ; but, judging from the promise of the present, India bids fair to become again a mighty empire in the East, and to outshine in its glory the splendor of the old Moguls."

Sixth. The improved condition and prospects of Christianity and of native Christians, as the result of the rebellion, is most marked and important.

The position of Christianity in India, and its disabilities, will be well understood from what has been already advanced. The condition of the native Christian before the Rebellion was a most trying one. He was cut off and proscribed by his heathen friends, looked down upon too often by European officials, refused all employment under Government, with no one to sympathize with him except a few pious persons and the missionary, the latter very often unable to help him, though his heart was distressed for him. Short as the time was that I had then been in India, I learned some most distressing cases of this kind.

The very last letter that I had from the martyred Missionary, Brother Campbell, of Futtyghur, was on this subject. He writes, "Poor Saul, whom you saw when at my house, is still without employment. I sent him to Cawnpore and Futtypore, but those places were full ; had more help and native Christians than could be well provided for. He is now at home near Agra, and writes to me that he is in a sad condition. Christians will not receive him, though he is willing to do any kind of work ; and his relations say, that if he remains with them in his native village he must become one of them, that is, a heathen. Poor fellow, I pity him, for I think him a good man ; weak, perhaps, but still, I trust, a 'chosen vessel.' O that God in his good providence would open up *some way* for these poor fettered souls (not a few) who wish to renounce heathenism and cast in their lot with the people of God, and cannot! For want of employment, we are obliged to turn off numbers who would gladly come, bringing their families with them, even very hopeful cases. O that the day may *soon* come when caste will be broken up! Then our converts will stand some chance."

That letter was written on the 15th of April. Eight weeks after the writer was "before the throne," and God in his mysterious ways was beginning to answer the martyr's prayer for the native Christians. Little did he imagine, when writing that letter, how soon and how fully Providence would "open up a way for those fettered souls!" The Christian public and the Government, immediately after the Rebellion, wanted them for situations of trust in far greater numbers than could be supplied. The Rebellion had tested and brought out the value of native Christians in a manner that admitted of no cavil or mistake.

Not one native Christian in India joined the mutineers, though their education would have made them valuable to them. It was also known that some conspiracies had been discovered and prevented by timely information furnished by native Christians. Notwithstanding the sufferings to which they were reduced during the Rebellion, as a body they stood nobly for Christianity and the British Government, though that Government had neglected and despised them. Many of them laid down their lives for their religion. Even under that fiery trial, it is asserted (see "Liverpool Missionary Conference," page 249) that only two of their number are known to have apostatized. At length the Government itself began to appreciate them, so that the Rebellion had hardly closed ere Sir John Lawrence, as Governor of the Punjab, and who soon after became Viceroy of all India, used the following language in one of his government orders: "The sufferings and trials which the Almighty has permitted to come upon his people in this land during the past few months, though dark and mysterious to us.

will assuredly end in his glory. The followers of Christ will now, I believe, be induced to come forward and advance the interests of his kingdom. The system of caste can no longer be permitted to rule in our service. Soldiers, and government servants of every class, must be entertained for their merits, irrespective of creeds, class, or caste.

"The native Christians, as a body, have, with rare exceptions, been set aside. I know not one in the Punjab, to our disgrace be it said, in any employment under Government. A proposition to employ them in the public service six months ago assuredly would not have been complied with; but a change has come, and I believe there are few who will not eagerly employ those native Christians competent to fill appointments.

"I consider I should be wanting in my duty, in this crisis, if I did not endeavor to secure a portion of the numerous appointments in the judicial departments for native Christians; and I shall be happy, as far as I can, to advance their interests equally with those of the Mohammedan and Hindoo candidates. Their future promotion must depend upon their own merits."

His Excellency then added suggestions to guide the Missionaries in selecting suitable persons to be presented for the purpose. Shortly after this Sir Robert Montgomery, the ruler of Oude, issued a similar paper. Other officials did the same. Merchants and traders also sought them, for they saw they could be trusted. Their value rose at once. Employment was thrown open to them, giving them a fair chance with other men, which was all we desired for them. The native Christian, who before the Rebellion could not obtain five dollars per month for his services, though an educated man and a faithful member of Christ's Church, within little more than a year from the date of martyr Campbell's letter, could command five or ten times that amount of salary. Missionary societies had, consequently, twice within five years, to raise the wages of their teachers and helpers in order to retain them, so great was the competition by other parties to engage them. The effect of this change upon their standing in society, the comfort of their families, and their own self-respect, as well as Christian usefulness, will be apparent. It was for them a great salvation, and most wonderfully wrought out.

The rapid growth of the Christian Church in India since that time, and especially of the native ministry, will be fully exhibited in the Statistical Tables which will follow the next chapter. To them the reader's attention is earnestly requested, that he may gratefully contemplate

"The silver lining to this cloud of grief"

with which a merciful God compensated the sufferings of his servants. What a change for the better, in the very respect which they so much desired, would Brothers Freeman and Campbell witness, could they rise from the dead and revisit the scenes where they suffered and died to bring about this result! What a justification, too, of dear Mrs. Freeman's words, in her last letter to her sister, when she said: "I sometimes think our deaths would do more good than we would do in all our lives; if so, His will be done!"

How intense the interest which that Rebellion awoke all through Christendom! how earnest the prayers which then went up to God for India! and how liberal the efforts since made to claim the land for Christ! All has been overruled for good. The vastness of India, the value of her evangelization as the heart of Asia, and the influence of her position, as the key to the salvation of the nations with which she has commercial relations—Affghanistan, Beloochistan, Eastern Persia, Bokhara, Herat, Thibet, Ladak, Nepaul, Western China, and others—all these must feel the effects of the mighty change which India is yet to undergo, and for which this Rebellion did so much to prepare her.

The hour had come when the inevitable conflict between human barbarism and divine civilization was to take place, and the words of Christ were to be realized in India—"I am not come to send peace, but a *sword*." Ere that sword could conquer the peace of righteous law and order, and place that great land in subjection to the influences which are all the more certainly and speedily to work out her redemption—as they are doing at this hour—the words of Simeon to the Virgin Mother of the great Peace-maker might have been addressed to the Futtyghur martyrs, and the victims of Cawnpore and Bareilly, as well as to those who lived to see the great victory of deliverance, "Yea, a sword shall pierce through thy own soul also, that the thoughts of many hearts may be revealed." They did not suffer nor die in vain. Their endurance unto blood, and the valor of those who, against such odds, fought their way to their rescue, have taught the men of Hindustan a lesson that can never be forgotten. They have been whipped into the alarming consciousness that their colossal and venerable systems of religion, in which they trusted, are utterly powerless ; that with civilization is strength ; and that Christianity is both invincible and inevitable. They have lost confidence and hope in their own systems, and the "thoughts of their hearts" are "revealed" in the candid and singular remark made to us one day by an aged native, when we pressed him upon this subject, as with a sigh he exclaimed, "It is so, Sahib ; for some reason that we don't understand God has left us and gone over to the Christian side ! I suppose what you say is true. My children, or grandchildren, will probably be of your way of thinking. But I'm too old to change ; I want to die in the faith of my fathers !" The tears flowed as he closed his remarks. They were shed because he felt that Hindooism is dying ! And so it is ; for already, thank God ! the blood even of the Sepoy race flows in the veins of the Methodist ministry in Oude and Rohilcund, while their children are singing in our Christian schools and churches, "Hosannah to the Son of David !"

CHAPTER IX.

THE CONDITION OF WOMAN UNDER HINDOO LAW.

AMONG the mercies resultant from recent events in India may be reckoned "the door of hope" which God has thus opened for the women of that land ; but to appreciate the hopeful possibilities of the present it is needful that we consider the past, and what, up to this hour, has been the condition of women there, under the law of her religion and the customs of her country. If she is rising at last in any respect, it is in decided defiance of the system that has so long repressed and wronged her, and her elevation therefore involves its overthrow.

On page forty-two we have presented a picture of the class whose legal relations we now more fully represent.

What is this woman, thus "gorgeously appareled," in her condition, character, and prospects ? Even the Zenana has had to give up its secrets, and the rest of the world may now know how the women of India live and die.

Of course every lady of intelligence has heard more or less of the condition of her sex in India, and has had her sympathy called forth by the wrongs which they have so long suffered ; yet few understand why these things are so, much less, what is the full measure of the disabilities to which this lady, or any of her sisters in India, is always exposed, without that appeal which other women possess to the divine rule of their religion, which forbids such treatment.

In other lands, and under the teachings and forms of a different civilization, the wrongs which women suffer at the hands of lordly and vicious men are the result of the current wickedness of those who oppress them ; but in India the abject humility, subordination, and implicit obedience of woman to every whim and wish which her husband exacts from her, is extorted under the express teachings of her cruel faith, and she is well aware that he can quote the only "scriptures" she knows to justify every demand and wrong to which she tamely submits. Her poor judgment and conscience are held fast in the terrors of a system that contains not one ray of hope of any change for the better for her; while this has been the condition of the hundreds of millions of women in India since long before the incarnation of Christ. All that period of time she has been sunk and suffering in this manner.

If ever woman had an opportunity of showing what she might become under the teaching and influence of a civilization where Christianity or the Bible did not interfere with her state, the women of India have had that opportunity; and now, after forty centuries of such experiment, what is woman there to-day? These pages shall faithfully declare it to the women whom Christianity has redeemed, and then let them judge for themselves the difference and its cause.

In rendering this service to the truth I shall be under no liability to exaggerate, nor shall I make a single unsupported statement as to her condition. The evidence shall be all her own, and chapter and verse—Code, Purana, and Shaster—shall give their testimony to the exact truthfulness of my descriptions. I feel assured that those who read these pages will lay them down with the conviction that a more atrocious system for the extinction of the happiness and hopes of woman than that which is contained in the legislation of the Hindoos never was devised by priest or lawgiver since the hour when guilty man first began to throw the blame, the burden, and the wrongs of life, upon the weaker sex.

The most ancient body of human law now extant is the Institutes of Menu. This unique and whimsical system of legislation —the offspring of despotism and priestcraft—fixed the social and religious position of woman in India nearly a thousand years before Christ. The full title of the Code—which has been translated from the ancient Sanscrit by Sir W. Jones—is, "Institutes of Hindoo

Law, or the Ordinances of Menu—Comprising the Indian System of Duties, Religious and Civil."

This is the fountain-head of those rules which constitute the laws of life for the women of India, and, terrible as many of them are in their undisguised deformity here, they have been made ever more hideous and horrible by the added ingredients of bitterness which they received as they flowed down through the ages, and were expressed in Puranas and Shasters, in traditional teachings, popular dialogues, in the Hindoo drama, and in their literature generally. We shall quote from these to illustrate and justify the representations given of woman's lot in that land

> "Where the skies forever smile,
> And the oppressed forever weep."

In drawing a picture of woman in India, we first speak of her *birth;* and here we are met with the terrible fact of female infanticide, so common in that land. This is an ancient, systematic, and prevalent crime among the Hindoos. Not especially among the poor or the debased, but prevailing chiefly among the Rajpoot families, some of the proudest and wealthiest of the tribes of India. The doctrine and practice, and the unblushing avowal of this unnatural crime, on the part of its perpetrators, are such as cannot be found anywhere else on earth. And the infernal custom has so drugged their consciences, that even the mothers themselves of these destroyed little ones have declared their insensibility of any feeling of guilt, even where the deed has been done by their own hands.

Girls are not desired, not welcome; and when they come, and must live—as British law now demands, where its power can reach them, that life must be held sacred—still they can be at least ignored, if not despised. Why, if my native friend had six children, three boys and as many girls, and I happened to inquire, "Lalla, how many children have you?" the probability is he would reply, "Sir, I have three children;" for he would not think it worth while to count in the daughters.

They cannot understand our Christian feelings in rejoicing over the birth of a girl with as sincere happiness as we would lavish upon our male children; and a case is actually on record, which shows how generally accepted is this idea in the native mind, where an English gentleman at Bombay actually received a visit of condolence from an intelligent native friend. A little girl had been born to him; and the polite Hindoo, having heard of it, had called to express his sympathy with the unfortunate parent!

The prevalence and extent of the horrid crime of female infanticide attracted, many years ago, the attention of the humane men whom England sent to rule her India possessions, and from the official statistics collected, which are now before us, we are able to give some accurate idea of the fatal devastation which, for ages past, this hellish cruelty has wrought upon the female life of India.

Mr. Wilkinson's reports were based upon a census taken in one locality where this custom was known to exist. By the simple, spontaneous admission of the guilty parties themselves, it turned out that in one tribe the portion of sons to daughters was one hundred and eighteen to sixteen; in a second, two hundred and forty to ninety-eight; in a third, one hundred and thirty-one to sixty-one; in a fourth, fourteen to four; and in a fifth, thirty-nine to seven. Now, as statistics in Europe and America have all shown but one result, namely, that the births of males and females are of nearly equal amount, the only inference to be drawn from this disparity is, that females equal, or nearly equal, in number to the difference here exhibited had been destroyed.

The murders, therefore, perpetrated in the first of the above tribes were seventy-seven per cent. of the females born. The aggregate result given by the census taken in this locality was six hundred and thirty-two sons to two hundred and twenty-five daughters. This is an average of thirty-six daughters to one hundred boys; or, in other words, of every one hundred females born sixty-four must have been cruelly immolated by their parents; or, in round numbers, about two thirds were destroyed, and but one third saved alive.

Some of the villages examined presented a more terrible exhibit than even this—as where he found only three per cent. of girls, and in one *no girls at all*, the inhabitants freely "confessing that they had destroyed every girl born in their village."

The guilty agents were generally the parents themselves, ofttimes the mothers, with their own hands. Sir John Malcolm positively states, in his Report on Central India, that "the mother is commonly the executioner of her own offspring." Professing to open the fount of life to her babe, she coolly and deliberately impregnates it with the elements of death, by putting opium on the nipple of her breast, which the child inhaling with its milk, dies. But the juice of the poppy is not the only ingredient by whose "mortal taste" so many unoffending victims fill the unmarked graves of India. The madar, or the dutterrea plant, the tobacco leaf, starvation, drowning, exposure in the jungle, and even strangulation, are the modes employed by these wretches for their fell purposes. "Without natural affection," truly!

Human language, with all its resources, furnishes a feeble and inadequate medium of expression for the horror which such deeds of hell awaken in the heart. Probably the celebrated Encyclopedist has as nearly expressed it as is possible when he says, "Infanticide, or child murder, is an enormity that our reason and feelings would lead us to reckon a crime of very rare occurrence. That it should exist at all is, at first view, surprising; that it should prevail to any extent is difficult of belief; that parents should be its perpetrators is in a high degree painful to imagine; but that mothers should be the executioners of their own offspring—nay, their habitual and systematic executioners—is such an agonizing contemplation, such an outrage on humanity, as every amiable feeling of our nature sickens and revolts at."

The most awful feature of the matchless enormity is found in the fact that Hindooism has dared to cover the deed with a professed divine sanction. On page 399 we have described the bloody deity, herself a female, under whose sanction these deeds, so inhuman, have been consummated. A fitting locality, as a general center for the hellish enormity, was long since found in that dreary island of Saugor, lying below Calcutta, and which few Christians have ever passed without feeling inclined to invoke upon the island and its shrine of blood the unmitigated curse of God and man. The sight of it fired the indignation of that great linguist, Dr. John Leyden, and led to the composition of those rugged, but honest lines of his, which describe the place and those deeds for which it was regularly visited, and which made it so infamous throughout the civilized world :

"On sea-girt Saugor's desert isle,
 Mantled with thickets dark and dun,
May never moon or starlight smile,
 Nor ever beam the summer sun!
Strange deeds of blood have there been done,
 In mercy ne'er to be forgiven;
 Deeds the far-seeing eye of Heaven
Vailed its radiant orb to shun.

"To glut the shark and crocodile
 A mother brought her infant here;
She saw its tender, playful smile,
 She shed not one maternal tear;
She threw it on a watery bier:
 With grinding teeth sea-monsters tore
 The smiling infant that she bore—
She shrunk not once its cries to hear!"

He then turns and addresses Kalee, and in the second verse following literally quotes the Shaster describing her:

"Dark goddess of the iron mace,
 Flesh-tearer, quaffing life-blood warm,
The terrors of thine awful face
 The pulse of mortal hearts alarm—
Grim power! If human woes can charm,
 Look to the horrors of this flood,
 Where crimsoned Gunga shines in blood,
And man-devouring monsters swarm.

"Skull-chaplet wearer! whom the blood
 Of man delights a thousand years,
Than whom no face, by land or flood,
 More stern and pitiless appears;
Thine is the cup of human tears,
 The pomp of human sacrifice:
 Cannot the cruel blood suffice
Of tigers, which thine island bears

"Not all blue Gunga's mountain flood,
That rolls so proudly round thy fane,
Can cleanse the tinge of human blood,
Nor wash dark Saugor's impious stain:
The sailor, journeying on the main,
Shall view from far thy dreary isle,
And curse the ruins of the pile
Where mercy ever sued in vain!"

This iniquity was openly and fearlessly practiced in India up to the time when the Marquis Wellesley, brother of the Duke of Wellington, was appointed Governor-General, and India's daughters will yet learn to revere and love the memory of that humane and intrepid man, who, in the face of the obstacles that arose around him on every side, when he attempted to deal with this "custom," never faltered till he had put the protection of Christian law over the life of every child in India. His Excellency honestly and bravely placed in the hands of the magistracy of India "A Regulation for Preventing the Sacrifice of Children at Saugor and other places, passed by the Governor-General in Council, on the 20th of August, 1802," "declaring the practice to be murder, punishable by death." In British India, so far as law could reach the case, he made infanticide to be regarded and punished as in England.

The Marquis Wellesley.

We present here an outline of the countenance of this true friend of woman, as that of one whose deeds of mercy will be held in everlasting remembrance.

It is no doubt true that children have been secretly offered to sanguinary demons in India, and many of the infants thrown to the crocodiles or sharks at Saugor by their mothers were immolated in fulfillment of religious vows. Even the desire for children has led to their destruction, the mother promising her deity, in advance, that if blessed with offspring, the first-born should be returned in sacrifice. In this case "the child of the vow" is carefully cherished for three or four years, and then the mother, tempting it a step beyond its depth, resigns it to the Ganges, or deliberately casts it toward the pampered alligator, and stands to see it bleeding within the monster's jaws! Again, it is not uncommon for a poor, sickly babe (under the blind infatuation of its parents, that its illness is caused by some malignant demon who has taken possession of it) to be placed in a basket and carried into the forest, and there suspended from a tree, and abandoned for three or four days and nights; and if, at the end of that time, the vultures, or ants, or beasts of prey, have not made away with it, and its sickness has departed, it is restored to its home.

But none of these abominable cruelties adequately account for the prevalence of female infanticide. We have to seek its causes in more unworthy motives than even these. In fact, the daughters of India have been sacrificed one generation after another, not to the superstition of their parents, but to their Satanic pride.

It is very difficult to convey to American readers, or to the common sense of a Christian lady, any adequate idea of the soaring and extravagant pride of family descent of such a race as the Rajpoots.

Multitudes of these Rajpoots are as poor as they are proud, and as immemorial custom requires, in the event of a daughter's marriage, not only her own "gift and dowry" to be provided, but the festivities of the occasion, lasting six days, to be furnished for all relatives and friends, priests, bards, and various functionaries, who must be "bidden" and provided for munificently, it is simply ruinous for all but the wealthy to dare the experiment, certainly more than once: hence the female children are still secretly murdered.

To this is added, what is equally difficult for Europeans and

Americans to understand or sympathize with, the general horror which parents in India feel in view of the supposed disgrace which would rest upon them and theirs in the event of their daughters remaining unmarried.

An additional explanation is found in the relation which a son bears to the *Shraad* of his father—those funeral rites at which he is to officiate, and which are considered essential to the happy transmigration and future welfare of the departed parent; so that the birth of a boy, and of each in succession, is an assurance of salvation to the father, while, as sacrifice and religious rites are all denied to women, a girl is regarded as of no moral moment whatever. She is a mere secular creature, whose life is considered as forfeited if the father concludes that there is no reasonable prospect of a suitable marriage for her, or that his means wont allow him to contemplate the customary nuptial expenses of his tribe. What girls are saved from death are usually those first born; the later ones have not a chance of life, those spared requiring their death as a necessity of their position and dignity.

This wholesale destruction of human life in the homes of India is a parental responsibility; but at whose hands have these innocents perished? By the midnight assassin, or the Indian tomahawk or scalping knife? No, no; let humanity shudder. They are the mothers—the unhappy mothers—who, in the name of false honor, demon pride, and hereditary fictions of rank or purity of lineage, have no compassion on the fruit of their own womb, who imbrue their hands in the blood of their new-born babes.

Say, ye happy American mothers, who have fondled your smiling babes, and clasped them to your bosoms as the most precious gifts of Heaven, if ever such a tale of woe as this has sounded in your ears? It will be a satisfaction to you to reflect that the lady missionaries whom your societies are now sending to that land, and who carry right into the center of these homes your Christian sentiments and feelings upon this subject, may be designed by God to work out a remedy for an evil which has hitherto defied human law and all that man alone could do for its extirpation.

May Heaven help them, until the day shall dawn when the mothers of India, exulting over their daughters—over each and all of them—as joyously as they have ever done over their sons, shall delight to direct their husband's loving attention to their female children, as the Christian poet has expressed it for them:

"O look on her, see how full of life,
Of strength, of bloom, of beauty, and of joy!
How like to me, how like to thee, when gentle,
For then we are all alike: is it not so?
Mother, and sire, and babe, our features are
Reflected in each other.
Look! how she laughs and stretches out her arms,
And opens wide her bright eyes upon thine,
To hail her father, while her little form
Flutters as winged with joy. Talk not of pain!
The childless seraphs well might envy thee
The pleasures of a parent! Bless her!
As yet she has no words to thank thee, but
Her heart will, and mine own too."

It seems a rapid transition, from describing the early childhood of the female sex in India, to speak of *betrothal*, yet the intervening space is not very extensive. The Hindoo Shasters say that a girl is marriageable when she is seven years of age, but that she may wait till she is ten years old. The term "marriage" is used in their writings to include betrothal as well as what we mean by the term. Reserved for a husband is, in their view, almost as sacred as being resigned to his care.

As soon as a little girl has reached her fifth birthday her parents begin anxiously to seek a marriage settlement for her. Their great concern henceforth relates to her nuptials. They would consider it a decided reproach if she saw her twelfth natal day without being at least betrothed. The whole matter is held in their own hands The poor girl has no choice or voice in her own destiny—all is arranged without consulting her views or affections in any way whatever.

The lawgiver Menu has laid the obligations heavily upon the father, so that he cannot escape the public sentiment. Menu ordains as follows: "Reprehensible is the father who gives not his daughter in marriage at the proper time;" and again, "To an excellent and handsome youth of the same class let every man give his daughter in marriage, according to law, even though she have not attained her age of eight years."

He carries up the responsibility to an awful height by declaring the neglectful father, whose daughter has not been wed at twelve years old, as incurring a guilt equal to that of the murder of a Brahmin for every additional month she continues single. He reduces, according to her age, the amount of the nuptial present which the father receives, and even deprives herself of the right to carry her ornaments from her home in the same proportion, and thus appeals to the mean motive of personal interest to hurry on her settlement.

The accountability is also pressed to avoid the condemnation of leaving his daughter *asancrita*, that is, destitute of the marriage sacrament. If he fails in this the law releases his children from all obligation of respect or obedience to him.

In the same chapter he also claims that "the wife of an elder brother is considered as mother-in-law to the younger, and the wife of the younger as daughter-in-law to the elder." This implies, what is generally a fact, that it is seldom that a young couple in India have the luxury of a separate home. The bride is generally taken to her father-in-law's residence, and receives her apartment within the inclosure surrounding the general home. The outer rooms are occupied by the males of the family, the inner or secluded ones by the women—hence called the Zenana. These inner apartments are never entered by one of the opposite sex, save by the father, her husband's brothers, or by children.

Harem—or as Mr. Lane spells it, *Hhareem*—signifies sacred, prohibited. The temple at Mecca is called *Al-haram*, that is, the sacred inviolable temple. The *Seraglio* of the Turks is a compound word, formed from *sura*, "house, apartment," and *ahul*, "family, domestic;" hence *Surahulio*, or Seraglio, the "family or female apartment." *Haram sera*, and *muhal sera*, are nearly synonymous words, and are often used to express the inner apartments in India. The common term is *Zenana*—from *Zun*, "a woman," Zunun, "women," an instance of the prevalence of the Persian language over the vernacular. (The *Calcutta Review*, No. IV.)

"Courtship," in our Christian sense, the maiden in India can never know. She is not allowed to see or converse with him to whose control she will erelong be handed over. She cannot write to him, for she can neither read nor write; all she is able to do is to follow the instructions, to "worship the gods for a good husband." She is taught to commence as soon as she is four years old. Her prayers are addressed chiefly to *Kama-dera*, the Hindoo Cupid. The books represent him as having for a steed an elephant composed of entwined female forms, and that elephant is darkness; his car is the south wind; his bow the sweet sugar-cane, with a row of green honey bees for its string, and charmed flowers for its fine arrows; his minister is spring; the ocean is his drum; his trumpeters are birds, and his conquering troops are women. He is especially worshiped where he celebrates his triumphs in connection with marriage festivals.

The maiden prays, and father and mother manage the business of selection. Each caste has its professional match-makers, whose aid is indispensable. When the negotiations have reached a certain definiteness, the Pundits are consulted to avoid mistakes of consanguinity, and then the astrologers, who pronounce upon the carefully preserved horoscopes of the boy and girl, whether they can be united with safety. These preliminaries all found satisfactory, the aid of the Brahmin is sought to ascertain if the family god favors the union. The stars, the gods, and men being a unit, negotiations are opened between the parents and relations as to the amount of gift and dowry, and when conclusions are reached here to their mutual satisfaction, the astrologer is again called in to ascertain and name a lucky day when the agreement may be registered and a bond for the dowry executed. This is done with due solemnity, and then the astrologer has again to ascertain and name a lucky day for the ceremony, which is accepted by the parents under their bond to see to the consummation of the engagement. This is the usual method, slightly varied in different localities. It is easily expressed in these few words, but what anxiety, what care and inquiry before these determinations can be reached!

No part of the Institutes of Menu is more definite and circumstantial than that which gives the law of selection in marriage. With the eye and taste of a whimsical connoisseur in female charms, the old legislator has prescribed the standard of excellence in age, caste, condition, and qualities, by which the Hindoo maiden is to be tested. Nor has he or his commentators forgotten the requisite compromises that will arise in such cases.

With great care and anxiety the questions of consanguinity, name, physical condition, motion, family, etc., have all to be decided upon. But let this singular law speak for itself.

As to relationship, "she who is not descended from his paternal or maternal ancestors within the sixth degree, and who is not known by the family name to be of the same primitive stock with his father or mother, is eligible by a twice-born man for nuptials and holy union."

The phrase "twice-born" refers to the investiture of high-caste men with the sacred string into the full immunities of their order, called a "second birth."

As to families outside the pale of selection Menu ordains: "In connecting himself with a wife let him studiously avoid the ten following families, be they ever so great, or ever so rich in kine, goats, sheep, gold, and grain—the family that has omitted prescribed acts of religion; that which has produced no male children; that in which the Veda has not been read; that which has thick hair on the body; and those which have been subject to hemorrhoids, to phthisis, to dyspepsia, to epilepsy, to leprosy and to elephantiasis."

The right family and the proper relationship having been carefully sought and found, the child's personal suitability is then examined; and first her age: "A Brahmin should, according to law, marry a maiden about a third of his own age." The exact proportion is not frequently realized; but whether the bridegroom be old or young, the Hindoo bride should not be over twelve years of age.

Her name is the next consideration, and the legislator has seriously provided for this also. Lovers in this land offer new names, and ladies accept them and lose their own. In India it is not so. There the wife is ever known only by her maiden name; hence the name is of vital importance, and the law gravely prescribes as follows: "Let him not marry a girl with the name of a constellation, of a tree, or of a river, of a barbarous nation, or of a mountain, or of a winged creature, a snake, or a slave; nor one with any name raising an image of terror. The names of women should be agreeable, soft, clear, captivating the fancy, auspicious, ending in long vowels, resembling words of benediction." Chapter iii, sec. 4.

A list of sixty-nine names of Hindoo ladies is before us as we write, and all of them answer to this requirement. They run thus: "Hira, Kaminee, Dasee, Munee, Pudma, Sidhoo, Bhowanee, Rutuna," etc.

The preliminaries we have already noted completed, the two children are then duly and properly betrothed by the officiating Brahmin. So legal, however, is the ceremony considered, that, should the boy die ere they come to live together as man and wife, the little girl is thereby considered a widow, and under the law of her religion is debarred from ever marrying any one else. Indeed, till British humanity interfered, many of them became suttees, and were actually burned with the dead body of the youth whom they never knew nor loved as a husband—being at once a virgin, a widow, and a suttee on the last wretched day of their singular life!

As soon as the ceremony of betrothal has taken place, the little girl enters on a new phase of her existence. Henceforth she is no more free to roam the fields and enjoy the lovely face of nature. Reserved for her husband, she can no longer be seen with propriety by any man save her father and brothers.

She is from that day "a *purdah nasheen*"—one who sits behind the curtains, within the inclosure which surrounds her mother's home, and her education commences.

What, then, is the education, so called, which the betrothed wife in her Hindoo home receives during her five or six years of training for her future life? Her mother is her sole instructor. But she can teach no more than she herself knows; that, however, she fully communicates. We may epitomize the young lady's education, the entire curriculum of it, under four heads, cooking, domestic service, religion, and their peculiar female literature.

The first qualification is to cook, not only well, but appropriately. Each caste has its own ordinances, and these are very minute and particular as to the kinds of food that may be eaten, their mode of preparation and serving, and the care required to preserve the cooking utensils from all contact with things or persons whose touch would pollute them. In fact, caste is preserved in the matter of food more carefully than in any thing else. A violation of her duty here would involve consequences at which she is taught to shudder. The health and life of her husband may be forfeited by an unintentional neglect of hers. Even where wealth and high position may excuse her from the drudgery of preparation, the Hindoo wife is not released from the careful superintendence of this vital duty. We in this western world have little idea of the importance attached to it there, where, indeed, it may be truly said that their "kingdom of God is meat and drink," and where the Christian freedom of the text, "Every creature of God is good, and nothing to be refused if it be received with thanksgiving," is a doctrine unknown and a liberty unenjoyed. By the little lady long, weary months are thus employed in the acquirement of these distinctions and customs.

Woman, ignorant though she be, is the depository of the system of Hindustanee heathenism. She was taught it orally by her mother in girlhood. In her memory are treasured up the "slokes' of her religion—the verses of the Shasters which illustrate the popular idolatry. She has learned the histories of her gods and the dialogues of her mythological legends, and with these she is now industriously storing the mind of the child whom she is training to be a Hindoo wife.

To these she adds the literature for females found in the books of her country. Space permits us to notice but one of those manuals of maiden education, which this mother is now teaching from her own remembrance—for she cannot read a word of it—to her little daughter to fit her for her future duties.

There are three leading deities in Hindooism. The first, Brahma, is not worshiped; he lost the right to be by his own unspeakable vileness. The other two, Vishnu and Shiva, divide between them the more special regard of the women of India; and as the two gods are in a state of hostility, their devotees join their respective factions and keep up the wordy contest. Vishnu and Shiva have consorts who, of course, take sides, each with her own lord and against the other. Lakshmi is Vishnu's consort, and Parvati that of Shiva. The two deities seem to have left the high dispute, so far as words are concerned, to be carried on by their ladies, between whom it is supposed to be progressing continually. The little book containing this celestial quarrel is a special favorite with the women of India; they learn it and treasure its sentences in their memory, and rehearse it, taking the parts at festivals and other occasions, for the amusement of the guests.

This abominable circle of endless strife, in every bitter invective uttered, refers to alleged facts in the mythological history of the parties named, and of course has a depth of meaning and pungency which it is impossible to convey to readers unacquainted with the legends of India. But enough is here intimated to cause the gentle heart of any Christian woman to compassionate the millions of her sex who are thus systematically debauched in their imaginations and affections by their very mothers, as they educate them thus to continue their own degradation and that of their offspring forever. How much such females need the Christian teacher, and what light the Holy Bible would bring to such homes, and what a contrast of loveliness, and purity, and goodness the story of our Incarnate God would be to such instruction, can be seen at a glance!

We have mentioned the present dawn of a better day. It is but the dawn. Dr. Mullen's statistics tell us that already there are 39,647 women and girls receiving an education in the Zenana schools in India. The number is by this time larger, and still increasing, yet what are these among 100,000,000!

The question of caste has an immense influence in the marriage arrangement of the Hindoos, and its discriminations against women are particularly mean and insulting to her nature; while the compromises constantly occurring show how the cupidity of the legislators, and of the violators of the code, outrage the professed inflexibility of their own regulations.

For instance, the Institutes ordain: "Men of the twice-born classes, who, through weakness of intellect or irregularity, marry women of the lowest class, very soon degrade their families and progeny to the state of Sudras. A Brahmin, if he takes a Sudra as his first wife, sinks to the region of torment; if he have a child by her he loses even his priestly rank."

In their absurd mythology, the deities and the souls of their ancestors are represented as suffering from hunger, which can only be appeased by human attention, the cooking and presentation of which is part of the wife's duty. The regular and frequent fulfillment of this service is considered to merit heaven. But these dainty deities and transmigrated folk are too fastidious to touch the offering, hungry though they be, unless proffered by high-caste hands. The result is, that the lady of low rank can never rise in India, while the favored few of high caste, with all their peculiar immunities, are sacredly reserved for themselves by these sacerdotal legislators.

The head of a family, a shade higher in caste, will not give his son in marriage to the daughter of a family a shade lower on equal terms. But he will do it on receiving a sum of money in proportion to the means of that family, the cash condoning the caste.

April and May are favorite months for the marriage ceremony among the Hindoos, though the rite takes place earlier in the year. But no father will have a marriage in his house during June, July,

August, and September, the universal belief being that the deity is then, during the whole rainy season, down on a visit to the celebrated Rajah Bull, and is consequently unable to bless the rite with his presence.

The ceremonies of marriage in India are too well known to need repetition here. Often, when traveling at night in my palanquin, I have been roused from my sleep by my bearers catching sight of an approaching marriage procession, with its torches, music, and shouting; falling in with the enthusiasm of each event, they would cry out that "the bridegroom cometh." First, the bridegroom would make his appearance, mounted on a fine horse, splendidly caparisoned—his own or borrowed for the occasion—and wearing a grand coat, decked out in tinsel and gold thread, with the matrimonial crown on his head, and his richly embroidered slippers, all very fine, his friends shouting and dancing along-side of him; and, of course, as he passes, we make our salaam and wish him joy.

Right behind the bridegroom's horse comes the palanquin of the bride, but she is vailed, and the venetians are closely shut, and on the little lady is borne to a home which she never saw before, to surrender herself into the hands of one who has neither wooed nor won her; a bride without a choice, with no voice in her own destiny; married without preference; handed over, by those who assumed to do all the thinking for her, to a fate where the feelings of her heart were never consulted in the most important transaction of her existence; beginning her married life under circumstances which preclude the possibility of her being sustained by the affection which is founded upon esteem.

When the procession has come within hailing distance of his home the watching friends go forth to meet the bridegroom, the bride enters her apartments, the door is shut, and the guests are entertained in other parts of the establishment.

Let us now consider her life as a married lady in her own home, surrounded by the cruel prejudices and customs which meet her at the threshold and subject her to their sway. What they are may be gathered from a few statements.

When I sit down at a table in this land, spread with Heaven's bounty for the family and friends, and look at the Christian woman who so sweetly presides at the board, and whose blessed presence sheds such light and gladness on the scene, I often sigh to think that no such sight as this is enjoyed in India, for that land is cursed by the iron rule of a system which denies to her the joys and charities of social life. No lady in India sits at the head of her own table ; no stranger can share her presence in hospitality ; her healing word or hand cannot be extended to the sick or to the whole. Woman's gentle, blessed ministries have no exercise in India. Her services are all selfishly reserved for him whom now she is taught to regard as lord and master, and on whom she is henceforth to wait in a state of abject submission and obedience that has no parallel in any other system in this world.

My lady readers will bear in mind that these conditions are all realized within the four walls of the "compound" which inclose the home of the Hindoo lady. That compound is the woman's world in India. In it she lives, and seldom leaves it till she is carried out a corpse. Ever while she inhabits it, she has "jealousy for her jailer, and suspicion as her spy ;" and fain would her husband draw all these bonds tighter when he is obliged to trust her in his absence. Thus saith the Shaster: "If a man goes on a journey, his wife shall not divert herself by play, nor shall see any public show, nor shall laugh, nor shall dress herself in jewels or fine clothes, nor hear music, nor shall sit at the window, nor shall behold any thing choice and rare, but shall fasten well the house door, and remain private, and shall not eat any dainty food, and shall not blacken her eyes with powder, and shall not view her face in a mirror ; she shall never amuse herself in any such agreeable employment during the absence of her husband."

Was there any insult ever offered to a lady's nature equal to that which this law has laid down, when it enjoins the Brahmin to suspend his reading of the Veda to his disciples should a woman happen to come in sight while he was so employed, and directs him not to resume the utterance of the holy texts until she has passed beyond the possibility of hearing them? *Her* ear is not pure enough to hear what the vilest male thief or sensualist in the Bazaar may listen to freely! Woman's religious knowledge must not rise higher than the Shasters. The "holy" Vedas are reserved for men, and for them alone.

These old laws were in existence when the New Testament was written; and in the provisions of that Christianity which threw its blessed protection over woman's nature and rights, did not the Holy Spirit glance at these wrongs, and provide the principle of their final overthrow when he said: "There is neither Jew nor Greek; there is neither bond nor free; there is neither male nor female; for ye are all one in Christ Jesus?"—one in the freedom, equality and privilege to which Heaven's impartial mercy was to raise the Pariah, the woman, and the slave, from the degradation to which heathenism, in its pride of power, had reduced those over whom it could thus safely tyrannize.

The Shaster renders her duty very definitely, as follows: "When in the presence of her husband, a woman must keep her eyes upon her master and be ready to receive his commands. When he speaks she must be quiet, and listen to nothing else besides When he calls she must leave every thing else and attend upon him alone. A woman has no other god on earth but her husband. The most excellent of all good works that she can perform is to gratify him with the strictest obedience. This should be her only devotion. Though he be aged, infirm, dissipated, a drunkard, or a debauchee, she must still regard him as her god. She must serve him with all her might, obeying him in all things, spying no defects in his character, and giving him no cause for disquiet. If he laughs, she must also laugh; if he weeps, she must also weep; if he sings, she must be in an ecstasy."

Menu declares, "Though inobservant of approved usages, [the services of their religion,] or enamored of another woman, or devoid of good qualities, yet a husband must constantly be *revered as a god* by a virtuous wife."—*Institutes*, sec. 154. Such is the law, and the popular sentiment is not better than the law even to-day, after these long ages of helpless woman's subordination and suffering.

She waits upon her lord, who is "her god, her guru, and her religion," as the Shaster phrases it. She lulls him to rest by the soft shampooing of his feet, and is at once his slave and stewardess. Her worth is well summed up by one of their poets, who describes the best condition she can know, when her bereaved husband thus laments her:

> "Dost thou depart, who didst prepare
> My savory food with skillful care?
> On whom alone of woman kind
> In ceaseless love I fixed my mind?
> Whose palms so softly rubbed my feet,
> Till charmed I lay in slumbers sweet?
> Who tendedst me with wakeful eyes,
> The last to sleep, the first to rise.
> Now weary night denies repose;
> My eyelids never more shall close."

Yet while living she might not walk by his side, even in the marriage procession; she may not even call him by his name nor directly address him; nor can a friend so far notice her existence as to inquire for her welfare, for the *Sacontala* lays it down as a rule of social life that "it is against good manners to inquire concerning the wife of another man." The face of any man, save her husband and father, and her own and husband's brothers, she must never see, at the risk of compromising her character. So inveterate is the prejudice occasioned by their education that many of the women of India have sacrificed their lives sooner than violate the rule. The writer heard of a case which sadly illustrates this. In the detachment which Major Broadfoot had to take from Lodiana to Cabul in 1841 there were wives of many native officers, and the Major, in the performance of his troublesome duty, had them each provided for their long journey with a howdah fixed on a camel's back. During the march one of these came to the ground suddenly, and there was a general halt, for the native lady had got entangled in the frame-work and had swung around beneath. An English officer, seeing her danger, sprang from his horse to rescue

Hindoo Woman and her Husband.

her; but his action was arrested by the other ladies, who saw his intention as well as the lady's peril, and from behind their curtains cried out that he must not approach her, as he could not save her unless by touching her person and lifting the vail that enveloped her. The astonished officer would have done it, nevertheless, had it not been that the poor lady herself implored him not to approach her—she would rather risk death. Her struggle to escape was in vain; the terrified and unwieldly beast actually trampled her to death before their eyes!

Look into the home where we left the young bride, and see her as she begins the duties for which she has been trained. She rises to prepare her husband's food, and when all is ready and laid out upon the mat—for they ignore such aids as chairs and tables, knives or forks, and take their meals with the hand, sitting on the floor—she then announces to her lord that his meal is ready. He enters and sits down, and finds all duly prepared by her care. Why does she still stand? Why not sit down, too, and share with her husband the good things which she has made ready? She dares not. He would not allow it—the law of her religion forbids it. She must stand and wait upon him. He "eats his morsel alone" truly. No wife in India can legally dine with her husband unless she becomes a Christian.

The opposite wood-cut, taken from a picture of a Hindoo home of the middle class, shows the situation of affairs generally. It is substantially the same whether the person be wealthier or poorer than the one here represented. The higher classes use more indulgences. The weather is warm and a fan is needed, or a fly flapper is required, for he considers that he cannot use his curry-stained fingers to drive the flies away or cool himself; so the duty in either case devolves upon the wife.

The fan is made of a fragrant grass called *khus-khus;* a basin of water is at her feet, and she dips the fan into it occasionally, shaking off the heavy drops, and cools her lord and master, who enjoys, as he eats, the fragrant evaporation. Or the mosquitoes may be troublesome, and provision is made also for this. The tail of the *yak*, or snow-cow of Thibet, white and bushy, inserted into an ornamental shaft, is ready at hand, and with it the lady whisks around him, and saves him from the slightest inconvenience.

The duty is patiently performed, and when he has fully satisfied himself, she removes what remains to another apartment—for her religion not only forbids her eating with him, but also prohibits her from eating, even what he may leave, "in the same room where he dines"—and then, and not till then, can she and her children eat their food.—*Code*, sec. 43.

Woman is absolutely, and without redress, in the power of her husband, and no one can interfere when it stops short of actual murder. In the western provinces of India the reckless treatment of woman was carried to its greatest extreme. Before British rule interfered there was positively no limit to the cruelty of native husbands.

Twenty years have not passed since similar tyranny might have been witnessed in the kingdom of Oude, (before the introduction of British rule there threw the protection of the law of Christ over woman's life, so far as it can reach her secluded existence.) An extract from a reliable work, "The Private Life of an Eastern King," will illustrate this. The writer says, speaking of Nussir-i-Deen, the late King of Oude: "Being irritated, the King retired into the female apartment, and we returned to our tents. Heaven help the poor woman who has the misfortune at such a moment to displease or disgust an irritated despot! An accidental sneeze, a louder cough than usual, nay, even an ungraceful movement, may bring down punishment terrible to think of—torture, perhaps, at the bare mention of which the English wife, or mother, or daughter would shudder. Such things take place but too often in the Hindoo zenanas of India. Magistrates know that such things often take place, but they are helpless to punish or prevent. But the zenana and the harem are sacred; and the female slave that revealed their horrid mysteries would suffer a lingering and excruciating death at the hands of the very woman whom her revelations might be intended to protect. The chief and the wealthy man who is disposed to be cruel can act despotically, tyrannically enough; but the king, with unquestioned power of life or death in his hands, if once infuriated or enraged, can torture or kill without question. 'My wife is about to be confined,' said a savage Hindoo Rajah to his European friend, a solicitor, 'and if she does not make me the father of a son, I will whip her to death with my hunting-whip.' The child was born; it was a daughter; the woman's body was burned two days after. How she died no one out of the zenana certainly knew. The fact of the threat only transpired long afterward, when it was the interest of the solicitor, to whom the remark had been made, to prove the Rajah mad in his later days in order to set aside a will."

The discrimination is against women as such. Menu and his commentators decree no equivalent punishment upon male violators of their law or customs, and he actually shields from all penalty the whole sacerdotal class who formed these laws, no matter how many or flagrant their crimes may be. No such "class legislation" was ever enacted as is exhibited in the following section of the Code: "Never shall the king slay a Brahmin, though convicted of all possible crimes; let him banish the offender from his realm, but with all his property secure and his body unhurt. No greater crime is known on earth than slaying a Brahmin, and the king, therefore, must not even form in his mind an idea of killing a priest." Sec. 380.

When General Havelock, in 1857, laid his hands upon these dainty and pampered Brahmins, and, finding them guilty of mutiny or murder, tried and convicted them like common men, and ordered them for punishment or execution, some of the poor benighted people whom they had thus deluded thought that the earth would surely quake or the heavens fall. But, in defiance of this unjust Code, they were strung up, and the earth was still, the sun rolled on in its course indifferent to their fate, and the spell of Brahminical inviolability was broken forever, after the long imposition and cruel falsehood of its claim. But in the breaking of that spell women in India had more interest, and gained more advantage, than in any event of the past generation. She knows it not yet, but it is nevertheless true that Havelock's grand march and Christian soldiership and justice snapped a galling link of that heavy chain that had so long encircled her mind and body.

Notwithstanding the inhumanity and deep injustice of Hindoo legislation for the ladies of that land, their married lives are not without honor and influence, nor their persons unsupplied with gorgeous clothing and ornaments. On the contrary, the law repeatedly requires these things to be supplied in abundance. But let the whole truth, as to the expressed design and motive of this generosity, be candidly stated, and then let the reader judge what is the value of this magnanimity to the heart of any noble woman. Is it for her sake, as true love would prompt, or is it for the gratification and interest of him who confers it all? The reply to this painful question I place before the reader.

Let it be remembered, as explanatory, that in India a woman's curse is considered to blast the person, the property, or the home against which it is uttered. Men stand in fear of it, for prosperity is impossible where it impends. The legislator (in Secs. 55–59 of the Code) has affirmed its liability, with the duty of marital liberality as a motive of prevention. Also let it be borne in mind that a husband's passion for sons, in view of the relation of his male offspring to his shraad and happy transmigration—as previously explained—is such, that all considerations are expected to bow to this desire.

Polygamy throws its terrors, either as a possibility or a fact, over the heart of every married lady in India. Creation and divine law have ordained woman to be queen of her husband's heart, and to reign without a rival. But heathenism has dared to overthrow that right, and sternly tells the loving and trusting wife that she must, and without complaining, admit a partner in her husband's affection, if he desires it. How often are long years of duty and fidelity thus rewarded, and the true, faithful heart is crushed for life, as she sees herself superseded by some youthful stranger, who has stolen her lord's heart and attention, and leaves her to pine in neglect and sorrow!

The right to become a polygamist, should he prefer it for any reason, must unsettle any man's heart, and be a barrier to true and permanent affection. That right to be thus unsympathetic and fickle, and to inflict this terrible wrong upon her whom he ought to cherish and cleave to, "forsaking all others, as long as they both should live," Menu fully grants in the following ordinance of his Code: "A wife who drinks any spirituous liquors, who acts immorally, who shows hatred to her lord, who is incurably diseased, who is mischievous, who wastes his property, may at all times be superseded by another wife; a barren wife may be superseded by another in the eighth year; she whose children are all dead, in the tenth; she who brings forth only daughters, in the eleventh; she who speaks unkindly, without delay; but she who, though afflicted with illness, is beloved and virtuous, must never be disgraced, though she may be superseded by another wife with her own consent."—*Code* VIII, Sec. 204.

Here is wide range enough from which to select a cause of dissatisfaction, in any hour of alienation or dislike. No tribunal or process is required; the husband is sole judge and executor of this facile law; and in a single day the virtuous and faithful lady may find herself superseded by some youthful addition to her home, or become a discarded outcast, without pity or redress on earth.

I have been often asked to what extent polygamy prevails in India. For reasons already manifest, it is not easy to give a sufficient answer to this inquiry. I fear it is more general than is supposed. Of course the crime is limited by its expense. It is a luxury that poor men cannot well afford; yet even they are not innocent of successional polygamy: they often forsake or change their wives, and then take others. Among the rich it is very common. Indeed, with that class it is viewed rather as an exhibition of wealth and splendor, and cases are not rare where ten or a dozen ladies may be found in the zenana of a Rajah or Nawab.

There are varieties in the law and usage of the different religionists of India in this regard, but all of them allow the practice. The Parsee faith and usage limits polygamy to a second wife, and then only where the first is childless and gives her consent to the introduction of the second. The Mohammedan is allowed by his Koran to take up four wives or concubines, and few of the wealthy among them limit themselves to less than this number, while it is notorious that they use their facilities of divorce with so little scruple that their license under their law is practically unlimited. The opulent Hindoos are restricted somewhat in the increase of their wives by the absurd expensiveness of their marriage ceremonies, but are limited in no other way as to the number they choose to take.

The law lays down the subordination which is to exist in a home where there are several wives. The first married remains mistress of the family. The others are designated *sapatnis*, or auxiliary wives, and the first is expected and required to treat them as younger sisters. Every additional wife added is thus instructed by the Hindoo authority called *Sacontala:* "Here, my daughter, when thou art settled in the mansion of thy husband, show due reverence to him, and to those whom he reveres; though he have other wives, be rather an affectionate handmaid to them than a rival."

Extremes meet, and that often when we would least expect them Who would imagine, in a country where such rules of social life exist, that we should meet with a custom so opposite to it in all respects as *polyandry?* And yet this singular and amazing relation existed in India twenty-five centuries ago, and lingers to-day in some localities to such an extent as to call for the legislative action of the English Government. It is bad enough to be one among many wives, but to be the wife of many husbands must be a wonderful relation for any woman to sustain.

India's greatest poem is the Mahabharata, and its lovely heroine, Draupady, is represented, at the great tournament, as throwing the garland of preference over the neck of the valiant Arjuna, whom she loves so well. But with him she accepts his four elder brothers, and is henceforth regarded by all five as their common consort. Singularly enough, there is not a word of reprehension for the relation, and the story ends with the reception of the entire family to the home of the gods. Sir William Jones, the great Orientalist, facetiously designates this family of the Pandian chiefs and their common consort as "the five-maled, single-female flower," and there is reason to believe that this curiosity bloomed then in other localities of the land besides Indraprasta. The Code must certainly have tended to its abolition, for except in the Ceylon Mountains, among the Nairs of the South, and very limitedly in the Himalaya Mountains, the daughters of India have ceased to lament the Dwaper Yug—a departed age—when they sang:

> "Prepost'rous! that one biped vain
> Should drag ten housewives in his train,
> And stuff them in a gaudy cage,
> Slaves to weak lust or potent rage!
> Not such the Dwaper Yug! O then
> One buxom dame might wed five men!"

Whatever may have been the motive for this unnatural alliance in the ancient days, the purpose in our own, as I learned in the Himalayas, is the gain to be realized by the sale of their fairer daughters to supply the zenanas of the plains, and the dearth of women thus occasioned led to the continuance of this unnatural custom; and so one vice created another, and that, too, its very opposite. The English Government has done what it could to repress the practice of polyandry where it still exists.

A widow in India is undoubtedly the most miserable of her sex anywhere. She is now more than ever under the tyranny of her cruel law, and the bitterest dregs of a woman's misery are then and henceforth wrung out to her. Her youth, her beauty, her wealth, give her no exemption whatever; the rules, relentless as death, enforce their dreadful claims upon her and crush her down. Formerly they were expected to become Suttees and burn with the man's body. British humanity, thank Heaven! has ended that hellish custom. So they live, but how much better than death is their condition let my readers judge, when they learn the facts in her case.

In the first of these pages I introduced a Hindoo wife as she appears in her best estate—a married wife in her full dress and jewelry. From a photograph, which has been engraved with equal fidelity, I now present a picture of a Hindoo widow as she appears in her weeds, sitting upon the ground in her sorrow. Her aspect and her attire show at first sight, even to a stranger, the agony of her condition, which will be better understood when the rules of her now hopeless existence are stated.

In the forms of their exclamations, when they first realize that they are widowed, there are terribly reflective phrases which imply that, for aught they know, they may be responsible for their husband's death; that not misery alone, but guilt also may fasten upon their wretched hearts. This arises from the fear that in the responsibilities of their caste duties, in preparing food, etc., they may have, even unwittingly, violated some rule of the Shaster, and that the gods have visited the violation with their vengeance in the sickness and death of the husband. The terrific fear thus seizes on the lacerated heart that they may be guilty of the death which they mourn! Her own children and friends, she justly fears, are entertaining similar thoughts concerning her, and this dreadful weight is enough to sink her to despair.

The day she becomes a widow, the lady in India falls to a lot little less terrible than death itself. All her ornaments and beautiful clothing—on which her poor, uninstructed mind has doted—are taken from her, so that "jewelless woman" is the well-understood designation for a widow. She is henceforth to wear the dun-colored robe in which the engraving represents her, on which there must be no seam, no fringe, no figure. Her *Tali*—the equivalent of the marriage ring in England—which her husband tied round her neck when he married her, is removed. From her forehead the bright vermilion mark is wiped away. Her raven locks are ruthlessly cut off. The terrible indignity is perpetual, for the head is henceforth shaven every ten days. The terrors of the "God of Hell," breaking forth against the departed husband, are employed to make her endure the degradation, for, says the *Casi-Candam*, "If matrons who have put off glittering ornaments of gold still wreath their hair in unshortened locks, the

Hindoo Widow, in her usual dress.

ministers of fiery-eyed Yama shall bind with cords the husband of her desire."

But even this is not the end of the widow's misery. She must henceforth consider herself as a creature of evil destiny, practicing severe austerities ; her weary limbs are no longer to repose upon a comfortable bed ; her food is to be taken but once a day, and then only of the coarsest fare ; and, lest her presence should involve the dreadful doom of a widow's condition, she is prohibited from ever appearing in the wedding ceremonies of another woman, no matter how nearly related to her. The higher in caste she is, the more rigorously are these rules exacted ; so that a Brahmin's widow is the most wretched of all : and this is "according to law"—a doom laid on willfully and wickedly by their legislation and its commentators. Menu ordains as follows : "Let her emaciate her body by living voluntarily on pure flowers, roots, and fruit ; but let her not, when her lord is deceased, ever pronounce the name of another man. Let her continue till death forgiving all injuries, performing harsh duties, avoiding every sensual pleasure, and cheerfully practicing the incomparable rules of virtue which have been followed by such women as have been devoted to one only husband."—*Institutes*, secs. 157, 158. To this the *Casi-Candam* adds : "On the death of their attached husband, women must eat but once a day, must eschew betel and a spread mattress, must sleep on the ground, and continue to practice rigid mortification. Women who have put off glittering jewels of gold must discharge with alacrity the duties of devotion, and, neglecting their persons, must feed on herbs and roots, so as barely to sustain life within the body."

Can any thing equal this cruel audacity of proscription to hearts which their system had already crushed ! Yet it may be matched by the willful blindness of our American and British transcendentalists, who profess to find in Vedic teaching and Hindoo philosophy sentiments and ethics which they deem and commend as even superior to our Christian faith and morality !

It was for the interest of Brahminism that these wretched widows, henceforth so useless and inconvenient, should die, and their valuables be divided in the ceremonies of the suttee For ages this was done, and the young and beautiful ladies of the land were immolated amid solemn religious ceremonies and music, before applauding crowds of priests, and pundits, and philosophers, while no voice was raised against these vile murders until the Christian missionary came to plead for the widow's life. Then a merciful God, in response to their prayers and efforts, sent that noble man, Lord William Bentinck, to India as Governor-General, and to him was given the honor to face the opposition of Pundits and Brahmins, and in 1829 to sign the law that extinguished these murderous fires forever. The women of India will yet hang his portrait in their homes, and gratefully cherish his memory as one of India's greatest benefactors.

Lord William Bentinck.

The law of Christ and the legislation of Christian countries permit a widow, where she chooses to do so, to create and enjoy the sunshine of a second home ; but from this right Hindooism has for twenty-five hundred years bitterly prohibited every widow in India.

The Code declares that she is bound by the law to her husband even *after* he is dead, and that to change her life is to sacrifice her claim to be a virtuous woman. Menu says : "A faithful wife, who wishes to attain in heaven the mansion of her husband, must do nothing unkind to him, be he living or dead ; while she who slights not her lord, but keeps her mind, speech, and body devoted to him. attains his heavenly mansion, and by good men is called *sadivi*, or virtuous. Let her obsequiously honor him while he lives, and when he dies let her never neglect him. Nor is a second husband allowed in any part of this code to a virtuous woman."—*Institutes,* secs. 151, 162, 165.

Let me remind the reader that these rules refer not only to the aged widows, whose long life-relation to their husbands might give some color to these stern demands, but as fully place the obligation upon the virgin widows who never knew the husband's care or love. The law is explicit here. Two authorities give the rule: "It is said to be unlawful for any to touch jewelless women, whose eyes are like the dewy cavi flower, being deprived of their beloved husband, like a body deprived of the spirit." "Nor must a damsel once given away in marriage be given a second time."

Old or young, faded or lovely, it is all one dull uniformity of woe. The number of widows is, necessarily, larger in India than in any other land on earth.

Can Christian ladies in this happy land wonder that these villainous laws have brought forth their fruits of death ; that women in India, being thus degraded by system and rule, have dragged the nation down into their own ruin, or that their sisters there have become demented and broken-hearted, so that they have so long and often preferred immolation to the sorrowful lot of a Hindoo widow? Alas! tens of thousands of them, after such married lives as theirs, ignorant, impulsive, and indolent, when the terrible alternative has stared them in the face, have either committed suicide, or else, bidding a long farewell to peace and virtue, have buried themselves for life in the hells which abound in every Bazaar in India!

The death and funeral of the Hindoo wife is a very sad topic. Those final scenes are complete contrasts to what such words express under Christianity. In our civilization, with all its honor, and love, and blessing for woman, as wife and mother, what tender thoughts and holy memories surround a wife's or a mother's grave! It is far different in the Land of the Veda.

The Hindoo wife and mother falls sick. Her case grows worse and the fear fastens upon her heart that she is dying. She must have sad anxieties for her children and their future, knowing well that none can ever be to them what she has been. Coming days of desolation lie before them. For her husband's future she can have little concern, as she knows that she is in no sense essential to his comfort.

The usual means are tried to restore her. Superstition and astrology do their best; but she is sinking. Her symptoms are reported to the Hukeem—the native doctor—and at last he pronounces that hope has fled. No time is to be lost now. If she is too far from the Ganges to be carried there before the vital spark has fled, preparations are made for the burning of the body. Within a few hours after death it is laid upon the pyre and quickly consumed. When the heap is cold, a small portion of the ashes and calcined remains, representing the rest, are taken and put into an earthen vessel to be carried to the sacred river; and the rest of the remains are left there to be, as I have so often seen them, tossed about by the hogs and pariah dogs, or scattered by the winds of heaven.

But, should the Ganges not be more than a few miles away, instead of being kept to be burned at home, the dying wife and mother is laid on a charpoy — the light native bedstead — and raised on the shoulders of four bearers. She leaves her home forever. unattended, however, by her husband; her eldest son instead goes with her, and they hurry her by the shortest route across the country to the sacred river. She is dying; the sun blazes upon her with its fierce rays, often as high as one hundred and thirty-eight degrees, and she is, of course, jolted and shaken by the runners; but they must go on, and she must bear it all. At length the river is reached — those banks where all Hindoos so much desire to die—and now they lift her off, and lay her on her back on the brink, with her feet in "the sacred waters," and the bearers depart, for no restoration is ever anticipated; none there grow better and return. They think that it would be fitting in such a case to prevent it. So the son takes his station by the dying mother, and every few minutes he wets her tongue with the sacred water, or puts the mud of the Ganges on her lips.

The sun sinks low in the heavens; the shades of night commence to fall, and the place begins to look very dreary, for the wolves and jackals which abound will come there to drink when it is dark; and the son, it may be a mere youth, timid and superstitious, thinks his mother is a long time dying. But he cannot immerse her till the heart ceases to beat; so he watches on, and wets her lips again. And there they are, alone, far from house or friends, in "the valley and shadow of death" together. At length the last gasp is over, and his final duty is ready. He goes outside into the water, and, taking her by the heels, draws her down into the river, and floats her out till the water is above his own breast, and then with a final push he sends her from him as far as he can into the river, and turns to the shore and makes his way home as fast as possible. She is left to her fate, no more to be thought of or protected. To her son, who thus deserts her —to her husband, who left her to die without his presence—it is nothing that the body of the mother and wife is rolling along with the current in the darkness, and that, most probably, within a few hours, and within a few miles of her dwelling, it will strand upon a sand-bar, and be discovered by the vultures, who, with the jackals, will fiercely contend together during the night as they feast upon it, or that the sun of the next day will shine on the gory and naked skeleton of the wife and the mother to whom, by their gloomy religion, even the rest of the grave is thus denied!

CHAPTER X.

OUR CHRISTIAN ORPHANAGES IN ROHILCUND.

THE preceding facts and doctrines will lead to an appreciation of the efforts made by the mission to educate and train some of the youth of India, so that we could present before the heathen the examples of Christian manhood and womanhood, and also have native helpers of both sexes on whose intelligence we could more fully rely than we could upon our adult converts. Our Boys' Orphanage was originated by the suggestion and liberality of the devoted Englishman mentioned on page 436. We present a woodcut of the present building, close to the city of Shahjehanpore.

In this institution one hundred and forty-eight boys are now receiving a good Christian education, under the direction of Dr. and Mrs. Johnson, whose devotion and ability, by God's blessing, have made that school the power for good which it is fast becoming.

The origin of this noble charity may be briefly given here, as it is one of the results of the Great Sepoy Rebellion, and intimately connected with the facts which have been stated.

The wages of a laboring man in India is *two annas* per day—the anna is three cents—so that millions of men in that land toil all day for six cents, and are grateful if they can only, even at that rate, obtain regular employment. This is their whole compensation, for they find themselves—as they would not, on account of their caste prejudices, touch our food—so the six cents have to pay rent, and clothe and feed them and their families! Of course, they could not live at all if their habits were not very simple, and the means of life very cheap. They eat only twice a day, rice and coarse flour, alternated, being their chief food, with a seasoning of curry; and they drink only water.

The result is, that these millions of toiling men are always on the very verge of want, living "from hand to mouth." Occasion-

Boys' Orphanage, School-house, and Chapel, at Lodipore. India. From a Photograph.

ally, two or three times in a score of years, there will occur a deficient rain-fall. This involves a scanty harvest and a pressure on the labor market, under which thousands are thrown out of employment for a period more or less protracted. They cannot be "forehanded," by savings from six cents a day, to meet these dreadful emergencies, and the result is, if relief does not soon come, hundreds of them are liable to starve to death.

One of these fearful experiences occurred in Rohilcund during the year 1860. So decided and quick was the calamity, that before the English Government ascertained its extent, and could originate public works to arrest its severity, large numbers of the people had died of want. The poor children were the last to succumb, for nature would lead the dying father or mother, heathen though they were, to give the final morsel to the child or children, in hope of saving them. The Government hurried on the measures of relief, and also sent around its police to give immediate succor to the living and to bury the dead.

From wretched homes, where a father or a mother, or both, lay dead, the surviving children were carried out and collected together. The orphan boys were assembled in one town, and the girls in another. There were hundreds of each. The Government could extend only temporary relief, and what was to be the fate of the rescued children became a painful consideration. The pressure was too great for friends of the dead to come forward and receive the bereaved and destitute, and the poor children thus lay between hope and despair. No Mohammedan or Hindoo hand was extended to save them. There was, however, one class of persons who were ready to receive a number of the elder and most likely girls, but they knew well that their proposal would be met with indignation by the English magistrates, and that they durst not make it. They had to deal with men who understood that there was something worse for a girl than even starvation and death. So the government waited, day after day, in hope that relief for these orphans would arise from some quarter.

Amid this fearful state of things, where Christian philanthropy was so much called for, the idea came to us that this emergency might be turned to good account, by our Mission seizing on the opportunity then presented, not only to save those ready to perish, but also to do a great work for the women of India and for Christianity, by taking up a number of these destitute children, particularly the girls, and training them for Christ and for usefulness.

We took the case to God, and laid it all before him. The more we prayed and thought over it, the more intense our zeal in the project became, till at length we could think of nothing else but those wretched children, and the way to save them, and what we might make of them in a few years by good care, and education, and Christianizing—and how much they would be to us in return as Christian women, Christian wives and mothers, meeting fully all this special want of our new Mission, and opening up in the future just such an agency as we required to reach the women of India.

The importance, also, of having a number of boys of our own, whom we could train up for God as Christian lads, free from the contamination of Hindoo homes, also commended itself to our best judgment and feelings as every way desirable. Yet still the girls seemed beyond all measure the more important proposition. But as the subject was considered and prayed over, it seemed essential that we should have both, and both in good numbers. So "a score" of each was given up, as far below the opportunity and the needs of our work, and at length our heart set its hopes upon the proposal of taking as many as would raise our number to one hundred boys and one hundred and fifty girls. It was a bold adventure to propose. We had no means in hand to provide for them; no shelter or support. But our feelings and judgment clung to the conviction that it was right and necessary to do this thing; and that the good of our Mission and the glory of God would be promoted by it; and that, somehow or other, the Lord and his Church would find the means to do it, and would sustain our effort, while the good results would justify it in the years to come.

Accordingly, the project was presented to the Mission. As was to be expected, the proposal, especially in its extent, awakened fear that it could not be done—that it would bankrupt the Mission to attempt it. To the inquiry, "Brother Butler, how are you going to sustain them? how will you feed, or clothe, or shelter, or educate them?" I could only answer in faith, "I cannot tell, but I believe the Lord will provide." The ladies soon heartily sympathized with the proposition, and encouraged me to go on and trust God, and erelong we were all united in the great and good enterprise.

I wrote to the Government; they were only too glad to consent, and have the children taken off their hands. We might have as many of each sex as we desired. English magistrates, in whose hands they were, were communicated with, and directed to make them over to us.

On going to Moradabad to receive our children, we found that the Mohammedan wretches connected with the magistrates' court, at whose disposal they had been placed, had actually distributed many of them in the houses of infamy in the city, to be brought up to a life of sin and shame! With an earnestness befitting the occasion, I placed the facts at once before the Governor, who acted with noble promptness, and the children were ordered to be immediately recovered and forwarded to us. The enemies of their souls and bodies were defeated, and we had the satisfaction of rescuing them from hands whose "tender mercies were cruel," and fulfilling in their case the letter and spirit of the divine Word, "Of some have compassion, making a difference: and others save with fear, pulling them out of the fire; hating even the garment spotted by the flesh." Poor girls! what a different fate did Christianity confer upon them, instead of the "deep damnation" of soul and body to which that vile and cruel Mohammedanism would have surely consigned them for time and eternity! They, and their children, and children's children, will certainly remember with adoring gratitude to God, and thankfulness to his people, the great salvation which was wrought out for them. I bless God, and shall always do so, for the part we took in their rescue.

They were sent on to us to Bareilly in native hackeries, fifteen or twenty of them to the load, drawn by four bullocks each, and were laid down at our door. I have four large photographs of these children as they now appear—every face of the one hundred and thirty-nine girls is there; and after twelve years' care and training what a contrast do they present! If I only had photographs of them as they were when laid down before us in 1860, in all their weakness and forlorn condition, so naked, filthy, and ignorant, what an eloquent sermon those pictures would silently preach, as they so wonderfully exhibited what Christian mercy and Christian education and grace could do, even for the poor wretched female orphans of an India famine! Can it be that these fine, healthy, hearty, educated girls in these graduating classes, year by year, so bright with intelligence and sanctified by the grace of God, were, only twelve years ago, just like the rest of the sad group in squalor and helplessness? Yes, it is so, and to the holy Trinity be the glory of the blessed change that has thus transformed them!

They were sent to us of all ages, from twelve or thirteen years down to the babe of three months, for whom we had to provide a nurse. Most of them were weak and emaciated, and a few of them dying, whom no care could save, so that we lost, out of the one hundred and fifty, about fifteen, who were too much reduced in strength and vitality to be saved.

What the Boys' Orphanage has become after twelve years may be best intimated by the picture, which presents Dr. Johnson and his theological class of thirteen young men. Educated and converted, they have been for some time seeking a higher preparation for the Christian ministry among their countrymen.

I have already mentioned the case of Maria, the first native of India who joined our Church in Bareilly, and who became one of the martyrs of Jesus at noon on the 31st of May, 1857. She dearly loved our means of grace, and particularly the class-meeting, where, with artless simplicity, she would tell how the Lord led her to hate sin and love holiness, and how sweetly her soul rested in Christ as her perfect Saviour. Her father was a Eurasian, and she spoke the

Theological Class in India. From a Photograph.

English language well. She had an unbounded zeal to do good, and an ardent hope for the elevation of her sex in India, though she knew their deep degradation far better than we did. But it was then a dark day in Bareilly.

Maria had been led to Christ while on a visit to Calcutta, through the instrumentality of the Baptist missionaries there. Thus, the first Church Member of American Methodism in India was contributed by the English Baptists, while American Presbyterianism donated the first Native Preacher to lay the foundation of our work in that land. No opening then appeared, even to her, by which we could reach and enlighten the daughters of India. Every door seemed shut, and we could not obtain a single female scholar to instruct or save. But Maria believed that the morning light would break soon, and a better day would dawn upon her country, and that it was near at hand. We would sit and converse with her, and then, with our hearts full of mingled hope and anxiety, would kneel down and implore God Almighty to come to our aid, and open a door of faith to those millions of souls so closely shut up. Prayer would give us renewed confidence, and help us to hang upon the naked promise of our God, while we struggled hard to answer the anxiety of our hearts as they would exclaim, "Watchman, what of the night?"

This precious girl, who, of all her race and sex in Bareilly, alone loved us for the Gospel's sake, seemed raised up to encourage and aid us in our new mission. She was likely to become as faithful a helper to my wife as "Joel" was to me. But the fearful Rebellion broke over the land, and Sepoy bigotry aimed to extinguish every vestige of Gospel light in India. Maria became a martyr for Christianity. Her blood baptized the soil of Bareilly and made it sacred forever for our mission and for Christ. And there, on the very spot where she fell, has sprung up a harvest of good for the daughters of India of the realization of which we had but feeble hope in those dark days before the Mutiny.

This wood-cut of the Mission-House and Orphanage at Bareilly represents the first spot in India where the denominational standard of the Methodist Episcopal Church was planted, in 1857, and from which the founder of the mission, with his wife and children, had to fly for their lives in May of that year. On the very ground now occupied by the house to the left stood the home of "Maria."

The site of our mission is on the edge of Bareilly, a city of one hundred and twelve thousand souls, hid in the trees of the picture. The Mission-House, where Brother and Sister Thomas and Miss Swain reside, is the tiled building to the left. Just over it is seen the top of the Orphanage, which is a square inclosure; in the foreground is the school-house, with its bell-tower; and in front of the school-house is the public road into the city.

I feel assured, with these reminiscences before my mind, that, were Maria alive to-day to read this account of what God has wrought for her sex in Bareilly since the 31st of May, 1857, and that, too, on the very ground occupied by her own homestead, her simple, gentle heart would thrill with a joy and gratitude for the priceless victories won for woman and Christianity in Rohilcund more intense and appreciative than can be bestowed upon these pages even by those who in this land may read them with the deepest interest. The reason is manifest. She knew the difficulties to be overcome, and the darkness to be illuminated, as none here can ever know it, and as even our missionaries to-day in India, who have "entered into our labors," cannot adequately realize amid their more hopeful opportunities and wider doors of usefulness. We were then in the valley of vision; around us were the moral skeletons, "very many and very dry"—no life nor sign of life—and, in our sadness and struggling hope in "Him that raises the dead, and calls the things that are not as though they were," the Divine Master was challenging our faith in his power. "Son of man, can these dry bones live?" All that we could answer was, "O Lord God, thou knowest!"

But a change has come, and by means which we then little anticipated. In that valley of the Ramgunga Maria died for Jesus, and the raging heathen, as they exulted over her lifeless body, concluded that they had killed the last woman of their race who would

The Mission House and Orphanage at Bareilly. From a Photograph.

ever become a Christian—that with her life would expire the only hope of reaching and ameliorating the lot of her sex in Rohilcund. How little they knew that Jesus is Jehovah! Nor did they imagine how soon He would dash to pieces, like a potter's vessel, the despotism which they built up that day upon the ruins of his cause. How much less did they anticipate that, on the very spot where they murdered his faithful handmaid, he would found an institution to be a Christian home for their own daughters, taken from their side when famine had laid them low in death, and that thus he would answer, in judgment to them and in mercy to their innocent offspring, their rage against him, and their diabolical efforts to overthrow his holy cause and to bind permanently the fetters of darkness upon the women of India! "Just and true are thy ways, thou King of saints!"

There stands that Orphanage to-day, one of the brightest hopes that shines for woman in the East; and of it may be said, that the little one has become one hundred and fifty, and the solitary female worshiper an exultant congregation of bright, happy girls, with a future of Christian usefulness before each and all of them. Truly, "Thou makest the wrath of man to praise thee, and the remainder of wrath wilt thou restrain."

Our early congregations in India, from 1857 to 1861, had, in one sense, a melancholy aspect. There would be from ten to forty men, chiefly young men, on one side of the room, offset by perhaps one woman or two, the wives of our native helpers, on the other side. No Christian families, no social aspect in our services. It was all a one-sided, unnatural-looking affair, with a certain monkish appearance that seemed dejected and forlorn. Woman was not there. The great want was felt deeply by the missionary as he rose to conduct the services. Nor was there then any way, or hope even, by which this dreary aspect could be relieved by female presence. We felt it the more because in India every young man looks forward to marriage as a duty as well as privilege. These young men, as they became attached to our congregations and converted to our faith, were met at the threshold by the forbidding and manifest fact that to all the other disadvantages of their position as Christians was added the consideration that only a life of celibacy remained to them. They could not return to heathenism for wives, for their friends would not give them; and, even if they did, our Discipline might put them out of the Church for marrying unconverted women; while, on the other hand, we had no Christian families from which they could be supplied. Such were their circumstances and the cheerless future that lay before them. I used to lie awake at night and groan over this aspect of our work, while the way to reach the minds of the women of the land, for want of a female agency, seemed as dark as did the prospects of our converted young men in reference to marriage.

These disabilities hemmed us in on every side, and made the progress and the future of our mission uncertain and doubtful. It was very discouraging. A Christianity without homes, or female schools, or daughters, without wives for our native teachers or preachers, without female worshipers in our congregations, wanted the first elements of perpetuity and completeness.

Every effort was made by our missionary ladies to obtain even day scholars from among the people, but such was then their bitter prejudice against educating girls that they generally treated the proposal with scorn. The ladies of our Bareilly mission made a vigorous effort in that city to obtain even a few scholars. They went from house to house, hired a suitable place in which to hold a school, bought mats and necessary equipments, offered even to pay the girls some compensation for the time expended if they would only attend; but at the end of three months they had only succeeded in inducing two children to come, and one of these was unreliable. At length, tired out, they had to abandon the effort as hopeless, until some change would come over the minds of the people in favor of female education.

I well remember what joy there was in November, 1858, when Providence put into our hands the first female orphan we ever received. She was a poor, weak little creature, was blind of an eye, and plain-featured—certainly no beauty; but she was *a girl,* and she was all our own to rear for Jesus and his Church—one of India's daughters. We rejoiced over her, and felt that she was a precious charge for India's sake. Dear, sainted Mrs. Pierce cherished her with a mother's love. She was baptized Almira Blake. After a while we obtained three or four more, but we were still pained to think how inadequate were these few to meet the great want of our extending mission. The opportunity of Divine mercy was, however, nearer than we then knew. God was about to meet our requirements, and thus lay the foundations of greater and wider usefulness for our mission than we were anticipating.

The kind ladies of our mission took this wretched group of girls in charge, and they were washed and clothed, and cared for and fed. Educational advantages were soon provided. Responses came pouring in from schools and individuals in America, pledging support for one or two, and sending a favorite name to be put upon their *protégé* at their baptism. Individuals in India also, and the Government itself, came to our help, and soon a comfortable orphanage and a school-house—shown in the picture to the right, with its tower and bell — and all necessary conveniences, were erected. To these have been added library, apparatus, pleasant grounds, and other requisites, until the establishment is acknowledged by all who see it, and by Sir William Muir, the Governor, who lately visited it, to be one of the best-arranged institutions in India, and an honor to the American Methodist Church. It is also a credit to the interest and diligence of Brother and Sister Thomas, who, in their long and devoted connection with it, have, under God's blessing, made it what it is to-day.

The Lord has graciously laid the claims of the Female Orphanage upon the hearts of our ladies. It is now under the special charge of the Woman's Foreign Missionary Society of the Methodist Episcopal Church, as a part of their work for women in India.

It is a beautiful sight to see the orphan girls on the Sabbath of God, in His house, so neat, and attentive, and devotional, and to hear them sing the praises of Him to whose mercy they owe so much, and then all bow down to worship in the true Biblical and

Oriental fashion. Their prayer-meetings and class-meetings are times of real interest, and in listening to them you realize that many of them are truly taught of God.

The number of female orphans is now nearly one hundred and fifty, about twenty having been added during the past year. The good fruits of the institution have so won the confidence of all who are acquainted with it that it has conquered prejudice and conciliated the interest and good-will of many even of the native nobility as well as the English magistrates, from whom the institution every year receives additional destitute orphans to be adopted into this Christian home and family, and trained freely upon our own principles.

From six to nine girls finish their studies and graduate each year. I here present, from a photograph, the last class that graduated, from which the reader will have a correct idea of their persons, style of dress, etc.

The girl on the left hand, standing up, is Julia Pybah, the middle one Mary Cocker, and the right hand one is Elizabeth Husk The first one sitting, left hand side, is Clementina Butler; the next, Rebecca Pettis; the next to her is Josephine, and the fourth is Grace Anable.

During a revival of religion, with which God was pleased recently to visit the Orphanage, over forty of these girls were soundly converted.

Thus God has justified our confidence when we first took these girls to train them up for him; all our hopes have been fulfilled. They have done well intellectually and religiously. More than twenty-five of them have already been married to our native preachers, teachers, and converts, and are now happy wives and mothers in their own homes, exhibiting before their heathen sisters what a Christian wife and mother is. Others of them have become efficient teachers and helpers in the work of visiting and instructing their countrywomen, as the columns of the "Heathen Woman's Friend" show. Probably the highest work which God had in view for these girls is that now in progress under the training of

Graduating Class. From a Photograph.

Miss Swain, M. D., who has a large class of the elder girls under instruction in the theory and practice of medicine, to fit them to go into the houses of the suffering ones around them as medical Bible women, healing the sick while they preach the Gospel. No words can be too ardent to express the importance of such an agency; and as to the view which is taken of its value by the people of the land, it is enough to mention the fact that the Nawab of Rampore, a Mohammedan sovereign in the vicinity, who lately visited the Orphanage, was so pleased with Miss Swain's medical class and its object, that his highness expressed himself greatly gratified, and asked their acceptance of a donation of a thousand rupees to aid their work. He has since conferred upon them his residence and grounds at Bareilly to become a Christian Hospital for the native women of Rohilcund.

The Ladies' Missionary Society of our Church has done well in taking this institution under its charge. It has elements of power, as thus directed, the value of which cannot be over-estimated. They will generously support it and develop its ability for good; and I doubt not it will justify all their confidence and expectations in its future history and success. From it must continually go forth influences which will mitigate the prejudices of the women of India, for they can understand the disinterested benevolence that thus seeks their own relief and welfare; and gratitude must surely incline them to examine into the truth and virtue of that religion whose mercy and good fruits will be so manifest in the benighted and suffering homes to which the graduates of the Bareilly Orphanage, and their devoted instructress, will bring help and healing in the days to come.

Earnest may be the prayers and strong the confidence of the ladies of Methodism in the Christ-like agency which they have thus made their own, and which, under their fostering care, will develop into a permanent power of Christian womanly goodness for long-neglected heathen women, the value of which they can never fully know till they find it in eternity, when they stand in the glorious presence of Him who, before his Father and the holy angels, will remember it all, and, acknowledging that each of them "hath done what she could"—to the body as to the soul, after his own blessed example—will tell it then "as a memorial of her."

The organization of the Missions into an Annual Conference, at the close of 1864, terminated my superintendency, while the toil and care to which body and mind were subject during these scenes, and in such a climate, were so exhausting, that release from further service there became indispensable. This release was kindly granted by the Bishop and the Missionary Board.

The progress of the Indian Church to-day is an encouraging contrast to the weakness and obstructions of sixteen years ago. Already some of our native Christian brethren are rising to positions of great trust and responsibility in the Church, the State, and the learned professions. We name but a few:—

Krishna Mohun Banerjea, Pundit Nilakantha Gore, John Devasagyam, and Goloknath Chattergi, not to mention others, are among the ornaments of its native ministry. Gunga Ram and Professor Ramchunder, show what Hindoos can become as cultured Christian teachers, as does Kalee Mohun Banerjea, among University graduates, and others equally worthy; while Government officers, like Behari Lal Singh, and Deputy Magistrates, like Tarini Churn Mitter, prove how worthily public positions can be filled by the followers of that faith: and their descendants shall yet occupy every office of their Government in the glad day when their Ganges shall flow only through Christian realms, and their fertile lands shall be cultured by a happy Christian population, whose redeemed country, no longer the LAND OF THE VEDA, "shall be called by a NEW NAME which the mouth of the Lord shall name."

India Theological Seminary at Bareilly.

The middle building is Remington Hall, the one to the left is Butler Hall, and that to the right is Ernest Kiplinger Hall.

CHAPTER XI.

RESULTS THUS FAR OF THIS WORK.

Explanatory Note.—In arranging for this new edition the extensive statistical tables formerly here have been superseded, being outgrown by the progress of the work. Other tables, presenting the results to 1894, have been prepared, and will here appear. Our readers can thus appreciate the great development which God has given to his Gospel, notwithstanding the fearful resistance with which heathenism met its introduction, as narrated in the early portion of this volume.

As a significant sample of this advance, made during the twenty-four years past, we present our Theological Seminary, the intellectual and religious center of our cause in India, which has already done so much to advance its interests in the past, and is getting ready to accomplish far greater results in the blessed future that is opening before it.

Equally necessary is it now to furnish a correct account of that development of grace which the Holy Spirit has recently granted to our Mission. Only a person who knows it thoroughly, and knows it all, could do this in a way to give full satisfaction. The publishers and the author both felt that the man who could best render this service to our readers was the beloved Bishop under whose administration the work has developed its present extension and power. Very kindly has Bishop Thoburn consented to render this service, for which the author heartily thanks him.

The new statistical exhibit will close the chapter.

I. *The Theological Seminary, Bareilly.*—While using every instrumentality available to spread the Gospel among the people no matter how humble their ability, our brethren in India are at the same time wide awake to the value and importance of the highest possible culture to meet the keen and violent heathenism that confronts their precious work. They cannot be intimidated by any show, or pretence, or bitterness exhibited by the enemies of the Lord Jesus and his cause. In their hearts is the full and patient persuasion that truly converted men, thoroughly trained, with the Bible in their hands and the unction of the Holy Spirit in their hearts, can cope with any resistance, and that such an agency is yet to lay low in the dust the proud and hostile heathenism of India. For such a result they cherish this evangelistic training center at Bareilly.

From the Report for 1894 we cull a few extracts to show the history and value of this institution to our work:

"The need of trained helpers was felt from the opening of the Mission. Rev. D. W. Thomas, one of the missionaries, in 1871 offered to donate from his private means $20,000 for the foundation of a Theological Seminary for India if the Mission Board would furnish $10,000 for some buildings. The proposition was accepted. Of this donation the editor of *The Christian Advocate* wrote at the time: 'We regard it as one of the most important benefactions, all things considered, that the Church has ever received.' E. Remington, Esq., of Ilion, N. Y., donated $5,000 of the money required from the Board for buildings. To these gifts a layman of Baltimore added $17,000 more. The seminary was opened in April, 1872, with a class of sixteen students. In 1876 Remington Hall, seen in the center of the picture, was finished, and dedicated by Bishop Andrews.

"Since opening the seminary over two hundred native missionaries have passed through the regular course of three years, and sixty have taken a partial course."

As the year 1888 opened upon our Mission with a wondrous visitation of grace, that has since added over fifty thousand souls to membership, it became more than ever apparent that our seminary must without delay have enlargement, both in buildings and resources, and this was accompanied with a divine call to an increasing host of young men on whose hearts God had laid "a burden for souls." Where to accommodate them and where to teach them if they could be accepted now became an anxious question. Two wings, one on either side of Remington Hall, became at once imperative, and were providentially provided for to the great joy of the faculty. The result is that the classes are doubled in number. This year the names of eighty-one students are on their roll, and this will probably soon rise to the requirement of accepting one hundred candidates every year.

The faculty gratefully acknowledge in their report the providential aid which so opportunely come to their assistance:

"Several friends have given $1,000 to found scholarships. As mentioned, Rev. E. S. and Mrs. E. R. Kiplinger gave $2,000 to build a lecture hall. A worthy physician gave his gold watch and jewels, worth $350, and laid the foundation of a library, for which also an officer in India contributed some $2,000. A sum of $2,000 was contributed by many friends to build a Butler Hall in memory of the founder of the Mission. We have now a total endowment of about $45,000, with buildings worth some $18,500. Many friends are sending very valuable aid for students and greatly enlarging our opportunity. We hope such help will continue."

Nor is the training of a native ministry all that this precious institution is doing for the work in India. There is here, in addition, a "Christian Woman's Training School," in charge of Mrs. M. E. Scott and Mrs. S. Dease, with Mrs. Mukerje and three teachers, for the training of the wives of the married students, which has been kept up for the past twenty years. These women are taught to read and write in Hindi and Urdu, and then take a regular course of Bible study and other subjects that prepare them to work among the women of the country. Forty-eight such are now enrolled, and one hundred and sixty have taken the course and gone out prepared to work in the villages and zenanas, as the necessity demanded, side by side with their husbands.

But the faculty need more financial help, and need it at once. Teachers have to be paid, appliances furnished, and many wants met. They greatly need a teacher of music (which is a very effective evangelistic agency in this field), and also an instructor in a simple course of medicine, which would give the preachers and their wives great access to the people in the villages, with one or two dormitories more for the accommodation of the students. They remind us in their report of the serious and important character of their position and work and of the high indorsement which it has received when they say to us that:

"This is the first Methodist Theological School organized in Asia. It should be raised at once to the highest effectiveness. Our immediate work is educating a native ministry for a population of forty million and in a language that can reach one hundred million. There is a pressing demand for trained men in a rapidly expanding work. Now is the time for a shoulder to the wheel. The great deep in India is breaking up. The Church should move with wisdom and power at this supreme moment. Anti-Christianity is trying to preempt the field. It is a burning shame that infidels and scoffers from Europe and America are found here doing the work of their father, the devil, villifying Christianity and withstanding the missionaries. The seare scattering infidel literature and trying to organize the natives against us. A native ministry under God must save India. If a trained ministry is needful anywhere, it is in a field like this. Our pressing work and rapidly growing Church demand it.

"What friends say of this institution: Bishop Foster, in his visit here, pronounced this "the most important missionary enterprise in India." Bishop Ninde wrote: 'I was strongly impressed while in India with the invaluable aid which this school affords to our work. The marked efficiency of our native ministry in North India is largely due to the vigorous and careful training so large a proportion of them have obtained here. The seminary should be liberally sustained and its facilities enlarged.' Bishop Thoburn wrote: 'Our Theological School at Bareilly has become more than ever a necessity to our work, especially throughout North India. It will continue to exert a blessed influence far and wide by educating men who will take the place of leaders.' "

With a full right do they appeal to the Church at home not only for the further financial help so much needed, but also for grace from heaven to increase the effectiveness of this fast growing work, when they say:

"Pray for us that we may train mighty preachers of the word. Give to the institution all you can till we are fully on our feet for the greatest mission work of modern times. Inform friends of the institution who may be able to help us."

The seminary stands on the highway of the city, and many of the thousands that pass it daily stop to gaze and think. They have good taste to admire its beauty, but they certainly feel that the people who erected it and the men being trained there are *in earnest* in the work which they are doing to spread their religion. Strangers and foreigners declare it to be a "credit to our denomination," and no doubt this representation of what it is will be a joy to the liberal hearts which furnished the means for its erection. It was wisely planned for the purposes which it was to serve, and was solidly yet economically builded. India has many evidences that good taste and economy may be united, and that beauty is about as cheap as deformity when one has prepared a good plan and works to it, as was done here.

I know I voice the thought of each member of the India Mission when I say that we may well pray that God may long spare to guide this precious institution its devoted principal, Dr. J. T. Scott, to whose eminent abilities and hard toil for twenty-two years are so largely due the extensive results which have been accomplished by it. I now resign the pen to the dear Bishop.

II. *Thirty-five Years of Progress.*—In the good providence of God I enjoyed the privilege of being one of the second party of missionaries sent out to join Dr. Butler in the work of founding a new Mission in North India. We landed at Calcutta, August 21, 1859, and after a few days spent in preparing for the journey set out for the special field which had been selected for occupancy by our Missionary Society. On Saturday afternoon we crossed the Ganges at Cawnpore, and set foot upon our own chosen field. Every object possessed a peculiar interest in our eyes, for we already regarded the land as, in one sense at least, our own. We were strangers, it is true, and among a strange people, but, like Abraham, by the anticipation of faith we looked upon the field as our own. Scarcely a dozen of the people would have confessed to any allegiance to us, however remote, in a religious or any other sense. A thousand obstacles confronted us, and we knew but too well that every inch of progress would be contested. We were none the less eager, however, to enter upon the task which God had set before us, and hastened on to Lucknow, where the pioneers of the Mission had already assembled, and were waiting to greet us.

We spent a week in Lucknow, during which the first annual meeting of our Mission was held, and here we were able to gain a clearer view of the field which had been chosen for us. Taking the Province of Oude, with the smaller Province of Rohilcund on the north, and the little mountain district of Kumaon, our field contained seventeen million inhabitants. It is not strange that we gave little thought to the limited territorial extent of our field, in the face of the immense population which confronted us. At that time this population amounted to almost half that of the United States, and as America had been more than all the world to us, it seemed as if we were going abroad to attempt the conquest of a new world.

As we took counsel together in reference to new mission stations, new schools, and other enterprises, and new plans for occupying all the region assigned us, it is not strange that our field seemed at times to assume imperial proportions. Even at that early time, some of us could not but feel as if we were about to lay the foundations of an empire. The only objection that was made, so far as I can now remember, to the field assigned us was that it was too large. It did not seem possible that we could occupy so much ground, and make anything like adequate provision for the exigencies which would be sure to arise in the progress of our work, nor did it seem to any one that the Church which had sent us out would ever be strong enough to attempt more than the limited task which had been proposed by Dr. Butler, and approved by our authorities at home. In those days a favorite idea, which was much talked about, and sincerely cherished by most leading missionary authorities, was that of dividing the heathen world into sections, each of which was to be assigned to some particular branch of the Christian Church in Europe or America, and thus the whole work distributed in such a way as to secure the most rapid consummation of the task, and also the best possible conservation of labor. Our own missionaries accepted this view, without giving it very much thought, and certainly without any misgiving as to its practical wisdom. As we then looked at the situation, the great empire of India was to be evangelized, and our share of the common work was the little field on the eastern side of the upper Ganges, where we had pitched our tents and hoisted our banners.

Before many years had elapsed, it began to be felt among us that the circumstances of the country were changing. Great lines of railway had been projected immediately after the mutiny, and as these, one after another, began to be opened, the people of India were quick to discover that the former isolated conditions, under which they had lived from time immemorial, were giving place to an entirely new order of things. Distant points were brought close together; long journeys could be made in a few hours; the ancient pilgrimages began to lose nearly all their merit when made upon comfortable railway trains instead of being prosecuted by long and painful marches on foot; provinces separated by wide distances of space seemed to be made neighbors, and people who had never seen one another before were brought into close contact. Almost immediately it was perceived that converts to Christianity would inevitably become more active and enterprising than other portions of the community, and that it would be impossible to expect them to remain within narrow provincial limits where their forefathers had chanced to reside. As these converts would go out into different parts of the empire, it was reasonable to expect that they would carry their preferences and ideas with them, and that this would almost inevitably result in the establishment of those forms of Christianity with which they had been familiar. It thus came to pass at an early day that a question was raised among our missionaries as to the possibility, and even probability, of our being obliged to extend our boundaries, especially on the western side of the Ganges, which at that time limited our progress in that direction. Dr. Butler was among the first, if not indeed the very first, to perceive the inevitable tendency of a work like ours, situated as it then was, to move forward without much regard for artificial barriers, and I can very well recall a proposition which he made near the close of 1863, for us to establish a mission station at a point on the western side of the Ganges, where there seemed to be a special call for us. In my own mind the proposal did not meet with a moment's favor. It seemed to me that we were already staggering under burdens which we could not carry, and that a great many long years, if not generations, must elapse before we could think of moving so far beyond our chosen limits. Nearly every one in the Mission looked with equal disfavor upon the proposal, and no one dreamed that within the short space of seven years our missionaries, after a careful canvass of the whole subject, would deliberately resolve to cross that river, which lay on our westward border like another Rubicon, and open work in a field which thereafter was to have no permanent boundary until it reached the sea.

Such an enlargement was inevitable from the first, although none of us were able at that early day to anticipate what afterward happened. If a similar attempt were to be made at the present time, if a body of twenty men, inspired with an enthusiastic confidence in the success of their work, moved by an ardent zeal for God and for the salvation of souls, and profoundly believing that the testimony with which they were intrusted was to be carried to the uttermost parts of the earth—if these men were to be put down on another continent, and told to confine their efforts within an area half as large as an average American State, the attempted restriction placed upon them would prove utterly futile. For a very few years they might be restrained within narrow territorial limits, but if successful in even a moderate degree they would be sure to break over the barriers, and move forward as God's Spirit and providence led them, precisely as the early Christians did when they once fully entered upon their mighty task of evangelizing the ancient Roman world.

In India an outward expansion of our work was inevitable for several reasons. In the first place, the men and women who were sent to our field were inspired by the spirit which has characterized practical missionary efforts since the days of Barnabas and Paul. The first disciples were more slow to take practical notice of our Saviour's specific direction to bear witness for Him to the uttermost part of the earth, and many Christians of the present day are prone to fall into the same error. The modern missionary enterprise has been from the first a practical protest against this mistake. In spirit it is utterly opposed to all barriers, artificial or otherwise, which are erected to limit its progress. Without waiting until all Antioch was evangelized Barnabas and young Saul set forth to bear witness in other cities, and this holy ambition to press on, and still on, into regions beyond, became from that time the inspiration of every Christian evangelist.

The men who were first sent to our Mission in India were animated by a like spirit. They were impelled forward, from one point to another, and no sooner had they gained a foothold in one city or town than they wished to establish themselves in the next city which lay in their pathway. This restless spirit of aggressive enterprise is inseparable from the earnest faith which characterizes every successful evangelist. A similar spirit manifests itself in England and America, but when once domiciled in a vast empire like India, with unlimited numbers presenting themselves in every direction, it would be little short of folly to expect men full of holy, aggressive zeal for God and souls to live for years and generations upon one bank of a great river, and refuse to carry the message which God has given them for all mankind to dwellers on the opposite bank.

There was something also in the ecclesiastical system which Dr. Butler introduced into his mission field which tended to make an extension of the work inevitable. Other systems may be equally scriptural and equally acceptable to God, but this system has some peculiarities in this special direction. It was not devised by any one man in a single day or a single year, but is the outgrowth of a movement extending over a long series of years; and as the product of an active movement it is adapted to the condition of things similar to that in which it first took shape. In other words, it can only work successfully while it is actively aggressive. It propagates itself as naturally as it makes provision for the immediate wants of that part of the work which is permanent. One of the most striking features of our work in India at the present time is the apparently natural manner in which Hindustanee presiding elders and superintendents of circuits adapt themselves to the system in which they have been religiously educated, and push forward their work into new regions.

The most successful workers that I have met in India are men who know very little about ecclesiastical systems, but who seem almost instinctively to use the system with which they find themselves connected to extend the work of God into new regions. A man, for instance, is given a new circuit. It consists of a central town, with three or four villages around him. At the end of two years he has ten or twelve villages within his circuit, in each of which is found a Christian congregation. Another year or two passes and a new group begins to form around each one of these villages or towns, and beyond these again there will be a further extension, until at length the man who originally had charge of a little circuit has a field large enough for a presiding elder's district. In a number of cases movements of this kind have actually occurred, under my own supervision, and nothing that I have witnessed in India has so encouraged me to believe that all India can yet be evangelized by simple men of God, raised up from among the sons of India, as the success achieved in this way. If no other reason existed for the outward extension of the work than this one peculiarity, the system introduced by Dr. Butler would in a large measure account for it.

But reasons of this kind will weigh less with the thoughtful reader than the fact that our people have been providentially led in extending the sphere of their labors, not only into regions immediately adjoining our first field, but to all parts of the empire. With the extension of the vast railway system of India thirty years ago, small colonies of Europeans and Eurasians were gathered into settlements at distances varying from one hundred to one hundred and fifty miles, for the most part along the leading lines of railway. These settlers were almost exclusively connected with the railways, and were, of course, Christians, in the general sense of that word, and were known as Christians to the people among whom they lived. Most of them were deprived of the ordinary privileges of the sanctuary, and, as always happens in such cases, very many began rapidly to forget their religious obligations when thus cut off from their early associations. In the providence of God, our missionaries were led to preach, not only to these people, but to other English-speaking people living in the larger cities, many of whom were in government service, while others were engaged in such kinds of private business as India affords. When the word was preached among these people God blessed it in a peculiar manner, and in a short time companies of believers were gathered together in a number of large cities, and from these centers the work spread, in the course of a few years, throughout the length and breadth of the empire.

During the first year or two no very definite plan was adopted in reference to this new work, but in the ordinary course of providence it happened, as it might have been expected to happen, that the people asked for church privileges and for pastoral oversight. It seemed not only natural, but in every way just, that their request should be granted, and it thus came to pass in the space of two or three years that churches of our own communion were organized at nearly all the important centers throughout the empire. This new work was destined to admit us definitely and permanently to a still more important work among the masses of the natives of India. Let me quote from *Light in the East*, a new book now in press:

"For some years it did not seem very clear what value would be permanently attached to our English work in India. Many of our friends in America looked upon it with great misgiving, fearing that it would divert the attention of our missionaries from the greater work of giving the Gospel to the Hindoos and Mohammedans. Others thought that among so sparse a population no important churches could be built up, and no material help received from the prosecution of the general work. Time, however, soon began to teach its lessons, and it was found that wherever a foothold had been gained among the English-speaking people a corresponding work was sure to manifest itself among the natives. It thus came to pass in due time that our missionaries were found preaching to the people, not only in the Hindustanee language throughout North India, but in Bengalee, Marathi, Gujarati, Tamul, Canarese, and Teloogoo, in other parts of the empire. As the years went by the work was extended into Burmah, and later still down the southeastern coast of the Bay of Bengal to Singapore and Penang. It is needless to narrate the successive steps by which our work was extended throughout all this vast region. It often seemed unwise to our best friends for us to plant our stations at so many distant points, but on the other hand it never seemed possible for us to hold back from doors which God so plainly opened before us. To sum up the result in a few words; our one Annual Conference in North India was at first reinforced by the creation of a second Conference; this in process of time was divided into two, and the two were again divided into four, so that we now have five Annual Conferences within the limits of India proper, and a Mission Conference, which includes our work in distant Malaysia."

This outline of our immense mission field is, of course, a mere outline as viewed upon the map. We do not pretend to occupy all the country, and as yet have no missionaries nor native preachers in some large cities and towns. Very recently a party of our missionaries have been exploring a vast region lying southwest of Calcutta, where no Christian worker of any kind is found. In a report recently sent to me by one of these missionaries it was stated that between six and seven millions of people were living in that region, among whom no one had yet preached Christ. In other parts of the country, no doubt, similar neglected areas might be found, but after making all due allowance we still find ourselves with a field extended so far beyond its original limits that our task may now be said to be ten times as great as the one which was originally set before us.

One interesting feature of the work in its more recent development is the creation of what we sometimes call "our foreign mission." I have spoken above of the extension of our work down the southeastern coast of the Bay of Bengal to Penang and Singapore. These large cities are not in India at all, nor in any way under the Indian Government, but belong to the colony known as the Straits Settlements. By the ordinary sea route down the coast, Singapore is nineteen hundred miles from Calcutta, and thus, both politically and geographically, the whole region is foreign to India, indeed as much so as Liverpool and the British Islands are to the United States. Led by providential indications, which space will not permit me to mention here, it was resolved at the beginning of 1885 to send an expedition to Singapore with a view to begin a new mission in that city, which should make itself felt among all the adjacent islands. The importance of Singapore, especially in the almost certain position which it is destined to hold in the future, had been appreciated by our missionaries in a way which Americans and Europeans could not at that time fully understand. A vast Chinese population is settling upon all those shores, and the future of that entire region will yet be in the hands of these colonists. We believed them to be accessible in a peculiar way to gospel influences, and felt sure that it was of the utmost importance to the future unborn millions that Christianity should gain a foothold, not only in the colony, but in all the adjacent islands, at the earliest possible date. We had no money with which to equip a Mission, and very few workers from whom to choose the first pioneers. Dr. W. F. Oldham was selected to lead the advance movement, and, with his wife, entered upon his work vigorously in the early part of the year.

The story of the founding of this Mission is one of peculiar interest, but cannot be detailed further here. Suffice it to say that a foothold was gained, while the Chinese received our missionary with unexpected favor, and in due time a church was built, a school building erected, and up to the present time the Mission has been making steady progress. We have now a vigorous Chinese Church at Singapore, a smaller Malay Church, an English organization, and regular preaching to the Indian colonists in the Tamul language. We have a second station in operation in Penang, while a third has been established at the town of Ipoh on the Peninsula. In every respect the Malaysian Mission has proved very successful, and in no part of our history has the hand of God appeared more manifestly present with us than in directing our steps to that remote part of the world.

The most marked feature of our Mission in India during recent years has been the wonderful development of the work among what are called the "depressed classes" This term is common to all low caste people, and is popularly applied to about fifty million of the population. All these millions live below the line of social respectability. Their children are seldom seen in the public school, although legally entitled to admittance. The ban of social prejudice against them is so strong they are practically excluded. In all the missions of India it has been noticed from the first that the majority of converts come from the depressed classes, and perhaps this fact has operated to some extent to create a prejudice in the public mind against missionary labor. Most persons forget that in the earliest and purest age of Christianity Christians were exposed to the constant taunt that their community was composed almost exclusively of slaves and wretchedly poor people. The same peculiarity has attended the progress of pure and undefiled Christianity in all ages. The simple fact in the case is that our Saviour deliberately adapted the conditions of membership in his kingdom to the wants of the poor, knowing that the vast majority of the human race belong to this class. Hence, those who work in accordance with the Divine will, and in harmony with the only possible conditions upon which the kingdom of Christ can be made to flourish in this world, will never shrink from receiving the poor, and will never feel surprised when they see the poor coming to them in unwonted numbers.

Some six years ago it began to be noticed in our Mission in North India that a movement of some magnitude was evidently setting in among this class of people. At the close of 1888 no less than eighteen hundred baptisms were reported, while several thousand converts were waiting to receive baptism as soon as the missionaries were willing to admit them to the privilege. Much attention was excited by this new development, but no one at that time anticipated so rapid and wide an extension of the work as has since occurred. The following year a still more marked increase took place, while in the third year the number of baptisms, including children, went up to the startling number of eighteen thousand. From that time to the present hour the movement shows no sign of abatement, but on the other hand is constantly spreading more widely, and apparently gaining a firmer hold upon the people. The total number of Christians of all ages in the mission at this time is probably more than eighty thousand, while all the reports for three years past indicate that fifty baptisms occur every day in the year. So far as can now be seen, there is no reason to anticipate any abatement of this work whatever, but on the other hand it seems certain that it could be extended almost indefinitely, if means could be found for conserving the work.

The people are extremely ignorant, and, unless instructed according to our Saviour's directions, it is found that they do not go forward in the Christian life, but, on the contrary, are almost sure to become unsatisfactory in many ways, and either go back to heathenism or bring a reproach upon their new faith. Hence the vital question at the present time is that of providing instruction for converts. The converts themselves are so wretchedly poor that they can do nothing in the way of self-help. If teachers could be sent among them, and they gathered into groups and instructed, at the end of a very few years we would be able to send out two or three thousand more workers, and the eighty thousand converts of to-day might then become two hundred thousand in the space of two or three years. A prospect of this kind ought to arouse the whole Christian Church, and call forth an immediate effort to meet an emergency so full of promise. Strangely enough, our friends in Christian lands, with few exceptions, fail to comprehend that this is a day of God's visitation in India. It requires the most strenuous efforts on our part to secure the slender aid with which we are able to carry on the work on its present basis; but we are looking forward constantly to increased resources, and trust that the time will speedily come when our converts will number at least one hundred thousand every year.

If space permitted it would make a very interesting story to lay before the reader, the steady and indeed remarkable progress which has attended what might be called the internal development of our Mission in India. A great work of this kind touches a community or a province at many different points. While the main object kept in view is that of evangelizing the people, other objects are always found in subordination to the main enterprise. Take, for instance, the work among women. Female education has been almost revolutionized since Dr. Butler first took up his residence in Bareilly. When I first entered the field, I can remember well that only a feeble attempt had been made to establish a girls' school, and that, aside from the very few Christian converts, there were not half a dozen girls who even nominally were receiving instruction in all that region. Now, however, we see not only a Christian college for women established at Lucknow, but what would have seemed absolutely impossible thirty years ago, a rival woman's college established in the same city for the daughters of Hindoos. The Mission established by Dr. Butler can also lay claim to the honor of introducing the first lady physician ever seen in India. The first Indian women ever educated in medicine were also trained in this same Mission, and it was not until the missionaries had successfully demonstrated the fact that lady physicians could gain access to the women of India, and that educated Indian women and girls could be successfully trained in medicine, that the much vaunted Lady Dufferin movement became a possibility. It would be impossible to give Lady Dufferin too much credit for the noble work which she has achieved for Indian women, but it should always be borne in mind that missionary ladies first made the movement which she leads possible.

It would be interesting also, if space permitted, to trace the successive steps by which a great publishing work has been set on foot in connection with our now widely scattered Mission. As early as 1860 Dr. Butler gathered a few rupees together with which to purchase a small press, and a very modest beginning was made in the way of printing at Bareilly. This press was afterward removed to Lucknow, where it has flourished greatly, and is at the present time perhaps the most vigorous Mission press in all the empire. A second large publishing house has been opened at Calcutta, a third at Madrás, and a fourth at the distant city of Singapore. Most of these enterprises are still in their initial stage, but there seems no reason to doubt that all four of these publishing houses will soon enter upon a wide sphere of active usefulness.

Our Sunday-school work has met with special success and proved an unexpectedly valuable auxiliary in our great work. I can remember very well the morning after I entered Lucknow in company with Dr. Butler that I was strangely moved when I heard two boys singing to a familiar tune a Hindustanee hymn. At that time perhaps not more than half a dozen children in all that region could have joined in the song, but now there are probably seventy thousand who could take up the strain if called upon. Many of the Sunday-schools are largely attended by adults as well as children, but, in view of the fact that the majority of our adult converts are themselves but children in knowledge, and in some respects in character also, the instruction received seems as well adapted to them as to those of younger years.

It remains to notice an important measure which was adopted some years ago for the better administration of our affairs throughout the vast region which we now occupy. At an early stage in our history it was felt that some central authority was needed which would be empowered to deal with all such interests as belonged in a peculiar sense to our own field in India and Malaysia. Questions of various kinds were constantly arising, for the settlement of which no provision had been made by our missionary authorities, and not a few of these questions were of such a nature that it would have been impossible for any party or parties on the other side of the globe to have satisfactorily dealt with them. In order to meet this want the General Conference of 1884 made generous provision for the organization of what was called a Central Conference; that is, a representative body of ministers and laymen meeting every two years, and authorized to deal with all questions of general interest to our own peculiar work. At the outset this measure was looked upon as pointing in the direction of ultimate independence, but those who advocated it were careful to raise no issue of this kind. Their object was simply to make a present provision for a present want, and the history of the past ten years has abundantly demonstrated the wisdom of those who first devised this plan for the better administration of the affairs of a very widely scattered Mission. The Central Conference meets every two years, and its sessions are constantly growing in interest and importance. It has to deal with common interests which affect the welfare of the work at points very widely scattered. Two of our presiding elders, for instance, live at stations which are no less than four thousand miles apart. Our missionaries and other workers are preaching in sixteen different languages. A meeting of this body is somewhat like a gathering of delegates from all the nations of Europe, with a few added from Egypt and the upper Nile. It is evident that as time goes on the gathering of delegates from such widely scattered communities will constantly grow in interest, while the feeling will become more and more deeply rooted among all our people that they are truly engaged in building up a mighty Christian empire which is to affect for good the whole of Southern Asia.

Perhaps I could not do better than to insert here a brief extract from *Light in the East*, containing a reference to the last meeting of the Central Conference:

"Early in last March our Central Conference held its biennial session in the city of Allahabad. Delegates were present from all parts of the empire, and also two, Dr. Luering and Mrs. Munson, from the distant Malaysian Mission. This Central Conference has authority to deal with all questions which pertain to our general interests throughout the vast field which we occupy in Southern Asia, and its last meeting was an occasion of extraordinary interest. A number of our Hindustanee brethren were present as delegates, and I was greatly struck with the impression made upon them by those who had come from such immense distances in the interests of our common work. It was also noticed that the old-time missionary spirit, which used to be manifested in the early years when the missionary enterprise was new to most Christians, developed itself in a remarkable way on this occasion. An extraordinary impression was made upon the delegates when Dr. Luering gave in simple language a report of his work in Borneo.

"All the interior of the great island of Borneo, an island, by the way, which is as large as France, is inhabited by tribes of wild people called Dyaks. These men, without exception, are said to be 'head-hunters;' that is, men who make it an object in life to possess themselves of the skulls of persons killed by themselves. It is said that a young man is not considered worthy of acceptance as a husband until he has killed somebody; and every man's standing is much influenced by the number of polished skulls which he is able to hang up under the ridge-pole of his bamboo dwelling. A common belief is entertained, when a man kills anyone and possesses himself of the skull of his victim, that as long as he keeps it he will have incorporated into his own person all the courage and other virtues which belonged to the murdered man; and hence every Dyak warrior is extremely unwilling to part with one of these trophies.

"After giving some details in regard to his life in Borneo, Dr. Luering went on to speak of the terrible ravages caused by this custom of head-hunting. During his comparatively brief stay he was able to master one of the Dyak dialects sufficiently to converse freely with the people, and among others a man of considerable local influence seemed to be much influenced by what he heard concerning Christ and his mission among men. He had frequently talked to Dr. Luering about becoming a Christian, and at times it seemed as if he was really inclined to take that decisive step. This man had no less than ninety skulls suspended in his dwelling, and his visitors would always see them occupying their conspicuous place, and know that an awful story of crime was probably connected with each one of them.

"When Dr. Luering received his summons to return immediately to Singapore, he called on this man to say farewell. It was a little after sunset, and the evening shadows were already beginning to fall upon the village. The Dyak was much surprised, and apparently sincerely sorry, when the missionary told him that he must leave next day, and that he had come to say farewell. The Dyak remonstrated warmly, and urged him to remain, but was told in reply that there seemed no prospect that, even if he should remain, he or any other Dyaks would give up their sins and become Christians. He was assured that possibly in a little time the man of the house himself would take that much-desired step, whereupon Dr. Luering said to him, 'If you are sincere, you will give me a token of your honest purpose. You have often told me you would be a Christian, and you now repeat it again; if you will become a Christian I will take the responsibility of remaining, to help the rest of your people into a better life; or, if you will even give me a pledge of your sincere purpose to become a Christian in the future, I will see to it that some one comes to you without delay. The pledge which I ask is this: let me take one of those skulls and carry it back with me to Singapore, and I will keep it as a token on your part that you wish us to return, and that you honestly intend to become a Christian man.' At the mention of so startling a proposal the Dyak grasped his long knife—a terrible weapon in the use of which they are fearfully skillful—and looked as if he would revenge the insult offered him on the spot. His friends also looked startled, for according to their notions no proposal could have been more insulting. The missionary, however, remained calm, and persisted in repeating his proposal. There was silence for a little time, and then the Dyak, pointing to his skulls, said to Dr. Luering, 'Take one.' The permission was immediately accepted, and the horrible trophy was carried back to Singapore."

It is given to few men of the present generation to see the work of their own hands, begun in the face of many obstacles and in the midst of startling perils, move steadily forth to such grand proportions as the Mission founded by Dr. Butler has assumed. He began the work among a people speaking one language; his successors preach in sixteen different tongues. He entered a field containing seventeen million souls; his successors are planting missions among three hundred and twenty-five million—one fifth of the human race. He lives to see his younger brethren coursing up and down as messengers of life and peace in a vast region which contains two and a half times as large a population as was comprised in the whole Roman Empire in the days of Barnabas and Paul. His sole assistant, Joel T. Janvier, still survives, but he is now a patriarch in the midst of a great host of men and women whom God has raised up to bear a noble part in the work. Instead of timid, doubting men, who at first came at long intervals to inquire concerning the way of life, the inquirers of the present day are numbered by the thousand. All the year round they stand before us, twenty thousand strong. Truly God has vindicated the counsel of his servant, verified the promises in which he trusted, and crowned his life with tokens of blessing, such as seldom fall to the lot of toilers in the Master's vineyard.

III. *Statistical Exhibit in* 1894.—Thus far Bishop Thoburn's article, connecting the past and the present, clearly shows "what God has wrought" among the heathen through the instrumentality of our Church. It now remains for me to present the results in statistical tables to enable our readers to comprehend the standing and significance of this great religious movement, and then weigh their own duty in regard to it. God's chosen instruments have evidently been "building better than they knew," for even here, before the first generation has passed away, we are allowed to behold, with adoring amazement, the divine growth of the precious seed, which they sowed with tears amid the dark and trying scenes of thirty years ago.

English rule some time since nobly struck off the shackles with which the Hindoo code and Brahmin pride had bound the common people of India, leaving them free to do the best they could for themselves. These downtrodden millions never before in the history of the world have had a chance to rise, but somehow, of late years, by the circulation of Gospel truth among them, they have grasped the great idea that in Christ and Christianity alone is there hope for them in this life and in all that may come after it.

The sympathy of the Saviour was especially given to this class. He rejoiced that "to the poor was the Gospel preached." His early ministry taught that God, who "made of one blood all nations of men," had forbidden these false distinctions and that any man was to be "called common or unclean." In this spirit our Mission went to this people, and the following table presents the blessed results so far realized.

We, first of all, present at suitable intervals up to 1888, and from that date yearly up to 1894, the numerical statistics, and then add to these the educational, financial, benevolent, and other aspects of the work.

NUMERICAL STATISTICS.

	Probationers.	Full Members.	Total.
1859	5	1	6
1863	97	89	186
1868	203	388	591
1873	599	1,173	1,772
1878	1,788	2,907	4,695
1883	2,819	3,393	6,212
1888	4,782	5,065	9,867
1889	5,770	6,517	12,287
1890	17,191	9,877	27,068
1891	18,017	10,615	28,632
1892	27,995	15,938	43,933
1893	36,971	20,961	57,932

Nor do these figures, wonderful as they are, show the full reality of this great ingathering. The statistical reports for 1894 are not yet all at hand, but from such as have reached us we realize that the increase for the present year will probably not fall below the past five years—and we may therefore already rejoice that the membership in our India missions is now fully seventy thousand souls!

The gracious outpouring of the Holy Spirit upon this work since 1889 has given us an average yearly increase equal to the creation of sixty new congregations of two hundred souls each per annum. During the past year in two of these Conferences (the North and Northwest India), the baptisms have amounted to eighteen thousand souls. So that American Methodism has been baptizing at the rate of fifty converts every day during 1893! Does not this look like the dawn of that morning for which the Lord Jesus has so long waited when he should "see of the travail of His soul and be satisfied"—the harbinger of that glad time when India will begin to supply her proportion of that "great multitude which no man can number?"

Even already it is noted that the work among the lower castes does not appear to have prevented successful endeavors among the higher castes. Bishop Thoburn says that an examination of the statistics shows that "the largest number of high-caste converts was reported from the very districts in which the largest number of low-caste people had been baptized." This is very encouraging. We are glad to have Christianity come with its ameliorating influences to the "depressed" classes; but we are also glad to have it appeal successfully to the educated and influential classes. It is in this way the terrible caste system of India can be, and will be, overthrown.

The genuine character of the experience of these converts is a constant source of joy to our missionaries, who frequently refer to it with gratitude. Low motives are not mixed up with it. They ask for nothing but to be taught "what they must do to be saved." Many of the women converts (once so timid), Brother Hoskins writes, "are now even more courageous than the men" to endure persecution for their faith.

"Methodist methods," as some are pleased to call them, have no secrets in them. They are simply the methods of the New Testament. Believing, as we do, that the Lord

Jesus, in the same sense and with the same intention, died for every one of these people, and authorizes us to offer to each a free and conscious salvation through repentance and faith in Christ, we earnestly urge its acceptance upon them, as we do on sinners at home. The Holy Spirit indorses the teaching and the offer, and the poor "weary and heavy laden" heathen turns from his idols to the living God and accepts Jesus as his Redeemer, and the work is done. He is saved, and knows it and rejoices, and then goes and tells others "what a Saviour he has found." This is all, and it is enough.

It may be doubted if converts anywhere have ever sought Christian baptism under a more intelligent impulse than what has led these thousands to us. Look at the facts. For thirty-five years our agency has been going through their villages teaching the way of salvation, distributing the Holy Scriptures, tracts, and books among them. We have also been giving a Christian education to thousands of their children, and the boys and girls have daily taken to their homes and there repeated and sung the texts and hymns which they have learned in their classes. For years these people have been discussing together this wonderful faith, brought thus to their doors, and now upon the good seed thus sown so widely the Holy Spirit has graciously descended and given it vitality, and this wonderful ingathering is the blessed result. In every one of our schools the Bible is read, hymns sung, and prayer offered. The first thing is to teach them to read the Bible in the simple village school; then follows the Anglo-vernacular school for wider training; then the orphanages, to raise teachers and preachers; then the boarding and high schools; then comes the Christian college, male and female, for special training. Adding the theological seminary, we have thus amply provided for the wide Christian culture of our membership and ministry. To all these we might add our numerous camp-meetings, which are practically for those people high schools of instruction in Christian experience as well as helps to its attainment. There has been no undue haste in our baptisms.

We next present the agency by whose labors these thousands have been drawn into the fellowship of our Christian faith. That agency, too, in its surprising growth and adaptation to meet the great demand, will be seen to be as marked a work of the Holy Spirit as is the ingathering of the multitude whom they are leading to Christ.

Agency.	Number.
Foreign and Anglo-Indian missionaries	84
Wives of missionaries	75
Native members of Conference	90
Native preachers not in Conference	462
Local preachers	362
Exhorters	668
Bible readers and colporteurs	498
Pastor teachers, about	400
School teachers, about	450
Lady missionaries, W. F. M. S.	48
Female teachers, 273, and Bible women, 250	523
Total	3,660

It is worthy of note here, as illustrating the devotion of these foreign missionaries to their work, that the records show that of the party of six who, with their wives, reached India in August, 1859, three of them are still at their work. Brother Downey and Judd died, and Brother Baume returned home; but Brothers Parker, Waugh, and Thoburn are in the field to-day. The record of the next party which came on the *Sea King* in March, 1861, and another in January, 1862, are equally encouraging. Brother Brown died, and Brothers Thomas and Hicks returned, but Brothers Johnson, Messmore, Jackson, Mansell, Scott, and Wilson, are still at the work. And yet, further, the next company, who arrived in India in 1863, can claim a share in this honorable mention, adding the ladies who still survive, and Brother Knowles, who joined us in 1858, and Brother Humphrey, now returning, and we have an aggregate, out of the twenty-five originally appointed, of fifteen still at work in India; that is, thirty-one years after the arrival of the third party, sixty per cent of the three companies are living and at work. Is there any other society that can show a higher percentage of surviving missionaries at their work after thirty-five years of toil in India?

We next present the educational statistics of the work in its different aspects, from the simple school to the college and theological seminary, for the culture of these thousands and their families, and for the training of a divinely-called native ministry to guide and guard this work of God in the future that lies before it.

	Number of Schools.	Number of Teachers.	Number of Scholars.
Day-schools	1,202	1,401	31,734
Sunday-schools	1,823	2,185	70,794
Boarding and high schools	14	34	1,346
Orphanages, boys	5	16	296
Christian colleges, male (363 preparatory)...	1	5	49
Christian colleges, female (151 preparatory).	1	4	6
Medical students in Agra College, male....	..	..	7
Medical students in Agra College, female..	..	..	21
Theological Seminary, Bareilly (206 graduates)	1	5	81
Training school for wives of students (178 graduates)	1	3	45
W. F. M. S. female orphanages	8	27	368
W. F. M. S. homes for homeless women...	3	9	100
W. F. M. S. pupils in schools and zenanas (besides 32,000 patients in hospitals and dispensaries in 1893)	302	345	31,259
Total	3,361	4,034	136,106

This table illustrates how thoroughly every interest of this foreign mission bearing on the evangelization and elevation of a great people, and looking to its wide extension among them, has been attended to.

It may be doubted if converts anywhere have ever sought Christian baptism under a more intelligent impulse than what has led these thousands to us. Look at the facts. For thirty-five years our agency has been going through their villages teaching the way of salvation, distributing the Holy Scriptures, tracts, and books among them. We have also been giving a Christian education to thousands of their children, and the boys and girls have daily taken to their homes and there repeated and sung the texts and hymns which they have learned in their classes. For years these people have been discussing together this wonderful faith, brought thus to their doors, and now upon the good seed sown so widely the Holy Spirit has graciously descended and given it vitality, and this wonderful ingathering is the blessed result. In every one of our schools the Bible is read, hymns sung, and prayer offered. The first thing is to teach them to read the Bible in the simple village school; then follows the Anglo-vernacular school for wider training; then the orphanages, to raise teachers and preachers; then the boarding and high schools; then comes the Christian college, male and female, for special training. Adding the theological seminary, we have thus amply provided for the wide Christian culture of our membership and ministry. To all these we might add our numerous camp-meetings, which are practically for those people high schools of instruction in Christian experience as well as helps to its attainment. There has been no undue haste in our baptisms.

The amount and value of the mission property in India accumulated for the accommodation and extension of the work, is a very encouraging portion of this exhibit. If I could here introduce the photographs of the principal items they would add greatly to the interest of this table. It is mostly paid for and free, and has no serious burdens upon it.

	Number.	Value in Rupees.
Churches and chapels	145	775,786
Parsonages	165	446,778
Publishing houses, Lucknow, Bombay, and Madras	3	195,000
Schoolhouses (besides hired halls)	179	446,928
Colleges and land	2	30,500
Theological Seminary	1	22,000
Orphanages, hospitals, etc.	...	100,000
W. F. M. S. homes, schools, etc.	...	446,500
Total		2,463,492
Equal, at three rupees to the dollar, to		$821,164

It now remains only to present the yearly contributions—the self-help, realized in India for the support and extension of this growing work of God—ere we close this exhibit of the condition which it has already attained.

BENEVOLENT COLLECTIONS, 1893.

	Rupees.
Missions	2,590
Sunday-schools	1,736
Church Extension	252
Tract cause	62
Bible Society	316
Children's Day	696
Dispensaries, etc	1,869
Total	7,521

EDUCATIONAL CONTRIBUTIONS.

English residents, for schools	9,333
Government grants, for schools	53,837
Fees from scholars	86,839
Total	150,009

MINISTERIAL SUPPORT.

Europeans	45,541
Natives, for their pastors	6,482
For Bishops and Presiding Elders	199
For Conference Claimants	622
Total	52,844
Total raised in 1893	210,374
Equal to	$70,127

The grants in aid of our schools are voted on the merits and results, which the government inspector of schools finds by his personal examination of them yearly, while the contributions of the English officers, civil and military, are given and continued on their intelligent conviction of the value of our work among the native people; and higher endorsement than both of these we cannot desire or look for.

Deeply grateful that I have been spared to present this exhibit of the work which I was honored to found thirty-eight years ago, I close this article, earnestly commending that work, in the flood tide of its divine prosperity and power of usefulness for the blessed future before it, to the sympathy and increased liberality of the ministry and membership of our Church. May God bless them all and our entire staff of workers in India, and their devoted and laborious Bishop, until we meet in that glorious presence where "he that soweth and he that reapeth shall rejoice together" forever, prays their humble fellow-servant in Christ.

WILLIAM BUTLER.

Newton Center, Mass.

GLOSSARY OF INDIAN TERMS

USED IN THIS WORK AND IN MISSIONARY CORRESPONDENCE.

(The common spelling is given in Italic, followed by the correct or phonetic spelling in Roman.)

Ab	'Ab	Water; e.g., *Do-ab*, two waters; *Punj-ab*, five waters
Abad	'Abád	A dwelling or city, as *Allah-abad*, City of God
Adawlat	Adálat	A court of justice.
Admee	'Admí	A man.
Allah	Alláh	The Arabic or Mohammedan name of God.
Alum	'Alam	The universe, or world.
Ameen	Amín	A native Judge.
Amreeta	Amrit	The water of immortality; the ambrosia of the Hindoo gods.
Anna	'Aná	A coin; the sixteenth of a rupee, worth three cents.
Ap	'Ap	Your Honor.
Asman	'Asmán	Heaven; the firmament or sky.
Asoor	Asur	A devil, an evil spirit.
Ata	'Atá	Flour, meal.
Attar	Itr	Essence, or rose oil.
Avatar	Autár	An incarnation; particularly of Vishnu, nine of which have taken place, the tenth is yet to come.
Ayah	'Ayáh	A maid or nurse.
Baboo	Bábú	Hindoo title of respect; sir, gent
Bagh	Bágh	A garden or grove.
Bahadoor	Bahádur	Brave, title of rank.
Bajra	Bájrá	A kind of millet.
Bana	Báná	The Word; the so-called sacred writings of the Bhuddists.
Bandy	Bándí	A gig or cart.
Banghy	Bahangí	A pole with ropes, for carrying baggage on the shoulder.
Bangle	Bangle	A bracelet.
Bap	Báp	Father.
Baraduree	Bárádarí	A building with twelve doors. A summer-house in a garden.
Barat	Barát	Marriage ceremony of bringing home the bride.
Basun	Básan	A plate, dish, or vessel.
Bawurchee	Báwarchí	A cook.
Bawarcheekana	Báwarchikhána	A cooking-place or kitchen.
Bazaar	Bázár	A market or trading-street.
Beegah	Bíghá	A land measure; about one third of an acre, but differing in the various provinces of India.

Begum	Begam	A princess or lady, (Mohammedan title.)
Belatee	Waláyatí	Foreign, European.
Bhadrnauth	Badrínáth	The Lord of Purity. The deity worshiped Bhadrinauth.
Bhugavat	Bhagavat	One of the names of Brahm. God.
Bhugavat-Gita	Bhagavat-Gita	A philosophic episode of the "Mahabarata."
Bhung	Bhang	An intoxicating preparation of hemp.
Bheestee	Bihishtí	A water carrier.
Bhoosa	Bhús	Food for cattle; chaff.
Bhoot	Bhút	A ghost or spirit.
Bihisht	Bihisht	Paradise, heaven.
Bouzees	Bonzís	The priests in China and Tartary.
Boodha	Budhá	Old man.
Boot	But	An idol or pagoda.
Brahm	Brahm	God; the Divine essence.
Brahma	Brahmá	The personal Creator.
Brahma-loka	Brahmá-lok	The highest of the sixteen celestial worlds of the Buddhists.
Brahmin	Brahman	Hindoo priest; the first of the four Hindoo castes.
Brahmo Somaj	Brahmo Somáj	A new sect of reformed Hindoos, styling themselves intuitional deists.
Brinjaries	Brinjárí	Carriers of grain.
Budgerow	Bajrá	A large cabin-boat; a pleasure-boat.
Buddha	Baudh	Gotama; a historical personage worshiped in Thibet, China, etc. Called Fo in China.
Buddhist	Buddhist	A follower of Gotama-Buddha.
Bucksheesh	Bakhshish	A present or gift.
Bungalow	Banglá	A house, usually thatched.
Bunya	Baniyá	A grain merchant or trader.
Burra	Bará	Great.
Bursat	Barsát	Rains, or the "rainy season."
Buttee	Battí	A candle or lamp; a lamp-wick.
Byragee	Bairágí	A religious mendicant, a worshiper of Vishnu.
Bylee	Bahlí	A native carriage drawn by bullocks.
Caranchie	Karánchí	A native carriage.
Caste	Zát	A division of Hindoo society, of which there are four principal: Brahmin, Kshatriya, Vaisya, Sudra.
Cazee	Qází	A Mohammedan Judge, who decides civil and criminal suits by the Koran.
Chand	Chand	The moon.
Charpoy	Chárpái	A light native cot or bedstead, usually made of bamboo and cords.
Chattah	Chhátá	An umbrella.
Cheetah	Chítá	A leopard; frequently used in hunting.
Chirragh	Chirágh	A small light or lamp.
Chitak	Chhatánk	A weight of about two ounces.
Chittee	Chitthí	A note or letter.
Chobedar	Chobdár	A bearer of a silver mace.
Chokey	Chaukí	A chair or stool; a guard station.
Chokra	Chokrá	A boy. Chokrí: a girl.

Chor	Chor	A robber, a thief.
Chota	Chhotá	Little.
Chota-hazree	Chhotí-háziri	A slight refreshment in the morning.
Chowk	Chauk	A market, yard, or court.
Chowkeydar	Chaukídár	A watchman.
Chowrie	Chaurí	A whisk for driving off flies.
Chuddur	Chaddar	A sheet or table-cloth.
Chumar	Chumar	A leather-dresser.
Chunam	Chunam	Lime.
Chupatti	Chapátí	A thin, unleavened cake of coarse flour.
Chupper	Chappar	A thatched roof.
Chuprassie	Chaprásí	A peon or messenger.
Churuk-poojah	Charkh-púja	An annual barbarous swinging festival.
Chutney	Chatní	A kind of pungent sauce or catsup.
Coolie	Qulí	A burden-bearer, a laborer.
Coss	Kos	The Hindoo mile; about two English miles.
Cowrie	Kaurí	A small shell used as currency; 5,120 to a rupee.
Crore	Karor	Ten millions; one hundred lakhs.
Curry	Kárí	A popular Indian dish, composed of meat cooked in a dressing of spices, and eaten with boiled rice.
Cutcha	Kachchá	Unripe; uncooked; green; imperfect; built of unburnt brick.
Cutcherry	Kachahrí	A court-house, or court of justice.
Dacoit	Dakait	A robber or river-pirate.
Dai	Dái	A wet-nurse; a midwife.
Dandy	Dandí	A light conveyance, or sedan, borne on the shoulders of two men.
Daroga	Dárogha	A superintendent; an agent.
Dawk	Dák	A post, letter post, or arrangements for traveling.
Dawk Bungalow	Dák Bungla	A rest-house for travelers.
Deccan	Dakhan	The South.
Deen	Dín	Religion, faith.
Devar	Dewá	A Hindoo name for the gods generally.
Dewan	Díwán	A chief minister; an agent.
Dewanee Khass	Diwán i Kháss	The audience-hall of the "Great Moguls."
Dharma	Dharm	Divine law, duty, virtue.
Dharma Shastra	Dharm Shástr	The Hindoo Code; religion, science, morals, law.
Dherna	Dherna	The custom of sitting in defiance before one's door to compel compliance with a demand.
Dhobee	Dhobí	A washerman. *Dhobin:* a washerwoman.
Doab	Doáb	A tract of country between two rivers; as that between the Ganges and Jumna.
Dooley	Dolí	A litter, or light palanquin.
Dozukh	Dozakh	Hell.
Durbar	Darbár	A court where a levee is held.
Durbeen	Dúrbín	A spy-glass or telescope.
Durga-Poojah	Durgá-Pújá	A yearly festival of the Hindoos, extending over fifteen days, in honor of the Goddess Durga.
Durvesh	Darwesh	A Mohammedan sage or beggar.
Durwan	Darwán	A gate-keeper.

Durzee	Darzí	A tailor.
Dustoor	Dastúr	Customs, manners, usage.
Dustoori	Dastúrí	Fee or percentage exacted by middlemen and servants
Dwaper Yug	Dwápur Jug	The third age of the world.
Eblis	Iblís	The Mohammedan name for the Devil.
Ed	'Id	A Mohammedan festival; their Easter.
Emir or *Ameer*	Amír	A chief or noble.
Eurasians	Eurasians	Descendants of Europeans and Asiatics sometimes called East Indians, or half-castes.
Fakir	Faqír	A religious mendicant.
Feringhee	Faringhí	A European; a foreigner.
Ferishta	Farishta	An angel.
Firdoos	Firdaus	Paradise; the heaven of the Mohammedans.
Firman	Farmán	A royal order, mandate, command.
Foujdar	Faujdár	A commander; an army officer.
Gunesha	Ganesh	A Hindoo deity: the God of Wisdom, represented with an elephant's head.
Ganges	Gunga	The holy river of India. From Gunga, the river, represented as a deity.
Gharree	Gárí	A carriage, cart.
Ghareewan	Gáríwán	A coachman.
Ghat	Ghát	A landing or bathing-place; flight of steps at a river; also, a pass in mountains.
Ghee	Ghí	An inferior butter used for cooking.
Ghogra	Ghógra	A river in Upper India, a tributary of the Ganges.
Gholam	Ghulám	A slave, a servant.
Ghora	Ghorá	A horse.
Ghur	Ghar	House, home, habitation.
Ghurra	Ghará	An earthen water-pot or pitcher.
Ghurree	Gharí	A clock. watch, hour.
Gomashta	Gumáshta	An agent, officer, or superintendent.
Goomtee	Gumtí	A river in Oude flowing by Lucknow.
Godown	Gudám	A store-house, cellar, warehouse, magazine.
Gora	Gorá	A white man: an English soldier.
Gossain	Gossáin	A religious mendicant worshiping Mahadev, (Shiva.)
Gonah	Gunáh	A sin, crime.
Gram	Gram	A kind of vetch, pulse, or peas.
Guddee	Gaddí	Pad, cushion, or seat; a throne or royal seat.
Guicowar	Gaekwár	Name of a sovereign in the South.
Gully	Galí	Street, alley, way.
Guroo	Gurú	A religious teacher, priest.
Guz	Gaz	A measure; a short yard.
Hackery	Hackery	A native cart drawn by bullocks.
Hadjee	Hájí	A Mohammedan who has made the pilgimage to Mecca.
Hukeem	Hakím	A Mohammedan doctor, a sage, philosopher.
Hakim	Hákim	A ruler, governor, king.

Hanuman	Hanumán	The deified monkey who was the ally of Rama.
Harem	Haram	Sacred, prohibited, the inner or women's apartments.
Hati	Háthí	An elephant.
Havildar	Hawáldár	A native sergeant.
Hazree	Háziri	Breakfast, presence.
Hejira	Hijrí	Flight; the flight of Mohammed from Mecca, 16th of July, A. D. 622; the Mohammedan era.
Hera	Hírá	A diamond.
Hookah	Huqqa	A smoking-pipe.
Hoolee	Holí	A Hindoo festival to commemorate the beginning of the new year.
Hoondee	Hundí	A native bank-note; a bill of exchange.
Howdah	Hauda	A box-seat on an elephant's back; an elephant's saddle.
Huck	Haqq	Equity, truth, reason.
Hurkaru	Harkára	A messenger, a running courier.
Hurrumzadu	Haramzáda	A rascal, a bastard.
Huzar	Hazár	A thousand.
Huzoor	Huzúr	Royal presence; "Your Honor."
Huzrat	Hazrat	Excellency, majesty, divine; a title accorded to superiors.
Huzrat Isa	Hazrat 'Isá	Jesus Christ.
Indra	Indrá	The God of Light. The leading ancient Vedic deity, sometimes called the God of Heaven, but now occupying only an inferior position.
Islam	Islám	The Mohammedan religion.
Istan	Istán or Sthán	A termination, signifying place or country, as Affghanistan that of the Affghans.
Izzut	Izzat	Honor, respect.
Jagheer	Jágír	A State or landed estate assigned by Government as a reward.
Jaghiredar	Jágírdár	A person holding a jagheer.
Jehan	Jahán	The world.
Jahaz	Jaház	A ship.
Jain	Jain	A kind of degenerate Buddhists.
Jat	Ját	A caste or sect; a tribe among the Rajpoots.
Jeel	Jhíl	A shallow lake or pond.
Jemmadar	Jamadár	A native subaltern officer; head-man of a village or class.
Jinn	Jinn	According to the Mohammedans, an intermediate race between angels and men.
Jotee	Jútí	A shoe or slipper.
Jowar	Joár	A kind of millet.
Juggernauth	Jaganáth	The Lord of the World. A god of the Hindoos, whose temple is at Orissa.
Juldee	Jaldí	Quick! quickly!
Jumma Musjid	Jama Masjid	Chief mosque at Delhi. The largest place of Mohammedan worship in India.
Jammaut	Jamáat	Assembly, meeting, congregation.

Jumna	Jamuná	A river of North-west India.
Jungle	Jangal	A thicket, desert, wilderness, wood.
Kaffir	Káfir	An infidel; impious rascal.
Kalee	Kálí	The Hindoo goddess of destruction.
Kali Yug	Kal Jug	The fourth or present age of the world; the black or iron age.
Kalpa	Kalpa	A day of Brahma, equal to 4,320,000,000 solar years
Karen	Karen	An aboriginal race in the hills of Burmah.
Kasi	Káshí	Magnificent; the ancient name of Benares, still so called by the Brahmins.
Katree	Khatrí	A military caste of Hindoos.
Khansama	Khánsámán	A steward or butler.
Kheleet	Khilat	A robe or dress of honor presented as a gift.
Keranee	Kiráni	A writer, clerk; a man of mixed blood.
Khuda	Khudá	God.
Khudawund	Khudáwand	Lord, sir, master.
Kitmutghar	Khidmatgár	A table attendant.
Kincob	Kimkhwáb	Brocade.
Kismut	Qismat	Destiny, chance, fortune.
Koh-i-noor	Koh-i-núr	"Mountain of Light." A diamond so called, formerly worn by the Great Moguls, and now by the Queen of England.
Koran	Qurán	The supposed revelation to Mohammed, collected by the Caliph Omar.
Kotee	Kothí	A house, mansion, dwelling.
Kotwal	Kotwál	Mayor of the city, police officer.
Kotwalie	Kotwálí	Mayor's office or police station.
Krishna	Krishn	The name of Vishnu in his eighth incarnation.
Kshatriya	Kshatrí	The second or military caste of the Hindoos.
Kulma	Kalma	The Mohammedan confession of faith: "There is no God but God, and Mohammed is his Prophet."
Kupra-wallah	Kápra-wálá	A cloth merchant.
Lac	Lákh	One hundred thousand.
Lamas	Lamas	The Buddhist priests of Tartary and Thibet, the chief of whom is called Dali, Grand Lama, or Living Buddha.
Larka	Larká	A babe, boy, child. *Larkee:* a girl.
Linga	Ling	*Membrum virile;* the indelicate form under which Shiva is worshiped.
Log	Lōg	Mankind, people.
Lohar	Lohar	A blacksmith..
Lungoor	Lungúr	A baboon; the black-faced monkey.
Maha	Mahá	Great, illustrious.
Mahabarata	Mahábhárat	The second great Sanscrit epic of the Hindoos, celebrating the wars of the rival Pandoos and Kuroos.
Mahadeva	Mahádev	One of the names of the god Shiva.
Maharajah	Mahárajá	A great king.

Maha Yug	Mahá Jug	A celestial age in Hindoo chronology, including 12,000 divine years, each of which is equal to 360 solar years, the Maha-Yug being equal to 4,320,000 years of mortals.
Mahout	Mahaut	An elephant-keeper and driver.
Malik	Málik	Master, lord, ruler.
Malee	Málí	A gardener.
Manjee	Mánjhí	Master of a vessel; a steersman.
Meidan	Maidán	A plain, ground, field-of-battle.
Mela	Melá	Hindoo fair or festival held for religious or commercial purposes.
Menu	Menu	The author of the legal and religious Code of the Hindoos.
Methur	Mihtar	A sweeper.
Mithuranee	Mihtaráni	A low-caste nurse.
Minar	Mínár	A tower, minaret, obelisk.
Mirza	Mirza	Prince, sir.
Mochee	Mochí	A shoemaker.
Mohulla	Mahalla	Quarter, district, division.
Mohur	Muhr	A gold coin, valued at sixteen rupees or eight dollars.
Mohurrum	Muharram	The first month of the Mohammedan year.
Moolk	Mulk	Country, region.
Moonshee	Munshí	A teacher of languages, usually a Mohammedan.
Moonsif	Munsif	Arbitrator, Judge.
Mootee	Motí	A pearl.
Moulah	Moulah	A Mohammedan priest, doctor, teacher.
Moulvie	Maulví	A learned Mohammedan.
Muntra	Mantra	Mystic verses or incantations of the Brahmins.
Musjeed	Masjid	A mosque; Mohammedan place of worship.
Mussal	Mashál	A light or torch.
Mussalchee	Mashálchí	A link-boy, torch-bearer.
Mussuk	Mashk	A leathern bottle for carrying water.
Mussulman	Musalmán	A term used, like Moslem, to denote all who believe in the Koran.
Musnud	Masnad	A throne, a royal seat.
Muezzin	Muazzin	The person who calls the Mohammedans to prayer.
Naib	Náib	Deputy or viceroy.
Namaz	Namáz	Prayer, (Mohammedan term.)
Nana	Náná	Maternal grandfather.
Nautch	Nátch	The dance, ball, etc.
Nabob	Nawáb	A Mohammedan title, viceroy, governor.
Nazim or *Nizam*	Nizám	Ruler.
Nimmuk	Namak	Salt.
Nimmuk-haram	Namak-harám	A traitor to his "covenant of salt."
Noor	Núr	Splendor, light.
Nubee	Nabí	A prophet.
Nuddee	Nadí	A stream, river.
Nugger	Nagar	A town, village, city.
Nullah	Nullah	A water-course, a ravine.
Nuzzur	Nazar	An offering.

Padishah	Pádsháh / Bádsháh	A king, ruler, emperor.
Paddy	Paddy	Rice; rice in the field.
Padre	Pádrí	A common term in India for a Christian clergyman; a priest, (Portuguese.)
Pagoda	Pagōda	A Hindoo place of worship.
Pahar	Pahár	A hill or mountain.
Paharee	Pahárí	A hill-man, mountaineer.
Palankeen / *Palanquin*	Pálkí	A litter for one person to ride in, the usual conveyance in India.
Parsee	Pársí	A sect found in Western India, the followers of Zoroaster, or the Persian Magi.
Parswanath	Parisnáth	The deity of the Jains.
Patan	Pathán	A term applied to the old Affghan Mohammedans as distinguished from the Moguls.
Pawn	Pán	The betel-leaf; the nut of the areca-palm, lime, and spice wrapped in a betel-leaf and chewed by the natives.
Peer	Pír	A Mohammedan spiritual guide; a sage.
Peishwah	Peshwa	A leader; originally the title of the chief minister of the Mahratta, later a royal designation of Bajee Rao and Nana Sahib.
Pergunna	Pargana	A district, township; less than a zillah.
Pice	Paisá	A copper coin; one third of an anna, value nearly one cent.
Pie	Pai	A copper coin; one twelfth of an anna.
Poojah	Pújá	Worship, prayer.
Pucka	Pukká	Ripe, finished, thorough, (as a burned brick,) perfect. Used to discriminate a true from a false Christian.
Punchaet	Paucháyat	A jury of five men.
Pundit	Pandit	A Brahmin learned in the Vedas and Shasters; a teacher of the Hindee or Sanscrit language.
Punkah	Pankhá	A large, wooden, covered frame, suspended from the ceiling, with a heavy, deep frill, kept in motion by a coolie, as a fan, to cool the air in a room.
Poor or *Pore*	Púr	A town or city; used in composition, as *Seeta-pore*, the City of Seeta.
Puranas	Purán	The especial designation of the eighteen books of the Hindoo legends or traditions.
Purda	Parda	A curtain or vail; partition, secrecy, privacy.
Purda-nashssn	Parda-nashín	A secluded lady; one sitting behind a curtain.
Purwana	Parwána	A permit, pass, or order.
Rais	Raís	A prince, chief, head, citizen.
Raj	Ráj	Empire, kingdom, government.
Rajah	Rajáh	King, prince, sovereign.
Ramadan	Rámzán	The name of a month; a fast of the Mohammedans
Ranee	Rání	Feminine of Rajah; a Hindoo princess or queen.
Rupee	Rúpí	A silver coin, worth nearly fifty cents.
Rutt	Rath	A four-wheeled carriage or car.
Ryot	Raaiyat	A peasant; a tenant or subject.

Sahib	Sáhib	Sir, lord, gentleman.
Satya Yug	Sat Jug	The first age of the world; age of truth.
Sepoy	Sipáhí	A native soldier.
Seraglio	Seraglio	From *Sura*, house, and *Ahul*, domestic; hence Suralio or Seraglio, the family or female apartments.
Sewalla	Shiválа	A temple.
Shadee	Shádí	Marriage, wedding, happiness.
Shah	Sháh	A king, a prince, (Mohammedan title.)
Shahzada	Sháhzáda	The son of a king.
Shastra or *Shaster*	Shástr	Hindoo Scriptures.
Shiva	Shív	The Hindoo God of Destruction, husband of Kali, and the third member of the Hindoo Triad or Trimurti.
Shesas or *Sheeites*	Shíah	One of the great Mohammedan sects; followers of Ali, the son-in-law of the Prophet, and esteeming the three Caliphs, Abubeker, Omar, and Oman, as usurpers. To this sect belong the Persians generally, the royal family of Oude, and most of the lower orders of Mussulmans in India.
Shroff	Sharráf	A native banker or money-changer.
Shytan	Shaitán	The devil, Satan.
Sheikh	Shaikh	A disciple, follower, scholar; the name of the religionists in the Punjab.
Sirkar	Sirkár	The State or Government.
Soma	Soma	The milky juice of the moon-plant mixed with barley and fermented, forming an intoxicating drink; used in the ancient Vedic worship.
Soonees	Sunnís	"Followers of the traditions," who maintain the lawful succession of the three Caliphs before Ali, and pay great respect to the traditions of Islam. The Arabs, Turks, Affghans, and most of the educated Mussulmans of India, are of this class, and style themselves Orthodox, the Sheeas being regarded as heretics.
Sowar	Sawár	A cavalryman, a mounted soldier or policeman.
Subadar	Súbadár	A governor of a province, a captain.
Subah	Súba	A province.
Sudder	Sadr	Chief, principal, as *Sudder-udawlut*, the Supreme Court of Justice in India.
Sudra	Súdr	The fourth or servile caste of the Hindoos; now vaguely applied to all low classes.
Sultan	Sultán	Sovereign, prince, (Mohammedan;) also a title formerly borne by the royal family of Delhi.
Sunnud	Sanad	A grant or diploma.
Surdar	Sardár	A chief, head-man, commander.
Suttee	Sátí	The ceremony of burning a widow with her husband's corpse.
Syce	Sais	A groom or horse-keeper.
Syud or *Said*	Saiyad	A prince; a descendant of Hossein, son of Ali, and grandson of Mohammed.

Taj .... Táj .... A crown.
Talook .... Táaluq .... A State or Barony, usually larger than a Zemeendaree.
Talookdar .... Táaluqdár .... A land-holder, a baron.
Tattee .... Tattí .... A mat made of cus-cus grass, kept wet, and suspended before a window to cool the room.
Tattoo .... Tattú .... A pony.
Thakoor .... Thákúr .... Idol, lord, baron.
Tharna .... Thána .... A police station.
Terai .... Taráí .... A swamp, marsh, or miasmatic region.
Thannadar .... Thánadár .... A police officer or constable.
Thug .... Thag .... A professional murderer and devotee of the goddess Kali.
Tola .... Tolá .... One hundred and eighty grains Troy weight.
Tonjon .... Tonjon .... A chair with a hood.
Tope .... Tōp .... A clump of trees; a cannon.
Tretu Yug .... Tret Jug .... The second age of the world; the silver age.
Tukht .... Takht .... Chair, throne, seat.
Tulwar .... Talwár .... A native sword.
Tussuldar .... Tahsíldár .... A collector of revenue.

Upanishads .... Upanishads .... Expository supplements to the Vedas.

Vaishnavas .... Vaishnavas .... The worshipers of Vishnu.
Vaisya .... Vaisya .... The third or agricultural caste of the Hindoos.
Vakeel .... Vakíl .... An envoy, prime agent.
Vedas .... Bed .... From *Ved*, learning, the most ancient sacred books of the Hindoos, of which there are four: the Rig-Veda, the Yajur-Veda, the Sama-Veda, and the Atharva-Veda.
Vedanta .... Vedánt .... A system of pantheistical philosophy founded on scattered texts of the Vedas.
Vishnu .... Vishnu .... The Preserver; the second member of the Hinduo Triad or Trimurti.
Vizier .... Wazír .... The chief minister in a Mohammedan sovereignty.

Wah Wah .... Wáh Wah .... Admirable! well-done! bravo!
Wilaet .... Wiláyat .... Country, region, abroad, foreign.
Wufadar .... Wafadar .... Faithful.

Yogee .... Jogí .... A silent saint
Yug .... Jug .... An age of the world

Zeen .... Zín .... A saddle.
Zemeendar .... Zamíndár .... Land-holder; collector of revenue of a district.
Zemeendaree .... Zamíndárí .... A province.
Zenana .... Zanána .... From *Zun*, a woman, the inner apartments in India.
Zillah .... Zila .... An extensive district.

INDEX.